A CULTURAL GUIDE TO THE GLOBAL VILLAGE

THOMAS E. NEHIL

MIDLAND, MICHIGAN

2002

FOURTH PRINTING

Pearson
Custom
Publishing

Cover Design by Lisa Bourdon-Krause
Graphics by Lisa Bourdon-Krause, Randy McDonald and Jeffrey Phillips

Please visit our website at www.pearsoncustom.com

ISBN 0–536–59816–9

BA 990209

 PEARSON CUSTOM PUBLISHING
75 Arlington Street, Boston, MA 02116
A Pearson Education Company

We are what we think.
All that we are arises with our thoughts.
With our thoughts, we make the world.
—The Dhammapada

Contents ▶ ▶

Foreword ▶ ▶

We are all now aware that the world is shrinking into one global village, to use Marshall McCluhan's colorful phrase. It now takes less time to circle the earth than it took in the 1700s to travel from Boston to Philadelphia. The price of wheat for the Iowa farmer is affected by the rainfall and wheat harvest in Russia. A large world audience watches Olympic games and World Cups as they are happening.

What is not so obvious is the impact of this shrinking on world cultures, the intangible realm of the spirit. For the wide differences between the way people behave in different societies and their different institutions are explained by their beliefs, their value system, their culture. These beliefs, too, are meeting each other on a regular basis. It seems almost certain that world culture will be strongly Western in nature as the world eagerly seeks the advantages of modern sciences and industrialization. At the same time millions of Americans are practicing Eastern meditation. Books entitled *Zen Catholicism* and *The Tao of Pooh* indicate an Eastern cultural influence in the West. There are also many signs of a return to cultural roots as a reaction to globalization.

Today the only suitable framework for understanding political, business and cultural changes is a world view. Only a world view can make the world in which we live make sense. The world community today can be no single tradition. Management is deeply involved in spiritual concerns—the nature of man and their values. Management is thus a liberal art because it deals with the fundamentals of knowledge, self-knowledge, wisdom and leadership; art because it is practice and application. Managers need to draw on all the knowledge and insight of the humanities and the social sciences—on psychology and philosophy, on economics and history, on physical science and ethics. They have to focus this knowledge to be effective. For these reasons, management must include the humanities. Management deals with people, their needs and wants. Today these people, whether employees, information sources or customers for our products and ideas, have a varied cultural background.

World history was once taken for granted as the only sensible basis for understanding the past and providing a guide for future action. Christians began with Creation and fit subsequent details into the framework of divine revelation. The other higher religions all have a similar world history. More recently all history was seen as moving toward a culmination in the modern national state, as Great Britain, Germany or the U.S. Foreign peoples joined the march of history and culture only when Europeans arrived with European culture.

These parochial ethnocentric views are no longer adequate. Recent popular phrases like "The Global Village" and photos from space picturing unforgettably "space-ship earth" underline the need for a world view.

▶ This Book's Objective

Give an overview of the world's principal cultural patterns and thus create:

1. An increased awareness of cultural differences.

2. A guide for fitting various countries' customs and value systems into a world cultural outline.

3. An openness and tolerance of other values, business customs and lifestyles while maintaining one's own cultural integrity.

The focus is on four cultural realms:

I. Western (or European)

    a. Latin Europe

    b. Northern Europe

    c. Latin America

    d. Northern America

II. Indian

III. Far Eastern (or Chinese)

    a. China

    b. Korea

    c. Japan

IV. Islam

Value areas detailed as formative to culture include:

- History
- Language
- Religion
- Concepts of time

It may be difficult to teach people to respect others unless we have some understanding of how they arrived at their point of view. The aim of this book is to present a broad world view that will help readers get a better perspective of their own culture and increase their understanding and respect of other cultures by better understanding their values.

For every main subject treated in this book, there is a vast library of information. Each library would provide a lifetime of reading and scholars have spent lifetimes of research bringing new light to misunderstood areas. This book is not a work of scholarship. No systematic effort has been made to record the sources of information. All subjects have been explored by numerous authors.

The book was written for students at Northwood University, Midland, Michigan, who have pleasantly surprised me by cheerfully responding to my lectures on world culture. The intention of this book is to give those students specializing in training for business or other disciplines, a global point of view consistent with the global viewpoint needed in modern decision making. It also should help the traveler, whether for pleasure or business, deepen understanding and enjoyment of other points of view.

In this survey book, I have borrowed freely from ideas expressed by others and I humbly give up any claim of priority. For those who may be interested, some of the authors who have most influenced my thinking include:

Arnold Toynbee
William H. McNeill
Christopher Dawson
L. S. Stavrianos
Barbara Ward
Huston Smith
Harold Goad
Peter F. Drucker

Thomas E. Nehil

Chapter 1 ▶ ▶

WORLD CULTURE: AN OVERVIEW

Culture will not be discussed as correct wine selection, poetry appreciation or musical knowledge, although these are manifestations of a cultured or cultivated (developed by education and training) person.

Culture will be discussed in terms of shared values or value systems.

If we describe culture in terms of value, we recognize we are surrounded by people of different cultures: Rural and urban, educated and uneducated, rich and poor, professional and laborer.

The business world is increasingly aware of corporate cultures and how important a healthy set of values is to company success.

> Values are the bedrock of any corporate culture. As the essence of a company's philosophy for achieving success, values provide a sense of common direction for all employees and guidelines for their day-to-day behavior. These formulas for success determine (and occasionally arise from) the types of corporate heroes, and the myths, rituals, and ceremonies of the culture. In fact, we think that often companies succeed because their employees can identify, embrace, and act on the values of the organization.
>
> —Deal and Kennedy
> *Corporate Culture: The Rites and*
> *Rituals of Corporate Life*

1. We will focus on the most important event of our time, the encounter between the West and the world, and the formation for the first time of a truly world community.

The scale is very large, necessarily so, for quite the same reason that a map of the world has a very large scale. But large scale patterns are just as real as small scale patterns, and no one supposes that a world map does not represent a view of the world as valid as their local county map. Both fill a need.

The recent drift in education has been quite opposed to large world views. We have settled for specialization. This emphasis on national and local affairs and interpreting the world from this local view are misleading. All people need a vision in which their own local unit can be seen in a global setting.

2. We will present a guide for fitting various countries' customs and value systems into a world cultural outline.

Today the only suitable framework for understanding political business and cultural changes is a world view. Only a world view can make the world we live in make sense.

Looking back on today, future historians will see that the really significant world event taking place in the second half of the twentieth century is the formation, for the first time, of a world community. It is happening rapidly, and it is happening on all fronts.

3. We will try to foster an openness and tolerance of other values, business customs, and lifestyles, while maintaining our own cultural beliefs.

The "ugly" American, also ugly Japanese, German, etc., are terms of approbrium. What do we understand by this term? The "ugly" people see their own values as the only values and are contemptuous of others.

The scene is Madrid. You have had a hard day touring. You and your spouse decide on a quiet early supper and then relaxation in the hotel room. Having looked up a restaurant and arrived by taxi at 6 P.M., you find the restaurant closed with a notice stating "Open at 8:00 P.M."

Now come the wrath and recriminations. Why don't they eat at normal times as we do in Detroit, as all good people do? No wonder Spain has such problems. Why don't they do it my way?

Okakura Kakuzo writes in his classic *The Book of Tea* soon after his arrival in America, "The average westerner, in his sleek complacency, will see the tea ceremony but another instance of the thousand and one oddities which constitute the quaintness and the childishness of the East to him."

Sleek complacency . . . the average westerner? Is that you? Is that me?

There are some very compelling reasons for tolerance and humility. History is full of beliefs everybody subscribed to that proved to be false.

Everybody knew the world was flat. If it were round, everyone would fall off. Everybody knew the world was the center of the universe. It was logical and supported by Scripture. For supporting a view of the solar system with the sun as its center, Galileo was forced to recant under threat of torture.

We still talk of sunrise and sunset and the sun moving across the sky. It's logical, observable and false.

There is hardly any problem that doesn't have a solution that is simple, logical and false.

All of Newtonian physics, the very basis of western science for the last 300 years, is now being rethought in the light of quantum physics.

As Mark Twain suggests, *It isn't what people don't know that hurts them; it's what they know for sure that ain't so.*

Tolerant, yes, but the second part of our objective states "while maintaining our own cultural beliefs."

While learning about Buddhism, we can treat the subject with respect and toleration without becoming Buddhists.

While appreciating the insights of the Koran and the logic of Islam's five pillars, we do not need to become Muslims.

A study of others' values should act to clarify our own values. What do I really believe?

While it's easy to see the problems and weakness of other cultures, can we humbly acknowledge some of our own?

Charles T. Vetter, Jr., in his booklet, "Citizen Ambassadors," gives a list of questions frequently asked Americans. It would be a worthwhile exercise to ask yourself how you would answer these questions. As you form your reply, try to think of why someone from another culture would question these particular aspects of American life.

1. Describe American family life for us. Is it true that the wife runs the husband and the children run the mother?

2. Isn't most American divorce, juvenile delinquency, and unemployment caused by women working outside the home?

3. Why do you put your old people in homes for the aged? Isn't this an example of your family life being destroyed?

4. Why is there so much crime and violence in the United States when you are such a law-abiding people? Is it safe to go anywhere? Won't I get mugged, or attacked, or robbed?

5. Why do white people in America hate black people, Mexicans, and other minorities?

6. Why are your Indians so poorly treated? Are they still being forced to live on reservations, and aren't they deprived of their rights and opportunities?

7. Why do your people know so little about us and our country? You know nothing about our people, our cities, our politics, our government. Doesn't this really prove that Americans are not interested in anybody else, especially our country?

8. Isn't it true that American businesses, the monopolies, the multi-national corporations, are really the ones that determine foreign policy in your country? Aren't the military industrialists and the scientists the ones that really control American foreign policy around the world?

9. Consider your American divorce rate. Is this breakdown of the family brought on by a system that inevitably produces an inferior quality of life, even though you have so many resources and fine people?

10. Why is it that Americans do not have strong philosophies and spiritual convictions? I expect that it is because you are such pragmatic, materialistic people. You do not have the spirit and the soul for philosophy or for conceptualizing profound ideas and principles.

Important in our world view is the development of the idea or value of respect. Without respect, the cultures of the world now being molded into one cannot communicate or cooperate. The wide differences between the ways people behave in different societies can be explained by differences in their institutions or forms of organization and by the differences in their traditional systems of belief. Differences in behavior between different cultures can be explained in terms of a common human nature influenced by different ideas of the truth. Respect is vital in all intercultural relations.

Maintain your own cultural integrity. Treat others with respect.

Before getting too far into the text, I think, in all honesty, I should let you know that I am a conservative, old fogy. I do not believe in multi-culturalism. I hear often from my politically correct, indoctrinated students that values are neither good nor bad, they are just different. What humbug! Tell that to the millions of Jews gassed to death during the Third Reich, the millions of Russian Kulaks killed by the Communist regime of Stalin, or the millions killed by Mao Zedong—madmen in power whose values were evil. Until recently only Nazis and Stalinists spoke of "political correctness." It is a purely totalitarian concept.

It is my hope that the themes presented in this book will help you better define your values, that you will have openness and tolerance "while maintaining one's own cultural integrity." Colleges that went deeply into multi-culturalism are precisely those where separatism and hostility are the worst and we can observe a resegregation. If you want to see multi-culturalism at work, look at Lebanon, Northern Ireland or the former Yugoslavia. It is very dangerous to discard social and cultural wisdom for the uncivilizing programs of embittered idealogues. Cultures are full of value judgments and much of the advancement of the human race has occurred because judgments were made that some things were not just different from others, but better.

It is not too much to say that we are seeing a rise in America of barbarism. In part, the rise of barbarism is a result of the disintegration of the family, which is itself the result of other factors. But the broken family does not see itself as a cultural problem. They see it as a personal lifestyle of choice.

Along with Kenneth Clark, I believe that order is better than chaos and creation better than destruction. I prefer gentleness to violence and knowledge rather than ignorance. I believe, along with Confucius, that we should strive to live in harmony and that everyday courtesy, which acts as a lubricant to the friction of daily life, should be practiced and taught, and the gentleman should be seen as an ideal.

Gentleman: The gentle man, one who does not knowingly hurt others in order to enhance his own ego. How strange this sounds to a culture that is entertained by violence. That makes heroes of Rambo and Conan the Barbarian. Make no doubt about it, Conan is a barbarian. He is not subject to laws. Barbarism is the absence of standards to which appeal can be made. Conan is completely self-centered and takes what he wants without appeal.

I have had students tell me they think they might prefer barbarism to civilization. I doubt they have thought about it deeply. All evidence of history suggests a life of infinite boredom, full of discomfort and deprivation. No books, no entertainment, no light after dark, and constant fear of attack by other barbarians; a melancholy existence with no hope.

If we teach that there is no culture but pop culture and that doing away with cultural or values emphasis will have no consequence but different teaching in the classroom, then we miss the point. As Thomas Sowell points out, "Cultures exist to serve the vital practical requirements of human life—to structure a society so as to perpetuate the species, to pass on the hard-earned knowledge and experience of generations past and centuries past to the young and inexperienced, in order to spare the next generation the costly and dangerous process of learning everything all over again from scratch through trial and error—including fatal errors."

Cultures exist so that people can know how to get food and put a roof over their heads, how to cure the sick, how to cope with the death of loved ones and how to get along with the living. Cultures are not bumper stickers. They are living, changing ways of doing all the things that have to be done in life. They are to demonstrate and to embody value, to create vision and to recall people to their responsibilities. A culture is perennially in need of renewal. A culture does not survive and prosper merely by being taken for granted; active defense always is required, and imaginative growth, too. Let us brighten the cultural corner where we find ourselves. I always thought T.S. Elliot's definition of culture sounded a little flippant but just about hits the nail on the head—"Culture may even be described simply as that which makes life worth living."

▶ A Big Picture

We tend to stress the differences and ignore the likenesses. People all around the world are, I believe, more alike than different, both biologically and culturally. But differences attract the attention. A commonly accepted division of world cultures, Eastern and Western, is fundamentally flawed. There are not two, but three, major historical civilizations; the Indian, the Chinese and the European. What distinguishes the three major civilizations from each other is the emphasis which is given to idealizing some traits, rather than others, and ignoring, suppressing, or perhaps despising others. These emphasized values are what make these three great historical cultures unique.

Of course, summarizing ideas of millions of people over a two-thousand-year period, is using a very broad brush. Nevertheless, certain persisting cultural traits do stand out. Outlining some of these different traits will help us toward our goal of achieving a world cultural outline.

First, let's remember Western culture has two basic pillars; the Judeo-Christian and the Greco-Roman. The great transcending concept of the Judeo-Christian tradition is that there is one God who has a plan with desires, wants and wishes. It is man's duty to discover God's plan, both for himself and for society, and carry it out according to God's wishes. To sin is to go against God's plan or wishes. God and his wishes are the measure of things. Greek

and Roman thought emphasized reason as form, order, regularity and the law. Real forms of real things can be known. Science as gaining knowledge about the nature of things is a European ideal inherited from the Greek faith in the logical structure of reality. Because man is a rational animal, both man and nature are inherently rational. Man is the measure of things. Down through the centuries, in the Western tradition, these two traditions have debated over which is ultimate in man and nature; reason or will.

Let me list some generalities:

Western culture encourages desire, Indians suppress desire, Chinese accept desire.

Man can have nothing but what he strives for. Advertising is good, satisfaction is good (Western).

Desire is the source of frustration. Frustration is evil. Therefore, desire is evil. Advertising creates desire and is evil (Indian).

Desire is natural and therefore good. Frustration is natural. Neither encourages or discourages ambition. Advertising is unnecessary (Chinese).

Western culture encourages activity, Indians encourage passivity, Chinese accept the need for both, each in turn.

To act is to be alive. To will is to act. Have initiative. Be inventive. Create (Western).

Being is more important than doing. Being is timeless. Action is temporal, temporary and illusory (Indian).

There is a time to rise and a time to go to bed; a time to work and a time to rest. Initiation of activity is symbolized by Yang, completion by Yin. Being and doing are nothing apart from being and Tao (Chinese). Western culture idealized being progressive, Indian the eternal, Chinese the present.

To will or desire is to lack what one wants. What is lacking can be filled only in the future. So expect the future to be better than the present (Western).

Time is not merely temporary but illusory. The greatest achievement is liberation from time and the endless rounds of reincarnation. The goal is eternal peace, passivity (nirvana). Withdraw from progressive, acquisitive, anxious and frustrating activities (Indian).

The present time is good. Whatever is natural is good and it is natural that the present is good. One should enjoy the present. The present is enjoyable and there is no need to hurry (Chinese).

Western culture wants to change things, Indians tend to regard change as illusory, Chinese see change as natural.

If we expect the future to be better than the present, then some change will have to occur. There can be no progress without change. Improve yourself, seek to improve others. Educate. Send missionaries (Western).

If ultimate reality is eternal, it does not and cannot change. If ultimate reality is good, goodness cannot be changed and improved. To believe things can be made better, is to mistake what is illusory for what is real. The only real change that counts is to escape, or liberation (Mukti), to nirvana (Indian).

Change is natural. The sun rises, the sun sets. If you are hungry, eat; sleepy, sleep. Nature (Tao) consists of changes, initiation (yang) is always followed by completion (yin). What is natural is good and natural changes are good (Chinese).

Western culture idealizes production of goods, Indians idealize non-attachment, Chinese emphasize enjoyment of life.

If desires are to be satisfied in the future, then we should work to bring about that satisfaction. If ends lie in the future, means are needed to achieve them. The work ethic urges greater efforts to produce more and better means (Western).

Every particular thing or value is temporary or illusory. To become attached to it as if it were real and of genuine value is to be misled. Non-attachment is better than attachment (Indian).

Enjoyment of life should be a self-evident value. Those misled into preferring means to ends, that is, devoting the present to producing future ends and postponing the enjoyment of life, are misled. It is equally natural to produce food as to eat it. Yang initiation and yin completion are both enjoyed while it predominates (Chinese).

Western culture focuses on God's will. He created heaven and wills everyone to get there, Indians envision dreams of quiescence, the Chinese conceive of the Tao as acting naturally and without exerting will.

The western hero is a producer who gets results. Skill, intelligence and efficiencies are high virtues and he excels most when he invents. (The Greeks hold that man is like a God because only man and God can create.)

The Indian hero is the yogin. By practicing yoga, he is aware of the quiescence of nirvana while still alive and is honored above all others.

In China, the ideal of Taoism is the ability to follow one's own nature without deviation or to live naturally, while in the Confucian ideal, each person is, by nature, social and he should follow his social nature of good will, appropriate behavior and right action. The ideal man willingly accepts his own nature and has no desire to deviate from nature's way.

Western culture tends to idealize reason, Indians idealize intuition, Chinese tend to accept apprehension.

If we understand the nature of something, then we can predict how it will behave and so avoid evils which might result or could be used for our benefit. Nature is understandable and what is understood is rational also. In a complex structure, we distinguish its parts, kill the animal, cut it up. If we can draw all this in detail, we have achieved understanding (Western).

Intuition grasps the unity of the whole. Intuition can provide certainty because it grasps all at once as a whole. Intuition does not take apart and put back together, it grasps the wholeness immediately. It is the quickest and surest way of knowing(Indian).

Experience comes both as a whole and its parts. A thing and its structure are not two different things. Each thing is a natural whole with its own natural parts. To see the parts separated from the whole is to miss something fundamental to what appears. To grasp the whole while ignoring the parts, is to ignore something essential to what appears (Chinese).

Alan Watts sums up the three views of the world. The West views the world as an artifact (something made), India views the world as drama (something manifested), while China views the world as drama (something grown). An artifact is made following a plan in the mind of the maker. In a drama, the actors play their parts as if real. In an organism, the principle of order in the universe unfolds itself. The West tends to emphasize definiteness, Indian indefiniteness, and China naturalism. This leads in the West to an encouragement of ambition and activity, progress and productivity; in India to suppression of desire, passivity, eternality and withdrawal of attachment; in China to an acceptance of change and continuance as natural, being present-oriented and enjoyment.

While itemizing some fundamental culture differences, don't lose sight of the fact there are more similarities than differences. Our common bond as humans make this so. Knowing some of the different emphases may be helpful in trying to understand persons from other cultures. Remember also that broad generalities are never completely true.

(I thank Professor Archie J. Bahm of the University of New Mexico for his philosophical comparisons.)

EAST
Man is part of nature
Knowledge is non-verbal
Life is a mystery to be lived

WEST
Man should conquer nature
Knowledge is verbal
Life is a problem to be solved

Most people without further study would intuitively be able to categorize the above statements as Eastern or Western. They are basically different points of view on some fundamental values. We, in the West, with our Christian inheritance, are dominated by an implicit faith in perpetual progress. This faith was unknown in Eastern culture or to Greece and Rome, for that matter. Christianity inherited from Judaism not only a concept of time as non-repetitive and linear, which is discussed in the chapter on "Time," but a distinct story of creation. By gradual stages, a loving and all-powerful God had created light and darkness, the heavenly bodies, the earth and all its plants, animals, birds and fish. Finally, God had created Adam and, as an afterthought, Eve, to keep man from being lonely. Man named all the animals, this establishing his dominance over them. God had planned all of this explicitly for man's benefit and rule; no item in the physical creation had any purpose except to serve man's purposes. And although man's body is made of clay, he is not simply part of nature; he is made in God's image. Judaism, in contrast to ancient paganism and Asia's religions, not only established a dualism of man and nature, but also insisted that it is God's will that man exploit nature for his own ends. Judaism made it possible to exploit nature in a mood of indifference to the feelings of natural objects.

Contrast this with the teachings of Taoism and Confucius. Here, we must strive to achieve harmony with nature. Disharmony with nature, including our own, is the cause of unhappiness.

"Standing on tiptoe, a man loses his balance;" "Nature does not have to insist;" "The earth is like a vessel so sacred that it is marred by the approach to the profane." We, in America, talk of "conquering Mt. Everest" and "how the West was won." A Chinese would go to Mt. Everest for the view, but not to conquer (see Far Eastern Culture chapter on Confucius and Taoism).

Let me tell a story. Two men hear for the first time about oranges. Both are interested to know more. The first man goes to the library and studies oranges. He learns where they are grown, the diseases, how to grow orange trees, types of oranges. He learns a lot about oranges. The second man goes to a store, buys six oranges and eats them. The question is, which man knows most about oranges? In my classes, most students opt for the man who ate them. What I would like to propose is that there are two kinds of knowledge.

Western culture tends to go to the library for answers. We get this from Greek science and that centuries-old tradition of discovering God's laws by breaking into parts. The Indians or Chinese have a tradition that emphasizes intuitive grasp of the whole. So the man who ate the oranges has a perfect right to say, "You don't know oranges, you simply know about oranges." While the man who read and studied oranges can say "How ignorant you are about oranges. All you know is about their taste." Both are right.

We have all had experiences such as mine. Living in Michigan, I had never seen an ocean until I was 14. I knew about oceans, could name them and something of their chemistry. One day, I went to an ocean and later crossed the Atlantic several times in a ship. Only then did I know oceans.

The chapter on India discusses the Buddha. He has a problem. He does not go to a laboratory or library. He goes out and by practicing prayer and fasting, achieves enlightenment.

How many Americans spend most of their time "pasting" and "futuring?" "Oh, if I had only said this or done this." And so many of my students talk about starting to live when they graduate, then start living when they are married, or perhaps when they get a job, or then perhaps once they retire. Life is a problem to be solved.

An Indian may go to a church service in America and wonder, "Is that all they do is talk? I thought we were supposed to listen, calling on God to solve problems." If we are quiet, God will reveal his wishes to you. Life is a mystery. Live each moment. Enter into harmony with nature, don't try to change it.

While I have enumerated differences, lets not forget that perhaps the most significant change is that today's cultures are integrating with each other. Each is being modified by this interaction. As long ago as 1946, F.S.C. Northrop, in a book called *The Meeting of East and West,* argued that East and West "can meet, not because they are saying the same thing, but because they are expressing different yet complimentary things, both of which are required for an adequate and true conception of man's self and his universe." He predicted that East and West values would unite in single thought systems, each absorbing the other's merits and each making up for the other's shortcomings.

▶ Three Models for Culture's Future Role

There has been a new interest in the role of culture by intellectuals recently with a flood of essays and books on culture as the basic force driving the world to act and organize as it does. The basic arguments have tended to group themselves around three models for the future.

The first model sees culture as playing a growing role in international relationship and conflicts.

Perhaps the most influential recent exposition of the clash of cultures in the world and their future impact on world affairs has been "The Clash of Civilization" by Professor Samuel P. Huntington. As this ambitious and provocative theory of culture has become a center of world debate, I would like to present Professor Huntington's views in some detail. His central point is that the fundamental source of conflict in this new (post-cold war) world will not be primarily ideological or primarily economic. The great divisions among humankind and the dominating source of conflict will be cultural. The principal conflicts of global politics will occur between nations and groups of different civilizations. The clash of civilizations will dominate global politics.

He names seven cultural centers that form clashing groups: Western, Confucian, Japanese, Islamic, Hindu, Slavic Orthodox, Latin American and possibly African. Along these "fault lines" or cultures

he writes one will find the battle lines of the future. Future wars will be culture wars. "Culture is the dominant framework for international relations, a principal basis for state actions and the chief source of conflict in world affairs."

Huntington sees the decline of the nation-state as the primary playing piece in world politics with a larger entity, culture, coming to the fore.

To support this view, we need only look at the continuing conflict in the former Yugoslavia, which is not a war between nations, but a cultural war involving Western Christians, Eastern Orthodox Christians and Muslims. See Figure 1-1.

A second model sees the world becoming one. This sees the rise of new technology creating our world.

The industrializing action of the world is the basis for an enormous homogenizing of global communications, travel, business and awareness. All industrialized societies must have rapid and regular communication with other people. There has been a great convergence as a result of world-scale enterprises. An American executive can feel more or less at home working in a Japanese company and vice versa. A computer programmer from the U.S. can work with other computer programmers from India or Thailand. There can be little doubt that industrial societies are showing many similarities and the process is accelerating. As Chinese Confucian values fade and everyone's lifestyles and world products converge, some argue logically the cultural differences are becoming less important. (Contrast this view with that of Professor Huntington.)

Free markets and access to the world's goods are the hope of all mankind. This process guarantees an increasing homogenization of all human societies regardless of their historical origins or cultural inheritances, and has a powerful effect in undermining traditional social groups like tribes, clans, extended families, religious sects, and so on.

Dozens of commentators have examined the emerging globalism and, of course, all business ventures have learned to think globally. Toynbee foresaw, "The evolving nature of the global economy is causing governments and businesses to reach past their cultural fetters and embrace globally shared models of governance, corporate structure, and economy. If this is true, then after continuing influence during the transitional period, cultures will decline as a factor influencing world affairs."

FIGURE 1-1

A border between Western or Latin Christianity and Eastern Orthodox Christianity has existed now for about 1,000 years. It has been a bloody border; you will note the line runs through Croatia, Bosnia, and Serbia and supports Professor Huntington's thesis.

Vaclav Havel writes that ours is the "first civilization in the history of the human race that spans the entire globe and firmly binds together all human societies, submitting them to a common global destiny." The result, Havel says, is an "amalgamation of cultures."

The third model holds there is both a new growing emphasis on cultural roots and a homogenous world of technology, communication and commerce. This point of view was expressed perhaps best by Benjamin R. Barber in an *Atlantic Monthly* article, "Jihad vs. the World." He sees two futures. First, a retribalization of large parts of the world with a breakdown of the nation state, as in Lebanon, into a world of culture against culture, people against people and tribe against tribe. A Jihad, or holy war, of hundreds of narrowly conceived cultures. Again, look at Lebanon, separatist movements in Catalonia, The Basque, Quebec, Bosnia and Kurds and Armenians. Countering the movement is the onrush of economic and ecological forces that demand integration and uniformity and that mesmerize the world with fast music, fast computers, and fast food—with MTV, Macintosh, and McDonald's, pressing nations into one commercially homogenous global network: one McWorld tied together by technology, ecology, communications, and commerce. The planet is falling precipitantly apart *and* coming reluctantly together at the very same moment. These two tendencies which he calls Jihad and McWorld are operating with equal strength in opposite directions. One divided by parochial hatreds, the other by universalizing markets. The one recreating subnational and ethnic borders from within making national borders weak from without.

Whichever model you emphasize, it appears that what has come from the West will still be at the core for every educated person in the world to come to grips with the present. Whether pro-western or anti-western, the world's material well-being all rests on western foundations, western science; tools and technology; production; economics; western-style finance and banking. None of these can work unless grounded in an understanding and acceptance of western ideas and of the entire western tradition. All societies are influenced by the western model. They are still engaged in conquest of the material world. As they proceed with their industrialization, they progressively embrace the "western ideas," in Huntington's litany, "of individualism, liberalism, constitutionalism, human rights, equality, liberty, the rule of law, democracy, free markets. . . ."

Tomorrow's educated person will have to be prepared for life in a global world. It will be a "westernized" world, but also increasingly a tribalized world. He or she must become a "citizen of the world"—in vision, horizon, information, but will also have to draw nourishment from local roots; enrich and nourish their own local culture.

I hope the reader will keep these three models in mind as we proceed to discuss four cultural realms.

Author's Note:

I have concluded each chapter with a "Study/Work Sheet" divided into three categories; **define or identify**, which lists key vocabulary and terms, **explain** which lists key ideas for the understanding of the chapter and finally, **discuss** which will itemize larger concepts presented. For the reader, it should be an excellent review of the chapter and a measure of the level of understanding. For the instructor, it can be a guide for teaching and a source for examination questions.

CHAPTER ONE

Define or identify:

- What is culture?

  Shared value or value systems

- What are the four subdivisions of Western culture?

  Latin Europe, Northern Europe, Latin America, Northern America

- What are the three subdivisions of Far Eastern culture?

  China, Korea, Japan

Explain:

- What are the three objectives of the book?

- What are the four cultural realms that will be the focus of the book?

- What are the four value areas that will be discussed as formative to culture?

• Use your opinions to answer Dr. Vetter's questions that a foreigner might ask about America concerning family, divorce, crime, and race relationships.

• Place the following statements in the Eastern or Western tradition:
Knowledge is verbal rather than non-verbal.
Acceptance of fate rather than control of fate.
Man is integral to nature rather than man is meant to conquer nature.

• Life is a mystery to be lived rather than a problem to be solved.

Discuss:

• What would you say were the characteristics of an ugly American?

• What would be the negative side of you as an American "going native" during your stay in Mexico?

• What does the book suggest is the most important value to develop in dealing with people from a different culture?

• What does the author see as the negative side of multiculturalism?

Chapter 2 ▶▶ ▶

Space and People

We think in images. Recently the world has received an important new image of itself, photographs taken from space. We now have a vision of Spaceship Earth, fragile, floating alone, a beautiful blue and white jewel in a black void. We can never again look at the world in quite the same way as we did before. It is a new picture of the world.

A picture of a thing, however, is not the thing, and a picture of the world is not the world. But it strikes us as a closer representation of the thing than a map. So we must start our view of the world with the realization that maps are our attempt to organize the world into meaningful patterns. We smile today at medieval maps showing Jerusalem as the center of a flat world which, in turn, was the center of the universe.

Today most maps of the world show countries well distinguished by sharp borders and distinct colors. This is not the way the world looks from outer space. In other words, these divisions are artificial, reflecting our present-day tendency to look at the world in terms of political units and primarily as nations. This map of the world is in a constant state of flux as new countries are formed, expand and divide politically, But, of course, there are various maps of the world, organization charts created to describe the world in answer to needs and points of view.

All flat maps are wrong for the simple reason the world is round. Thus, these representations of reality exaggerate the size of land as it gets farther from the equator. Canada and the USSR are exaggerated in size relative to Mexico and India. Distances and directions are also distorted. Distances nearer the equator will appear shorter than the same distances north or south of the equator. Most disconcerting to a flat map reader, which nine times out of ten looks at the globe with North America in the center, is to find that his flight from New York to London will proceed North from New York and fly over Greenland, rather than east on a direct line. Only by using a globe and a string will this "great circle route" be confirmed as the shortest path. (See Figure 2-1.)

▶ Latitude and Longitude

One very useful way for the world traveler to look at the world is in terms of latitude and longitude. When the Europeans started on their world voyages of trade and discovery and confirmed the world was actually round, they needed a way of knowing where on the surface of the sphere they were. A system was worked out that divided the world into a grid using sun, stars, and time to place location on this grid.

Starting at the equator, the distance to the north or south pole is approximately 6,000 miles, and the angle from the center of the earth between the equator and its poles is 90 degrees, a right angle. These degrees are called degrees of latitude. If you are at 45 degrees latitude, you are halfway between the equator and the North Pole (about 3,000 miles

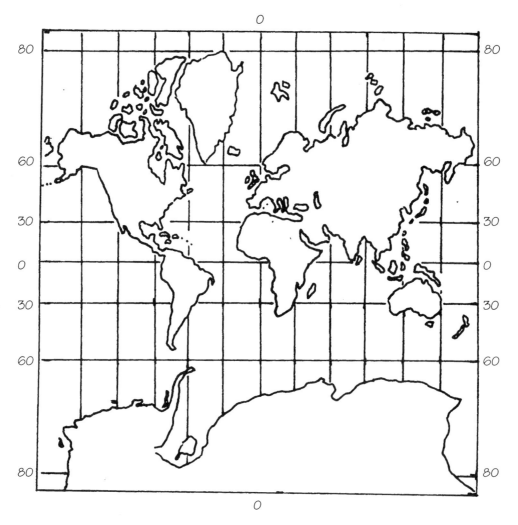

FIGURE 2-1 A commonly used Mercator projection contains gross distribution of size in high altitudes; i.e., Greenland appears larger than South America.

each way). Latitude can be determined by the position of the sun and the date, which plots the course of the run between its Tropic of Cancer and Tropic of Capricorn.

The more difficult job is to locate your position East and West. The ability to do this was a key element in the conquest of the oceans and subsequently the world by Europe. The solution came with the precise clocks that were starting to be produced in Europe in the 1200s: simply divide the world around the center into a 360-degree circle. These are degrees longitude.

The earth is approximately 24,000 miles around at the equator. Knowing that the earth rotates once every 24 hours and comparing local sun, as they observed it, to the time shown on the clock, each

hour of time difference translated into 15 degrees of longitude. Today we have time zones of approximately 1,000 miles (24,000 miles divided by 24 hours). Longitude starts at 0 at a line north and south through the location of the British Royal Naval Research Center in Greenwich, England; the days start at the International Date Line in the middle of the Pacific.

So time runs East to West at about 1,000 miles an hour with longitude with the day starting in the middle of the Pacific. Climate runs north and south with latitude. Our time cycle is based on the daily rotation of the earth around the sun, and climate is affected by the yearly cycle of the sun between the Tropic of Cancer and the Tropic of Capricorn. (See Figures 2-2 and 2-3.)

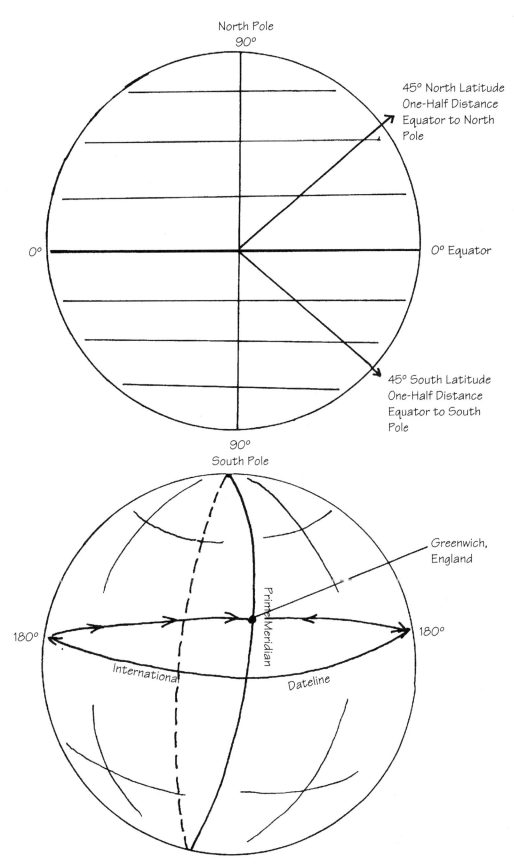

FIGURE 2-2 June 21—Summer Solstice. December 21—Vernal Equinox (sun farthest from equator)
September 21—Autumnal Equinox. March 21—Vernal Equinox (sun directly overhead at the equator.

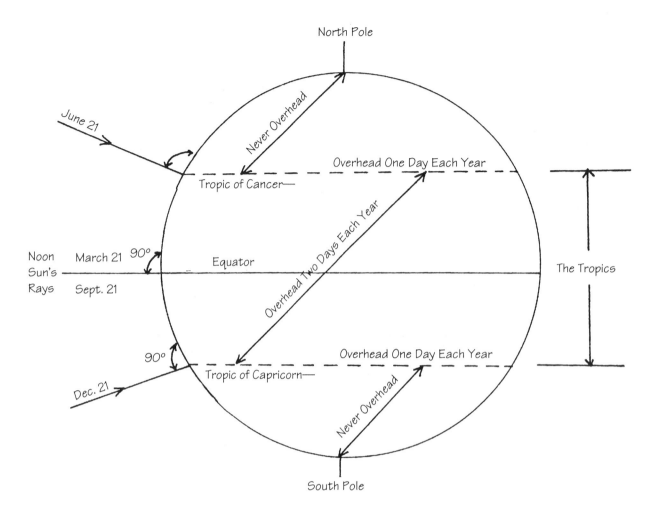

FIGURE 2-3 Latitude—Planes parallel to the equator. Longitude—Planes passing through both poles or planes parallel to the axis.
June 21—Summer solstice (sun furthest from equator)
December 21— Winter solstice
September 21—Autumnal equinox (sun directly overhead at the equator)
March 21—Vernal equinox

▶ Cultural Implications

People have always placed enormous significance on the sun's movements. Very early, the key dates were sanctified by religion. From Stonehenge to the Mexican Toltec pyramids, orientation marked the equinox, when the sun stands directly over the equator. March 21, is the first day of spring and September 21, the first day of fall; the solstice occurs when the sun stands at the tropic lines June 21, the beginning of summer, the longest day of the year, and December 21, the beginning of winter and shortest day of the year.

Today these dates are still remembered by midsummer's night celebrations in Scandinavia at the summer solstice, Christian Easter which is set at the first Sunday after the first full moon after the equinox, and Christmas at the winter solstice. The return of the longer days at Christmas is identified with Christ's birth and the coming of the light into the world. Christ, the light of the world, conquers darkness. Easter, the time of planting and the earth's fertility, is commemorated both by the fertility symbols of eggs and bunnies and by Christ rising from the dead. Christ's rising conquers death.

These, of course, are European in origin, and the dates are quite out of sync when we move to the Southern hemisphere where the seasons are reversed. Christmas in Sydney, Australia, and Buenos Aires falls on their longest days and hottest season, and Easter, rather than the beginning of spring, is the beginning of their winter. (See Figure 2-2.)

▶ Physical Distance/Time Distance

Modern transportation and communication have changed the way we must think about the world and distance. The basic physical framework is a constant. The earth is 24,000+ miles around at the equator and the miles from New York to Paris remain the same. However, to be meaningful, this distance must be translated to time. The earth turns toward the sun at a rate of about 1,000 miles per hour (one time zone). As the SST (Super Sonic Transport Plane) can travel from Paris to New York faster than 1,000 mph, it is possible to arrive in New York earlier than you left.

Electronic communication is instantaneous. If I mail you a letter, it takes a couple of days. If I phone you, our communication is direct and instantaneous. All plane travellers have had the experience of taking more time to get the thirty miles to the airport through heavy traffic than the air travel time of 600 miles to the next city. So time and distance must be united to understand the world and its people. How far can I go in a day? On foot, 20 miles; in my car, 600 miles; by air, 20,000 miles.

▶ Climate

Climate has had and continues to have a major influence on cultural patterns. The temperate lands (i.e., those outside the tropics) are generally the lands of dependable rain, mild sunshine and fertile topsoil. They also contain a great part of the world's mineral resources. Most importantly, the steady and invigorating alternation of warmth and frost creates a climate in which man and beast are favored, and pests and parasites are not.

The area between the Tropic of Cancer and Capricorn is less favored. Here the flood and heat, the scorching sun, the torrential downpours leach and wash away the soil. Disease and parasites breed in the steaming rivers and forests or else perpetual sun dries out the land and leaves it an empty desert.

Cultural patterns and values arise as a response to the climatic condition. Climate dictates the crops to be grown, clothing to be worn and value to be rewarded or punished. Sometimes, as with the Eskimos, the culture becomes very specialized, fixed and isolated. The nomads of the Asian steppe used the horse and superior mobility to conquer the world in the 1200s. Northern foods tend to be bland and high in calories, whereas, further south, food gets spicier. The siesta of Spain and Greece is a sensible adjustment to the hot mid-day sun.

Some historians and philosophers have even developed a climatic theory of civilization. According to this theory, high civilizations do not arise in the tropics or Arctic regions because its climates are too severe. In the tropics it's too hot to be active and life is a relatively simple matter since food is abundant. In the polar cold, the weather is so severe the people must spend most of their energy just finding food and staying alive. They don't have time for building cities and other developments. But in the middle latitudes where the temperature is neither too hot nor too cold and there is an invigorating variety of temperatures and weather conditions, civilization can be built.

▶ Where the People Are

Two major trends in population need to be remembered to put the world today in proper perspective. First is the rapid increase in world population which is completely out of any growth pattern of 5,000 years of recorded history and secondly, the movement from the countryside to the city.

The gross numbers give an idea of the world trend. In the twentieth century, population seems to spring off the end of the graph. (See Figure 2-4.)

World population edged up from the levels made possible by early agriculture to perhaps 400 million by the fall of Rome. Over 1,500 years later, it reached its first billion. Thereafter, the acceleration began as a result of rising production on farms and in factories as the Industrial Revolution was followed by a steady fall in the death rate. The second billion arrived after only three hundred years in 1900. The third took only 50 years, 1950, and in the late '80s the world's population reached an estimated 5 billion.

Individual countries and area increases are uneven, but generally stunning. Up to 1800, all of Europe did not succeed in reaching a total population of over 180 million. Between 1800 and 1914, the population of Europe went from 180 million to 460 million and this at a time when millions were leaving to populate North and South America, Australia and South Africa.

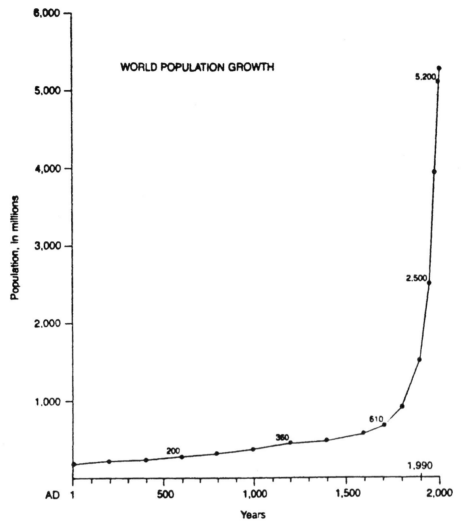

WORLD POPULATION GROWTH

FIGURE 2-4 World Population Explosion. The world's population increased steadily from 1700 to 1900, then began to increase rapidly. Since about 1950 it has "exploded" with a very rapid increase rate.

It is estimated that in 1650 Europe and the Americas had a population of 113 million; Africa, 100 million; and Asia, 330 million. It is common to think of the world's non-white populations as jostling and pushing out white populations. Actually, the last few hundred years have seen the European peoples settle the Americas, the temperate lands of South Africa, Australia, and New Zealand. As the Russians pressed east, Asia was settled by Europeans. By 1940 the populations of the Americas and Europe had risen six times and the Americas over twenty times, while Africa had not risen by even 50% and Asia had only tripled.

The numbers alone are also misleading, for in the 400+ years from 1550 to today, Europeans were expanding into what were without exception the best lands of the earth—the temperate lands. While we have traditionally focused on European colonialization of Africa and India, the really significant feature of the last few hundred years has been European colonization and settlement of the world's more or less empty lands. Total population in continents with predominantly European population, Europe, America and Australia, went up from a fourth of the world population in 1750 to more than a third in 1950.

▶ Urban Growth

The growth of cities and the urbanization of both developed and underdeveloped areas of the world are the most distinctive and universal features of the world today. The migration of large numbers of rural people to the growing industrial centers together with the mass migration from Europe to the empty areas of the world are the two elements of a large redistribution of the world's population.

The world-wide process of urbanization continues as a smaller and smaller percentage of the population is now required for feeding the rest. In the United States, for example, less than 5% of the population is engaged in agriculture today. The other 95% seek their livelihood in some city.

Similar percentages are true for Europe and Japan. In Australia, an overwhelming majority of the population is located in five big cities. These developed countries are able to live and, indeed, create an agricultural surplus from 5% of their population because of great technical leaps forward in farming procedures that make it possible for one land owner to cultivate 600 acres and more.

In non-industrialized countries, the pull of urbanization is more economic than technical. Subsistence farming barely supported the existing population before the population explosion began. If the additional millions were to remain on the land, they would starve. So they flock to Calcutta, Mexico City, Cairo. Here they may well go hungry, too, but as centers of government and industry, many more possibilities for survival are present.

In addition, cities attract rich and poor alike as centers of activity, entertainment and opportunity. Major cities in the non-industrialized world from Lima to Baghdad to Rangoon are surrounded by shanty towns where dreams of a better life overshadow the grim reality of the slum life they have chosen.

All over the world advanced and backward cities alike are growing on a scale and at a pace that would indicate that separate cities will coalesce into a megapolis. Already the northeastern section of the United States is coagulating into a megapolis stretching from Boston to Washington, D.C. while Los Angeles, Mexico City and Tokyo swell to the size of countries. Some feeling for the population percentages of a country contained in their principal metropolitan area indicates the principle city's dominant position, Tokyo 35%, Oslo 15%, Paris 17%, Copenhagen 30%, Sydney 20%, Ring City, Holland 34%, Buenos Aires 20%.

Size is, however, only one characteristic of the big city. It has overpowering economic significance as a manufacturing, commercial or financial center and quite often all of these. In addition, large metropolitan areas exert a strong cultural eminence. Here are located universities, the symphony orchestra, museums and art galleries, the theater and opera houses. And, finally, the city exerts strong political power as a massive concentration of highly organized prestige and authority.

The growing migration of people from rural to urban areas is largely a result of a desire for greater access to sources of education, health care and improved job opportunities. These attractions can be considerable to individual families, for once in the city, perhaps three out of four migrants make economic gains. Income can roughly triple for an unskilled laborer with a move to an urban area. The family income of a manual worker in urban Brazil is almost five times that of a farm laborer in a rural area.

Industries also benefit from concentrations of laborers and consumers. Large cities provide big, differentiated labor markets and the exploitation of economies of scale for water supplies, electric power, health services, food distribution and other social services made possible in large urban centers.

Although there are some benefits from urban growth and migrants experience some relative improvement in their living standards, intense urban growth without commensurate investment in services eventually leads to profound problems. Slums populated with unskilled workers living hand to mouth puts excessive pressure on sanitation systems, water supplies and other social services. At some point, the disadvantages of unregulated growth begins to outweigh the advantage for all concerned.

While it is true that a majority of mankind still consists of subsistence farming peasants because of their predominance throughout Asia and Africa, it is clear that the trend is to urban life. This trend is having a profound effect on the social environment, traditional values and psychological adjustment of people around the world. Since the beginning of historical times, the city was marked off as a huddle of human beings separated from the normal open country and endless wilderness beyond. Today, the exception is not the city; it is the park or greenbelt which must be fenced off to keep megapolis from engulfing it.

▶ Rich Industrial North— Poor Agricultural South

If we judge the economic lives of our ancestors by modern American standards, it is a story of almost unrelieved wretchedness. The typical human society has always given only a small number of people the leisure and means for a humane existence.

Only during the last two hundred years and in a few places in the world have progress and prosperity touched the lives of a large section of the population. These places—Western Europe, the United States and Canada. Australia and Japan—contain an unusually high proportion of people who are better fed and healthier, enjoy more possessions and are more secure than most of the rest of the world, and than the ancient Indian, Greek, Roman, and Islamic cultures; in other words, than at any other time in history.

We speak of developing countries when we refer to the other areas. This phrase has nothing to do with levels of culture or contribution to civilization. The phrase means simply that a society has not yet crossed the threshold to the modern, high-technology society often referred to as the West. Included are immensely old and well-developed civilizations such as India or China, long- established societies in Latin America and very old continuous political units such as Egypt and Iran.

Besides developed and developing areas, we also speak of the rich manufacturing north and the poor agricultural south. A purely arbitrary figure of $3,000 Gross National Product per capita serves as a level at which an area begins to emerge into a developed condition. In most of the underdeveloped world, annual per capita incomes of less than $500 are the rule. In the developed countries, the GDP per capita figures illustrate the vast discrepancies:

United States	$24,700
Sweden	$17,600
Germany	$16,500
Japan	$20,400
India	$1,300
Somalia	$500
Uganda	$1,200

It is easy to see why these countries in the underdeveloped world are attempting to import western technology, industrialization and government practices. (GDP figures vary according to variable exchange rates. Also, these figures are dated and are cited for comparative purposes.)

The failure to attain meaningful Third Word development during the recent decades is evident in various social statistics. In 1981 the richest fifth of the world's population received 71 percent of the world's product, whereas, the poorest fifth received 2 percent. Differences in food consumption contributed to differences in health conditions. Life expectancy in the developed countries in 1981 was 72 to 74 years; in the poorest of the underdeveloped countries it was 42 to 44 years. Infant mortality (death before age one) in the developed world in 1981 fluctuated between 10 to 20 deaths per 1,000 live births; in the poorest underdeveloped countries the death rate was 200 per 1,000. The 1974 World Food Conference set the goal that within a decade no child would go to bed hungry. But the 1984 World Food Conference had to face the fact that hunger had not been alleviated—that 400 to 600 million people remained chronically hungry.

The move from poverty to wealth is, of course, an advance in material well being. It is also a move away from death as life expectancy goes up and mortality rates go down. It is a move from famine and hunger with a decline in malnutrition and related disease. It is a move from illiteracy, superstition, ignorance and life within a narrow village setting, to literacy, education, with greater possibilities and individual choice.

We must understand that poverty and wealth have powerful cultural implications and establish values. Improved incomes mean that early years working can be spent in school, a future of farm work can be changed to a trade or a profession. A hut can be exchanged for an apartment in town. Rich societies differ from the poor not only in having more money, but in having an entirely different way of life for their members.

Rich and Poor*

Television sets:

United States	1 per 1.2 persons
Sweden	1 per 2.2 persons
Germany	1 per 2.5 persons
Japan	1 per 1.2 persons
India	1 per 45 persons
Uganda	1 per 145 persons

Telephone:

United States	1 per 1.3 persons
Sweden	1 per 2.3 persons
Germany	1 per 1.7 persons
Japan	1 per 2.2 persons
India	1 per 131 persons
Uganda	1 per 314 persons

Physicians:

United States	1 per 391 persons
Sweden	1 per 394 persons
Germany	1 per 313 persons
Japan	1 per 570 persons
India	1 per 2,189 persons
Uganda	1 per 20,720 persons

*Taken from the 1996 World Almanac

▶ Facts About Our World

- Area of the world's surface is about 196,951,000 square miles (510,100,000 square kilometers)

- Population of the world in 1988 totaled about 5,014,000,000.

- Largest continent is Asia, which covers 16,968,000 square miles (43,947,000 square kilometers).

- Smallest continent is Australia, which covers 2,966,150 square miles (7,682,300 square kilometers).

- Most populous country is China, which had about 1,097,000,000 people in 1988.

- Distance around at the equator, about 24,000 miles. (Note: 24 hours/day—24 times zones—time zone approx. 1,000 miles.)

Worksheet ▶

CHAPTER TWO

Define or identify:

- Tropic of Cancer.

- Tropic of Capricorn.

- Longitude 0.

- International Date Line.

- Rich—industrial North.

- Poor—agricultural South.

- Solstice.

- Equinox.

- Where is the sun directly overhead on March 21, June 21, September 21 and December 21?

- What is a time zone?

- If it is 12 noon in Michigan, what time is it in London, England?

- If it is summer in Michigan, in what season is Argentina?

Explain:
- I am at 45 degrees north latitude. Am I closer to the North Pole or the equator?

- What is the approximate distance around the earth at the equator?

- Name some countries you would put in the rich industrial north and some you would put in the poor agricultural south.

- Greenland is farther from the equator than Brazil. Why, on flat maps, does it look larger, even though it is smaller?

- I am 100 kilometers from Paris. How far is that in miles?

• I have 10 kilograms of potatoes. How many pounds do I have?

• Is it farther from New York to Paris or Buenos Aires? Going to Paris, I would pass through time zones; going to Buenos Aires, I would change seasons.

Discuss:

• What are the distortions we get from a flat map?

• When I leave New York for Europe, I head toward Greenland, which is north of New York. Why?

• How does the sun's movement fix the dates for the Christian celebrations of Christmas and Easter? What is the significance or symbolism?

• What are some of the cultural implications of moving from poverty to wealth?

Chapter 3 ▶ ▶

SOURCES OF CULTURAL VALUES
Language, Religion, Time, History

▶ LANGUAGE

> Language is not simply a reporting device for experience, but a defining framework for it.
> — Benjamin Whorf

Language and culture are so tied together that it is not an exaggeration to equate language with culture. Language is all pervasive. It enters into, influences and is, in turn, influenced by every form of human activity without exception. That everything we do, think or create influences language is fairly evident. What is not so obvious perhaps is that language, in turn, affects all our actions and thoughts. It is well established that the change of language on the part of a speaker, for example, is accompanied by changes in gestures, mannerisms, even humor.

I believe we can all relate to the feeling Frederick Buechner in his novel *Godric,* puts in the mouth of a pilgrim returning to England after a long pilgrimage to Rome. "An onion's an onion, no matter how you call it. A man's a man, a tree's a tree and God is God, but when a Norman names them or a Dane or a Roman, there's something lost. The ear takes comfort from the sounds of home, and the outlandish speech of foreign folks makes all seem strange."

To put it another way, (*language is not a universal means of communication; it is really a means of communication within a particular culture which understands all the meanings. Each language signifies and perpetuates a particular world view.*) It forms a frame of reference which molds the thoughts of its users.

The picture of the world varies from one language to another. The words in each language reflect the primary emphasis and technology of the culture. The Arabs, for example, are said to have six thousand words for camel, its parts and its equipment—a specialization not needed by a German. Eskimos have many more words for snow than English, but are short of words for business and airplanes.

There is an inward as well as an outward speech, for there are two functions of language: **social** for relating with others and **private** as the individual uses it to express and define emotions and ideas. Language should not be regarded as solely an instrument of conscious reason, rather than of feelings and imagination. It is also much more a vehicle for conveying information. There are always subtle overtones of traditional associations for the speaker who grew up with it in its native culture. This is why language is such a key to culture, and without speaking the foreigners' language, it is difficult to really understand the culture. *There is nothing as powerful as the spoken language for distinguishing one culture from another.*

The strong cultural role of language helps us understand the cultural tensions and their political overtones in countries that have been politically united for years. If two languages are spoken in a country, there are two separate cultures, as illustrated by Flemish and Walloon speakers in Belgium. Recent events in Canada caused by the sharp divisions between the English and French speaking regions are evidence of language's force to mark off cultures. Spain is dealing with separatist movements among Basque and Catalan speakers seeking to preserve their special cultures. Just as languages and cultural groups develop inside national borders, so can language and cultural groups can stretch across national borders, as with Germany and Austria or North and South Korea.

The institution of the nation state originated in Europe, as we will explain later. Most of these nation states in Europe coincided approximately with language groupings, such as England, Germany, France, Finland, etc. European peoples have been very conscious of language and nationality and the relationship between the spirit of nationalism and language identity.

In recent years, the European institution of the nation state has been taken up by the world. These new nation states have not fit as neatly to the local linguistic map as was the case in Europe. For one thing, throughout a large part of Asian languages do not occur within neat geographical limits. They can even be mixed up in alternate houses on the same streets in the same towns. In this different setting, languages, in India, for example, are grouped by occupations and trades among individuals and don't fit political boundaries at all.

One of the major reasons for the political instability of Africa is that the borders of the new nation states were drawn by Europeans with very little regard to local tribal cultures and languages. Tribes with centuries-old traditions find themselves in different countries and often subject to persecution, if in a minority. The linguistic unity typical of the western countries where the nation state started is not typical of Africa as it is divided today.

Language could be called the soul of a people. For language forms thinking while expressing thoughts. All words contain an emotional content from the associations which they awake in the mind of the speaker or listener as well as the specific rational message. As children learn to think, the few first words they learn, as well as stories and songs, form a feeling and character. A national language embodies the national habits of thought and feeling, and in the course of generations, these habits mold the language itself.

National words and habits of speech are keys to the character of a people. For example, the modern American uses many words from business and entertainment just as the nineteenth century English drew heavily on sports and games, and the ancient Roman used words from the fields to explain military formations. Recall the Arabs' many words for camel.

The language we happen to use shapes our world view. Intolerance is probably based on linguistic differences more than any other factor. It is no accident that the Greeks coined the word *barbarian* in imitation of the supposed unintelligible Bar-Bar sound of those whose language they did not understand; that in many languages, the term for foreigner coincides with the word that means dumb or silent; or that the Italians called syphilis the "French disease."

Language is the key to the history and literature of a culture and the outlook and education we receive. Take, for example, the difference of outlook on European colonization between an English speaking American and a Spanish speaking Mexican. Most Americans, because of their English language information, would feel the superiority of the English colonization to that of the Spanish. The English settlers were not afraid of hard physical work, while the Spaniard, whether soldier or aristocrat, looked down on manual labor and left others to do it for him.

In religion, the English version would emphasize Spanish cruelty to the Indians and the Inquisition. Lust for gold would be accepted as fact and included in thousands of stories and books. In Mexico, our Spanish speaking neighbors would learn that Latin-American culture is superior to that which exists in North America. Not the Inquisition, but the Christian faith of the Catholic missionaries and the humanistic and spiritual life which they fostered is praised and contrasted with the history of the English exclusion of the Indian from their society. The Spanish interests in art, literature, and music are contrasted favorably with American preoccupation with trade, money and machines.

Who Speaks What

There are approximately 3,000 languages in the world and several thousand additional dialects. Because each language reflects cultural differences, this could be taken as a rough estimate of the number of different cultures in the world. Fortunately for understanding the main outlines of world culture, there are large areas of language dominance. Over 95% of the world's population speak one of the most common one hundred languages, and half speak one of the ten leading languages.

English is the language that has enjoyed by far the fastest growth in modern times. It's not concentrated in one area, but has the advantage of being widely distributed over the globe, thanks to the fact that the British Empire girdled the globe and English speaking colonists established their language in North America and Australia. English is, in fact, becoming the world's language for business, travel, and learning, filling the role once played by Latin in medieval Europe.

The present world role of English comes not only from the British Empire and English settlers, but also from the economic, technological and military power of the United States. American multinational business is found around the globe along with American businessmen, tourists and American troops. Movies have for years been a big American export, and now we have television in popular English originals. In fact, entertainment is an American-dominated industry, and wherever you go American songs will be heard in English.

As a result, English has become the most useful second language for anyone to learn in order to get a job, travel, or pursue higher studies and scientific research. In France, Germany, Russia and Japan, English is by far the predominant foreign language being studied in the schools. African international conferences are conducted in English as in India, where 33 major tongues are spoken. It serves as a *lingua franca*.

A word of warning however. Just because the foreigner is speaking English, does not mean this learned language is taking the place of his native language in setting core values and attitudes. Numerous languages in history have served the international role now being played by English: Greek at the time of Alexander, Church Latin throughout the Middle Ages, and French at the time of Louis XIV. Native languages and cultures remained. It is quite possible that the more the world becomes one, the more assertive people will become about their native culture and language, as we are seeing today in Quebec, Catalonia, Scotland and Ireland, to name a few. The more English becomes a world language, the more sensitive will the Arab and French be of their native language, and the show of respect the foreign speaker shows in an effort to communicate with them in their own language.

As we look back on the development of the major world languages, we see they started in a capital city and spread to other cities and eventually grew into national or international tongue. Athens, Rome, Paris, London each, in turn, extended its language and its particular culture. The values carried by the language attained a spiritual influence far wider, deeper and more lasting than any military, commercial and political empire.

Today there is a world exchange in language being brought about chiefly by the development of world-wide communication. If English is to be the principal world language, it is important that we who are lucky enough to have been born to it find a fresh interest in language as a whole and in our own English in particular. Language is a carrier of sentiment and image and values. We should treat it with respect, recognizing what a powerful tool it is.

In the Beginning

In the beginning was the word. At some time, early man began to communicate by vocal noises more elaborate than grunts and barks. The distinctive quality of man is that he is a talking animal. Our present day languages have all evolved and continue to change. Languages multiplied and spread over the face of the earth. Probably hundreds of thousands of languages have been spoken since the beginning. Today something like 2,800 are spoken, and over 1,200 of them are spoken by American Indian tribes, most of which number only a few thousand speakers. Some 700 are used by African Negroid groups, many of which are quite small.

The Top Twenty Languages*
Mother-tongue Speakers (millions)

1. Chinese (1,000)
2. English (350)
3. Spanish (250)
4. Hindi (200)
5. Arabic (150)
6. Bengali (150)
7. Russian (150)
8. Portuguese (135)
9. Japanese (120)
10. German (100)
11. French (70)
12. Punjabi (70)
13. Javanese (65)
14. Bihari (65)
15. Italian (60)
16. Korean (60)
17. Telugu (55)
18. Tamil (55)
19. Marathi (50)
20. Vietnamese (50)

*Cambridge Encyclopedia of Language, Cambridge University Press, 1987

Numbers, of course, are not the same as influence. Of the languages of the world, the languages of Europe are the most influential today and of the languages of Europe, English stands above the others. The languages of Europe are dominant because Europe, after 1500 AD, spread its culture throughout the world and it is also from Europe that the great revolutions in science, industry, and politics took place.

Indo-European Roots

The common mother tongue of all European languages, now long extinct, is called Indo-European. We know of the common ancestor through the clues found in the languages that have come from it. For example, English *mother*, Sanskrit *matar*, Greek *meter*, Latin *mater*, and Iranian *maithai* are obviously related. The Indo-European mother tongue started to be spoken about 8,000 years ago, probably in the open lands where Europe and Asia meet. Today its descendants are spoken and written all over the earth.

The history of the languages of the world might have been different had the Chinese spread their influence globally, as they might have; instead they turned inward. It was Europe that became a world explorer and colonizer between the fifteenth and eighteenth centuries and in so doing, were continuing a process that had begun several thousand years earlier. In the plain of what is now southern Russia, there existed a society whose everyday conversation contained the root words of almost all the languages now spoken in Europe, and many of those in southern Asia. The dispersal of this mother tongue, or "speech community" of closely related dialects, lasted many centuries until, through migration and conquest, it spread all over Europe. The original language had vanished and its dialects, through years of change and local usage, had grown into distinctive language groups.

Those of Europe were beginning to take shape as Greek and Latin, Celtic and Germanic, Slavonic and Baltic; in Asia, the same roots had changed into early Iranian forms and Sanskrit, parent of most of India's modern tongues. The change became, with time, so great, common communication was no longer possible. "Branches," Italic, Germanic, and Slavonic, evolved to form distinctive families of their own, and Latin and German had moved to another continent. There are now far more speakers of Spanish, Portuguese, and English in the Americas than there are in Europe. Russian, the most widely spoken of the Slovanic languages, has spread with the Russian empire across Asia.

See Figure 3-2 for a summary of the Indo-European family, today the languages of about one third of the human race.

The Languages of Europe

The Latin Family

The Romance languages, descended from the Latin of Rome, include five of Europe's official languages: Italian, French, Spanish, Portuguese, and Romanian. (See Figure 3-3.)

The Latin languages of Spain and Portugal are, next to English, the most successful of European colonizing languages. From the United States to Cape Horn, Spanish is the official language with the exception of Brazil (Portuguese). It is also the language used by millions of Americans, a total in excess of 300 million people. As Latin America's population is one of the fastest growing in the world,

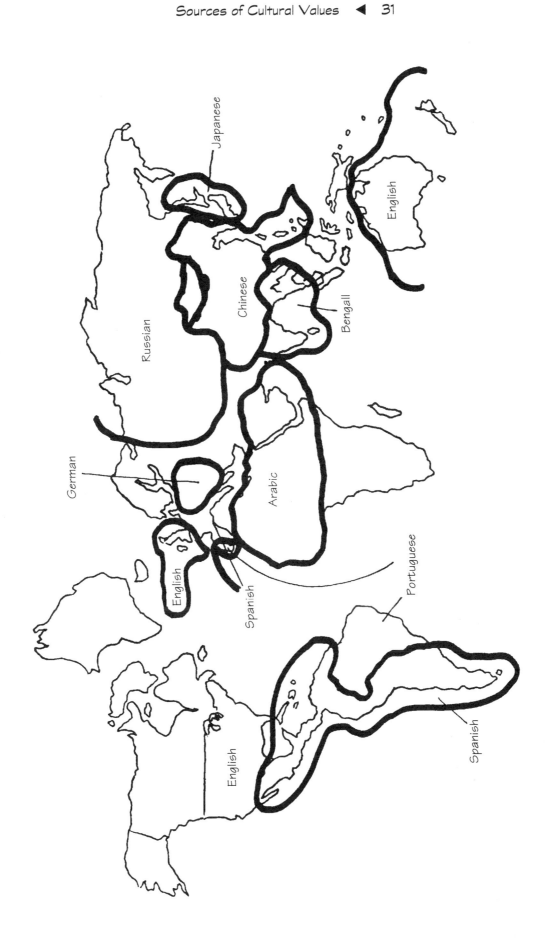

FIGURE 3-1 Distribution of the World's Major Languages

FIGURE 3-2 The Indo-European Family Today

Albanian		
Armenian		
Balto-Slavic	Burgarian	
	Czech	
	Latvian	
	Lithuanian	
	Polish	
	Russian	
	Serbo-Croation	
	Slovenian	
	Slovak	
	Ukrainian	
Celtic	Breton	
	Irish (Celtic)	
	Scots (Celtic)	
	Welsh	
Germanic	Dutch	
	English	
	German	
	Scandinavian –	Danish
		Icelandic
		Norwegian
		Swedish
Greek		
Indo-Iranian	Bengali	
	Farsi	
	Hindi	
	Pashto	
	Urdu	
Romance	French	
	Italian	
	Portuguese	
	Romanian	
	Spanish	

the number is expected to increase rapidly by the year 2000. This means that Spanish and Portuguese will retain and improve their importance among the world's languages. It is worth noting that the native American languages have not been completely destroyed; they are still used by about twenty million.

The Germanic Family

From their beginnings in northern Europe around the Baltic Sea, the Germanic languages are now heard throughout northern Europe. The spread of German was a result of the great migrations of German speaking tribes after the collapse of the Roman Empire. There are two important branches, the *Scandinavian* languages of Norway, Sweden, and Denmark and *English*, the most important international language.

The Slavonic Family

With Latin and German, Slavonic is one of the three most important language groups in Europe. It appears to have developed later than either of the others. The beginnings seem to have centered in western Russia during the first centuries AD, and to have expanded gradually during the next 700 years. From the common Slavonic tongue there emerged an eastern branch ("Three Russians"); a western branch (modern Polish and Czechoslovakian); and a southern branch (Serbo-Croat, Slovene, Macedonian, and Bulgarian). (See Figure 3-4.)

The Story of English

In richness, good sense, and terse convenience, no other of living languages may be put beside English.

— Jacob Grimm

Because of the present dominant role of English in the world today, English has become the most useful second language for anyone to learn and is the foreign language of choice in non-English speaking schools.

The making of English has three important elements. In the simplest terms, the language was brought to Britain by Germanic tribes, the Angles, Saxons and Jutes, hence Angle-ish, influenced by Latin and Greek when England became Christian, and finally transformed by the French-speaking Normans.

The roots go back to the Central European language group called the Indo-European, as we discussed. Their descendants are the languages of Europe. English has much in common with all these languages. A word like brother has an obvious family resemblance to its Indo-European cousins: broeder (Dutch), bruder (German), phrater (Greek), brat (Russian), brathair (Irish), and bhratar (Sanskrit).

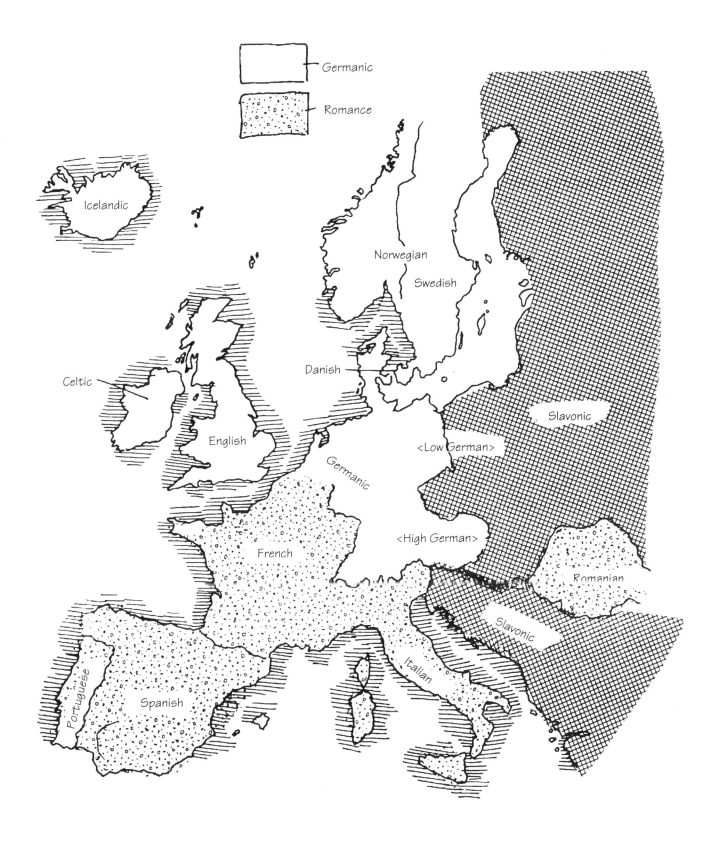

FIGURE 3-3 The Germanic and Romance Language Division of Europe

FIGURE 3-4 The Slavonic Languages of Europe

The Anglo-Saxons

According to their own record of events, *The Anglo-Saxon Chronicle*, the first invaders of the British Isles—the Angles, Saxons and Jutes—sailed across the North Sea from Denmark and the coastal part of Germany, still known as Lower Saxony, in the year AD 449. They brought their language and overcame the Gaelic speaking native tribes whose language survives in parts of Scotland, Ireland and Wales. In the course of the next 150 years, they set up seven kingdoms (Northumbria, Mercia, East Anglia, Kent, Essex, Sussex and Wessex) in an area which roughly corresponds to present-day England. They called the dispossessed Britons wealas, meaning "foreigners," from which we get the word Welsh.

To this day the feeling of animosity between the English on the one hand and the Welsh, the Scots and the Irish on the other, can be strong. The Welsh campaign for bilingualism; the Scots proudly retain separate legal and education systems and frequently make known their feeling of difference from the English, and the Irish have been at war with the English now on and off for nearly eight centuries. The extent to which the Anglo-Saxons overwhelmed the natives is illustrated by the fact that instead of Celtic words blending with the invaders' language, only a handful were ever used.

To the Celts, their German conquerors were all Saxons, but gradually the terms Anglii and Anglia crept into the language, generally referring to the invaders. The people started using Angelcynn (Angle-kin) and their language was Angle-ish. By AD 1000, the country was generally known as Angleland, the land of the Angles.

While modern English has used few Celtic words, many of the finest writers in English—for example, Swift, Burns, Burke, Scott, Stevenson, Wilde, Shaw, and Dylan Thomas—are of Celtic origin. English was greatly enriched by the poetic mind of the Celts, and it was the scattered people of Scotland, Ireland and Wales who took the English language with them as they explored and settled around the world.

The Norman Invasion

In 1066 the victory of the French-speaking Norman invaders at Hastings changed the face of English forever. Harold, the English loser at Hastings, was the last English-speaking king for nearly three hundred years. It was an event that would make the English we speak today quite different from what went before.

William, the Norman French conqueror, brought with him his own followers whom he put in positions of authority. He took over the English church: Norman bishops and abbots gradually took over in the cathedrals and monasteries. For several generations after the Conquest, all important positions in the country were dominated by French-speaking Normans.

After 1066 the overwhelming majority of English people felt the humiliation of being second class because of language. Religion, law, science, literature were all now written and spoken in French or Latin, as words like felony, perjury, attorney, bailiff, and nobility testify. English dropped out as the language of learning. In court, church, and government circles, French was established as the cultivated and Latin as the professional language.

English did, however, survive. English, both written and spoken, was simply too well-established, too vigorous, and too hardy to be wiped out. It is one thing for the written record to become Latin and French (writing was the skilled monopoly of church-educated clerks), but this did not prevent its use as the popular speech of ordinary people. The English speakers had an overwhelming population advantage, and they were not going to stop speaking English to each other because they had been conquered by a foreigner.

Almost immediately the Normans began to intermarry with those they conquered. By 1300 English began to reassert itself among educated classes. Chaucer by 1370 was writing his classic *Canterbury Tales* in an English which had absorbed French rather than being absorbed by it.

Today two main streams run through English: The Germanic Anglo-Saxon, constituting our basic vocabulary of the most intimate and commonplace words, and the French, Latin from which come many words of law, food and etiquette. Mann evolved to man; mete became meat; hus to house; etan, eat; and drincan, drink. The modern English speaker still uses old English father, mother, brother and sister as well as walk, run, laugh or sleep for key actions. Probably 55 percent of the words we use, including the most common, are German in origin.

The French Latin origin from the Norman invasion of 1066 form the balance. Old English calf, pig, ox and sheep became veal, pork, beef and mutton. Many of the words coming from French reflect a master-servant relationship move to the Noman dominance after the conquest.

The resources of two languages have given English a rich and sophisticated vocabulary. We can *begin* and *end* in English or *commence* and *finish* in French. There are thousands of English-French doublets, such as kingly German and royal Latin.

An English speaker is in a uniquely advantageous position to learn new languages. Our German heritage opens all the languages of this group; (German, Danish, Swedish,) while our French heritage opens up the Latin languages (French, Spanish Portuguese and Italian).

Glance through the attached lists to see examples of the English-German and English-Romance connections. Also note the Romance language similarities. You will see how closely related all these languages are. It is great fun when you start becoming aware of word origins and relationships.

ENGLISH	SWEDISH	DANISH	DUTCH	GERMAN
TO COME	komma	komme	komen	kommen
came	kom	kom	kwan	kam
come	kommit	kommet	gekomen	gokemmen
TO FIND	finna	finde	vinden	finden
found	fann	fand	vond	fand
found	funnit	fundet	gevonden	gefunden
TO FLY	flga	flyve	vliegen	fliegen
flew	flog	floj	vloog	flog
flown	flugit	flojet	gevlogen	geflogen
TO RIDE	rida	ride	rijden	reiten
rode	red	red	reed	ritten
ridden	ridit	redet	gereden	geritten
TO SEE	se	se	zien	sehe
saw	sag	saa	zag	sah
seen	sett	set	gezien	geseh
TO SING	sjunga	synge	zingen	singen
sang	sjong	sang	zong	sang
sung	sjungit	sunget	zezongen	gesunge

ENGLISH	FRENCH	SPANISH	PORTUGUESE	ITALIAN
barn	la grange	el granero	o celeiro	il granaio
barracks	la ceserne	el cuartel	o quartel	la caserna
bridge	le pont	el puente	a ponte	il ponte
building	le batiment	el edificio	o edificio	l'edificio
castle	le chateau	el castillo	o castelo	ilcastello
cathedral	la cathedrale	la catedral	a catedral	il duomo
cemetery	le cimetiere	el cementerio	o cemiterio	il cimitero
church	l'eglise (f)	la iglesia	a igraja	la chiesa
consulate	le consulat	el consulado	o consulado	il consolato
corner(street)	le coin	la esquina	a esquina	il canto
courtyard	la cour	el patio	o patio	il cortile
dock	le bassin	la darsena	a doca	il bacino
embassy	l'ambassade (f)	la embajada	a embaixada	l'ambasciata
factory	l'usine (f)	la fabrica	fabrica	la fabbrica
farm	la ferme	la granja	a granja	la fattoria

ENGLISH	SWEDISH	DANISH	DUTCH	GERMAN
Good morning!	God morgon!	God Morgen!	Goeden morgen!	Guten Morgen!
Good evening!	God afton!	God Aften!	Goeden avond!	Guten Abend!
Good night!	God natt!	God Nat!	Goeden nacht!	Gute Nacht!
Good day!	God dag!	God Dag!	Goeden dag!	Guten Tag!
Good-bye!	Adjo!	Farvel!	Tot ziens!	Auf Wiedersehen!
Good health!	Skal!	Skaal!	Proost!	Prosit!
Thank You! (accepting offer)	Ja, Tack!	Ja, Tak!	Alstublieft! Graag!	Bitte! Bitte schon!
No, thank you! (refusing offer)	Nej, Tack!	Nej, Tak!	Nee, dank U!	Nein, Danke!
Thanks! (for favor done)	Tack!	Tak!	Dank U!	Danke!
Don't mention it!	Ingen orsak!	Aa jeg beder!	Niet te danken!	Nichts zu danken!
Excuse me!	Ursakta!	Undskyld	Excuseer! miq!	Entschuldigen Sie!
I beg your pardon	Forlat!	Omforladelse!	Pardon!	Verzeihung!
Please, show me . . .	Var sa god och visa mig . . .	Vaer saa god at vise mig . . . !	Wijs mij . . . alstublieft!	Bitte, Zeigen Sie mir . . . !
How are you?	Hur star det till?	Hvordan har De det?	Hoe gaat het?	Wie geht's (ihnen)?
Very well, thank you	Tack, utmarkt	Tak, udmaerket	Goed, dank U	Gut, danke
Come in!	Stig in!	Kom ind!	Binnen!	Herein!

ENGLISH	FRENCH	SPANISH	PORTUGUESE	ITALIAN
good morning	bonjour	buenos dias	bom dia	buon giorno
good day	bonjour	buenos dias	bom dia	buon giorno
good evening	bonsoir	buenas tardes	boa tarde	buona sera
good night	bonsoir bonne nuit	buenas noches	boa noite	buona notte
good-day	adieu au revoir	adios hasta luego	adeus ate a vista	addio

ENGLISH	FRENCH	SPANISH	PORTUGUESE	ITALIAN
good trip	bon voyage	buen viaje	boa viagem	buon viaggio
your health	a votre sante	a su salud	a sua saude	salte
many thanks	merci bien	muchas gracias	obrigado	tante grazie
don't mention it	il n'y a pas de quoi	no hay de que de nada n'est rien	nao ha de que	prego non c'e di che
I beg your pardon	je vous	perdone usted demande	perdoe-me pardon	le domando scusa
excuse me	excusez-moi	dispenseme	desculpe	permesso
I am sorry	je suis desole	lo siento	lamento muito	mi rincresce
please	s'il vous plait	por favor	se faz favor	per piacere
with pleasure	avec plaisir	con mucho	com muito gusto	con piacere gosto

ENGLISH	FRENCH	SPANISH	PORTUGUESE	ITALIAN
good	bon	bueno	bom	buono
how are you	comment allez vous	como esta usted que tai	como esta que tal esta	come sta
so so	comme ci, comme ca	asi asi	assim, assim	cosi cosi
come in	entrez	adelante	entre	avanti

I often tell my classes that one day I will teach them a vocabulary of over 500 words in four foreign languages. I keep my promise and it usually takes about 15 minutes. Consider a single word "nation"—French-nation, Spanish-nacion, Portuguese-nacao, Italian-nazione. Any word that ends in "ion" in English you now know in four languages by using the above "ion" changes. Why be afraid of foreign languages? Speaking English, we have easy entry to thousands of words in both the German and Romance languages:

ENGLISH	SWEDISH	DANISH	DUTCH	GERMAN
country	land	Land	platteland	das Land
ice	is	Is	ysdas	Eis
nature	natur	Natur	natuur	die Natur
wind	vind	Vind	wind	der Wind
arm	arm	Arm	arm	der Arm
blood	blod	Blod	blold	das Blut
finger	finger	Finger	vinger	der Finger
calf	kalv	Kalv	kalf	das Kalf
cat	katt	Kat	kat	die Katze
crab	krabba	Krabbe	krab	die Krabbe
rat	ratta	Rotte	rat	die Ratte
apple	apple	Aeble	appel	der Apfel
fruit	frukt	Frugt	vrucht	die Frucht
gold	guld	Guld	goud	das Gold
silver	silver	Slov	zilver	das Silber
mother	moder	Moder	molder	die Mutter
bread	brod	Brlod	brood	das Brot

and hundreds more . . .

ENGLISH	FRENCH	SPANISH	PORTUGUESE	ITALIAN
air	l'air	el aire	o ar	l'aria
gay	la baie	la bahia	o baia	la baia
desert	le desert	el desierto	o deserto	il deserto
east	l'est	el este	o leste	l'est
valley	la vallee	el valle	o vale	la valle
fever	la fevre	la fiebre	a febre	la febbre
muscle	le muscle	el musculo	o'muscolo	il muscolo
animal	l'animal	el animal	o animal	l'animale
tiger	le tigre	el tigre	o tigre	la tigre
fountain	la fontaine	la fuente	a fonte	la fontana
hospital	l'hospital	el hospital	o hospital	l'ospedale
port	le port	el puerto	o porto	il porto
theater	le theatre	el teatro	o teatro	il teatro
cigarette	la cigarette	el cigarillo	o cigarro	la sigaretta
salad	la salade	la ensalada	a salada	l'insalata
actor	l'acteur	el actor	o actor	l'altore

and hundreds more.

► RELIGION

> It is well said, in every sense, that a man's religion is the chief fact with regard to him.
> —Thomas Carlyle

In our definition of culture, we stated that "culture will be discussed in terms of shared values or value systems." An important element of a person's value system is religion. There are four major areas in which it should be a guide.

1. It is a way to truth. It relates people to a goal and by symbols and ritual leads them to that goal.

2. It should provide answers to some of the basic questions of life and provide a feeling of security and certainty.

3. It is a consistent value system guiding actions and indicating right and wrong.

4. It is community, going to church, worshiping together, praying together and giving its people an identity.

What are some key questions that religion attempts to answer?

1. Why do I exist?

2. What is true and real?

3. How did the universe begin?

4. Why do things happen the way they do? What is the meaning of suffering?

5. How does life end?

6. Is there immortality?

7. What is right and wrong, moral, immoral?

8. What is the good life?

The major religions are similar in some respects, but they also differ.

All religions *share*:

1. In a belief in a **power** greater than man which is the source of life and should be worshiped.

2. In having "**holy writings**" containing some statement of the story of the religion and its main beliefs.

3. In having "**holy places**" which deserve to be visited, such as the founders' birthplace or the scene of some important religious incident.

4. In having a number of **important people**, founders or prophets, missionaries, other historical characters now worshiped or revered, such as the Christian saints.

5. In having a set of **symbols** by which the religion is identified. (Some of those symbols are included in Figure 3-5.)

6. In having a **place of worship** in a building and containing an altar-like structure or center for worship.

7. In having a **liturgy** of observance, "holy days" concurring with seasons or natural phenomena depending on the country.

8. In their belief in "**some sort of golden rule,**" "brotherhood of man," "good will to men," "do unto others as you would have them do unto you."

FIGURE 3-5 The symbols of the Great Religions

La Llalia Lla Allah, Muhammed Rasul Allah. This is the Shahada, expressed in Arabic. It expresses the very kernel of the Islamic faith.

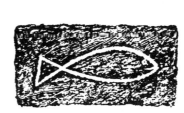 

The fish Christ (in Greek) for symbolism in Christianity. PX Chi Rho—Ch—Christ.

The Menorah

The Star of David

The eight-spoked wheel, the Buddhist symbol of the Noble Eightfold Path.

The Chinese character above represents the "Tao" or "Way." It can be used as a symbol of both Taoism and Confucianism. To Confucianists "Tao" came to mean the way of morality, and to the Taoists the way of nature.

The ancient symbol of Om. (Om is the most sacred mantra or syllable in the Vedas, and is used in meditation and prayer. A mantra embodies in sound some type of supernatural power.)

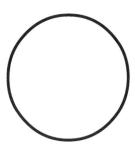

The sun is the symbol of the Shinto goddess of the sun, and is the national symbol of Japan.

The Bah-Kua, ancient symbol of yang and yin, a concept that is fundamental to Chinese philosophy.

Religions are not monolithic and quite often seem quite contradictory. Compare a Quaker meeting and a solemn high mass at St. Peter's, Rome. Both are expressions of worship within Christianity.

Compare the intricacies of the Christian doctrine of the Trinity and a charismatic prayer meeting.

Consider the Greek gods on Mount Olympus and the Jews' Yahweh.

Consider the doctrines of compassion for one's fellow man and the terrible wars and crimes committed in the name of religion.

While it is true many beliefs are shared by the world's major religions, as in the phrase "there is one God but many ways to Him," there are also differences. The principal differences divide along four main lines:

1. Some religions are messianic—that is, they believe that some one person, divine or human, will save humans from eternal oblivion. Others see their god as too remote to operate this way.

2. Some religions believe humans are basically evil. Others suggest that they are good but corrupted by society's rules. Others believe that they are a part of nature and neither evil nor good except in the sense that they do not conform to nature.

3. Some religions believe that a select group of men act as official intermediaries between their god and the common man. The "power" or authority given this group is different for each religion. Other religions believe worship is a personal matter and no priest class exists.

4. Some religions believe their god can communicate personally with each human being—can be contacted, persuaded, involved. Others suggest that their god is unreachable—man is on his own to find the answers. Others believe that their god is "immanent" (i.e., can be experienced and known) or their god is "transcendent" (i.e., beyond the limits of experience and knowledge).

Why is a study of religion important to our study of world cultures? *Because*—religion is part of all cultures and of all history—and a study of it helps us to:

1. *Understand Differences* between nations and cultures—both political and philosophical.

2. *See Similarities* in views of the world by all humans.

3. *Appreciate Our Own Beliefs* by seeing them alongside those of others.

4. *Relate Our Religion to Others* in terms of origin, antiquity, source, beliefs,etc.

5. *Keep from Being "Superior"* in our own point of view which leads to feelings of hostility.

6. *Work for Mutual Respect* (i.e., a world-view of religion) via a meaningful exchange of ideas between religious groups.

There are hundreds of different religions in the world, but we will consider eight that are major influences in the four culture realms under consideration:

Judaism—The religion from which come both Christianity and Islam

Christianity—Root of western culture

Islam—Root of Islamic culture

Confucianism and Taoism—Roots to the Chinese or Far Eastern moral ethical system along with Buddhism

Buddhism—A root of Far Eastern culture

Hinduism—The formative belief of Indian culture

Shinto—Unique contributions to Japanese Culture along with Zen Buddhism

In the discussion of these eight religions, it will be helpful to make a broad classification.

Theistic Religions. In these religions the concern is man's relation to God. The great theistic religions are Judaism and its daughters Christianity and Islam. These three religions all go back to Father Abraham and are sometimes call "Abrahamic" religions. Mecca is called the "City of Abraham" and all three hold many similar beliefs. But above all God has a plan and reveals his plan which is man's duty to carry out. God speaks to Moses in the burning bush, God gives the Ten Commandments and God speaks through his prophets. Islam holds that Muslims, Jews and Christians are "people of the Book and are on the right path."

Humanistic Religions. In these religions the concern is primarily man's relation to man. Confucianism is a prime example. When they asked Confucius about what happens when we die, he replied he didn't know and neither did anyone else. His concern was to see how humans could live in harmony. It is highly ethical, but not God centered as Christianity. I usually refer to it as a moral ethical system rather than a religion. To a certain extent this is true of Taoism, Buddhism and Shinto. For example, any effort to come to grips with Buddhism involves encountering a number of obstacles—not least is its extensive technical terminology. But the first, and in some ways most persistent, barrier that Westerners are likely to encounter is the fact that, coming from a Judeo-Christian background, they impose upon it the perspectives and categories which provide the norms of their habitual thinking about religion, whether they are particularly "religious" or not. It takes some time and reflection to come to terms with the style of a religion which, in some senses, dispenses with the notion of God altogether, conceives salvation as extinction rather than redemption and is, in many of its forms, indifferent to whether or not its followers adhere to another faith at the same time.

Origins

Religions originate with man seeking answers. Human beings wouldn't be human if they didn't wonder about the world about them. What makes lightning flash? Where does wind come from?

People also wondered about themselves. Why did they get sick sometimes? Why does everyone die eventually?

Questions. What are the answers? What early man did was put together what seemed to be the most logical answers in the light of their experience. The wind must be created by a tremendously huge and powerful man, one who never died. Such a being was a god. Since men and women married and had children, perhaps the plants of the world were the children of the sky (a god) and the earth (a goddess). The rain which made the plants grow was the marriage between them.

Every group of human beings found explanations in such stories. Probably the best and most inventive were the ancient Greeks. They called such stories "myths" which is a Greek word that simply means tale or story.

Since the gods controlled natural forces, it was wise to treat them with respect. They had to be asked to send rain when it was needed and pleaded with not to send disease and misfortune. For that reason, animals were sacrificed and beautiful temples were built for them, songs were composed to praise them. Thus religion grew up about the explanations, and rituals were established.

Consider a famous Greek myth or story of explanation.

Demeter, goddess of agriculture, had a daughter, Persephone, who while playing in the fields of Sicily was carried off by Hades, god of the underworld, who had fallen in love with her. Demeter searched for her without success for a long time and in her sorrow refused to let the ground bear grain. Mankind was faced with starvation.

Zeus then persuaded Hades to let Persephone return provided she had eaten none of the food in the underground kingdom. At the last moment, though, Hades tempted Persephone into eating four pomegranate seeds. As a result, Demeter had to allow Persephone to remain underground with Hades four months of every year, one for each seed.

While Persephone was underground, the earth bore no grain, the trees lost their leaves and ever the sun scarcely shone. Only with Persephone's return did the goddess of agriculture allow its earth to return to life.

This explains why winter comes each year.

Religion unites and religion can divide. As we strive for global understanding and respect for other cultures, we should remember we all have our own perspectives, but they no longer need be cast in hard molds of enmity to the rest. Religion has been a great humanizing force. It has also made many wars unusually cruel and inhumane. Consider the following comments about what we profess and what we do.

Totem, tribal, racial, and aggressively missionising cults represent only partial solutions of the psychological problem of subduing hate by love; they only partially initiate. Ego is not annihilated in them; rather, it is enlarged; instead of thinking only of himself, the individual becomes dedicated to the whole of his society. The rest of the world meanwhile (that is to say, by far the greater portion of mankind) is left outside the sphere of his sympathy and protection because outside the sphere of the protection of his god. And there takes place, then, that dramatic divorce of the two principles of love and hate which the pages of history so bountifully illustrate. *Instead of clearing his own heart the zealot tries to clear the world.* The laws of the City of God are applied only to his in-group (tribe, church, nation, class, or what not) while the fire of a perpetual holy war is hurled (with good conscience, and indeed a sense of pious service) against whatever uncircumcised, barbarian, heathen, "native" or alien people happens to occupy the position of neighbor.

—*The Hero With a Thousand Faces*
Joseph Campbell

The world is full of mutually contending bands: totem-, flag-, and party-worshippers. Even the so-called Christian nations—which are supposed to be following a "World" Redeemer—are better known to history for their colonial barbarity and wars between themselves than for any practical display of that unconditional love, which was taught by their founder, Jesus Christ:

> I say unto you, Love your enemies, do good to them which hate you. Bless them that curse you, and pray for them which despitefully use you. And unto him that smiteth thee on the one cheek offer also the other; and him that taketh away thy cloak forbid not to take thy coat also. Give to every man that asketh of thee; and of him that taketh away thy goods ask them not again. And as ye would that men should do to you, do ye also to them likewise. For if ye love them which love you, what thank have ye? for sinners also love those that love them. And if ye do good to them which do good to you, what thank have ye? for sinners also do even the same. And if ye lend to them of whom ye hope to receive, what thank have ye? For sinners also lend to sinners, to receive as much again. But love ye your enemies, and do good, and lend, hoping for nothing again; and your reward shall be great, and ye shall be the children of the Highest: for he is kind unto the unthankful and to the evil. Be ye therefore merciful, as your Father also is merciful.

—Luke 6:27-36

Can we apply Christ's words to Russians, Iranians, Iraqis, Red China?

500 BC

In the religious history of the human race no period is of greater significance than that around the year 500 BC which we will be emphasizing. The year 500 BC is called the Axis year for its importance in defining world culture. Consider the amazing series of coincidental events; in different corners of the world at about the same time in history, three of the great religions had their beginnings, while two others underwent profound changes.

In the Near East, the Babylonian Captivity destroyed the Jewish state, and the hardships suffered during the period of exile forced the Jews to reassess their rituals and practices. Many of the rites of modern Judaism had their origin in this period.

In Greece, the old Homeric theology was being challenged and eventually supplanted by the rise of philosophy, which was to achieve in time the concept of monotheism and develop certain codes for man's earthly conduct.

In northern India in 567 BC Gautama, the Buddha, was born, who was destined to found one of the great religions of modern man.

At about the same time in China, Confucius preached a moral ethical system, the base of which was the proper conduct of man and which still numbers millions among its adherents.

At the same time also, there arose among shepherd tribes in Iran a religion which became in time the state religion of the Great Persian Empire Zoroastrianism, inspired by the prophet Zarathustra or Zoroaster. We will not have room in this book to discuss Zoroaster, but all the others will be central to a culture under discussion.

▶ TIME

> O let not time deceive you. You can not conquer time.

— W.H. Auden

One of the greatest sources of friction and misunderstanding for an American dealing with a foreign culture is the different attitudes and values placed on time.

All who have travelled in the East find an immense contrast between the calm acceptance of the

Orient and the restlessness of the West. No doubt aspects of a technical and industrial civilization contribute to Western activism; a deeper cause for difference, however, is a different relation to time. The roots and implications of these different attitudes was already discussed in some detail in the first chapter's discussion of cultural value differences.

The Orient has a conception of time entirely different from that of the West, and this difference belongs to the religious and philosophical sphere. In all profound Oriental philosophy and religion, time is treated as something irrelevant and illusory compared with eternity. Reality is beyond and above the time-process and is changeless.

Change means imperfection. Just as people looking for change do so because they are not satisfied, so nothing that is subject to change can be looked upon as true being. That which exists must have duration, persistence; it must be changeless. It is not possessed by an urge to get what it does not have, to become what it is not yet. True being is eternal. This idea is common to the whole Eastern world, although there can be different interpretations.

An extreme expression of this idea is where found in India where the world itself is changeable and therefore is unreal. Reality is eternal . . . the One and All which cannot change, and therefore has no relation to time. It is timeless, motionless, self-satisfied eternity; therefore it is the deepest desire of the Indian thinker to enter into or to share in that motionless eternal being, in Nirvana.

For a contrasting view on time, consider these words of Lin Yutang, a Chinese interpreter of differences between East and West.

To the Chinese, therefore, with the fine philosophy that "Nothing matters to a man who says nothing matters," Americans offer a strange contrast. Is life really worth all the bother to the extent of making our soul a slave to the body? The high spirituality of the philosophy of loafing forbids it.

The three great American vices seem to be efficiency, punctuality and the desire for achievement and success. They are the things that make the Americans so unhappy and so nervous. They steal from them their inalienable right of loafing and cheat them of many a good, idle and beautiful afternoon. Our quarrel with efficiency is not that it gets things done, but that it is a thief of time when it leaves us no leisure to enjoy ourselves and that it frays our nerves in trying to get things done perfectly.

The tempo of modern industrial life forbids this kind of glorious and magnificent idling. But worse than that, it imposes upon us a different conception of time as measured by the clock, and eventually turns the human being into a clock himself. This sort of thing is bound to come to China, as is evident for instance in a factory of twenty thousand workers. The luxurious prospect of twenty thousand workers coming in at their own sweet pleasure at all hours is, of course, somewhat terrifying. Nevertheless, this is what makes life so hard and hectic. A man who has to be punctually at a certain place at five o'clock has the whole afternoon from one to five ruined for him already. Every American adult is arranging his time on a pattern of the schoolboy—three o'clock for this, five o'clock for that, six-thirty for change of dress; six-fifty for entering the taxi and seven o'clock for emerging into a hotel room. It just makes life not worth living.

What a common critique about American values involving time!

Americans overseas are psychologically stressed in many ways when confronted by time systems such as those in Latin America and the Middle East. In the markets and stores of Mediterranean countries, one is surrounded by other customers vying for the attention of a clerk. There is no order as to who is served next, and to the northern European or American, this is nothing but confusion. Often Americans are very upset when asked to wait in a room full of people by an official or businessman running behind schedule. Particularly irritating to Americans is the way in which appointments are handled. Appointments just don't carry the same weight as they do in the United States. Things are constantly shifted around. Nothing seems solid or firm, particularly plans for the future, and there are always changes in the most important plans right up to the very last minute.

In contrast, the American finds little in life that escapes the need for disciplined use of time. In fact, social and business life, even sex life, are apt to be completely time-dominated. Time values are so thoroughly woven into our way of thinking that we are hardly aware of the degree to which they determine and coordinate everything we do, including our relations with others. By scheduling, we compartmentalize; this makes it possible to concentrate on one thing at a time, a pattern that makes us feel comfortable and in control. Important things are taken up first and allotted the most time; unimportant things are left to last or omitted if time runs out.

To Americans and people of northern European tradition such as England and Germany, time is linear and divided into segments or time periods going forward into the future and backward to the past. It is also treated like a commodity. Time is spoken of as being saved, spent, wasted, lost, made up, accelerated, slowed down, crawling, and running out. This way of thinking and expression indicates the basic manner in which time is thought of as a building block.

Scheduling is used as a classification system that orders life. With the exception of birth and death, all important activities are scheduled. It should be mentioned that without schedules, it is doubtful that our industrial civilization could have developed as it has. Both "time" and "space" affect the behavior of everyone in western culture.

"Time," especially, causes us to be oriented toward calendars, dates, "the course of history," timetables, clocks, hourly wages, races against time, accounting, compound interest, actuarial statistics. The concept of time drives us to look ahead in planning programs, schedules, appropriations, balanced budgets. Our deep concern about time causes other cultures, whose traditions permit a less hurried outlook, to regard us as a bit imbalanced.

Looking to the future fits our feelings of optimism, modernity, progress. Some Mexicans say we are so concerned about the future that we aren't able to enjoy the present. Americans might say of Mexicans that they are so caught up with the present that they won't make a future. Various cultural orientations to past, present and future are very different, and each culture makes judgments about the other based on its own orientation.

M-Time and P-Time

In Edward Hall's influential writings on time as it affects culture, he has distinguished two kinds of time: "monochronic" (M-time) and "polychronic" (P-time). These correspond as an example to the North American and Mexican preferred modes respectively. M-time values taking care of "one thing at a time." Time is linear, segmented. (American football is a very 'M-time' game.) "Time is money" is very American and M-time. M-time people like neat scheduling of appointments and are easily distracted and often very distressed by interruptions.

In contrast, P-time is characterized by many things happening at once, and with a much "looser" notion of what is "on time" or "late." Interruptions are routine, delays to be expected. Thus it is not so much putting things off until *manana*, as some Mexican stereotypes would have it, but that human activities in reality just don't proceed like clockwork. Even in Japan, a culture that is known for a hard work ethic, U.S. business people are seen by the Japanese as much too time-bound, driven by schedules and deadlines which stand in the way of developing human relationships. Some Western Europeans, on the other hand, are more time conscious than Americans, notably Germans.

It is not easy to adjust to time value differences. The American view of time as linear and segmented is a minority view from a global perspective. We tend to be future and youth-oriented while the past plays an important role in making decisions and guiding actions in most of the world. Age in most cultures means experience and wisdom. When traveling, the American should remember the younger person defers to one who is older. Older organizations are more respected too. An example would be an American company in Japan which may take years to establish the needed trust. A company founded earlier than another would have more prestige and inspire more confidence.

It is the Chinese culture that instills the most respect for age. It extends beyond people to buildings, institutions, or even plants like the very old Bonsai. American culture respects qualities of innovation, change, and vitality.

American attention is often directed toward the near future—one, two, perhaps five years from now in contrast to the typical Oriental view. Because Americans expect and value change, and like to work with known quantities they tend to make short-term plans. To a foreigner we may seem preoccupied with short-term deadlines and schedules. Their goal is present but open to a more flexible schedule. ◀

Vagueness in fixing dates by foreigners or the demand for specific times by Americans can cause friction. A proposal may be made by an American team, and the Japanese may respond, "We will study the matter." That is too vague for many Americans who will press for something more specific: "How soon can you get back to us? In one or two weeks? In a month?" But that, in turn, makes the Japanese uneasy.

Americans and Orientals differ in dividing time concerning work and leisure.

Americans, having worked their required hours, feel they are then on their own time while the Japanese or Korean worker will feel obliged to continue working or to go out to socialize with business associates or staff. The American has divided time into work time and private time and resents intrusions on "private" time.

On the other hand, Orientals can feel frustrated and left out when all of their American colleagues leave work and head for home. They feel there is no chance to really get to know these people or to become friends or to hear and say some things that don't get said at the office.

Each culture places a different emphasis on past, present and future. In the United States, the future with inferred progress seems to be valued the most. Our history has been one of starting a new country and building a nation. The frontier valued youth and achievements ("onward and upward," each son better than his father) and independence. This undoubtedly has much to do with our optimism and future orientation. Generally, there is much less enthusiasm for saving an old building than for erecting something new. General Electric's slogan: "Progress is our most important product" appeals to Americans. The U.S. child typically has little concern for or knowledge of his family history and a word like ancestor sounds foreign.

Valuing the past, however, does not mean a society has to ignore the present or resist change. Japan has a culture with the Confucian emphasis on the past ("ancestor worship"), but it has also shown itself to be a society influenced by the philosophy of change in all things.

Differences in the concepts toward time often are among the first value differences sensed by a person in a new culture. One is likely to sense a difference in the pace of life, so that things seem too slow or too fast. And these attitudes toward time are not changed by urging people to work faster or be on time.

Linear Time—Circular Time

The word *traditional* refers to the older concept of time, the one associated with preindustrial societies. This attitude to time can be called more circular or less linear than that employed in industrial societies, for the older concepts more closely reflect the cycles that are the pattern of nature. In preindustrial societies, changes between day and night and the yearly cycles of the seasons are the model for deciding when to plant, as well as setting dates for religious highlights such as Easter and Christmas.

In the traditional view, time is perceived as a circle. The natural events which measure time—the movement of the sun, the phases of the moon, the tides, the seasons of the year—all recur, and appear a part of nature's plan. Most Asian religions have developed notions of time involving vast cosmic cycles during which all creatures undergo a series of re-births (discussed under Hinduism). Taoism and Hinduism accept notions of circularity as ways to survive. Taoism teaches melding into nature. Hinduism teaches living with people, animals, plants, rocks, and spirits, and especially with oneself. Its teachings are effective for survival and indicate that life in reincarnation can be lived in a better way.

Buddhism teaches escape from circularity, not into the world but out of it onto a higher plane. One strain of Mahayana Buddhism in China preached that the compassionate Maitreya Buddha would return when the world fell into extreme depravity. It gave rise to some revolutionary movements. All three of these religions have aroused interest in the West among people seeking a road from movement to rest.

But the God-seeking religions—Judaism, Christianity, Islam—abhor paganism, a faith that preaches living in harmony with people, animals, plants, rocks, and spirits. Jews and Muslims must break with all paganism and submit to God. Christians must die spiritually and be born again, like Saul who became Paul when he gained faith in the risen Jesus. Christianity especially envisages a break in the life of individuals, communities, and the world so that darkness can give way to light. The idea of revolution in the West came from Christianity.

Revolution and death go together, not the peaceful dying of circular life, but the hideous deaths states have for millennia inflicted on those they particularly loathed, like the crucifixion of Jesus or of rebellious wretches in Japan before modernization. Yet revolution and hope also go together. And hope gives direction, which circularity never does.

Theistic religions of Judaism, Christianity and Islam believe that direction—the straight path leading toward the face of God—must be chosen even if it means undergoing the torments that Jesus did.

Existence itself is a cycle in which being and non-being alternate. The symbol for both Hindu and Buddhist is a wheel.

Preindustrial societies differ widely in how accurately they measured time. In some societies, periods of the day were roughly divided into work time, cool and hot time, and no-work time, for example. It is a mistake to think that these workers didn't work hard because their hours were tied to natural events. Peasants did back-breaking work to get the hay in on time and harvest done before a storm. It is more precise to describe the activity as periods of leisure alternating with periods of intense activity done as natural events dictated.

This older version of time still exists not only in less developed countries of the world, but within more developed countries. The life in the city can be quite different than life in a farming village. Attitudes toward time have impact on economic attitudes. Measuring time by natural events does not work in a modern factory system. In industry, everything must proceed to a precise time schedule. This applies not only to the operation of an assembly line, but to workers showing up on time and finishing work on time. The pace of a factory is a regular rhythm as opposed to the periods of idleness and intense activity of an agricultural economy.

An example from the Hopi Indians, cited by Edward T. Hall, illustrates how a traditional view of time can bring trouble to nonagricultural work projects.

For the Hopi, time is not fixed or measurable as we think of it. It is what happens as the corn matures or a sheep grows up—a characteristic sequence of events. There is a different natural time for everything. Hopi houses were often in the process of being built for years and years. The Indian had no idea that a house should be built in a given time span, as a house had no natural time system such as

the corn and sheep had. This way of looking at time cost the government untold thousands of dollars on construction projects because the Hopi could not conceive of a fixed time in which a dam or a road should be built.

Another aspect of the traditional view of time is the emphasis on the present versus the long-run future. Industrialization and economic development are difficult to achieve without long-range planning.

Abstract, Lineal Values Toward Time

In contrast to the circular concept of time is a more abstract, lineal version. This concept we could designate as modern; but in fact, the idea goes back to the early Jews and is part of our Judeo-Christian heritage. This Judeo-Christian time concept was quite radical in its day, for it defined a unique, non-repetitive history with a beginning (Creation) and a vision of the end (Apocalypse) to all things.

In this scheme, time is thought of less as recurring natural events than as a linear progression. The Jews could not accept the idea that sense and purpose of history lay outside time and history repetitive. God's will was worked out in time and progressed to a purpose. The universal ancient belief in revolving cycles of change in which the end brings back the beginning was repellent to the Jews, for it did not give God a role in history and made senseless creation and salvation. Judaism and subsequently Christianity has never dismissed time as an illusion as it comes from the hand of God.

Monasteries and the Development of Mechanical Time

Lewis Mumford described with sharp insight how the clock was the critical machine for the development of industry. The first use of measurement in the study of nature was in the measurement of time. The breaking of time into measurable units arose in part out of the routine and the purpose of the monastery. Within the monastery, order and learning were the ideals; outside was irregularity, chance, and striving for power. In the seventh century, the Pope ordered that the bells of the monastery be rung 7 times in the 24 hours to regulate the monk's life. It became necessary to develop a means of keeping track of these prescribed hours and assuring their regular repetition. Although the mechanical clock did not appear until the thirteenth century, the habit of order and the conscious regulation of time periods of prayer, work, and rest had become part of a monastic way of life.

Some historians point to the Benedictines, the great working order (at one time there were 40,000 monasteries under Benedictine rule), as contributors to the rise of modern industrial society. They note that the monasteries helped give human enterprise the regular collective time discipline of the machine; for the clock is not merely a means of keeping track of time, but of coordinating people's work. The clock and precise time were essential to a smooth running system of production and transportation. The clock kept time completely independent of seasons, sickness, and natural events and helped create the understanding of time as an independent world of measurable sequences.

"Idleness," wrote St. Benedict, "is an enemy of the soul." The fixing of a daily schedule of prayer and work was putting order as a way of progressing in God's work, both worldly and religiously. When the monks joined the world to their religion: (*laborare est orare*—to work was to pray), St. Benedict's rules set aside times for work, study, eating, and sleeping; rules gave penalties and penance for the latecomers; rules spelled out how to maintain the clock and its nightly adjustment, so that it would be sure to wake the monks at the proper time.

Punctuality and Time Pressure

Especially after the Industrial Revolution, precise measured time became the rule. Industrialists taught workers that punctuality was a virtue. If time is a collection of hours, minutes, and seconds, time becomes a commodity. Time is to be well used, to be saved, not wasted. In 1923, the Soviet Time League, realizing the importance of time to industrialization, was obliged to report every waste of time encountered. They distributed leaflets saying:

> Measure your time, control it!
> Do everything on time! Exactly to the
>   minute!
> Save time, make time count, work fast!
> Divide your time correctly, for work and for
>   leisure!

This was exactly the attitude of the early industrialists. At the time of the American Revolution,

ninety percent of Americans worked on farms, and the pace of life was regulated by the natural cycles of agriculture. As the United States industrialized, the artificial time of the clock and of the assembly line came to regulate the rhythm of life.

More recently, Frederick W. Taylor and his time-and-motion studies were important steps in the development of scientific management. According to studies cited by McClelland, this sense of urgency is especially strong among individuals with a high need for achievement. Such individuals are acutely aware of the rapid passage of time. It is precisely this tie-in of achievement and time urgency that characterizes the American in the eyes of many foreigners.

Our time measurement and increased productivity have resulted in less leisure. Anthropologists have calculated that preindustrial societies reached their goals by working, on the average, no more than eight hundred hours a year (twenty forty-hour weeks). High achievers in the United States today work several thousand hours a year.

Measuring Time

Any repetitive change is different from other changes that don't repeat. The rising and setting of the sun suggest repetitive change. The first people to keep time probably counted such natural repeating events and used them to keep track of events that did not repeat. Later, people made clocks to imitate the regularity of natural events. When people began to count repeating events, they began to measure time.

Units of Time Measurement

For early peoples, the only changes that were truly regular—that is, repeated themselves evenly—were the motions of objects in the sky. The most obvious of these changes was the alternate daylight and darkness, caused by the rising and setting of the sun. Each of these cycles of the sun came to be called a day. Another regular change in the sky was the change in the visible shape of the moon. Each cycle of the moon's changing shape takes about 29 1/2 days, or a month.

The cycle of the seasons gave people an even longer unit of time. By watching the stars just before dawn or after sunset, people saw that the sun moved slowly eastward among the stars. The sun made a full circle around the sky in one cycle of the seasons. This cycle takes about 365 1/4 days, or a year.

For hundreds of years, people tried to fit days and months evenly into a year or a period of several years. But no system worked perfectly. Today, the calendar is based entirely on the year. Although the year is divided into 12 so-called months, the months have no relation to the moon's actual cycle.

There is no regular change in the sky that lasts seven days, as does the week. The seven-day week came from the Jewish custom of observing a Sabbath (day of rest) every seventh day.

The division of a day in 24 hours, an hour into 60 minutes, and a minute into 60 seconds probably came from the ancient Babylonians. The Babylonians divided the imaginary circular path of the sun into 12 equal parts. Then they divided the periods of daylight and darkness into 12 parts each, resulting in a 24-hour day.

The Babylonians also divided the circle into 360 parts called degrees. Other ancient astronomers further divided each degree into 60 minutes. Later, clocks became accurate enough to need smaller units than the hour.

Clockmakers, following the astronomers' division of the degree, divided the hour into 60 minutes and the minute into 60 seconds. In this way, the face of a clock could easily show hours, minutes, and seconds. A clock face has 12 divisions. Each of these divisions equals one hour for the hour hand, five minutes for the minute hand, and five seconds for the second hand.

By most standards, probably the outstanding technological achievement of the high Middle Ages was the invention of the clock in the late thirteenth century. The clock is important technologically because in the pursuit of ever more accurate timekeepers, the clockmakers' shops became the research centers of western knowledge of the mechanical arts. Friction, precision metalwork, and the varying behavior of metals and other materials at different temperatures and under different loads were studied. It also had a more subtle social importance, cultivating the sense of time crucial to the organized collaboration of large numbers of people.

Some clock faces are divided into 24 hours. On such a clock, 9 A.M. would be shown as 0900 and 3 P.M. would be 1500. This system avoids confusion between the morning and evening hours.

Time Zones

Local and standard time

Clocks in various parts of the world do not all show the same time. Suppose they all did show the same time—3 P.M., for example. At that time, people in some countries would see the sun rise, and people in other lands would see it high in the sky. In still other countries, the sun could not be seen because 3 P.M. would occur at night. Instead, clocks in all locations show 12 o'clock at midday. Every place on the earth that is east or west of another place has noon at a different time. The time at any particular place is called the local time of that place. At noon local time in one town, the time might be 11 A.M. in another place west of the town or 1 P.M. in a place to the east. The local time in the other places depends on how far east or west observers are from their town.

If every community used a different time, travelers would be confused and many other problems would be created. To avoid all such problems, standard time zones were established. These zones were set up so there would be a difference of one hour between a place on the eastern edge of a time zone and a place on the western edge. The local time is at the meridian (line) of longitude that runs through the center of the zone and is used by all places within the zone. Thus, time throughout the zone is the same.

Worldwide time zones were established in 1884. The meridian of longitude passing through the Greenwich Observatory in England was chosen as the starting point for the world's time zones. The Greenwich meridian is often called the prime meridian. The mean solar time at Greenwich is called Greenwich Mean Time (GMT) or Greenwich Civil Time (GCT).

An international conference in 1884 set up 12 time zones west of Greenwich and 12 to the east. These zones divide the world into 23 full zones and two half zones. Both the 12th zone east and the 12th zone west are half a zone wide. They lie next to each other and are separated by an imaginary line called the International Date Line. The line is halfway around the world from Greenwich. A traveler crossing this line while headed west, toward China, loses a day. A traveler who crosses it traveling eastward gains a day. A few places do not use standard time zones. For example, the polar regions have weeks of constant sunlight or darkness. (See Chapter 2, Figures 2-2, and 2-3.)

▶ HISTORY

> There is a history in all men's lives, *figuring*
> the nature of times deceased.
> —Shakespeare, *King Henry IV*

Our culture and beliefs are formed by history and ideas we may feel are quite modern or even our own probably go back to some philosopher or historical event of many years ago. The goals and values of the Michigan auto executive, the Texas oil field worker, or the Italian grape grower are a mixture of ideas and experiences gathered from here and there through the centuries with adaptations to serve their peculiar needs.

A few questions to modern Americans about their beliefs would show side-by-side ideas that have come down almost unchanged for centuries. These ancient ideas would be found right beside the latest scientific knowledge and new political ideas put together in an unorganized jumble somehow forming a frame of reference that acts as a guide through the problems of the day. And we all need these ideas to give a feeling of security and direction.

A person today will believe that water is made of hydrogen and oxygen, that Jesus rose from the dead and sits at the right hand of God, that burning the American flag is cause for a jail sentence, and that restraint of trade is un-American with very little sense of the origin and meaning of these beliefs. Our minds are like a *warehouse full of wildly different and often contradictory ideas that are not very well explored. This diversity is accepted with little strain.*

While it is certainly interesting to explore the events of history and how they make up the set of values that form an individual's beliefs and cultural groups, it is also of utmost importance for an understanding of what's going on in the world and for achieving our goal of a world view that includes our understanding of cultures other than our own.

Ideas are much more lasting than the tools of the world's culture and the ideas which we find in the minds of the modern men of Europe, Asia, Islam and the Americas have roots that go back into the foggy past. It is through ideas that we identify ourselves with our ancestors, far more than buildings or race. This is clearly the case in America where, despite our relatively new history, we are as much a part of European culture as France or England. To understand the religion, the art and the morals of today, we must understand the events and accomplishments of the past that have created today's attitudes.

Values and the ideas that form them are living, and like all living things, must change and adapt to the environment in which they live. We are apt to regard the body of our beliefs as we do mountains: they are fixed and unchangeable, have probably always been there and will remain in about the same form. Christianity, democracy, private property, the English language must always have been, we reason, and must be destined to endure forever.

We don't have much trouble accepting change in material things because we have observed constant change. Changes in ideas, however, we are less apt to recognize. The difficulty is not that people believed differently than we do today, but it is almost impossible to realize from our point of view that they really believed such strange things, and they believed them just as sincerely and without question as most of us hold our beliefs.

A tracing of the history in each of the four great cultural realms should make it easier to achieve a sense of where the ideas and values of that culture originated. If our minds are a warehouse of beliefs inherited from the past, then to understand their values, we must understand their life history. What formative events of history have shaped our values and our neighbors' on planet Earth?

In the Beginning

Human history begins with the emergence of Homo Sapiens from proto-human populations. The process was undoubtedly very slow, but by about 100,000 years ago, scattered hunting packs of physically modern kinds of man roamed the savanna lands of Africa and perhaps also inhabited regions with suitably mild climates in Asia as well. These earliest human communities depended in part on skills inherited from their proto-human ancestors. The use of wood and stone tools, for example, seems to have started long before fully human populations had come into existence. Elementary language and habits of co-operation in the hunt were also proto-human in their origin. So, perhaps, was the domestication of fire.

A distinguishing feature of the Homo Sapiens that would enable them to develop the culture which we feature in this book was a prolongation of infancy and childhood. This meant a longer time when the young depended on parents, and a correspondingly longer time when the elders could teach their offspring the arts of life.

From the child's side, slower aging meant prolonged period of change and a much-increased capacity to learn. Enlarged learning capacities, in turn, increased the frequency of selective preservation of inventions and discoveries made, presumably, more or less at random. When this occurred, cultural evolution began to outstrip the comparatively slow pace of biological evolution. Human behavior came to be governed far more by what men learned in society than by anything individuals inherited biologically through the marvelous mechanisms of the DNA molecules.

When cultural evolution became more important than biological evolution, history, in its strict and proper sense, began. About nine-tenths of Homo Sapiens' time on earth saw men confined to a life of hunting and gathering, using simple tools of wood and stone, becoming familiar with fire, and living, so far as we can tell, in an almost unchanging way from generation to generation.

As long as men lived mainly by hunting, and supplemented animal flesh with whatever they could pick up—grubs, insects, edible roots, stalks, and seeds—they lived a roving life like the few surviving primitive hunters of modern times. Very likely bands were small, numbering from twenty to sixty persons under normal circumstances.

The comparative stability of the earliest hunting style of life suggests that adjustment to the environment became very exact. Each band inherited adequate customary responses to every situation that might arise. In the absence of important changes in the environment, perhaps human life would still be using the patterns of behavior that these small roving bands worked out. If so, human cultural evolution would have assumed a pace more like that biological development which needs centuries for even minor changes. Instead, humans have burst into a pattern of constant accelerated change.

The stability of early man's adjustment to his environment was shaken by climactic changes. Along the northern limits of human habitation, time and again, climate and ecological changes faced man with a series of new challenges to their powers of adaptation and invention. This is our best guess about what unleashed the marvelous human potential for evolution from the rigid habits that served them well in an unchanging hunter-gatherer society.

The climate changes that triggered a human cultural explosion were related to the retreat of the glaciers in the northern hemisphere. Glacial ice began to melt back from Europe and northern Asia and America about 30,000 years ago. On the bared ground, tundra and thin forest first developed. In Europe the warm waters of the Gulf Stream established a comparatively moist and mild climate. As a result, vegetation grew lushly and supported a large population of grass and plant eaters: mammoth, reindeer, bison, and many more. This, in turn, constituted a rich food resource for primitive peoples to prey on.

But before men could effectively kill these animals, some inventions were needed. In particular, humans had to learn how to sew skins together to make an artificial pelt that might keep hairless humans warm in a very chilly landscape. This, in turn, required awls and something to serve as "thread"— perhaps sinews and thongs of raw hide. The necessary inventions were made, allowing bands of hunters, who were physically all but indistinguishable from modern men, to invade the tundra and forest of western Europe some 25–30,000 years ago. Earlier Neanderthal man disappeared as the Homo Sapiens advanced.

Other populations, taking a different strategy, learned to exploit water resources by inventing simple boats, nets, and fish hooks. Relatively stable communities thus developed, since boats had to come back to harbor and there were only certain spots where suitable shelter from storms could be had. Great rubbish piles, composed mainly of the remains of shellfish, accumulated on such sites. They allow modern archaeologists to study the sequence of occupation and to trace changes in tool assemblages through time.

Changes Brought About by Agriculture

It was probably between 7000 and 6500 BC that a few human communities located in the Middle East around the Tigris and Euphrates rivers began to cultivate crops and tame animals, and, thus, take charge of their destinies. Wheat and barley were their most important crops; sheep and goats, their most numerous domesticated animals.

The early communities had a practice known as slash and burn. By slashing off the bark all around their trunks, the tree died and this exposed the forest floor to sunlight, so that seeds planted in the loose leaf mold around the standing trunks of the dead trees could grow. Then after two or three crops had depleted the soil, fertility could be renewed by burning the dried-out trees and scattering the ashes over the ground. Then, five to ten years after the plot had first been carved out of the forest, primitive farmers moved on.

Having exhausted the soil of their small plots, they simply repeated the whole cycle elsewhere, letting their abandoned fields grow back to woods and slowly return to something like their original state. This state of cultivation still survives in a few remote parts of the world.

Early farmers developed a number of new skills, including basket weaving and forming clay pots for storing grain and other possessions. Also, as they were not always on the move, houses, looms for making cloth, oven-fired pottery suitable for boiling cereals and other foods, and the arts of baking and brewing all came rapidly into use. The settled village community replaced the roving band as the key organization of human society. The discipline of regular hard work in the fields, together with the need for knowing the rhythm of the seasons and division of time to identify the right season for planting, made the farmers' life quite different from that of the hunter. Planning was needed to allocate food during times of hunger and to save enough seed for the next planting. Courage and killing skills, so necessary for hunters, were not required of farmers.

With the move to a farming society, human numbers vastly increased. Instead of remaining a rather rare species, mankind began to form village groups, and their farming activities changed the environment that, without their presence, would have balanced plant and animal life.

The first great landmark, then, of human history was the agricultural revolution which produced more food and made possible a population increase. In several areas, a hunting and gathering style of life gave way to farming and grazing of cows, sheep, and goats.

One of the earliest and most important of these transitions took place in the Middle East, perhaps between 8500 and 7000 BC. Then, through migrations and borrowings, grain cultivation spread into Europe, India, China, and parts of Africa. The cultivation of plants became central to the support of human life in most parts of the globe.

The second great landmark in mankind's history was the emergence of cities from which we get our modern word and concept of civilization. Cities started in the Middle East. The earliest civilized or citified communities developed in the valleys of the Tigris-Euphrates and the Nile between about 3500 and 3000 BC The Indus Valley followed suit soon afterwards.

At first, civilized complexity required very special conditions. This condition required a river so irrigation could guarantee a rich crop year after year without moving; and when irrigation was needed, large numbers of people had to cooperate in digging and diking. An agricultural surplus could then support specialists such as weavers and potters and even a leisured priestly class that could develop writing, mathematics, and astronomy.

It took about a thousand years before mankind began to extend city complexity from river basins to rain-watered land. The invention of the plow was fundamental here. It permitted ancient farmers to harness the strength of animals to the tasks of cultivation, and thereby allowed the individual farmer to increase his food production very substantially. This made available an agricultural surplus such as had previously been reserved for irrigated land.

In addition to food production, civilization demanded new organization of the social order. It required a sharp emphasis on authority between those with authority and the peasant majority to force the farmers to part with their surplus crops in order to support the soldiers, administrators, and cities that the ruling classes gradually built up.

An important development was the growth of sea trade, which allowed rulers of islands such as

Crete to gather the fruits of the entire Mediterranean coastline and to sustain a palace city at Knossos in Crete on the strength of sea trading.

Another part of the great change in mankind's organization was the use of horses by the peoples of the plains in southern Russia and the arrival of these people as conquering warriors. This happened soon after 1700 BC, when techniques of chariot warfare were perfected somewhere to the north of Mesopotamia. Chariots gave dominance to warriors who knew how to tame horses, and since the great center of horse raising was on the steppes, it was warrior tribes of central Asia and the Ukraine, speakers of Indo-European tongues, who reaped the principal advantage. (The implications of this on language was previously discussed.) These warriors overran all of Europe, western Asia, and India. Others, who had acquired the techniques of chariot warfare, also conquered the peasants of the Yellow or Huang Ho River Valley in China.

In Europe, India and China, interaction between already settled agricultural peoples and the new masters of the land laid the groundwork for the emergence of three new and enormously successful cultures we will examine. The pace of their development was roughly comparable, so that by 500 BC

a distinctive European type of civilization had emerged in Greece; an equally distinctive Indian style of civilization had formed in northern India; and in the middle stretches of the Yellow River, Chinese civilization had likewise asserted itself.

The Middle East had a more complicated history. Empires arose here which led to an unstable political unification of the entire civilized area of the entire Middle East. A decisive formulation of a distinctive world-view took place among the Jews, whose religion, as shaped by the prophets of the eighth to sixth centuries BC, was to exert as much or more influence than the Buddhism of India, the Confucianism of China, or the philosophy of Greece.

All of these key world views had found their initial expression before the end of the sixth century BC. By 500 BC, as we begin our discussion, an initial phase of world history came to a close. From this date until today, these early cultures; European, Indian, Chinese and Mid-Eastern (Judaism and Islam) have been the basic formative world views.

We will now explore these four distinctive culture realms that emerged which most people today still use as their value system, Our starting point will be that period around 500 BC.

Worksheet ▶

CHAPTER THREE

Define or identify:

• Name the languages of the Latin family and the Germanic family.

• Many immigrants to America came from countries speaking Slavonic languages. Can you name a few?

• The book will discuss eight world religions. Name the eight and place them in the proper cultural realm.

• Which language has become the *Lingua Franca* of the world?

• Civitas—Civilization.

Explain:

• Why does English contain a mixture of both German and Latin origin words?

• Why does the western view of time as linear have Jewish origins?

- Why is the symbol of Buddhism a wheel?

- How does religion unite?

- How does religion divide?

- Identify some nations of Europe today that are Slavic, German, Celtic, Latin, Scandinavian.

- What are the two basic contributing factors in the formation of modern English?

- What do we mean by civilization?

- What are the four rivers that were the source of the earliest civilizations?

- When we speak English, why is it related to the language of northern India?

Discuss:

- What are some of the reasons language is so important in distinguishing our culture from another? (myths, history, values)

- Why is the year 500 BC called the axis year for its importance in defining world culture?

- What do we mean by linear time and circular time? How could it change attitudes toward progress?

- Some historians paint the medieval monasteries as contributors to the rise of modern industrial society. What is the connection?

- Why would people tend to be more punctual in industrial countries?

- "Our culture and beliefs are formed by history and our heads are filled with a mixture of ideas and experiences gathered from here and there through the centuries with adaptations to serve their peculiar needs."

- How did the development of agriculture tie with the advancement of civilization?

Chapter 4 ▶ ▶

WESTERN CULTURE_____

▶ Western Culture and the Rest of the World

The Western or European cultural realm will receive, and deserves to receive, particular attention in our survey of the four cultural realms. It is the cultural realm of the United States and continues to be the dominant culture of the world as we are becoming a global community. Indeed, global history since 1500 can be seen as a story of the impact of Europe on the rest of the world. Increasing European dominance of mankind, especially after 1750, and the efforts of these impacted cultures to survive the European onslaught are a central theme of the last several hundred years. This perspective helps explain the state of modern Japan, Communism in China, and the anti- Western attitudes of Muammar Khadafy and Ayatollah Khomeini in Islam.

The cultural encounter between Europeans and the rest of the world's people is a central theme of modern history and of this book. World history since 1500 may be thought of as a race between the West's growing power to dominate the rest of the world and the increasingly desperate efforts of other peoples to maintain their own cultural integrity. The two options they have used have been to cling more strenuously than before to their peculiar cultural inheritance or, when that failed, to borrow aspects of western civilization—especially technology—in the hope of finding a way to protect themselves

By the early 1900s, one country in the whole inhabitable globe was not controlled by western culture: Japan. Other non-European countries were considered sovereign and independent: China, Siam, Afghanistan, Persia, Ethiopia, Liberia and Haiti. But these were all greatly under European influence and had their policies controlled and their economies dominated by western powers.

Although European empires have fallen apart since 1945, it remains true that, since the end of World War II, the scramble to copy science, technology, and other aspects of western culture has accelerated enormously all round the world. So even the break-up of western European political mastery of the globe has coincided with an unprecedented, rapid westernization of all the peoples of the earth.

If a world society or a world civilization can be said to exist, it is the result of European influence Interaction between the Islamic, Indian, and Chinese cultures, on the one hand, and western innovation on the other, has been and will likely remain, a central theme of modern history. This theme will dominate nightly news and international conflict. The phrase "the West and the rest" is apt.

During the last hundred years, traditional patterns of society in each of the great cultural regions described in this book have collapsed, and Chinese, Indian, and Muslims have reacted very differently to the problems facing them. The Muslims have been the least successful, for they can neither abandon the traditions of Islam nor can they successfully live any longer within its narrow traditions.

The Japanese are the most successful, having been able to maintain political independence and traditional cultural patterns while building a formidable industrial and military strength by means of a massive borrowing of Western science and technology.

China, after a late start, is now opening up to Western technology and ideas of industrial organization. The progress toward a modern, industrial, consumer society is proceeding rapidly. Likewise, India is desperately trying to reconcile modern Western techniques of production and marketing with their traditional values.

China and India seem to occupy halfway positions. They have better come to grips with the industrial and political revolutions, but have made less tangible progress toward the realization of their hopes than the Japanese. The effort to conscious modernization or westernization still commands the central place in the hopes and strategies of all the non-Western peoples of the world.

▶ The Western Tradition

What then is European and Western culture? Europe is a community of peoples who share in a common spiritual tradition that had its origins three thousand years ago in the Eastern Mediterranean and which has been transmitted from age to age and from people to people until it has come to overshadow the world.

Two pillars of tradition support our western heritage: One, the classical tradition of the Greeks and Romans, our Greco-Roman heritage, and two, the Jewish and Christian religious tradition, our Judeo-Christian heritage. These two great heritages have molded a society different than any that went before. Western culture has its roots in two profound traditions: the Greek and Roman view of law and the Judeo-Christian vision of souls all equal in the sight of God.

For the Greek, the essence of citizenship, what distinguished the polis—the city-state—from the barbarians outside, was that people lived in the Greek city according to laws which they, themselves, had helped to frame. There was not full equality; slaves and women were excluded. But the citizen enjoyed equality with his fellow citizens before the law, and the law was the final protection of his integrity and equality against the threat of tyranny; either the tyranny of a single leader or the possibly more dangerous threat of an arbitrary ma-

jority. Here in its first emergence in history could be found a definition of the "rights of man" in terms of his rights against a dangerously sovereign government.

The other key statement of equality is expressed in Christian theology, in the vision of souls standing equal in the sight of God. During the Middle Ages, cathedral and church were the educators of the common people. A favorite theme in those days was the 'Doom,' or Last Judgment, carved above the doors of cathedrals or painted on the walls of parish churches. From these vivid pictures of Heaven and Hell, the people received with graphic force the sense of human equality. Among those called to heaven would be the shepherd, the peasant, the woodman, the carpenter, while those descending with tortured faces to hell were often kings, princes, dukes, and bishops.

Here, expressed with the most dramatic sense of contrast, is a deep root of western culture's equality: the belief that souls are equal before God and that, therefore, as human beings, they are equal despite differences of class, race, or culture. Clearly, once you believe this, revolutionary ideas such as self-government can prosper.

These beliefs in equality, for example, gave the cities with their merchants and bankers and rising middle classes in medieval Europe an independence they enjoyed nowhere else. And without the self-confidence and security of the merchant class, the later evolution of capitalist society would have been inconceivable.

The drive for equality worked right on through the rest of society. It works on to this day. In England's Civil War, it was John Lilburne, a soldier in Cromwell's Army, who gave classic expression to the drive which would dominate politics for the next four hundred years: "The poorest he that is in England has a life to live as the richest he."

In Europe the drive for equality has been the inspiration of revolutions beyond number. In recent times, it underlies the growth of socialism, trade union organization, the emancipation of the workers, and the whole concept of the modern welfare state. The idea of equality has worked through every level of western society, liberating new classes and letting loose new political forces into the world.

Here is a second great revolutionary Christian idea: the idea of what one might call belief in this world, an immense interest in this world, in its processes, in its laws and construction, in the ways in which it can be made to work to human ends and purposes.

Equality before God and belief in this world spring essentially from three sources: Greek thought, Judaism, and Christianity. It was in the Greek vision of law that science acquired its fundamental confidence in a material universe predictable and orderly enough to be explored. The world makes sense from the Judeo-Christian religious inheritance through the idea that the whole of creation is God's work, and, as such, must be of immense interest and value.

In spite of the temptations of religious pessimism, Christianity has never dismissed as "illusion" what comes from the hand of God. Other societies have lacked this essential insight into the value of created things. In Hindu culture, for instance, the world is Maya, illusion, a fevered dance of fleeting appearances which mask the pure reality of uncreated being. (We will explore this further in the chapter on Indian culture.)

▶ Progressive Living

Perhaps the sharpest difference in western tradition from the basic ideas of other civilizations lies in its vision of reality as an ongoing drama, as an immense dialogue between God and mankind which will end in an outcome of fulfillment and bliss. All traditional societies feel themselves bound to a "melancholy wheel" of endless recurrence. Seasons, the life cycle, planetary order, all revealed the return of things to their origins, and life swung round in the orbit fixed by destiny. (See previous reference, "Time," on linear and circular time.)

Marcus Aurelius, wisest of Roman emperors, believed that at forty a man had experienced all there was to experience. Greek, Roman, Chinese, and Indian cultures saw no vision of progress to new possibilities, no sense of the future as better and fuller than the present. All contained the underlying fatalism of traditional civilization. It is only in the Jewish and Christian faith that a Messianic hope first breaks upon mankind.

In Christianity, the hope is expressed in religious terms of deliverance and salvation. Over the

centuries the idea became changed into this-worldly terms. Nothing is more western than the dominant idea of progress, of getting forward, of being able to see hope ahead, and of working for a better future, not hereafter, but here and now. The West's steadily increasing interest in material things, belief in this world, and in the value of the exploration of nature are based on this Judeo-Christian concept.

We take this attitude so much for granted that it is easy to forget how recent it is and how entirely its origins lie in our Western society. The scientific spirit, drawing on the Greek sense of law and the Judeo-Christian respect for the handiwork of God, is perhaps the most profoundly distinguishing feature of our Western culture.

Modern science could hardly arise in Hindu society since one does not devote a lifetime to exploring an illusion. It did not prosper in China, for, in spite of orderly government, rational rule, and intense intellectual interest stretching back through millennia into the past, the dominant Confucian class turned its back on science and preferred instead the consideration of human relations and urbane life. Islam showed no interest in the industrial revolution.

But in Europe, the aftermath of the Wars of Religion following the Protestant Reformation turned educated opinion to science in which, it was hoped, the clash of religious dogma and the horrors of the wars of religion could be left behind. As a result, in the seventeenth and eighteenth centuries, all over western Europe, especially in Britain, the inventors and experimenters set to work to explore matter and improve technology. They revolutionized the use of iron. They invented all types of new machinery. They invented the steam engine. The age of the railways and the factory system opened up ahead. In other words, we have the beginning of the industrial revolution that is still shaping our modern world profoundly. (This western based revolution will be explored later in more depth.)

An emancipated and self-confident merchant class, with a strongly developed credit system, had savings to pour into these new technologies. They were joined by enlightened gentleman farmers and by sturdy self-reliant artisans, all ready to experiment and back the experiments with their own—and other people's—savings. This combination of new technology and expanded saving made possible great increases in productivity. Much more could be produced by each pair of hands in each working hour. The surplus could be reinvested in further expansion. This process depended on keeping general consumption low. The mass of workers did not at first profit from the new system. Herded into the towns, ignorant, unorganized, they contributed to the massive new saving by working for wages which were much lower than their true productivity. But the savings were used by entrepreneurs who reinvested them to expand the whole scale of the economy.

Out of these savings came what one might call a "break-through" to a new type of economy. Fresh capital was applied to all the processes of production; the expansion of each helped the expansion of all with a sort of internal momentum. This combination finally put the economy into orbit as the new type of advanced, capitalized, industrialized, technological society that we see around us, in the industrialized nations.

In the five centuries since 1500 western modes of thought and action have taken over the world. All societies have had to change age-old tribal values and patterns of life. Citizens now had political rights and a claim to equality. Humans could participate in a developing history full of hope and material progress. These were the new images people around the world acquired, enlarging their purpose and significance. The old customs and fatalities could only fight a losing battle. Western culture was at work incorporating the twin influences of its Greco-Roman and Judeo-Christian traditions which had been dramatically focused by the Renaissance (Greco-Roman) and Reformation (Judeo-Christian).

From 1500 onwards, the forces of dynamic change gather strength. The stream becomes a torrent. In Western Europe, energy, innovation, enquiry, confidence are characteristics of the new Europeans. Violence begins pouring out all over the earth, burying old ideals, overlaying old societies, creating a wholly new political and economic landscape. The first impact of western culture was often terrifying to those whose lives had been spent in peculiar unchanging environments before the arrival of the Europeans, such as in the Americas or Australia.

The original breakthrough to what we call modern society clearly belongs to the side of freedom in the western tradition, to innovation, personal initiative, and untrammeled experiment. Eighteenth-century entrepreneurs could draw confidence from hundreds of years of constitutional rule in which their rights vis-a-vis the government had been guaranteed by law and their property protected against the violent closing and expropriation normal under absolute monarchy. A tradition of law.

The new technology on which they drew had been the invention of free minds working in the spirit of free enquiry exploring God's work. Their actual operations—in investment and trade and foreign commerce—were felt to be liberating acts, consistent with the western idea of progress. Without all this vigor and risk, this breakaway from old forms, the shape of the modern world is hardly conceivable. This unique western tradition is still impacting the world.

▶ Time Table

In our outline of the development of Europe and western culture, we will build five dates. These dates are not, of course, that specific, but are accurate enough for the purpose of giving a sense of history and development and to provide focus to the key developments.

500 BC Height of Greece
    "Man is the measure"
    Man is like a god
    Greek idea of law
    Science—the universe has laws
    A healthy mind in a healthy body

0 Height of Rome
    "Captive Greece holds her rude conquerors
        captive"
    The empire and Latin Europe.
    The Code Justinian.
    Constantine and the Christian empire.

500 AD The Dark Ages
    St. Benedict—to work is to pray.
    The tribal grouping and languages of Europe
    Equal in the sight of God
    Christendom

1000 The Revival of Europe
    Triumph of the church.
    The cathedrals
    The university
    Brother Sun, Sister Moon
    The "re-birth"

1500 The Rise of Europe
    Conquest of the oceans
    The world become one
    Applied science
    The nation state

▶ The Two Foundation Traditions of Western Culture

Greeks—Reason
Man is the measure
The universe makes sense
Man is like a god

Jews—Faith
God is the center
God has a plan
We must carry out God's will

Roman
    Law and Order

Christian
    The Universal Church

Greco—Roman   Judeo-Christian

The empire becomes Christian
The church incorporates the Roman language, law and tradition

Western Culture

Worksheet ▶

CHAPTER FOUR

Define or identify:

- In 1900, what was the one country in the world not controlled by Western culture?

- 500 BC; 0; 500 AD; 1000 AD; 1500 AD.

- Greco-Roman.

- Judeo-Christian.

Explain:

- The two pillars that support our western heritage: Greco-Roman and Judeo-Christian.

- Why, in the Christian tradition, might those going to heaven be shepherds and peasants while those going to hell were kings, princes and bishops?

- Hindu—the world is illusion.

- Judeo-Christian—this world is of immense interest and value.

- The book relates a story about two men learning about oranges. How would you classify eastern and western traditions as they relate to eating the orange or finding out all about oranges in the library?

Discuss:

- Why is western or European culture given particular attention in this book?

- What are some differences between our Greco-Roman and our Judeo-Christian traditions?

- Equal in the sight of God.

- Equal in the sight of the law.

- The western tradition of progress.

Chapter 5 ▶ ▶

THE CLASSICAL
TRADITION_____
Greece and Rome

As discussed in the section on language, the Indo-Europeans or Aryans moving from central Asia around the year 1700 BC began filtering in to the Balkans and to the area of modern Greece as well as the western part of present day Turkey. They came as separate tribes, and the key to their success was the perfection of chariot warfare. Chariots gave the power to conquer to warriors who knew how to tame horses.

Since the great center of horse raising was the steppes of Central Asia, these speakers of Indo-European tongues overran all of Europe, western Asia and India. Others who acquired the techniques of chariot warfare also conquered the Yellow or Huang Ho River Valley in China. These new masters, interacting with the pre-existing agricultural peoples, laid the groundwork for three new and successful cultures, European, Indian, and Chinese.

By 500 BC, a distinctive European culture had emerged in Greece, another in northern India; and along the Yellow River, a Chinese culture had likewise matured. The great distinctive cultures of the world were in place, which together with Islam form the basis of our four world cultural realms, which are the focus of this book.

When the Persians first attacked mainland Greece in 492 BC, the philosopher, Confucius, was teaching in China. A dedicated reformer, he urged a return to the moral standards of an earlier epoch. His doctrine was one of several great creeds which arose almost simultaneously and won millions of followers in the East.

Persia, itself, intermittently warring with the Greeks, was being converted to another new creed: Zoroastrianism, based on the beliefs of the teacher, Zoroaster. This esoteric religion outlasted the Persian Empire and spread such momentous concepts as a day of judgment and the all-pervasive struggle between good and evil.

A third creed spreading at this time was born of the teachings of a semi-legendary Chinese philosopher, Lao Tzu. Partly in reaction to the feudal wars that were disrupting China late in the Chou Dynasty, Lao Tzu taught that salvation lay in renouncing society and retiring into a life of solitary contemplation, becoming one with nature.

In India, where the great mass of the people found in their religion little but obscure ritual and the need for costly sacrifices, Gautama Buddha arose to offer them the comforts of a gentle philosophy of life ruled by compassion and self-denial.

500 BC is often called the Axis date, because the fundamentals of the great world cultures are being defined. Western culture is taking shape in Greece

and will be passed to Rome to form the great classical tradition of western culture.

▶ GREECE

An Outline of Greek History

Not too long ago, it was thought that classical Greek civilization sprang more or less full-fledged out of nothing. True, the great classics of Homer, the *Iliad* and the *Odyssey,* told of a war of the Achean Greeks against Troy about 1200 BC, and of cities such as "golden Mycenae" in Greece, and "wide-eyed Knossos in Crete;" but the epics of Homer, who is thought to have lived in the middle of the ninth century BC, were regarded as mere legends, not as having something of history in them. Then, in 1870 AD, the German businessman, Schliemann, found not one but nine cities on the hill of Troy.

Six years later, Schliemann went to the reputed site of "golden Mycenae" in southern Greece. It was here, according to Homer, that Agamemnon, the leader of the Greeks against Troy, had ruled; and here Schliemann discovered inside the outer wall untouched tombs. From them he took: golden cups, beautiful bronze daggers decorated with lions or birds in gold, and golden death-masks.

This find was enough to prove that there had been a high civilization in Greece from about 1700 BC forward, centuries before the classical Greeks of 500 BC. Then in 1900 AD, in search of the center of this culture, the Englishman, Sir Arthur Evans, bought a small hill on the supposed side of "wide-eyed Knossos" in Crete, sank a shaft, and struck stone. Today the remains of the six-acre palace of the Minos, the name of the ruler of Knossos, are exposed for examination. Evans named this newly-discovered civilization "Minoan." It reached its peak from about 1600 to 1400 BC.

So, long before the Greeks of classical times, there had been an advanced civilization which was centered in Crete and had spread northward into the Greek peninsula. The basic stock at first was the small, black-haired, olive-skinned Mediterranean race. There were people, too, from Asia Minor' and then, shortly after 2000 BC, big and predominantly fair-skinned intruders began to infiltrate northern Greece. At about the same time, incidentally, a similar people was pushing into North Italy, speaking a language akin to Latin. They will found a city named "Rome." These people we now know as the Indo-Europeans or Aryans.

In Greece these newcomers, although of differing tribes, we call the Achaeans. They came in small bands, driving their herds and flocks and bringing with them: their ox-carts, their horses, and rough chariots, and their wives and children—a people in search of new homes. By 1700 BC, they were in southern Greece. These people, then, are "the bronze-armored Achaeans" of whom Homer sings. They spoke an archaic form of Greek. Their power endured for two centuries, from 1400 to 1200 BC. They had their splendid palaces and fortress-cities. They traded with Egypt. They crossed the Aegean and settled in Asia Minor.

In the twelfth century BC, another Greek-speaking people, the Dorians, took over in southern Greece, swept across Crete, and reached Asia Minor. Many refugees from Greece also fled across the Aegean to the coasts there and settled away from the Dorians. The Dorians hated cities. The rich Achaean fortresses were sacked. The Aegean world slipped back into barbarism. Out of these dark ages, about the middle of the ninth century BC, the classical Greeks began to emerge. In general, they spoke some form of one of the three major dialects of Greek: Aeolic, Ionic, and Doric. They lived in small and primitive but intensely patriotic city-states called "Polis." Corinth, for example, possessed only 376 square miles of territory.

They all called themselves "Hellenes" and anyone who did not speak Greek was a "barbarian." This term was not at first derogatory. It simply meant anyone using an incomprehensible language—a "bar-bar" sort of person. Their Greek homeland they named "Hellas."

The homeland was a bare, rugged and poor country. By its nature, it forced people to develop fiercely independent city-states and to turn to the sea. The country side favored the growth of small city-states, each separated from its neighbor; and the Greeks, themselves, never achieved anything like a modern nation-state. Also, it turned the people to the sea. No part of ancient Greece was more than fifty miles from the sea, and a boat could easily find a harbor. These harbors in the Greek world were countless, and the Mediterranean is a practically tideless sea. In summer, too, for most of the season, the Aegean is a glassy pond. It was inevitable, then, that the Greeks, settled as they were on both sides of the Aegean as well as in the islands, should become mariners and traders.

The Phoenician traders of the eastern Mediterranian soon sought out the new Greek communities, bringing them goods and the alphabet, and giving them a push toward civilization. Inland from the Asia Minor Greeks, the country of Lydia, which was in touch with Mesopotamia, invented coinage and passed it on to the Greek cities. Then, about 750 BC, a combination of circumstances set the Greeks hunting for new homes; and a wide dispersion of Greeks and their culture begins.

One cause was over-population, which is always a problem in a poor country. Another was the development of wealth and trade. This, in turn, sparked a struggle for political power between the old land-holding nobles and the newly-rich merchants. The side which lost often emigrated. To these motives, we must add the love of adventure. From the eighth century BC to the sixth, the maritime cities of the Greek world were aboil with new ideas and new discoveries.

The settlers were in search of farmland but were also looking for ship-timber, hides, and native ores. The Greeks put colonies along the Dardanelles, the Sea of Marmora, and the Bosphorus. The primary purpose was to control the passage into the Black Sea. One of these colonies, Byzantium, was to become Constantinople; and today we call it Istanbul. They founded Cumae and Naples, for which their name was Neapolis: "New City." They took over the eastern part of Sicily. Syracuse, Naples, Messina, Girgenti, Taranto, Brindisi, these names all go back to the original Greek colonies. The settlers went still farther west. Modern Marseilles was ancient Greek Massalia. Through this port, by following the Rhone and Seine rivers, Greek traders appear to have reached England. Meanwhile, so many colonies were established in Sicily and Italy that it was called "Greater Greece." (See Figure 5-1.)

We know from the Greek philosophers, Plato and Aristotle, what the Greeks looked for in a site for a colony: first, tame natives, then good land, spring water, a harbor, a city-site not too near the sea for fear of pirates, and timber for ships. Each new colony became a center which radiated outward the Greek way of life as a stove radiates heat.

Romans and Etruscans, too, felt the influence. To give one example only, it was from the Greeks that the Romans got the alphabet which they, in turn, passed along to us. Greek colonization was one factor which assured the impact of Greek culture on the Western world.

As the Greeks' horizons broadened, there was a rapid increase of knowledge, the rise of a new and highly individualistic poetry, and the beginning of Greek philosophy.

The Persian Wars

No country, even in 500 BC, can live to itself alone. The Persians to the East, growing in power, took over the Asia Minor Greek states. They went on to capture Babylon and to conquer Egypt. Under Darius, they crossed into Europe to subdue Thrace. When the Asia Minor Greeks revolted, and Athens sent twenty-two ships to help their brothers, the stage was set for the great struggle between the vast Persian Empire and the Greeks.

The odds seemed to be heavily favoring the Persians. They had reconquered the Greeks of Asia Minor. Their empire stretched from central Asia and the frontiers of India, Egypt, and the Mediterranean Sea. They were reputed to be invincible. Many Greek states sent earth and water as symbols of submission to the great king, Darius.

Two states, however, spearheaded resistance. One was Dorian Sparta, a polis in which the individual was nothing and the state everything; but it did have the best fighting men in Greece. The other center of resistance was Ionian and democratic Athens. As every history book tells: when in 490 BC a large Persian army landed on the coast of Greece at Marathon. 9,000 Athenians and 1,000 Plataeans charged and broke the resistence; 6,400 Persians were slain and 192 Athenians killed, who are still commemorated by a mound which was put up over where the fighting had been hottest.

Marathon proved that the heavily armed Greek hoplite, as the Greek soldier was called, could shear through light-armed Persians like a knife through butter. Herodotus added in his famous history of the Persian wars, "Freemen," he said, "fight better than slaves."

In any case, the myth of Persian invincibility was shattered. Meanwhile, Darius died. He was succeeded by his son, Xerxes. In 480 BC, Xerxes moved

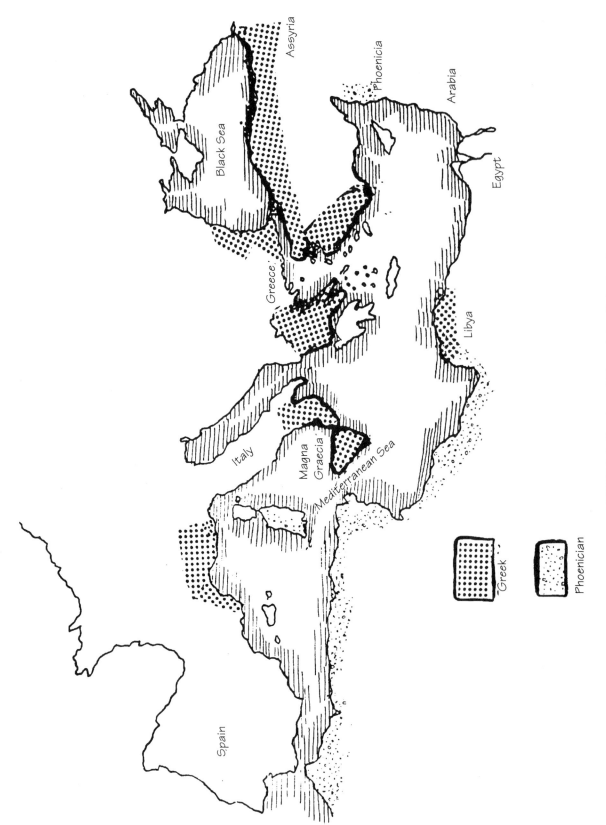

FIGURE 5-1 Greek and Phoenician Colonization

on Greece with a huge fleet and an army so immense that Herodotus says, "It drank the rivers dry."

But in addition to the Greek army, there was now an Athenian fleet. At Salamis in 480 BC, led by the Athenian squadron and Themistocles, the Greek fleet defeated the Persians. In the next year, the Persian army was beaten at Plataea. In the same year, the western Greeks beat back the Carthaginians in Sicily.

The significance of the victories is that the defeat of the Persians and Carthaginians was the torch to set fire to the brilliance of the great age of the Greeks. There was a tremendous upswelling of confidence. Like the English after the defeat of the Spanish Armada, the Greeks felt that there was nothing they could not attempt.

This was especially true at Athens. When the conservative Spartans withdrew from the Pan-Hellenic alliance, the Athenians formed the Ionian Confederacy of Delos. As its leaders, they reopened the route to the Black Sea and freed the Greek cities of Asia Minor. Then, initially almost without knowing what they were doing, they turned the League into an Athenian Empire. They attacked Cyprus. They conquered a small land-empire. They invaded Egypt.

Alongside the commercial and political expansion marched a terrific development in art and literature. The great war with Sparta from 431 to 404 BC put a stop to Athenian political supremacy; but her cultural achievement continued and endured. It has been said, and with a good deal of truth, that in the fifth century BC: "the history of Athens is for us the history of Greece."

In a very brief form, we have attempted to tell something about who the Greeks were and how they came to spread out around the Black Sea and along the Mediterranean coasts. The political and economic changes which took place from the eighth to the close of the sixth century BC have been sketched, and the significance of the Persian Wars has been indicated. In the fifth century BC, a set of values and ideals was defined in Greece that was to endure and give to modern western culture many of its basic values.

Our Greek Values

Greek ideals have exerted a strong influence throughout European history. The Romans who incorporated Greece into their empire were deeply impressed by it. Despite their confidence, they always thought that in much of art, letters and thought they could never do as well as the Greeks.

When the Italian Renaissance (to be discussed later) of the fifteenth century AD brought an intensified interest in the ancient world, Rome at first held the attention. But behind the imposing Roman tradition, scholars and poets felt the presence of something more powerful and more attractive. Slowly the full impact of the Greek performance was revealed. So great was Greek prestige that Greek ideas on medicine, astronomy and geography were accepted with unquestioning faith until the 17th century when the birth of a new scientific spirit inaugurated the era of experiment and inquiry into which we ourselves have been born.

Even today, the Greek view of life excites and inspires us. Greek thought and Greek assumptions are closely woven into the fabric of American lives almost without our knowing it; and for this reason alone, we are right to wish to know about the Greeks. A people should pay attention to their origins, and the modern world is far too deeply indebted to Greece to neglect what it has inherited.

At the center of the Greek outlook lay an unshakable belief in the worth of the individual, "Man is the measure of things." In centuries when large parts of the earth were dominated by the absolute monarchies of the east, the Greeks were evolving their belief that the individual must be respected not as the instrument of an omnipotent overlord but for his own sake. They sought at all costs to follow their individuality, and in this they were helped by the nature of their country. In Greece, where every district was separated from the next by mountains or the sea, central control of this kind was impossible. Men were forced to be, not specialists in this or that profession, but masters of a whole range of crafts and accomplishments. Each separate group was deeply aware of its own being, and within each group its members were aware of their responsibilities.

Life was hard for the Greeks, but this made them conscious of themselves and their worth. Without this self-awareness they would never have made their most important contribution to human experience: the belief that each person must be honored for individual worth and treated with respect just because he is himself. Just as they detested the thought of being conquered, so in their own circles a man claimed for himself the freedom to do all of which he was capable, to realize his full potential within his society, and to speak what was in his mind, to go his own way without interference from other men. The belief in freedom was sustained by a deep respect for personal honor and nurtured by a love for action.

This feeling among the Greeks may have started as something vague, but it was deeply felt; and it matured into reasoned philosophy which long after shaped, and still shapes, so many attitudes we call "American." It was based on convictions which we take so much for granted today that we can hardly imagine what efforts must have been made to establish the philosophy or what its absence meant outside Greece.

It has its own dangers, of course, especially the risk that in asserting their own claims men would pay too little attention to their neighbors and reduce society to anarchy which is a real problem in America today. As in America, Greek states did suffer gravely from internal dissensions. Nevertheless, they survived as centers of order because the Greek belief in liberty was inextricably associated with the existence of law, much as we say the United States is a government under law.

The Greeks did not invent law or originate the notion of it. Codes of law existed in Babylonia when the Greeks were still little better than savages, and the Mosaic Law of Israel is also ancient; but Greek law, which emerged in the seventh century BC, differed from these in several respects.

First, it was not intended to carry out the will either of an omnipotent monarch or of a god: the government of will. Greek law was aimed entirely at improving the lot of mortal humans.

Second, while these earlier systems could be changed virtually at the will of a king or a priest, Greek law was usually based on some kind of popular consent and could be changed only by being referred to the people for their approval.

Finally, Greek law was expected to secure life and property for all members of a society, not just for a select group of leaders or priests. The Greeks regarded themselves as vastly superior in this respect to the Persians, who being utterly dependent on their king's whim, were, in the Greek view, no better than slaves. Note again Herodotus, "Free men fight better than slaves."

From the first Greek lawgivers stems the whole of the West's legal systems. The Romans, great lawmakers in their own right, learned from the Greeks. In turn, the comprehensive Roman Code of Justinian gave rise to most modern legal systems. The belief in Roman law emphasized and strengthened an ethnic pride which shaped the whole political development of Europe.

A Greek state or Polis consisted of a city and of the lands around it which provided its livelihood. Each state formed its own habits, rules and government; as a consequence, local loyalties were remarkably strong. Beyond this, the Greeks had a second loyalty, vaguer perhaps and not always paramount but in the end irresistible.

Though they quarreled and fought with one another, they felt strongly that they were all Greeks: those who spoke some form of the same language, worshiped the same gods, and obeyed the same customs; in all these respects, they saw themselves as vastly superior to other races or nations. The world consisted of Greeks and barbarians. Though they never created a truly national state such as those of the modern world, they presented a strong contrast to the multinational empires of Babylonia or Persia. The latter comprised a large number of different peoples held together not because they shared a common culture or ideal, but simply because they were subjects of a despotic ruler.

The Greeks' sense of personal achievement and of a man's obligation to make the most of his natural gifts, led them to give to the works of their hands the same care and attention that they gave to the structure of political life. In the Greek view, anything worth doing was worth doing well, and the remains of their household pottery have a remarkable distinction. Even objects of everyday use such as coins are masterpieces of relief sculpture in gold or silver.

In the major arts, notably in sculpture, this sense of fine workmanship was inspired and reinforced by something more exalted. Greek sculpture was meant to be seen in public places, principally in temples; and it had to be worthy of the gods. It had to have a nobility and dignity, yet, it could not be too remote from everyday things for the gods were believed to be always at work in every day things. All this explains why Greek art at its best never aimed at the violent, gross, grotesque, or tricky effects. Instead it showed men in the full strength of their natural, muscular bodies and women in the graceful drapery of their finest clothes.

The Greeks were a people who lacked inhibitions in speaking about themselves; and as might be expected, they loved words. They had at their disposal a wonderfully subtle, expressive and adaptable language, and they made full use of it. With the Greeks as with many peoples, poetry came before prose. Poetry, in fact, became almost a second religion; and it was created with all the care and insight that was accorded to the visual arts. Poets were highly esteemed. If a man, any man, had something important to say, he often said it in verse, which in the early days, meant that he said it in song for almost all Greek poetry was originally sung or spoken to music.

The arts were not the only creative fields in which the Greeks excelled. The nature of the physical world excited their curiosity and led them to make spectacular scientific hypotheses. Before them, to be sure, much of a practical nature had been accomplished in such fields as astronomy and engineering by Egyptians and Babylonians. The Greeks' unique contribution was to provide a theoretical basis for these applied sciences. They sought general principles, and in the process became not only the founders of science but of philosophy meaning literally: "love of knowledge." To the Greeks, the two fields were closely related, both being the means by which men could seek to find out more about the nature of things, and moving both by argument and proof from one hypothesis to another. (See Figure 5-2.)

If in their practical way the Greeks needed astronomy for navigation and an understanding of weights and stresses for building, they strengthened and broadened this technical knowledge with theories and general principles about the nature of matter and space and motion, which they expressed in mathematics, especially in geometry. Then, they often reaped the benefits in other fields. Pythagoras set a firm foundation for music, for example, by discovering the numerical ratios of the lengths of string that would produce a seven-note scale. Music is beautiful, of course. The Greeks asked why and provided a scientific theory.

The Greek myths are beautiful and sophisticated and are a part of our western cultural heritage and literary tradition; but it was the Greeks who also introduced a way of looking at the universe that was quite opposite that of the myth makers. Those who made the myths saw the universe as essentially like human unpredictability. While men were like gods, the gods were like men. The new view of the Greeks saw the universe as a machine governed by inflexible laws. The Greek philosophers set about discovering just what those laws of nature might be. In their search for nature's laws, the philosophers assumed that if the right approach was used, the secrets could be discovered; and that when found, they would be comprehensible.

So to progress, humans had to work out a system for learning how to determine the underlying laws from the observed data. To progress is to use reason. While we may use intuition to guide our search, we must use sound logic to test particular theories. The steps the Greeks set up were three: first, you must collect data; second, you must organize the data into an orderly array; third, you must derive from your orderly way of observation some principal that summarizes the observations. The Greeks named their means of studying the Universe Philosophia, "love of knowledge," or maybe a better translation would be "the desire to know."

While Greek science was developing on a theoretical basis, it also saw the need for observation and experiment. When medicine flowered in the fifth century BC under the inspiration of the great physician Hippocrates of Cos—American doctors still take the oath of Hippocrates—it made its first task the collection of data from which deductions could be drawn. Thus, in the identification of diseases, a Greek doctor set great store on the correct description of symptoms, and proceeded from that point to do what he could to effect a cure. Medicine was, of course, very much in its infancy, and doctors were much better at diagnosing a complaint than in knowing what to do for it; but, at least, they had made a great advance over the old days when illnesses were thought to be curable by amulets, magic charms and the like. Again, we see the Greek

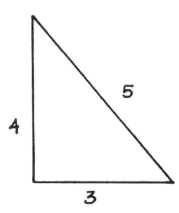

TECHNOLOGY • HOW IT WORKS

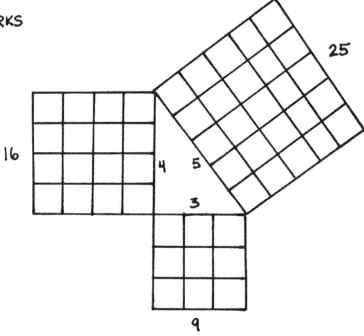

$$A^2 + B^2 = C^2$$

SCIENCE • WHY?
        WHY IT WORKS

• HOW?
SUBSTITUTE ANY NUMBER
FOR A, B, OR C AND SOLVE

FROM THE SPECIFIC TO GENERAL LAW

$$c^2 = (a-b)^2 + 4 \times \tfrac{1}{2}\, ab$$
$$= a^2 + b^2$$

FIGURE 5-2 Technology and Science

search for reasons. In surgery the beginnings were primitive enough; but by experimenting on animals and learning something about the principles of physiology, the Greeks were able to deal with fractures and dislocations which were common among athletes, and with wounds, especially head wounds, received in war.

The spirit which inspired Greek research into nature was also at work on human actions, and it made the Greeks the first true historians. Their accounts of past events gradually changed from legend to verifiable fact; "What I write here," said Hecataeus of Miletus at the beginning of the fifth century BC, "is the account of what I thought to be true; for the stories of the Greeks (of other centuries) are numerous, and in my opinion ridiculous."

In pursuing truth for its own sake the Greeks were hampered by no rigid theology. Since they were not tied to creeds, they were free to ask questions about the scheme of things. Such inquiries, far from being thought impious, were often regarded as a quasi-religious activity because they showed the wonderful workings of the gods. Note our reference earlier: *Nothing that comes from God can be thought unworthy of study.* Though Greek gods to us may seem mere superstitions, they had something impressive in common. They were, to a high degree, embodiments of power whether in the physical world or in the mind of man. From them came literally everything, both visible and invisible; and it was the task of the mortals to make the proper use of what the gods provided. Much of modern science is based on this moral justification.

Because the gods were the sources of power, men honored every kind of power and wished to display it in their own lives. This applied equally to war, the arts, athletic games and thought. If a Greek did well in any of these, he was making a proper use of his divinely provided gifts; and to that extent, he was getting nearer to the gods. This is what Aristotle means when he said: "We must be immortal as far as we can." Thus the Greeks stood of two minds in relation to their gods, at once eager to be as much like them as possible, yet knowing that humans must not attempt this too eagerly, lest they imagine that they were gods, a principal cause of a man's downfall.

This ambivalence proved a great value. From it came the characteristic Greek mixture of energy and moderation, both in life and the arts. While the Greeks zestfully tried every form of action, they tempered it with the maxim: "Nothing in excess;" and they praised the desirability of the Mean; the middle state between attempting too much and not attempting enough. Needless to say, they did not always achieve the Mean, but it was at least an ideal, and it set its mark on their civilization. They felt it to be a driving strength which came from the gods, and they knew that it was their task to make the most of this not by seeking pleasure and sensation—though, of course, they enjoyed these as the reward for their efforts-but by shaping their lives to rational and desirable ends. As the Greeks set out to make the best of their natural gifts and to be worthy of their human nature, they dedicated themselves:

—to noble toil,

—to creating something new and splendid,

—to keeping their bodies as fit as their minds,

—to making order out of disorder,

—to living in harmony with their fellow citizens.

Not too bad.

Greek Religion

The religions of the ancient Greeks are extinct. They now belong to: history, literature, music and museums. Today, no one on earth worships the Olympian gods: Zeus, Apollo or Venus. Yet, they reflect Greek thinking and enter the mainstream of our western culture, not only because of Greece, but also because of their influence on Rome and Christianity.

Greek religion was essentially a blending of the beliefs of a nomadic, warlike people from the north who invaded Greece sometime during the twelfth century BC, and those of an agricultural and domestic native society whose gods reflected its own peaceful attitudes. As these two cultures settled down, merged and blended, the patterns of a new religion began to emerge. There was in reality no such thing as a "national" religion, since each city-state in Greece worshiped its own deity and had its own beliefs.

To begin with, Greek religion was basically polytheistic with literally scores of major and minor gods were worshiped; and each city had at least one patron god. In addition, Greek religion possessed no sacred writings nor books equivalent to the Bible, nor was there a professional clergy in the true sense, although numerous prophets and official priests conducted public ceremonies.

Further, there was no evidence of a moral or ethical code designed to regulate the behavior of man, although such a code was operative in Greece independent of religion. Finally, Greek religion was unique in its failure to advocate the existence of an evil power or the presence of evil spirits in the world. Even Hades, god of the Underworld, was not represented as an evil being. Their gods had human failings. Zeus, king of the gods, was constantly henpecked by his domineering and jealous wife, Hera. The other gods were also subject to the frailties of human nature: Ares, the god of war, was a drunken bully, for example; and Aphrodite, the beautiful goddess of love, was promiscuous.

Probably to an extent greater than any other religion known to man, the religion of the Greeks and the Romans, who copied them, had a foundation of myth and legend. This is an indication that, in the early stages at least, these societies lacked a true religious base; and their level of scientific knowledge remained at the same time in a fairly primitive stage.

In answer to the basic questions which have always puzzled mankind: "What is the origin of the earth? Of mankind? Why does it rain?", imaginative, often poetic stories called "myths" evolved. (See story of Demeter in Religion section.) Frequently, these myths had roots in historical reality. For example, the many amorous affairs of the god Zeus with various young ladies of both heavenly and earthy origin probably represent the actual union of the early Aryan invaders of Greece with the native peoples of the country. As well, the exciting archaeological discoveries at Troy, Mycenae, Crete and elsewhere indicate the substantial reality of many stories once considered pure fiction; but in the Greek experience at least, it is probably fair to say that myths are *neither conscious poetry nor valid science, but the common root and raw materials of both.*

Greek mythology, and to a lesser extent Roman, has had a deep influence on western civilization. The stories continue to inspire authors, musicians and artists as they have through the ages. To the average Greek, for whom life was most difficult, the gods must have appeared fickle indeed. So it was with fear and awe but with love that mankind worshiped the gods. Thus, in worship, it was the ritual itself which was of importance rather than the sentiment behind it. Throughout the country, rituals had a similar format and every Greek worshiped in much the same way as every other Greek.

While most cults were mechanical in their observance and the individual subject to the will of fickle gods, some of the more thoughtful cults developed a belief in the soul and afterlife. This was to be determined by one's moral behavior and a new attitude toward mankind's ethical behavior. Indeed, many of the doctrines and beliefs embraced by later Christians appear to have had a substantial following among devotees of the mystery cults. Among these, are the doctrines of heaven, hell, and purgatory; the nature of the soul, the belief in the resurrection of a slain god; and the ritual eating of the body and blood of a god-symbol, which may have had a direct or indirect influence in the development of early Christianity.

Eventually the real outlet which provided the Greek with an opportunity to release their intellectual energy lay in the realm of philosophy. By the fifth century BC the Greek thinkers had harnessed the rational force of philosophy to religion, and produced some important religious concepts. Indeed, the wedding of religion and philosophy is among the greatest of the contributions of Greek civilization to posterity. By the fifth century BC, the Greeks had developed a highly elaborate, ritualistic-oriented religion, which, though rich in mythology, art and literature, lacked the emotional appeal to sustain its practice among the majority of the people. For the educated minority, the slack was taken up by the genius of philosophy then in full flower in Greece. For the majority, the traditional Homeric faith slowly ceased to function, as it was eclipsed in turn by the popular Eastern cults, and subsequently by Christianity. To Christianity, in the area of both art and ideas, the Greeks contributed to a great deal. (See listing of Olympian Gods.)

The Decline of Greece

The potential instability of Greek individualism became real after the magnificent achievement of the unified Greeks in defeating the mighty Persian Empire. After maintaining a precarious balance among themselves, the Greek states began to separate into two camps: Athens or Sparta. Soon war became inevitable. The war was called the Peloponnesian War (431–404 BC) and is well documented by the famous book on the subject by the historian Thucydides. The Greek polis or city-state exhibited a fundamental flaw, for it soon became apparent that the greatness of one polis involved the eclipse of the freedom and greatness of its neighbor. This flaw has been repeated in our century as we have experienced the tragic inability of the European nation state to resolve differences.

Within the heartland of Greek civilization, the Peloponnesian War was drastically disruptive of polis life. In many city-states, sentiments of solidarity among the citizens were strained and even destroyed by the hardships and opportunities of the war. What happened cannot be better described than in Thucydides' own words:

> . . . the whole Hellenic world was convulsed; struggles being everywhere made by the popular chiefs to bring in the Athenians, and by the oligarchs to introduce the Lacedaemonians [i.e., Spartans]. In peace there would have been neither the pretext nor the wish to make such an invitation; but in war, with an alliance always at the command of either faction for the hurt of their adversaries and their own corresponding advantage, opportunities for bringing in the foreigner were never wanting to the revolutionary parties. . . .

Thus, every form of iniquity took root in the Hellenic countries by reason of their troubles. The ancient simplicity into which honor so largely entered was laughed down and disappeared; and society became divided into camps in which no one trusted one's neighbor.

The Greek city-states never entirely recovered from such shattering experiences. In Athens after the war, an underlying suspicion and mutual dislike divided the few from the many, the rich from poor; and similar sentiments pervaded other Greek cities.

The old Periclean concept of citizenship, with its demands upon the whole man, could not be maintained. Individualism, political passivity, and the sense of personal alienation from the commu-

nity all gained ground. Many see in the Greek experience parallels to our problems. The Peloponnesian War had the professed purpose of restoring the freedom of the Greeks, but the practical result was far different.

After 404 BC, victorious Sparta intervened in the affairs of other cities even more highhandedly than Athens had done; and Thebes and Macedon later did likewise. In truth, the separate sovereignty of scores of small city-states was no longer practicable in an age when greater fleets and armies could be created and maintained by tribute and plunder. Yet, even in the third and second centuries BC, despite locally successful efforts at the federal government level, Greek particularism proved too strong to allow either a stable union within or firm control from without. Only the crushing military superiority of Rome brought intercity warfare to an end.

Single and separate cities, where the citizens' voices could perhaps still be heard, had lost control of their own fates. Greece as a whole had become a mere pawn on a military and diplomatic chess board which was dominated by governments commanding professional armies and navies and financial resources vastly greater than any city could hope to match.

With the decisive loss of local polis sovereignty which was an event signalized by the Macedonian conquest in 338 BC, Greek civilization and culture lost much of its initial elan.

Alexander the Great

Alexander succeeded his father, Philip, to the throne of Macedon in 336 BC. Philip had already imposed his will on a divided and weak Greece. When Alexander ascended the throne at age 20, Macedonia's power was firmly established. Alexander from his power base was able to dream of a unified world. Alexander admired Greece, and his favorite reading was the *Iliad*. Alexander saw himself as a second Achilles. Aristotle, Alexander's boyhood teacher, imbued his young pupil with a love of Greek art and poetry and instilled in him a lasting interest in philosophy and science.

The principal empire of the near East was Persia, which Alexander had reason to believe he could defeat. In 334 BC, he crossed the Hellespont separating them before. Soon after he defeated the Persian forces, he successfully pursued the Persian King Darces to his death. Now, Alexander was officially the Great King of Persia. In his new role, he headed east to take possession of the remaining Persian provinces. After two years, he reached and subdued Bactria and Sogdiana. He now controlled all the lands that had belonged to Darius, the Persian who had earlier attacked the Greeks.

After completing his conquest of the Persian Empire, Alexander turned south and headed into India. Nearly two centuries before in the reign of Darius I, the Persian Empire had included part of that subcontinent. Determined to recapture it, Alexander crossed the Hindu Kush mountains, followed the Kabul River down to the Indus River and crossed overland, and advanced deeper into India. Like most men of his time, he believed that the Indian continent was a small peninsula jutting eastward; and that at its uttermost extremity was located the body of water simply called "Ocean" that encircled the world. His men had other ideas. As they were tired and yearned for home, they refused to march. He turned his army toward home. In 323 BC, he reached Babylon when a fever struck him, and he died. He was not yet 33 years old.

With his death, the political structure of his Empire disintegrated almost immediately. The Indian conquests reverted to their own rulers; and Alexander's generals, grabbing for sovereignty of scores of small city-states which was no longer a practicable strategy in an age when greater fleets and armies could be created and maintained by tribute and plunder. Yet, even in the third and second centuries BC, despite locally successful efforts at federal government, Greek particularism proved too strong to overpower, soon divided what was left. One general, named Seleucus, seized most of Persia and formed the Seleucid Empire; another, Ptolemy, established the dynasty of the Ptolemies in Egypt; and a third, Antigonus, became King of Macedon. In Greece, Athens and Sparta were again independent city-states, while most of the other states joined in one of two new alliances. Alexander's successors in Asia claimed to carry on his rule, and they followed at least some of his patterns. They modeled their cities on the Greek city-state and adopted the Greek language as the "lingua franca" of their world. They even appropriated Alexander's titles and attributes, and stamped their coins with his image.

In Bactria and India, petty rulers for many centuries claimed to be his direct descendants. The Indian King Chandragupta saw in Alexander's success the possibility of uniting India under a single monarchy. The Mirs of Badakhshan believed that their horses were descended from Alexander's horse, Bucephalus. Greek art influenced the art of all of western Asia and left an enduring mark on the sculpture of India. Greek design infiltrated Persian design, and from there moved to the Far East. Objects showing Greek influence have been found at the western end of the Great Wall of China. Several hundred years after Alexander's death, Roman legions pushing into the eastern Mediterranean and Asia found the residue of his system still working and learned from it some of the arts of ruling an empire.

Alexander's career was the sunset of Classical Greece. After Alexander, Greece was never the same. Politically, it maintained its independence, but it never regained its former power; and after two centuries was conquered by Rome. Culturally, its influence after Alexander was wider than it had ever been; but it was also more diffused and less homogeneous. The opening of Asia to Greek trade inevitably broadened the Greeks' outlook; and at the same time introduced essentially alien ideas into their cultural life. Classical Hellenism was modified by Asian influences and became Hellenistic. In this form, Greece influenced Rome, Egypt, and large areas of Asia; but Greek civilization had lost the brilliance of its early days.

The Olympian Gods

Greek Name	Function	Roman Name
Zeus	King of the Gods	Jupiter
Hera	Queen of the Gods	Juno
Athena	Goddess of Wisdom	Minerva
Apollo	God of the Sun, Prophecy, Music, and Medicine	Apollo
Artemis	Goddess of the Hunt and Moon	Diana
Hermes	Messenger of the Gods	Mercury
Hestia	Goddess of the Hearth	Vesta
Hephaestus	God of Fire	Vulcan
Hades	God of the Underworld	Pluto
Aphrodite	Goddess of Love	Venus
Demeter	Goddess of Agriculture	Ceres
Dionysus	God of Wine and Drama	Bacchus
Poseidon	God of the Sea	Neptune
Persephone	Goddess of the Underworld	Proserpina

▶ ROME

As with the Greeks, wandering tribes of Indo-Europeans entered a new territory around 700 BC and settled in Italy. One of these tribes, the Latins, founded their city, Rome, which was destined to bring not only Greek culture to our western heritage, which is our Greco-Roman tradition, but also because of its conversion to Christianity which is our Judeo-Christian tradition, Rome stands a key player in the development of European and western culture.

An Outline of Roman History

Rome owed its beginnings to a river, a ford, and the Seven Hills. As in very early times, there was a vigorous trade in salt from the mouth of the Tiber along the river to the tribes of the interior. Some sixteen miles from the Tiber's mouth, navigation ends. At this same point an island makes a ford possible, and low hills give shelter. This is where Rome began. The Romans date the founding of their city at 753 BC; but excavations have proved that the first primitive settlements on the site of Rome go back to before 1,000 BC.

Those first settlers may have comprehended that the Seven Hills controlled both the river traffic and the north-south trade by way of the ford. For that matter, in Roman times the road from Rome to the Sabine Hills nearby was still called the "Via Salaria," which means "the salt road."

But these first inhabitants of Rome could not have foreseen that the site of Rome made it natural for it-the city of Rome will now adopt a feminine gender, being referred to as "she" or "her"-to become the mistress first of Latium and then of Italy. For Rome, being on the Tiber is about half-way between the sea and the hills; and the plain of Latium, which is roughly forty miles wide and twice as long, is close to the center of Italy.

In 753 BC, Rome was a small community. Its people, the Romans, were Latins mixed with Sabines. The Latins spoke an Indo-European language, which they called the "lingua Latina," the "Latin tongue." (See Chapter 3, "Language.") Down the center of Italy, through the Umbrian, Sabine, and Samnite country were other Indo-European tribes.

All these peoples were intruders from the north, cousins to the Greeks. In Venetia on the east coast of Italy were Illyrian settlers. In Liguria, in the northwest of Italy and on the fringes elsewhere, were Mediterranean stocks.

Indo-Europeans, Mediterraneans, Illyrians, all three were in a primitive stage of culture. Civilization, as we know it, began in the Near East, in Sumer and Mesopotamia. The harbors and plains of Italy are on the west coast. Civilization came to Italy later than it did to Greece. When it did appear, it was brought by Carthaginians, Greeks, and Etruscans.

The Carthaginian influence was never very strong, but the Greeks made a lasting; and in the end, the major impact. Starting as early as the eighth century BC, they planted their colonies in Sicily and fringed Italy with settlements from Brindisi around the heel and toe of the country and as far northward as Naples and Cumae. In Sicily, the Carthaginians checked them. In Italy, the Etruscans blocked their expansion to the north. (See Figure 5-1.)

The Etruscans are a mystery people. The usually accepted view is that in the eighth century BC they landed on the west coast, north of Rome, in that part of Italy which is still called Tuscany after them. They were highly civilized. It is thought that they came from the east. As the decades went by, they reached out northward over Umbria and into the valley of the Po. Mantua is the site of one of their foundations. So is Milan. Later, they were to be pushed out of the Po valley by an onrushing surge of the Celtic Gauls.

Before that time, however, the Etruscans had also moved south over Latium. Rome was for a while an Etruscan city. When, in 509 BC, it became a free republic, there was little hint of the splendor that was to come. Rome had lost the hold on Latium which the Etruscans had given her. Her total territory was about ten miles by twenty-five.

For roughly a century, Rome fought a savage struggle for mere survival. Fortunately, she soon became once more the leader of the Latin League of Latium. But there were the savage hill-tribes to the east and south. To the north were the Etruscans. Then, just after Rome had captured the Etruscan city of Veii, the Gauls raided south. Before the fierce rush of these warriors who fought naked except for shields and swords and gold torques around their necks, the Romans broke. Rome was sacked and burned.

The Gauls withdrew, and, luckily for Rome, they had weakened the Etruscan power. Stubbornly, the Romans started again. In desperate war after war, they finally, by 272 BC, became the unchallenged masters of all Italy south of the Po Valley; but, no sooner was this achieved when Rome was drawn into two climactic conflicts with Carthage. When, in 202 BC, Hannibal was beaten at the battle of Zama, Rome emerged as the principal power of the western Mediterranean. Spain, Sicily, Sardinia, and Corsica were her possessions; and she had moved northward to the Alps. The Roman empire had begun.

During this same period, until 287 BC, there had been vicious internal strife in Rome between plebeians and patricians. The plebeians achieved political, economic, and social equality. Yet one result of the coming Carthaginian wars was to place a new nobility of wealth and office-holding in control of the Roman state. Thus began what is called the "Rule of the Senate," which was a permanent body of some three hundred magistrates and ex-magistrates. Meanwhile, there was still a distinction between the Romans, the original inhabitants of Rome, the Latins of the plain of Latium, and the Italians. These distinctions were later to disappear.

It was in three centuries of constant warfare that the character of the early Roman was formed. A people struggling for survival have little interest in philosophic speculation or in the search for beauty. Harsh, unbending discipline, dogged endurance, narrow bigotry, devotion to the practical—these were the qualities needed. The ideal Roman virtues were simplicity, seriousness, dignity, and piety—the proper performance of one's duty to the gods, to the state, and to one's family.

Such people can only understand what they can grasp and hold. Yet, when they came into contact with Greek culture they recognized its superiority. In 272 BC the Romans captured the Greek city of Tarentum, which is now Taranto, on the instep of Italy. The Greek prisoners became the tutors of the Roman children. And thus was begun the process by which, to quote the famous cliche, "captive Greece took her rude conquerors captive." That trend was intensified and accelerated by Rome's conquest of Greece and the Hellenistic Near East.

After the desperate struggle against Carthage and Hannibal, from 218 to 202 BC, the Roman people deserved a breathing space. Instead, they were plunged into wars with Macedonia, and with Antiochus the Great of Syria. There was a third Carthaginian War which ended in the obliteration of Carthage. Spain revolted, but the rebellion was crushed. By 133 BC the Romans were the unchallenged masters of the Mediterranean. The empire was now established.

On the whole, the conquest of the Near East was merely a training exercise for the Roman legions which were, by this time, the most efficient fighting machine the ancient world ever devised.

The Romans discovered that war could be made to pay. The loot of the Near East flooded into Italy—gold, silver, paintings, statues, jewel-studded tables, golden thrones, and the like. Above all, there was a host of war-captured slaves.

In that flood of wealth the old Roman character began to dissolve. Banking and capitalism sprouted and flourished. The ruling class, the senators, were either silent partners of the capitalists or used the governorships of the Roman provinces to plunder those provinces. Self-indulgence became the rule. The Romans still paid lip-service to the old Roman virtues. In practice they became gross and greedy materialists.

The enormous wealth was limited to a small class. The main mass of the Romans and Italians were either starving peasants or debt-ridden farmers or people on the dole. Italy had become, as the historian Mommsen puts it, "a society of beggars and millionaires." Meanwhile, Rome's republican constitution, which had been framed to govern a small city-state, creaked and groaned as it strove to administer an empire.

The result was a century of internal struggle. When Julius Caesar defeated Pompey the Great, it seemed as if ravaged Italy might have a rest. But Caesar's assassination in 44 BC set off a new round of civil wars. When in 31 BC Octavius, the adopted son of Julius Caesar, defeated Mark Antony and Cleopatra at the battle of Actium, the Romans gladly gave up political freedom for a dictatorship which assured tranquillity. Octavius, as Caesar Augustus, became, in effect, the first emperor of Rome.

And then for two centuries, from the battle of Actium until the death of Marcus Aurelius in 180 AD, the Roman empire experienced a peace and prosperity such as the world has seldom seen since.

True, there were frontier wars. In the last century of the republic, Pompey tightened Rome's hold on the Near East and Julius Caesar had conquered Gaul. The battle of Actium added Egypt. During the first century AD there was an adjustment of the northern frontier and Britain was conquered. The Emperor Trajan occupied Mesopotamia and what is now Romania; Mesopotamia was soon given up, but Dacia, as Romania was called, was held until Aurelian withdrew from it in 270 AD. Even today Romanian is a Latin language.

There was, too, more than one bloody revolt of the Jews. In Rome itself, in the first century AD, several emperors met violent deaths. But all of these happenings scarcely affected the security of the empire as a whole; and from 96 to 161 AD there was an era of almost uninterrupted peace. The ancient world lay cradled in the Pax Romana (Roman Peace).

Roman Empire and Trade

Let us take a look at that empire. From north to south, it stretched from northern Britain, and from the Rhine, the Danube, and the Black Sea; to the Atlas Mountains, the Sahara Desert, and into the Sudan. On the west it was bounded by the Atlantic, on the east by the Arabian Desert and Mesopotamia. What is now France, Switzerland, Austria, and parts of Germany belonged to it. So did Spain, North Africa, Macedonia, Greece, and the Near East. The empire was about 2,000 miles from north to south and 3,000 from east to west. Its area was roughly two-and-a-half million square miles, and its peak population is estimated at a hundred million. Thus, it was a sizeable empire for any age. (See Figure 5-3.)

The Roman Legions kept the Roman world secure. Within the Roman empire there were great

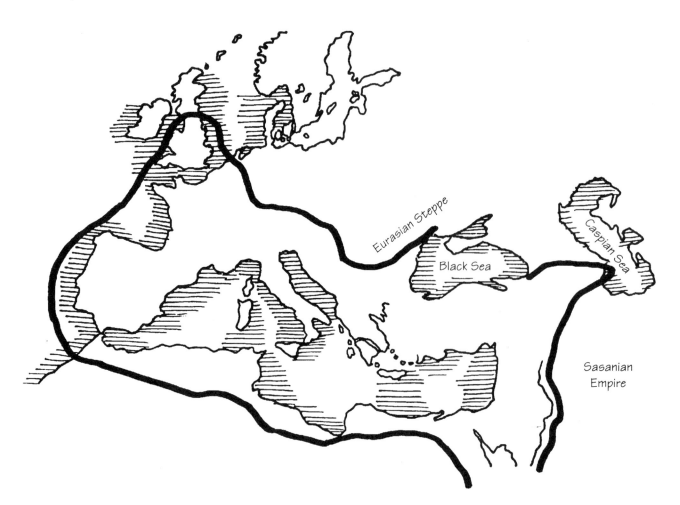

FIGURE 5-3 The Roman Empire at Its Height

cities and prosperous municipalities with a large measure of local self-government. There were many Roman citizens. The Romans had been forced to give the franchise to the Italians. By the time of Christ's birth all free men south of the Alps were Roman citizens. Julius Caesar granted citizenship to whole towns and tribes outside of Italy and to those who had served in the army, whatever their nationality. He also planted colonies of citizens all over the empire and even admitted provincials to the Roman Senate.

Augustus was more conservative, but there was an increase of 900,000 on the citizen roll during his reign. In this way Roman citizenship was widely extended. Thus, St. Paul, though a Jew, was proud of his Roman citizenship. Under later emperors, such as Trajan and Hadrian, the citizen franchise included the upper class of every city in the empire except in Egypt. Finally, in 212 AD, every free man in the empire was made a citizen. (Note "free man"—slavery was widely practiced.)

Citizenship helped the Romanization of the empire, particularly in the west. So did the network of roads and the trade which flowed along them. The total mileage of those roads is estimated at 47,000. The oldest of them was the Appian Way, built from Rome to Capua in 312 BC As the Roman power reached out, so did the roads. Along them the legions marched. And along them flowed the never-ending traffic, travellers on foot, carriages; wagons; transporting goods, post-horses, and the like.

The Roman roads were the arteries of the empire. They were built to endure. Today, for example, you can still walk on patches of the Appian Way where St. Paul once trod.

Those roads were all marked at intervals with the distance from the golden milestone which stood in the Roman Forum. Quite literally, all roads led to Rome. Under the empire a passenger, freight, and express system was organized. For the imperial couriers, there were post-stations for the changing of horses. For the transport of goods, there were mansiones, which in English means waiting-places. These mansiones maintained riders, drivers, conductors, doctors, blacksmiths, wheelwrights, and about forty beasts and the appropriate amount of rolling stock. The empire could be kept moving smoothly.

There was even a well-organized passenger service. By the fourth century AD, first- and second-class tickets were being sold, and from the first century AD the Romans had sleeping carriages in service. Free passes were issued, good for from one to five years or during the life-time of an emperor. Under the empire every Roman of any pretension at all was likely to make the "grand tour" to Athens, Ephesus, Antioch, and down the Nile.

To the great roads must be added the seaways. To the Romans the Mediterranean was Mare Nostrum, which means "our sea." It was furrowed by countless merchant ships, carrying passengers and freight.

The empire was, in fact, a great place for business. In foreign traffic, traders found their way to Denmark or up the old amber route from the Danube to the Baltic and across it to Sweden. Furs and slaves poured through the Brenner Pass into Italy. In the Near East, Greek merchantmen worked their way to Somaliland and beyond. The Roman traders pushed by land into Abyssinia.

The most exotic trade was to Arabia Felix, India, and China. Part of this was by caravan route from Syria, either to Arabia for spices and gold-dust or to India for gems and cottons or to China for silk. The Romans called the Chinese the "silk people," and in 97 AD a Chinese envoy travelled to Antioch in Syria to establish relations with the Graeco-Roman merchants.

The more popular route to India and the far East was from Alexandria via the Red Sea and the Indian Ocean. Each year as many as 120 ships set out for India. They carried gold and silver plate, metals, tools, weapons, trinkets, luxury goods, and Roman currency. Hoards of Roman coins belonging to the first half of the first century AD have been dug up in southern India. After the reign of Nero, these hoards are also found in north India.

Another interesting item is the discovery of a statue of the Hindu goddess of prosperity, Laksmi, at Pompeii, the town which Vesuvius buried in 79 AD It is known, too, that at least one Greek merchant crossed the Malay Peninsula and sailed up the coast, while in the reign of Marcus Aurelius a group of Graeco-Roman traders reached the court of China.

From this brief outline, you should have gathered an idea of the immense volume of trade and the great prosperity which the Roman empire enjoyed in the first two centuries of our era. The luxury was equal to anything the world has seen since. But there was also a solid and prosperous middle-class. Banking and credit capitalism were well advanced. Checks were used, letters of credit were common, and Roman currency was valid anywhere. It seemed so solid it would last forever.

But the colossus had feet of clay. The loss of freedom under a dictatorship brought inevitable spiritual and political repercussions and this is the key to a culture's vigor. The growth of a top-heavy bureaucracy and of a benevolent paternalism went unnoticed. Most of the inhabitants of the empire did not care. The extension of Roman citizenship, the levelling influence of a world-wide trade and prosperity, and the excellent government of the provinces under the imperial administration, left them contented so long as they could make money.

There was slavery, but slavery was an accepted fact. There was an idle and unemployed proletariat which had to be kept quiet by doses of "bread and games" or as we would say today "welfare." But the empire was an Eden for the banker, the capitalist, and the ordinary businessman. Consequently, only a comparative few cried warnings of the dangers to come. The first two centuries of our era were, in fact, as materialistic an age as any until the present. Everywhere a man was judged not by what he was but by what he owned. As the businessman Trimalchio said in one of the two Latin novels left to us: "If you have a penny, that's what you're worth"—much as we speak of a $100,000 a year man or woman.

Like early Greek religion, the religion of the Romans developed essentially from a blending of the beliefs of the native peoples with the gods of the surrounding civilizations that they conquered. The most important of the influences were those of the Etruscan to the north of Rome, and the Greeks in southern Italy.

In time, as Rome's imperial thrust spread to Asia and Africa, the religions of these conquered areas were also imported and amalgamated with the existing religions in Rome. It is a tribute to the Roman sense of practicality and religious toleration that each new cult, with the notable exception of Christianity, was received with open arms rather than with fears and persecution.

Roman Religion

The religion of the Romans, like others at that time, retained many aspects of its primitive ancestry. The Romans believed they were surrounded by invisible spirits and powerful forces which they called numina. The numina were present everywhere in nature: in the air, trees, groves, springs and fountains, rivers and hilltops.

To the practical-minded Roman, the immediate task was to identify these forces and harness their power in his behalf. Consequently, all worship, whether of a public or private nature, assumed the form of a contract between man and gods: prayer and worship were to be offered dutifully in return for services rendered. In only the rarest of cases was worship of the gods imbued with the sentiment of love.

As befits an agricultural society where the basic unit is the family, the majority of spirits came to be identified with some aspects of the farming household. Chief among these were the Lares, guardians of the household, and the Penates, guardians of the pantry or cupboard. Each family had a shrine containing images of these spirits in the home, and according to tradition a candle was kept perpetually burning before the shrine.

Equally important to the family were Vesta, goddess of the hearth or fireplace used to heat the home, and Janus, guardian of the gateway. It is said that Janus was always the first god mentioned in any prayer, and for this reason to him went the honor of having the first month of the year, January, named in his behalf.

Another early belief, important though difficult to grasp, was the Roman concept of the genius, the true spirit of man, or his spiritual double. The genius was thought to reside in every male and was the inspiration behind each man's deeds. It was in fact the genius, rather than the man himself, which was honored when a feast or banquet was held for an individual. Today we usually mean something quite different when we speak of a certain person's genius, but our usage had its origin in this early Roman concept.

As the Roman conquest spread across the Mediterranean many new gods were invited to Rome. From Egypt Isis and Osiris and from Persia Mithras, the sun-god, exerted an immense appeal to Roman manhood through its emphasis on honor, courage and combat.

Most important of all, however, were the Greek gods who, with all the elaborate mythology which enshrouded them, were especially attractive to the educated segment of Roman society. With only minor changes, the Romans absorbed most of the major Greek gods into their pantheon. In some cases, (Apollo, for example) the Romans even retained the original Greek name. (See previous chart of Greek and Roman Gods.)

From the Etruscans, the Romans learned the secrets of augury. It was thought that the will of the gods could be discovered if one carefully followed certain ritual practices. For the Romans this meant the precise observations of the entrails of birds or the eating habits of chickens. In time, this ritual became so important that no significant personal or state function would ever be undertaken until the approval of the auspices, the "forecasts," was secured.

Another medium of prophecy, also imported from the Etruscans, centered about the oracles of the Sybil, or prophetess, of Cumae. The oracles were contained in three books and formed the entire sum of what might be called Rome's sacred writings. These were the most honored of Rome's religious relics, but the actual content of these books is a mystery to this day, since none of them survived the destruction of the Empire.

After the death of Julius Caesar there was strong pressure within the Roman state towards emperor-worship. At first, this took the form of worship of dead rulers. Augustus Caesar had resisted all attempts to make himself a god while still alive. However, he was deified after his death, and beginning with Caligula, later emperors became living gods.

The practice of emperor-worship had the dual effect of providing a unifying symbol for Rome's scattered subjects in the far-flung empire, as well as instituting an official head for the Roman state religion. Also, it should be noted, making an emperor a God could not be reconciled with the Jewish and Christian belief in one God.

By the first century BC, however, it was already evident that the old religion was essentially discredited by its failure to provide moral and ethical sustenance. Being ritualistic in form and content, it could not provide the much-needed ethical and moral guidance for the vast majority of the people. So long as the ideal of empire and conquest had been maintained, the desire to serve Rome had replaced religious ideals; when the empire was consolidated and later declined, the traditional virtues also declined, and there was no meaningful religion to replace them.

The answer for many Romans lay in the new philosophies dealing with ethical behavior. The most influential of these were Epicureanism and Stoicism. Epicureanism, with its emphasis on the pursuit of pleasure and avoidance of pain, attracted many of the young Roman nobles, but it was Stoicism which captivated the greatest intellects of the Empire, including the emperor, Marcus Aurelius.

For the ordinary Roman, there was little consolation. Even the attempt to amalgamate the various religious cults through the institution of emperor-worship was a failure. What was needed was a faith which could appeal to men on an individual basis and set before them new goals and challenges. Increasingly throughout Rome and its western empire after the first century AD, that religion was Christianity.

The Decline of the Empire

There were ominous signs of change. In the last years of Marcus Aurelius' 161 to 180 AD reign, Rome's borders of the Rhine, the Danube and the Euphrates were all endangered at once. Although it would be another 200 years before those borders were breached in any strength, Marcus Aurelius' time was increasingly taken up with military matters. He was often at the frontiers, moving from camp to camp, personally leading his armies (and between battles, finding time to write down his rightly famous meditations).

The military campaigns eventually put a severe strain on the treasury and on civilian manpower. With so many men called up for military service, provinces along the borders began to turn to barbarian peoples for help on their farm lands—leading, ironically, to the appearance of barbarian settlements within Rome's borders. And, as a final portent of trouble, plague spread through the Empire, demoralizing the people and undermining the economy.

In the century after Marcus Aurelius, the Roman Empire crumbled. There were civil wars between 180 and 285 AD. Of 21 emperors, all but two met violent deaths. The middle class was squeezed out of existence. Farmers and laborers were transformed into serfs. When Diocletian put the empire back together in 285 AD there was little of the old prosperity left. But the bureaucracy continued to grow and personal freedom to shrink. The cost of the Army doubled between 96 and 180 AD.

To add to the troubles was plague. By 180 AD at least one-fourth of the population had perished. A further major plague ravaged the Empire from 252 to 267 AD An ever-increasing taste for the brutal and brutalizing spectacles of the amphitheater and circus were symptoms of a deep spiritual rot and loss of personal freedom. In Europe the Germans broke through the barrier of the Rhine and Danube. Diocletian, taking charge in 285 AD, succeeded in driving the barbarian back. But he ruled a new Roman Empire. No one could approach Diocletian without prostrating himself on the ground and kissing the hem of his garment. We've come a long way from early Roman ideals. Furthermore, he appointed three other Caesars and divided the empire into four prefectures. His own capital was not at Rome but at Nicomedia in Asia Minor. The army was reformed and enlarged and was composed chiefly of Germans and Sarmatians or else of the sons of veterans.

To cure inflation, Diocletion in 301 AD issued an edict fixing prices and wages. Death was the penalty for breaking the code. Still prices continued to rise.

The local senatorial class was now made up of all who owned fifteen acres or their equivalent. They had to serve as tax-collectors without pay. If they attempted to enlist in the army or to join the clergy to avoid their duties, they were forced to return to their jobs. Finally, they were forbidden to change their residences or to dispose of their own property without permission. The crushing cost of the army and of a top-heavy bureaucracy had to be met. Thus, the middle-class was taxed out of existence.

The principle of strict regimentation was imposed on farmers and on free labor. Farmers were tied to the soil and, by law, the son of a farmer had to become a farmer. Similarly, the son of a baker or of a metal-worker or of a dock-worker each had to follow the profession of his father. Furthermore, all artisans, traders, shop-owners and the like had to furnish each year to their city and to the state a specified amount of their products at a price fixed by the state.

There was no escape from this relentless regimentation. Regimentation was the end result of the abdication of political freedom and of the pursuit of materialism. The state had become a despotism. The new and dreary type of empire still possessed sufficient power to hold the frontiers against the barbarians for another century.

In 324 AD Constantine the Great became emperor under the sign of the Christian Cross. He subsequently issued an edict of toleration for Christianity. With this edict, Christianity becomes the official religion of the Roman Empire.

But the despotism was tightened rather than eased; and it is an interesting note on the state of morals of the age that within three years of his championship of orthodox Christianity at the Council of Nicaea, Constantine put a nephew to death, drowned his wife in a bath, and murdered a son. Life was hazardous.

Constantine placed his capital at Byzantium, which became Constantinople. Thus Rome was now no longer the center of the empire, but the empire had two capitals, Rome and Constantinople. Finally, in 395 AD, the former Roman world was formally divided into an Empire of the East and an Empire of the West. (See Figure 5-4.)

The eastern empire survived until the capture of Constantinople by the Ottoman Turks in 1453 AD. In the west, Visigoths, Ostrogoths, Vandals, Franks, and Huns burst over the frontiers and the Jutes, Angles, and Saxons planted themselves in Britain. In 410 AD Alaric and his Goths sacked Rome. Then, in 476 AD, the last of the Caesars, Romulus Augustulus, was dethroned. The Germanic kingdoms took the place of the Roman Empire. The empire that seemed destined to last forever had disappeared in the West.

▶ Byzantium

For a long time the general view of the history of Western civilization relegated to a minor place one of the most fascinating and influential ages in the human record. It is remarkable that Byzantium, a vast empire and a brilliant cultural entity that lasted more than a thousand years was almost disregarded by most historians of the West.

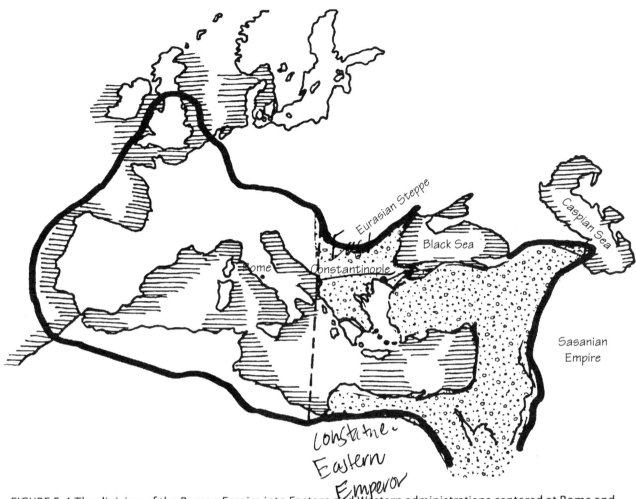

FIGURE 5-4 The division of the Roman Empire into Eastern and Western administrations centered at Rome and Constantinople.

A Divided Christendom

Capital—Rome
Language—Latin
Latin Christian (Roman Catholics)

Capital—Constantinople
Language—Greek
Greek Orthodox Christians

We, in the European tradition have been taught that Western civilization had its origins in ancient Greece. Behind the ancient Greek world itself lay the impressive if sometimes shadowy forms of several other civilizations—among them Assyria, Egypt, India and Minoan Crete. But it was in ancient Greece that the key elements of these earlier civilizations were fused into a pattern of civil and cultural life that we now recognize as specifically Western. The Greeks, however, failed to practice their political thought on any scale larger than that of the city-state.

It was only three centuries later, with the rise of Roman power and the consolidation of Roman rule, that western civilization for the first time acquired a pattern for political order. Rome absorbed and preserved Greek culture within a political structure that covered Europe and the Mediterranean. Yet it was an Empire destined to disintegrate. After some five centuries, between the fourth century and the early sixth century, the great barbarian leaders—Alaric, Attila, Clovis, and Theo-doric—swept into Italy and other parts of the empire in the West. Rome's old ruling classes were destroyed and the West sank into that period of its history known as the Dark Ages.

The next great phase in this general view of western civilization is represented by the Renaissance, and the revival of learning and culture which took place in Italy and elsewhere from 1400 onward. The "rediscovery" of the literature and art of the ancient Greco-Roman world, that had lain hidden for so many centuries under a blanket of ignorance, brought light into the darkness.

This version of history (as are most) is of course an oversimplification. It is also a misrepresentation. The fall of Rome did indeed usher in a time of barbarism for western Europe. The ancient world, the classic world of Greece and Rome had died, but a new era was taking shape out of the ruins of the Roman Empire. The early period from 500 AD to 1000 AD (which we will discuss in the next chapter) would see the peoples of Europe settle into their basic groupings out of which were formed the present nation-states of Europe, Russia, Germany, England, France, etc.

But from the year 1000 AD western Europe reached one of the high points of world culture, examples of which are still very visible in the great Gothic cathedrals. (This will also be discussed in the next chapter.) It should be remembered that, though Rome fell, the Roman Empire continued centered on the "New Rome" Constantinople. This continuation of the Roman Empire is referred to as Byzantium. It endured for some eleven centuries, and formed a strategic bridge between antiquity and the modern world. It not only preserved the two unifying elements of the Roman Empire—Roman law and state organization, and the inherited tradition of Hellenic culture—it added a third and even more powerful organizing force: Christianity.

The place of Byzantium in history has been shrouded by neglect and misunderstanding. A part of the reason for this is no doubt the enmity of Latin Christendom. There is, however, a sizable part of the world that regards Byzantium as a major source of its cultural heritage—the Balkans and western Russia. To these sections of Europe more than to any others did Byzantium transmit its rich heritage of tradition and invention. The Orthodox Christian religion, the Cyrillic alphabet, the very way of life of these people may be traced to Byzantine origins. The Byzantines' greatest success as missionaries of Christianity and civilization came in the Slavic regions of Eastern Europe.

In 863 the King of Moravia asked Emperor Michael III for a teacher who could preach the Christian faith to his subjects in their own language. A Byzantine monk named Cyril evolved a Slavic alphabet and set out to convert the Moravians. Although his attempts with them failed, his followers succeeded among the Bulgarians. By the tenth century other countries, including Russia, had joined the Orthodox fold, and Cyril's written language eventually became the basis for the culture of the entire Slavic world.

Though indebtedness to Byzantium may be obvious in Eastern Europe, it is more subtle and more grudgingly recognized in the countries of the West. The revival of Greek ideas during the Renaissance would have been largely impossible had not Byzantine scholars studied and preserved the ancient literature. There is another major debt western Europe owes Byzantium. From the rise of Islam in the seventh century until the fall of Constantinople in 1453, the Byzantine empire's stand against the armies of Islam saved the West from invasion many times.

The idea and attraction of the Roman empire did not die. The ideal of the Pax Romana remained through the Dark Ages. And it remains an ideal. The Goths, the Franks, the Lombards, and the rest of the European kingdoms, especially in Italy and France, believed themselves to be carrying on the Roman tradition. With Charlemagne the idea of the universal Roman empire was revived; and it fascinated Europe for centuries.

The German Kaiser, or Caesar, king to the Holy Roman Empire, reflects this fascination as does the the Russian Czar or Caesar, heir to Augustus in Moscow, which Russians referred to as "the Third Rome," after Rome and Constantinople, the second Rome. The Imperial Roman eagle is still today at the back of the Reichstag in Germany and on the seal of the United States "E pluribus unum."

Above all, the empire left behind it a great inheritor, the Christian Church. Through it, more than by any other single agency, a spark of culture was kept alive. It was the Roman empire that put a major value imprint on Europe and, subsequently, on the United States and the rest of the new world.

▶ Three Channels of Our Roman Heritage

Today, 1,500 years later, the heritage of Rome is an essential ingredient of Western culture: it has shaped and become a part of our thought, institutions and the languages. Sometimes the influence of Rome is plain to see, as in the classic style of a public building, or in scientific terms constructed on Latin roots. Often, however, the Roman element is hard to distinguish, for it has been so woven into the pattern of daily experience that it takes on the appearance of a being completely ours.

But the path followed by Roman ideas and fashions is never difficult to make out. The heritage has been passed on to the modern world through three principal channels: through the Roman Empire of the East, Byzantium, which lasted until the Turks captured Constantinople in 1453; through the Roman Catholic Church; and through the conscious adoption of Roman styles throughout European history.

The first channel, the Eastern Empire (or Byzantium), preserved the Roman way for a thousand years after Rome itself had fallen to the barbarians. Constantine's Eastern capital of Constantinople was a replica of old Rome on the Tiber. It had seven hills and 14 regions, as did Rome; many of its buildings were exact reproductions of Roman originals; and it had a senate patterned after the Roman version.

The emperors who reigned from this second Rome on the Bosporus did not regard the loss of the West as fatal. They continued, in the tradition of Constantine, to rule as Christian emperors. The great civil service developed by the Caesars continued to function and expand. The army remained organized along Roman lines.

In the Eastern Empire, Roman elements were mixed with Hellenic and Oriental culture. Massive Roman-style buildings were decorated with lacy surfaces and ornate Byzantine mosaics, and Oriental domes were introduced. The Roman toga gave way to a brocaded robe that came down directly from the mandarin robes of China. Latin remained the official state language (until the late sixth century), but the common spoken language was Greek—a somewhat vulgarized form of the classical language, and the direct ancestor of modern Greek.

In time communications between East and West broke down, and the Church of the East split with the Church of Rome. In 1053 the patriarch of Constantinople closed all churches that adhered to the Roman liturgy, and the following year the pope's legates reacted by excommunicating the patriarch. Despite these conflicts, the Eastern Empire remained a great preserve of Roman tradition and influence. As late as the fifteenth century, inhabitants of Constantinople still referred to themselves as Romaioi—Romans.

From Byzantium, Romanism and Christianity spread even farther into the East. The Byzantine church fathered the church of Russia, explained in more detail in the section on Russia; for a time, the patriarch of Constantinople appointed church fathers in that country. But when the Ottoman Turks captured Constantinople the grand dukes of Moscow proclaimed themselves successors to the great Constantine, and sixteenth century Moscow called itself the Third Rome. The grand dukes even claimed to be descended from a brother of the first Roman Emperor, Augustus. Roman coins were used in Russia for many years, and parts of the Justinian code were worked into Russian law.

Russian is written in Cyrillic script named after St. Cyril and is based on Greek, the script of Great Orthodoxy rather than the Latin letters of western Europe.

The second channel of Roman influence, the Catholic Church, remained throughout the Middle Ages as the only effective unifying force in the old territories of the Western Empire. Retaining Rome as its capital, it kept Roman tradition alive through its organization, its laws, its language, and, above all, through its universal outlook. The unity of all Europe which the Church fostered was a conscious continuation of the unity which Rome had put together. The Catholic Church always worked for a united Christendom.

From the viewpoint of the Church, even Rome's pagan past was part of the Divine plan: the Empire had prepared the ground for the Church. The organization of the Church, in turn, was constructed largely on the Roman model. Regional dioceses corresponded to the Empire's territorial divisions; the word "diocese" had originally been used administratively by Diocletian. The hierarchy of the Church corresponded to the Roman administrative apparatus. For example, the early bishops were assigned to Roman districts called curia, each of which had its own civil official. Ecclesiastical law was strongly influenced by Roman jurisprudence, discussed later.

With the decline of the Roman state, the Church became the chief carrier of Latin culture. Church schools continued to teach Latin, and over the centuries, it endured as a functioning language only in Catholicism. In the years following Rome's decline, a good Christian education continued to include the great works of Roman literature. Christians did not feel any incongruity in referring to Seneca as one of their own, or in praising Vergil and other Roman writers.

The old Roman works were not only studied and taught but also transcribed by monks and preserved in the libraries of monasteries and abbeys. In the Middle Ages, when education was at a low ebb, some classical writings were so rarely reproduced that by the time the Renaissance dawned copies were hard to find. But the Church had preserved them, and it was because of these Church copies that so much of the Roman heritage could be handed down. Even in that age, there was never a time when literary men did not know Vergil. Thus the great fourteenth century poet Dante wrote the Roman poet Vergil into his masterpiece, *The Divine Comedy*—and in the lowest reach of the underworld, where archtraitors are punished, Dante placed Brutus and Cassius, the betrayers of Caesar, along with Judas Iscariot, the betrayer of Christ.

Third and most important of the ways in which Rome shaped our culture was the sheer impact of Roman ideas and objects. The actual relics of Rome—its language and literature, its architecture and its law—constitute perhaps its greatest legacy.

Not the least of these relics was the memory of Rome's grandeur, which inspired the leaders of Europe for centuries. When Clovis established a new Kingdom of the Franks in Gaul in the late fifth century, he acknowledged the sovereignty of the Roman emperors—in both Rome and Constantinople—although by that time their power had dwindled to their own reduced realms. It was the idea of the Roman emperor to which Clovis bowed.

Centuries later, when Charlemagne reunited most of western Europe under a single ruler, he claimed to be reconstituting the old Roman Empire, and he dreamed of restoring the tradition of the Caesars. He journeyed to Rome for his coronation in 800 and was crowned in Saint Peter's Basilica to a chanted salute: "To Caesar Augustus, crowned by God, great and peaceful Roman emperor, long life and victory."

Successors to Charlemagne carried this process by naming their kingdom the Holy Roman Empire. Though this empire ultimately shrank to a confederation of German principalities, emperors like Frederick Barbarossa and the Hapsburgs continued to rule using the dream of Rome until 1806 when the Holy Roman Empire was dissolved.

The work of the political theorists who shaped modern thinking was largely a continuation of the thoughts of the ancients. The ideals of the Roman Republic are basic to the writings of men such as Machiavelli and Thomas More, Rabelais and Montaigne, and the "philosophes" who paved the way for the French Revolution.

Roman Architecture

The Founding Fathers of the American Republic also studied and consciously emulated the Romans. They quoted liberally from Roman authors and often signed themselves by Latin names. (Thomas Paine called himself Atlanticus.) John Adams spent nights alone in his room declaiming the orations of Cicero aloud. Rome left its mark in language. (See Chapter 3, section on romance languages.) which are the roots to perhaps half of all the English words we use. In architecture, Thomas Jefferson led a Roman revival. He designed his own house, Monticello, in what was essentially the Roman style (via Palladio); he modeled the Virginia state capitol after the Maison Carre, an old Roman temple in Nimes, France; and he designed the library of the University of Virginia as a small-scale pantheon, of brick and wood instead of marble. The architecture of the old Roman republic, he believed, was ideally suited to the structures of the new American Republic.

The city of Rome, showplace of the Empire, was the model of all the great metropolises of Europe in later centuries. Roman architects and builders seized on ancient concepts and coupled them with a new building material—concrete—that enabled them to overcome all ancient limits of height and space. Roman concrete was little different from the concrete we use today; the only improvement introduced in modern times has been the reinforcing of the concrete with steel rods. Using this relatively cheap, crude material, which could be easily handled by unskilled labor, Roman architects and engineers were able to devise grandiose structures without worrying much about the cost of executing their plans. Majestic arches and domes quickly became the distinctive feature of their work.

The original arch was a simple semicircle of bricks and stones, each slightly wedge-shaped to form the curve. The Romans, desiring to roof over great areas, adapted the arch to this purpose by lengthening it into a tunnel-like structure, called a barrel vault. To support such a vault, massive walls were required. But later Roman engineers devised the technique of building two barrel vaults that intersected at right angles; the result, called a groined vault, was supported at its corners by four great piers.

With the weight thus distributed, the walls could be light because they were not bearing the full load of the structure. They were less expensive; furthermore, windows could be cut into them to brighten the interior. Roman methods of constructing such vaults served as a basis for architectural developments over the next thousand years, and are reflected in many of the resplendent cathedrals of medieval Europe. (See Figure 5-5.)

The old plan of the Forum Romanum has never lost its broad appeal; in the great cities of later centuries, the frequent arrangement of imposing structures around large areas of open space has continued the Roman ideal in practice—as in Washington, D.C., for example, where the Roman-style capitol building stands at the end of the great Constitution Mall.

The Romans' accent on utility in building was nowhere more strikingly reflected than in their great roads and aqueducts, monuments of engineering skill. Rome laid down roads wherever its authority extended—to facilitate trade as well as troop movements. The Romans spent five centuries in completing a road system to every corner of the Empire. Roman roads eventually covered a distance equal to 10 times the circumference of the earth at the equator.

Each mile along the Roman roads was marked by a six-foot circular pillar, measured from the Golden Milestone in the Forum Romanum. The main arteries were so well constructed that some are still in use today—including the first one, the Appian Way, built some 2,200 years ago.

Roman Law

Of all Rome's intellectual bequests, the one that may have been most characteristic of the Roman mind was its thousand years of law. Rome not only extended her rule over all Europe, she was responsible for ideals in men's minds. This ideal was "authority," based on an abstraction called "law" and independent of ties of blood or affection, of sympathy or antipathy, of religion or ownership, can exist as a relationship between human beings.

The word "justice" stems from the Latin word for law, "ius," and the Roman concept of impartial justice, even more than the Roman laws themselves, has shaped Western legal tradition. Regardless of political changes—from Republic to Empire and under emperors liberal or authoritarian—Roman law based on human wisdom and consent continued its development. Then, around 527 AD a codification of the entire system was ordered by the Eastern Emperor Justinian—the Corpus Iuris Civilis, or Body of Civil Law.

The concept of justice, and of the rights of individuals, embodied in this Code remains in force in modern legal codes throughout the Western world.

Just a few of the Code's provisions will show its continuing impact on our ideas of right and wrong:

- No one is compelled to defend a cause against his will.
- No one suffers a penalty for what he thinks.
- No one may be forcibly removed from his own house.
- Anything not permitted the defendant ought not be allowed the plaintiff.
- The burden of proof is upon the party affirming, not on the party denying.
- A father is not a competent witness for a son, nor a son for a father.
- The gravity of a past offense never increases ex post facto.
- In inflicting penalties, the age and inexperience of the guilty party must be taken into account.

The law codes of most western nations were derived from or were deeply influenced by the Roman Justinian Code. The Napoleonic Code in France was directly and consciously modeled on it. In Ger-

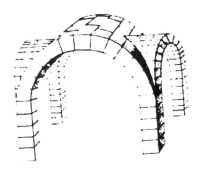
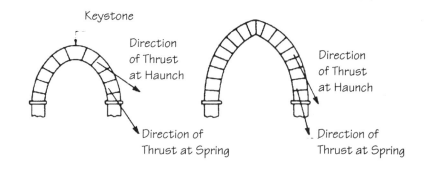

Keystone

Direction
of Thrust
at Haunch

Direction
of Thrust
at Haunch

Direction of
Thrust at Spring

Direction of
Thrust at Spring

Greek (600–100 BC)

Roman (100 BC–AD 500)

Byzantine (AD 300–1000)

Gothic (1200–1400)

Renaissance (1400–1600)

Baroque (1600–1700)

FIGURE 5-5 Our Architectural Heritage

many Roman law was applied whenever it did not run counter to local legislation until 1900, when a national law system was devised.

Although England (and the U.S., Canada, and Australia) developed a native "common law" of their own—which differed from Roman law in placing its emphasis on precedent rather than on written statutes—it too had roots in Roman judicial principles and practices.

The influence of Rome and Greece, whether seen in the practice of a courtroom or the style of a church, in literature or the politics of a state, remains as a vital force, shaping the ideas and the material works of us all.

What, then, are a few of the ways in which Rome still influences us today? There is, first of all, language. As you know, all the Romance languages are descended from Latin; and no educated English speaker can, as in this very sentence, speak or write anything but the mot elementary of sentences without using words derived from Latin. Nor is it any accident that the very forms of our letters are Roman. Architecture is a word derived from Greek and the Greco Roman architectural tradition can be seen in our nations capital, particularly the Supreme Court building and the Lincoln Memorial.

The Romans gave us the arch, the vault, and the dome. Their inspiration is evident in St. Peter's of Rome and St. Paul's of London and most of our state capitals. They also built for permanence. Roman roads and Roman concrete are like the best of the Romans—solid, efficient, and enduring. In sculpture, except for portrait busts and their sculpture of animals, the Romans were inferior to the Greeks. In literature, the Greeks were also superior. But in law they took over the "natural law" of the Stoics and made it into the *ius gentium*, the law of nations. They are, in fact, the originators of law as we know it, through the influence of it is Code Justinian.

Their greatest achievement, perhaps, was in their ability to rule an empire with even-handed justice and, gradually, to infuse a sense of unity through the whole. Order, discipline efficient administration—these were some of the qualities which Rome passed on to western civilization.

We in the West have owed to the Greeks and Romans an enormous proportion of our cultural property. That does not mean that we have always consciously imitated those peoples. But whether we know it or not, they have been our models, even in the United States today, when deliberate attempts have been made to bring other legacies into play. What would any of the essential branches of our life consist of without the long, varied, preceding story of the Greeks and Romans, and the contributions that they handed down to us?

We are what we are, and we hope to be, because of what we learn from the classical civilization, and that remains true however much—like the Greeks and Romans themselves—we have adapted and modified what we have learned, for our own use. For whether we like it or not the past of Greece and Rome lives on in us.

Worksheet ▶

CHAPTER FIVE

Define or identify:

- Hellene—Hellas

- Barbarism

- Greater Greece—Magna Grecia

- Marathon

- Polis

- Hubris

- The Persian War

- The Peloponnesian War

- Mare Nostrum

- New Rome, Byzantium and Constantinople

- The Code Justinian

- The division of the Roman Empire

Explain:

- "Freeman fight better than slaves." Herodotus.

- Greek religion was polytheistic.

- Man is like a god.

- "Captive Greece took her rude conquerors captive."

- Rome, "A society of beggars and millionaires."

- The Roman idea of genius.

- Why did the Jews refuse to worship the emperor and why were they persecuted?

- How do Hitler and Mussolini illustrate the Greek idea of hubris?

- Can you match the great contributions of science, religion, and law with the Greeks, Romans and Jews?

- How did Europe come to blend the Greco-Roman tradition with the Judeo-Christian?

- The Roman Empire broke into two parts, East and West. What was the capitol of each? The language of each? The religion of each?

- What is the difference between science and technology?

- Outline the Roman Empire at its furthest extent.

- Why did North Africa become Christian?

Discuss:

- "Man is the measure of things."

- Greek law

- Greek science—the universe is rational, discover the laws. Not *How* but *Why*?

- A healthy mind in a healthy body, nothing in excess.

- Alexander the Great and the spread of Hellenism.

- What were some causes of the fall of the Roman Empire?

- The Emperor Constantine and the Empire becomes Christian.

- Justice holds the scales to weigh truth and falsehood and she is blindfolded.

• We discussed the two main streams of western culture, our Judeo-Christian and Greco-Roman traditions.

    a.   Discuss what you see as the meaning of those two traditions.

    b.   What are some of those values you see as generally accepted in America today?

    c.   What are some conflicts between those two values you can observe in America today?

Chapter 6 ▶▶

Dark Ages and Revival

The status of Europe in the year 500 AD was indeed dark. Roman law and order were no more. The Germanic peoples were on the move. The remains of old Roman England for example were being wiped out by Germanic tribes called Angles (hence Angleland, England and our language English). (See Chapter 3, "Language.")

For us today it is difficult to imagine the fall of a civilization. As we look around, America looks so solid and its institutions so well established that it's difficult to think that it could collapse. Could people ever forget how to read and write? Instead of warm centrally heated houses, could people go back to living in huts, allowing roads to grow over, watching farms return to woods? So must it have seemed to a Roman at the time of Augustus.

And yet it happened. And it was a disaster. There should be no glamour applied to the term barbarism. Conan and Rambo are barbarians. Some young people might glamorize Conan, but barbarism and the breakdown of law are darkness, unrelieved boredom, and suffering.

Imagine yourself and spouse with a prosperous farm and children in northern France in the year 500. One day appearing to the east is a tribe of barbarians out for loot. They burn your farm and murder your children. You pull yourself together, start anew and make progress. Again a tribe appears and loots your farm. Barbarism would be very unglamorous to you.

In addition there is no place of escape. Everywhere the rule of law has broken down. There is no relief. Stagnation is everywhere—not just stagnation but fear. Hunger and disease stalked early medieval man. Ravage by enemies near and far was a constant threat, and too often a reality. Law and order, the twin pillars of the Roman imperial system, lay in ruins. An individual's sole hope of protection rested in local chieftains powerful enough to fend off the enemy.

Rome's Germanic conquerors made their debut on the stage of history as uncouth, unlettered, simple warriors—men who apparently loved battle and booty above all else. For the next several centuries the barbarian experience was a classic example of a timeless process—the meeting and merging of two peoples widely separated in levels of attainment. By this process, we read how the crude early Romans had benefitted from their conquest of the sophisticated Greeks. By this same process today, half the world is seeking to absorb the technology of the West, an interplay of cultures.

While the great classical cultures of Greece and Rome were collapsing and barbarism became the rule over most of Europe, many of the tribal groups were finding new homes and establishing their language and social institutions. (This is discussed in some detail in our chapter on language groupings which will correspond later to national identification.) Slavs, Germans, Celts and Scandinavians were gaining dominance in areas of Europe where they continue to this day.

The years 400 to 1000 AD were a political and social seeding time. In little more than six centuries the Germanic invaders created a new and vital society to replace a decadent classical society and transformed the Western world from a single state facing the Mediterranean into a collection of independent kingdoms facing the North Sea and the Atlantic— the nucleus of Europe. From these raw, warlike kingdoms rose the first modern nation-states that will go on to dominate the earth.

The foundations of modern European culture were laid in the centuries following the fall of Rome by a revolution. Unable to continue on the basis of the old political order, society reorganized itself on the basis of Christian principle. We can only understand Europe and its historical development by the study of Christian culture, for this forms the center of the whole process.

It was as Christendom that Europe first became conscious of itself as a society of peoples with common moral values and common spiritual aims, in other words as a culture. The new entity, Christendom, was a spiritual commonwealth that united all believers across the constantly changing boundaries of the barbarian kingdoms. Faith was the patriotism of the new order.

This revolution was inspired and engineered by the Church. No other agency in the West, during or long after the Empire's collapse, could have filled the political vacuum left by the weak Roman emperors and illiterate Germanic kings. The Church alone had a constructive attitude toward society and a disciplined organization capable of putting ideals into practice. Moved to serve the general welfare by an unshakable conviction in its mission to all mankind, the Church took the lead in the West, with political results as significant as its later contributions to art, architecture and the revival of learning (which will be discussed later). The Church provided and worked to instill social ideals and moral values. It brought the West under the great civilizing influence of Christian doctrine. It furnished trained personnel who sustained civil government while the barbarians made their painful transition from a semi-nomadic existence to a more-or-less settled agrarian life. These and other achievements proved so decisive that it is almost impos-

sible to imagine what course western history might have taken if the Church had fallen along with the Roman Empire.

The Church prepared for its role as leader by making significant gains in the last century of Roman rule. Benefiting from the establishment of Christianity as the state religion of the Empire (remember Constantine), the Roman Church grew rapidly into a wealthy, well-staffed group of self-governing regional churches. It taught the same beliefs. This uniformity of religious teaching was possible because the western churches generally accepted the Bishop of Rome or the Pope's views on questions involving doctrine. The popes claimed even broader authority, maintaining their right to set standards for Church conduct as well as doctrine. Both these powers, the popes declared, were their inheritance from St. Peter, the first Bishop of Rome.

Within the Church bishops were established in the main urban centers. The bishops were placed in the middle of things where they could respond swiftly to the need of their district. As the empire collapsed, the bishops were on hand to take over some of the essential functions with some sort of competence, learning, and discipline.

▶ Monasticism and the Christian Tradition

A key element in the formation of Europe during these dark times was the monastery. Western monasticism as it is now known was born in Italy around 529 AD. Its father, the holy and aristocratic Benedict of Nursia, was then just another pious hermit in the hills east of Rome. From his personal experience, Benedict concluded that most men, unable to discipline themselves, seemed to need a firmly organized environment. Benedict led a handful of disciples to a lonely hilltop between Rome and Naples, called Monte Cassino, and there he founded a monastery that operated on a full cenobitic, or communal, basis. For the monks' guidance, Benedict set down his program and ideals in a remarkable document that he called "A little rule for beginners."

St. Benedict's Rule was the first great practical creation of the post-Roman West. In an age when even simple local institutions (such as the law courts) were mostly makeshift and ineffective, the Rule blueprinted a complete social system that actually worked. Every monastery was self-sufficient. The monks were required to follow a balanced daily routine of prayer and manual labor. Through their work as farmers and craftsmen they supplied all their meager needs by themselves and by trading surpluses with others.

The organization of the monastery provided independence and permanence. The monks elected their own governing abbot, whose only superior was the pope, and they submitted to the abbot's decisions in all matters, worldly and spiritual. To insure the stability of each little commonwealth, a new pledge was required of the monks. In addition to their classic vows of poverty, chastity and obedience, they swore to remain within the monastery until death, unless specifically given permission to leave.

The rule of St. Benedict became the rule of western monasticism. The immense missionary effort of bringing the great traditions of Roman law and Greek humanism to the barbarians was supported by that great Christian institution, the Benedictine monastery. The people needed some refuge of tranquility and order from the whirlwind of disaster and some example toward the rebuilding of their society. Monks were not unknown to the primitive Church but as in Oriental monasticism, they were men who turned their backs on the world. As in the Oriental tradition fasting in the deserts, withdrawn on the top of pillars, they gave witness to the transitory nature of the world.

St. Benedict, (note the contrast with the attention to this world described as the western tradition) conceived his rule essentially in social terms. His monks would labor and study as well as pray. In fact, the famous doctrine "Obrare est orare" states labor *is* prayer. They would seek out the wilderness left by invasion and warfare and make it blossom again. They would persevere to document the traditions of ancient learning and set up schools to transmit it to coming generations. Among all the darkness of the dark ages in isolated spots, the Benedictine monestary gave order (see Chapter 5, "Time") and kept alive the flickering light of learning and culture.

When Europe rediscovered Greek science, the Benedictine concept that to work is to pray had deep consequences. Science and technology were not unknown in the Classical world, nor for that matter in China and India. But the classical world was built on slave labor. There was great disdain for physical labor. Science was an intellectual exercise. Indeed, Aristotle describes a slave as "a human tool." No Christian could look on another human being, all equal in the sight of God, as a human tool. One of the elements of the European genius is to take science and apply it to make it work; not only to understand the mechanics of a windmill but to use this discovery to grind wheat. Man is the craftsman who masters the forces of nature and forces them into the service of men as required in the Christian message of *to work is to pray*. The moral and social revolution of Christianity would abolish slavery and rehabilitate manual labor and mechanical arts. It would establish the dignity of labor.

The monks of the West, by introducing manual labor into their monastic rules, made work a part of the Opus Dei—work of God. One saw them clearing forests, draining swamps, transforming marshy woods into cultivated farms and abbeys, which in turn became the sites of towns, villages, and finally of great cities. The early Christians opposed corrupting idleness, declaring, in the words of Paul, that "If any one will not work, let him not eat." Legally, the slave in antiquity was a thing, a bit of merchandise to be used and abused at will (and in the United States before the Emancipation Proclamation). As Aristotle had said, a slave is a "living tool." The slave had no will of his own; he was a body without the power to say no; he had no rights; he had neither family nor legal marriage nor recognized paternity.

Christianity—by declaring that all mankind descended from the same couple, that they were all children of God, all equally redeemed by the passion of Christ, and all equally worthy as brothers—established the equal dignity of men without exception of condition, race or nationality. Christianity revolutionized the social positions of slaves and the humble by providing religious sanctions for their individual dignity; every human, made in the image of God, possessed a free soul.

> The Christian slave is, before God, the equal of the rich man, of the free man, and of his own master.

He is admitted on a footing of complete equality into the Church, the love feasts, to the sacraments, into the ranks of the religious hierarchy, and finally to a common burial.

If baptized, the Christian could even be superior to his own master, were the master still an initiate (catechumen) or under a public penance.

A slave can become a priest, a bishop, even a pope like Calixtus, the escaped slave.

His marriage is valid; his paternity is recognized; his chastity is defended; the Christian ideal of family is founded.

▶ The Revival of Europe

By the year 1000, the year in which many timid people had feared that the world would come to an end, the long dominance of the barbarian wanderers was over. The Dark Ages were over, and Western Europe was prepared for its first great age of civilization. There is a return of confidence. The Dark Ages following the end of Roman law suddenly gave way to an extraordinary burst of energy. One of the high points of world culture, comparable in many ways to the miracle we described that took place Greece in the sixth century BC, appeared in Europe.

The evidence of this heroic energy, this confidence, this strength of will and intellect, is still visible to us. Even alongside modern construction using modern power, the Gothic Cathedral remains an impressive construction. These great and beautiful monuments of stone at first rose out of a small cluster of wooden houses, as if by a miracle. A part of the miracle is that it all happened quite suddenly—in a single lifetime.

This effort needs a new social and intellectual background. It requires wealth, stability, technical skill and, above all, the confidence necessary to push through a long-term project. These great cathedrals show that at the end of the tenth century there was a new power in Europe, greater than any king or emperor: the Church. The Church was not only an organizer; it was a humanizer.

Every culture requires a certain amount of natural prosperity in addition to a great deal of technological progress, and western Europe now had both. One of the reasons for this was the absence of slavery, a practice that inhibits innovation. Christian ethics left no place for slavery, as we have noted. Conditions of Europe called for labor-saving devices. The monks of the Rule of St. Benedict were the first to combine intellectual and spiritual power with sweat. They introduced advanced methods of agriculture—specifically, three field rotation system of farming and the development of the heavy wheeled plow with its ability to dig into the heavy sod of northern Europe to a depth of eight inches or more. Horsepower became more effective. A horse could not pull a heavy plow without choking from the nape circling its neck. The horse collar resting on the horses shoulders increased its pulling capacity four to five times.

A good example of the European mind set can be illustrated by the water mill and wind mill. Both the Greeks and Romans knew about them, but used them very little because of the abundance of slave labor and lack of good streams. Medieval Europe used water especially as a generalized source of power, for sawmills, grinding grain and crushing ore. In the Doomsday Book Census of England in 1086, 5000 mills were listed.

But far more important than the material advance was the return of confidence—confidence in the society in which one lived, belief in its philosophy, belief in its laws, and confidence in one's mental powers.

▶ Triumph of the Church

When we opened the book and talked about culture, we warned not to think of culture and civilization as music appreciation, poetry, and art exclusively. These can be the results of culture, or the signs of a cultured person. Culture and a society can have these amenities and be quite dead. We described culture as value systems.

How had all these new values and confidences suddenly appeared in Western Europe? There are many answers but most important was: the triumph of the Church. It could be argued that what we call western culture was basically the creation of the Church, the Church as a setter of values. The

Church took the leadership for a number of reasons.

Men of intelligence naturally and normally took holy orders, and could rise from obscurity to positions of immense influence. In spite of the number of bishops and abbots from royal or princely families, the Church was basically a democratic institution where ability—administrative, diplomatic and sheet intellectual ability—made its way. And the Church was international. It was, to a large extent, a monastic institution following the Benedictine rule and owing no territorial allegiance. The great churchmen of the eleventh and twelfth centuries came from all over Europe, or as they viewed it, Christendom.

The ordinary man living a narrow and monotonous life drew inspiration and direction from his Church. One can only imagine the impact on the believers coming from their dark homes and shops as they entered one of the great cathedrals, with its spectacular construction, tapestries, candles, gold altar, music and stained glass windows. Is it any wonder they followed the Church's lead.

The great profusion of beautiful things in the church was based on a revolutionary idea first proposed by the man who could almost be said to have invented Gothic architecture, the Abbot Suger. He was responsible for the building of St. Denis, the royal chapel in Paris. He argued that we could only come to understand absolute beauty, which is God, through the effect of precious and beautiful things on our senses. He said, "The dull mind rises to truth through that which is material."

This was really a revolutionary concept in the Middle Ages, and there would be a reaction during the Protestant Reformation. It was the intellectual background of all the sublime works of art of the next century and in fact has remained the basis of our belief in the value of art, until today, that it raises our mind to truth.

His St. Denis incorporated the pointed arch, the high windows and the great emphasis on light of the Gothic style. The shaft with its cluster of columns, passing without interruption into the vault and the pointed arch—made stone seem weightless: the weightless expression of man's spirit. The Gothic Cathedral is the epitome of the Great Awakening that starts in Europe around the year 1,000. (See Figure 5-5.)

It would be a mistake to conceive of the flowering of Europe in the centuries after 1000 without a realization of the still primitive life of most people. Living in cramped and dark quarters doing boring and often degrading work, people lived unpredictable and harsh lives. It is easy to understand the need for the consolations of religion. Charles V, the French king adorned his royal chapel with his collection of relics and, by the time he was thirty, in the year 1368, had acquired, among other objects, the top of John the Baptist's head, Christ's swaddling clothes, the crown of thorns, and a flask of the Virgin's milk. (One has to imagine how this might have been acquired.) It is difficult to understand the Medieval mind. A well known and lurid example of the afflictions and unpredictability of these times is the plague which affected Europe on and off for 300 years.

▶ The Black Death

Out of the East came a terrible pestilence. Medical historians now believe that it was a variety of the bubonic plague. Contemporary accounts labeled it the Black Death, because of the dark skin blotches with which it began. The Black Death killed its sufferers after an agonized period of one to three days in which they spewed up blood, fell into delirium, and broke out in boils, carbuncles, and lumps the size of eggs.

Medieval writers blamed the plague on the Mongol hordes which had swept west from Asia and were besieging the Genoese trading station of Kaffa on the Black Sea. Among Asians, the plague was no stranger. Whenever a soldier succumbed, his corpse would be catapulted over Kaffa's walls. Rats carried the disease aboard homeward-bound Italian vessels, and in April 1348 it struck in Florence. Later that year it overran the rest of Italy and France. England's turn came in 1349, Germany's and Scandinavia's in 1350. Estimates of the death toll range from one fourth to one half of Europe's entire population.

The effects of war that occupy so much space in history books were as nothing compared with the tragic consequences of the plague. Food supplies ran short because, in many places, there was no one left to cultivate the soil or to supervise the cultivators. Commercial enterprises slumped. Schools, universities and charitable services shut down for lack of qualified personnel to run them. Crafts suffered irretrievable losses through the death of guild masters who could pass their skills on to apprentices. The sharp break in continuity extended to the most basic institutions; for decades afterward, litigants in court cases were not expected to be familiar with the old unwritten laws that had governed their fathers and grandfathers.

The dimensions of the disaster led to the widespread conviction that the plague represented divine retribution for human sins. Many Europeans, disenchanted by the Pope's move to Avignon, already tended to be introverted and individual in their faith. The fright and horror stirred by the plague now sent them to extremes. Some lost faith completely and formed cults for the worship of Satan. Others indulged in frenzies of religious excess. Many joined the Flagellants, who believed that they could be purged of sin, and thus escape punishment from on high, by flogging themselves with leather scourges studded with iron spikes. Other Europeans sought solace in superstition, personal revelations and mystical ecstasies. Treatises on the art of dying became immensely popular. Death haunted everyone.

The plague also cast a long shadow in the form of social unrest. In a number of European countries the previously well-ordered structure of medieval society began to be shaken by violent uprisings of peasants and artisans against nobles and wealthy merchants.

France saw the first major eruption. There occurred an uprising known as the Jacquerie, for Jacques, the nickname of the peasant. Jacques nursed a special fury of his own, directed at the local lord who, although he had failed to shield his tenants from the destruction of war and the depredations of mercenaries, blandly continued to insist on his usual rents and services.

Banding together, peasants put the torch to manor houses and set upon their masters. But staves and scythes were no match for swords and lances. The insurrection was crushed, and brutal reprisals followed in short order. Known troublemakers were hanged outside their own cottages and entire villages were burned to the ground.

An interesting commentary on the mentality of the age and how far we have come in our thinking is some of the reaction to the plague. Overwhelmed by the occurrence, men at all levels looked for answers. Both the Pope and the king of France sent urgent requests for help to the medical faculty at the University of Paris, then one of the most distinguished medical groups in the western world. The faculty responded that "the plague was the result of a conjunction of the planets Saturn, Mars and Jupiter at 1 P.M. on March 20, 1345, an event that caused the corruption of the surrounding atmosphere." We are still a long way from modern medicine and the benefits of applied science.

But change does come. The great, indeed the unique, merit of European civilization has been that it has never ceased to develop and change. It has not been based on a stationary perfection, but on ideas and inspiration.

▶ St. Francis of Assisi

About the time the great cathedrals were rising, a man named Francesco Bernadone, in the Italian town of Assisi, had a change of heart. His new vision helped to reinvigorate European society and the Church.

One day when he had fitted himself up in his best clothes in preparation for some chivalrous campaign, he met a poor gentleman whose need seemed to be greater than his own, and he gave him his cloak. That night he dreamed that he should rebuild the Celestial City. Later he gave away his possessions so liberally that his father, who was a rich businessman in the Italian town of Assisi, was moved to disown him; whereupon Francesco took off his remaining clothes and said that he would possess nothing, absolutely nothing. The Bishop of Assisi hid his nakedness, and afterwards gave him a cloak; and Francesco went off into the world, singing a French song.

He began looking after lepers, who were very common in the Middle Ages, and rebuilding with his own hands abandoned churches. One day at Mass he heard the words "Carry neither gold nor silver, nor money in your girdle, nor bag, nor two coats, nor sandals, nor staff." He took these words literally as well. He threw away his staff and his sandals and went out bare-footed onto the hills. In all his actions he took the words of the Gospels literally. He said that he had taken poverty for his Lady, and when he achieved some still more drastic act of self-denial, he said that it was to do her a courtesy. It was partly because he saw that wealth corrupts; partly because he felt that it was discourteous to be in the company of anyone poorer than oneself.

From the first, everyone recognized that St. Francis (as we now call him) was a very special person. When, with his first twelve disciples, he managed to gain access to Innocent III, the Pope gave him permission to found an order. It was an extraordinary piece of insight, because St. Francis was not only a layman but had no theological training. He and his poor, ragged companions were so excited when they went to see the pope that they began to dance. It is pleasant to imagine the scene and its effect on the self important officials.

St. Francis died in 1226 at the age of forty-three, worn out by his austerities. On his deathbed he asked forgiveness of "poor brother donkey, my body" for the hardships he had made it suffer. He had seen his group of humble companions grow into a great institution. Typically, in 1220 he had, with perfect simplicity, relinquished control of the order. He recognized that he was no administrator. Two years after his death he was canonized and almost immediately his followers began to build a great basilica in his memory. This was a strange memorial to the little poor man, whose favorite biblical saying was, "Foxes have holes and the birds of the air have nests: but the Son of Man hath no where to lay his head."

I have included these notes on St. Francis as a contrast to modern glorification of capital accumulation and possessions. His message was to sanctify poverty. Even today his belief that in order to free the spirit we must shed all our earthly goods is the belief that all great religious teachers have had in common—eastern and western, without exception. We will be discussing the Buddha, Lao Tzu, Confucius and Mohammed. It is an ideal to which, however impossible it may be in practice, these fine spirits and others down to our own time will always return.

By demonstrating that truth with such simplicity and grace, St. Francis made it part of the European consciousness. By freeing himself from the pull of possessions, he achieved a state of mind which gained a new vitality in late eighteenth century thought through the nature worship of Rousseau and Wordsworth. It was only because he

possessed nothing that St. Francis could feel sincerely a brotherhood with all created things, not only living creatures, but brother fire and sister wind.

This philosophy inspired his hymn to the unity of creation, the "Canticle of the Sun." Today with the increasing awareness of the environment and our certain knowledge that uncontrolled exploitation and pollution will doom mankind, the simplicity of St. Francis' message and his conception of "brother sun" and "sister moon," the unity of all nature will perhaps become a major inspiration again. He remains the guiding spirit of the environmentalists.

▶ The University

Because their massive stone structures still exist, the cathedrals are the most striking examples of the heights reached in the 12th and 13th centuries. In addition, medieval civilization produced great contributions to culture that have survived to enrich each era since. Universities were founded. The beginnings of modern Western literature emerged. A philosophy of ethics developed. Esthetic tastes were expressed in cathedral architecture, in fresco painting, in polyphonic music. Fresh breezes blew through the realms of political and scientific theorizing. Imaginative enterprise and speculative inquiry pervaded every endeavor.

The vital spark of this cultural explosion was the spread of education. In earlier medieval times, learning had been a privilege primarily enjoyed by the clergy. St. Benedict, founding the western monastic system in the sixth century, had directed the monks to read and to study. In response, Benedictine abbeys had developed a kind of rudimentary schooling in Latin and in the arts of lettering and illumination. Charlemagne, dreaming of a new society in the eighth century, had widened opportunities for scholarship through a decree that every monastery have a school to teach all those "who with God's help are able to learn." The Emperor himself set an example with a Palace School for his own children and those of his courtiers.

Even as the monastery schools taught candidates for the monastic orders, cathedral schools taught candidates for the secular clergy. There was a crucial distinction between the two. Attached to the cathedrals, which were an integral part of town life, cathedral schools were more readily accessible to laymen. As more towns were established and more cathedrals were built, these schools proliferated throughout Europe, most notably in France—at Tours, Rheims, Chartres, Paris and elsewhere. Among the students they attracted, a rising number came from the bourgeoisie and talented serfs.

The curriculum of the cathedral school was limited to grammar, rhetoric, logic, arithmetic, geometry, music and astronomy—the seven liberal arts, so called because in ancient Rome their study had been reserved for *liberi*, "freemen." At first the learning was confined to the reading the church fathers and a few other authorities such as Boethius whose *Consolation of Philosophy* attempted to reconcile the misfortunes of man with the concept of a benevolent, omnipotent God.

Learning was soon to be liberalized, however, with the advent of an era of great schoolmasters. After the Crusades began and Mediterranean commerce expanded, intellectual contact with Islam would become less and less of a rarity. Christian Europe would be introduced to Arabic medicine, astronomy, mathematics and philosophy. At Constantinople, as well as in Sicily and in Spain, Moslem and Jewish scholars would be kept busy turning out Latin translations not only of Arabic lore but also of ancient Hebrew and Greek writings they had preserved. Westerners would travel to the East to study the works of Aristotle in his own language.

Out of these rather moderate beginnings was to evolve the University, a uniquely European contribution to the advancement of knowledge. To this day University buildings in America from Yale to the University of Chicago feature medieval gothic style buildings that remind us of their origins.

▶ Abelard and Aquinas

These ideas were spread by the great teachers in the new schools. A most notable teacher is the celebrated Abelard. "The first key to wisdom," Abelard asserted, "is assiduous and frequent questioning. . . . For by doubting we come to inquiry, and by inquiry we arrive at the truth." This idea, commonplace to the Greeks, was hardly so to medieval Europeans. Abelard's astounding work won the applause to some, but alarmed as many others.

Among those alarmed was the great St. Bernard. "The faith of the righteous believes," he declared, "it does not dispute." This outlines very clearly the age old European conflict of Faith and Reason represented by those two pillars of western culture—the science of our Greco-Roman tradition and the faith of our Judeo-Christian tradition. Abelard was condemned for heresy and concluded his life in a monastery. Despite his condemnation, Abelard's method of inquiry persisted and flourished.

By the thirteenth century all Europe had a thirst for learning which the church would not satisfy. Intellectual enterprise as a way of life thrived even in the shadow of that fearsome new institution, the Papal Inquisition. Established in 1233 to stamp out the Albigensian heretics of southern France, the Inquisition's courts of inquiry kept a sharp eye on maverick scholars as well. Nevertheless, the seeds that Abelard had planted in the medieval mind sprouted all around the continent. Less than 100 years after his death universities thrived at Paris, Orleans and Montpellier; across the Channel at Oxford and Cambridge; at Bologna and Padua. And the university is a major cultural contribution of the middle ages.

The step that signaled the birth of the universities was the grouping of students and masters into guilds. As craftsmen had done before them, they banded together for mutual interest and protection, and called themselves a *universitas*, the medieval name for any corporate group. In Italy, where the majority of students were mature men pursuing advanced study in law and medicine, their guilds came to exercise great power. Students hired and paid teachers, determined the courses to be given, and fined any lecturer who skipped a chapter. Examinations were given at the end of the course of study, which generally took six years. About midway through, the student was questioned orally by his master or by a committee of masters. If he passed, he became a baccalaureat, entitled to serve a master as an assistant teacher. Upon completion of his studies he became a master and could teach on his own. You can see the origins of our bachelor's and master's degrees.

In addition to lectures, the method of teaching was the disputation, in which two or more masters, and occasionally the students, debated text readings, employing Abelard's question-and-answer approach. It was in this context that medieval men developed Scholasticism, a process of painstaking arrival at logical conclusions through questioning, postulating, examining and arranging details into a system of logic. It trained students to think. It did much to overthrow unquestioning acceptance of the authors. It led to a new ordering of Christianity into a systematic philosophy.

The writings of the Greeks were appearing in Europe in great volume. Aristotle's doctrines about the nature of the universe were leading men to doubt revelation. The beginning of that conflict between faith and science in our Greco-Roman and Judeo-Christian traditions was under way. The Church needed an answer. They received it from Thomas Aquinas, a Dominican monk of brilliant mind. He saw no conflict between faith and knowledge that could not be reconciled by reason. Rather than denounce the tenets of pagan thinkers such as Averroes, Maimonides and Aristotle out of hand, he examined their writings point by point, refuting some and reconciling others with Christianity.

The result was his *Summa Theologica* (a summation of theological knowledge), a titanic treatise of 21 volumes dealing with the Christian viewpoint on such matters as logic, metaphysics, theology, psychology, ethics and politics. Accepting Aristotle's principle that every effect has a cause, every cause a prior cause, and so on back to a First Cause, Thomas declared that the existence of God could be proved by tracing all creation back to a divine First Cause, or Prime Mover. Also following Aristotle, he declared that the goal of life is the acquisition of truth.

Although his position caused a great ruckus, in the end the Church declared that Thomas was a saint and his writings were accepted as completely in accordance with Christian dogma. The great majority of medieval people comforted themselves, in their short and difficult lives, with hopes of a better life in the world to come. Increasingly, however, there came the humanists, who honored man's worldly aspirations and sought his well-being here and now. With the Renaissance, the humanist point of view would triumph, and its triumph still endures and is dominant in our culture. The emergence of humanism was no accident, but rather a testament to the vision of men like Abelard and Thomas Aquinas.

Superstition and ignorance would linger. But learning at last had passed into the mainstream of society, and thought was venturing farther afield than it had since the height of Greece nearly 2,000 years before.

▶ The Medieval Values

Professor Frederick B. Artz in his book on the Middle Ages gives this summary picture:

> In society, the great medieval thinkers held that all men are equal in the sight of God and that even the humblest has an infinite worth. In economics, they taught that work is a source of dignity not of degradation, that no man should be used for an end independent of his welfare, and that justice should determine wages and prices. In politics, they taught that the function of the state is moral, that law and its administration should be imbued with Christian ideas of justice, and that the relations of ruler and ruled should always be founded on reciprocal obligation. The state, property, and the family are all trusts from God to those who control them, and they must be used to further divine purposes. Finally, the medieval ideal included the strong belief that all nations and peoples are part of one great community.

It is understandable why many first-rate thinkers of our day look back on the Middle Ages as a high point in man's cultural achievement.

FIGURE 6-1 Cultural fault lines are areas of war and conflict

▶ The Renaissance

The educational and intellectual environment of Europe changed with the Renaissance, from roughly 1350 to 1600. The Renaissance began first in Italy and thus reflected the conditions and values of contemporary Italian society. This was a bustling urban society based on flourishing industries and on the commerce between industries and on the commerce between western Europe and the wealthy Byzantine and Islamic empires. Prosperous cities such as Venice, Genoa, Florence, Milan, and Pisa were dominated by great merchant families, who controlled politics as well as trade and crafts. These families were the patrons of Renaissance artists and writers.

There is no doubt the people of the time saw themselves as a "new birth," since Renaissance Italians invented the term "Dark Ages." They looked back on the barbarian invasion of Rome as the end of the light, and on the intervening ten centuries as a period of night. It was, to them, both a joy and a duty to bring light again, to breathe life into the literature, the monuments and the values that had made Rome great. Therefore, the emphasis was on the secularism and humanism of the Greek and Roman world—its concerns with this world rather than the hereafter; its focus on pagan classics rather than Christian theology.

At the center of most Renaissance art and literature was the human being—the new Renaissance man who was the molder of his own destiny rather than the puppet of supernatural forces. Remember the Greek "Man is the measure of things;" the classical tradition gains at the expense of the Christian. A person no longer needed to be preoccupied with supernatural forces; instead, the purpose of life was to develop one's potential. "Men can do all things if they will," wrote Leon Battista Alberti (1404–1472), and his own attainments show he meant it. He was an architect, mathematician, and archeologist, as well as a playwright, poet, art critic, organist, singer, and in his youth, a well-known runner, wrestler, and mountain climber. He was an example of the ideal person of the age, the "uomo universale," or what is termed today the "Renaissance man."

Changes in Education

The worldliness and individualism of the Renaissance were reflected in its scholarship and education. The father of Renaissance literature, Petrarch (1304–1374), stressed the value of the classics as a means for self-improvement and a guide to social action. Likewise the new boarding schools of the Renaissance trained not priests but the sons of merchants. The curriculum emphasized classical studies and physical exercise and was designed to educate the students to live well and happily and to function as responsible citizens.

During the Renaissance, as today, to get rich and to stay rich required a relatively high standard of education. First and foremost, this education was useful: a man could not be successful in commerce and industry without knowing how to read and write and being skillful at figures. But the ways of the Renaissance world required something further. More business meant more partnership agreements, more complicated wills—in short, more law. Legal studies boomed steadily throughout the Renaissance, attracting the largest enrollment at universities, and causing professors of law to be paid among the highest of academic salaries. As the city-states grew, the business of government became more complicated, creating a demand for well-educated secretaries at home and for diplomats who could speak with persuasion and eloquence abroad.

There was, then, a steadily increasing pressure for a more practical kind of education than the one provided by the theological studies of the Middle Ages. Professional skills were needed—also worldly attitudes. The humanistic program of studies took shape to provide them. This program involved the reading of ancient authors and the study of such subjects as grammar, rhetoric, history and moral philosophy. By the fifteenth century, such a course was officially known as *studia humanitatis*, or "humanities," and the men who pursued this knowledge came to be known as humanists.

The Renaissance spirit is most strikingly expressed in its art. Since the church no longer was the sole patron of the arts, artists were encouraged to turn to subjects other than the traditional biblical themes. Such themes continued to appear quite commonly, but in the works of such masters as Leonardo da Vinci, Michelangelo, Raphael, and

Titian, emphasis shifted more and more to portraits designed to reveal hidden mysteries of the soul, to paintings intended to delight the eye with striking colors and forms.

The Renaissance, starting in Italy, spread its new ideas to northern Europe in the sixteenth century. The printing press, which accelerated the circulation of books and ideas, helped the rapid diffusion. Printing was particularly influential in northern Europe because literacy was more widespread there than in Europe's southern and eastern regions. The flood of printed matter stimulated popular agitation concerning political and religious issues and so contributed substantially to the Reformation and the following religious wars.

What is the significant contribution of the Renaissance to world culture? The new emphasis on human beings and on what they could accomplish was more conducive to overseas expansion than the preceding medieval inward-looking emphasis. But this can easily be exaggerated. The fact is that Renaissance Europe was not scientific. Its leading figures tended to be more philosophical than scientific. Keeping many medieval patterns of thought, they persisted in admiring and believing the incredible and the fantastic; they continued to seek the philosopher's stone that would convert other metals into gold; and they still believed in astrology and confused it with astronomy.

The Renaissance or rebirth does not fully explain the origins of European expansion before 1500. There was a generalized intellectual ferment in western Europe that had no counterpart in the rest of the world. This was uniquely European and is fundamental to explaining the rise of Europe and the spread of its culture.

In China, Confucianism continued to dominate society. Its respect for age over youth, for the past over the present, for established authority over innovation made it a perfect instrument for the preservation of the status quo in all its aspects and very antipathetic to change. This atmosphere of conformity and orthodoxy prevented continued intellectual development and helps to explain why China fell behind the West in technology, despite its brilliant initial achievements in developing paper, printing, gunpowder, and the compass that the Europeans were to use so effectively. These early inventions were not followed by the formulation of a body of scientific principles.

The situation was basically the same in the other cultural centers. In the Ottoman Empire, for example, the Muslim colleges emphasized theology, law, and rhetoric at the expense of astronomy, mathematics, and medicine. The graduates of these schools knew nothing about what was being done in the West and were not interested in finding out. No Muslim Turk believed that a Christian infidel could teach anything of value, a dangerous attitude.

Far-reaching changes were taking place in almost all phases of west European life. The end result was the emergence of a new type of dynamic, aggressive modern civilization, which was of a different nature from the traditional agricultural civilizations of the rest of the world. Europe began the process of modernization, which has persisted at an ever-increasing pace to the present day and which has determined the course of modern world events.

From the viewpoint of world history, the significance of this modernization process is its leading to European domination of the globe. Modernization (i.e. applied science) provided the Europeans with not only superior economic and military power but also with superior political and commercial organization. A tremendous gap began opening between the modernized and those who were not. This gap is being closed in our day by countries around the world as they absorb modern technology and market economies.

Religious Turmoil

After many attempts at reform and years of protest at certain abuses of the church, the age-old unity of western Christendom was shattered. By the end of 1520 Martin Luther, who had started as a reformer, broke irrevocably with the Church. This break signaled the beginning of many new sects. In Switzerland, for example, John Calvin preached predestination—each individual's fate was decreed by God before birth.

The religious division of Europe eventually showed almost half the German states Lutheran, along with the Scandinavian kingdoms of Denmark-Norway and Sweden-Finland. In England, Henry VIII was a good Catholic in doctrinal matters and enjoyed as much control over the Catholic clergy as did the French king. Yet Henry eventually established the independent Church of England (1534) because he was determined to divorce his wife, Catherine of Aragon.

The resulting destruction of the old ideal of Christendom compelled each religious group to accept the fact that the leadership of any universal church was not feasible. This was to lead to the gradual acceptance of religious toleration, although the process was slow and is not yet fully accepted.

The emphasis by Protestants on the reading of the Bible led to greater literacy, which opened doors to other books and ideas. In certain respects the Reformation enabled women to move forward. Protestant leaders rejected the medieval Catholic belief in the moral superiority of celibacy. Instead they considered married life desirable for three reasons: procreation of children, sexual satisfaction, and mutual help and comfort between partners. This attitude toward marriage and family encouraged the new idea of a single standard of morality for men and women, and also the equally novel idea of the right of a prospective bride or groom to select their own partner.

As far as the immediate legacy of the Reformation was concerned, it shattered the universal medieval Church into a large number of local territorial churches. The common feature of all these local churches was their control by the government. Regardless of whether the church remained Catholic in doctrine or adhered to one of the Protestant faiths, it was the government and not the church that controlled church appointments and church finances.

The decisive legacy of the Reformation was the transfer of power from church to state. In this sense, the Reformation represents a stage in the evolution of the modern all powerful nation-state. The expansion of Europe may be explained in part by the new militancy of the Christian Church. Christianity asserted itself as a universal religion and became very aggressive. Missionary spirit was especially active in the 1500s because of the centuries of armed conflict with Islam and the conflict during the Reformation.

Worksheet ▶

CHAPTER SIX

Define or identify:

- Obrare est orare

- The rule of St. Benedict

- Gothic style

- The Black Death

- "Brother sun, sister moon"

- Europe in 500 AD

- Europe in 1000 AD

- St. Thomas Aquinas and the "Summa Theologica"

- The Renaissance

Explain:

- How does western monasticism differ from the Oriental tradition?

- How do you think law relates to barbarism and civilization?

- The University, the cathedral and the return of confidence.

- Why does the book feel the Renaissance in Europe was the prelude to the European domination of the globe?

- What do we mean by Gothic architecture? Why would Yale, University of Chicago and Duke University all have Gothic buildings?

- I go to France and the guide tells me Notre Dame de Paris was built in 900 AD. How do I know this is false?

- In which countries of Europe would I be more likely to find a church dedicated to the Blessed Virgin — Latin countries or Northern countries?

- Why was Michelangelo's David naked?

Discuss:

- The role of the Christian church during the Dark Ages.

- Why did the Christian church object to Aristotle's description of a slave as a "human tool"?

- The year 1000 and the return of confidence.

- St. Francis of Assisi's attitude toward poverty and riches.

- The conflict of faith and reason. The medieval ideal man versus the renaissance ideal man.

- The break up of Christendom and the rise of the nation-state.

- What are some differences between the Christian hero and the Renaissance hero?

- Why is Conan the Barbarian a barbarian?

- What is the ugly side of barbarism?

Chapter 7 ▶ ▶

1500 AND THE RISE OF EUROPE

The encounter between the World and the West may well prove, in retrospect, to be the most important event in modern history.
—Arnold J. Toynbee

The year 1500 AD has come to symbolize the advent of the modern era and a turning point in world as well as in European history. Shortly before that date, Europeans, especially the Portuguese, had made technical improvement in navigation that made sailing for long periods out of sight of land not too dangerous. Once they had mastered long-distance navigation, European sailors found no seas beyond their daring, nor any ice-free coast too challenging. In quick order, daring captains sailed into far and undiscovered oceans: Columbus (1492) to America, Vasco da Gama (1498) to India, and Magellan (1519–1522) around the world were the most famous. But there were many others.

What had always before been the unknown fringe of Europe became, within little more than 30 or 40 years, well travelled sea lanes, bringing every one of the world's cultures within easy reach by water. Now, the land-based balance between European and Asian culture was changed and within 300 years sharply changed in favor of the Europeans. Only Australia and the smaller islands of the Pacific remained isolated for a while; yet by the close of the 1700s, they too began to feel the impact of European culture. Europe was forging the entire world into one.

Western Europe, or more specifically those lands facing the Atlantic, was the principal winner from this abrupt change in world relationships. Europe now became the meeting place for new ideas from every corner of the globe. This allowed Europeans to adopt many ideas and skills of other peoples and stimulated them to adjust and consider in a new light ideas and technology within their own now greatly enlarged cultural heritage.

Many cultures wilted under the new world order. The American Indian civilizations of Mexico and Peru were the most conspicuous victims being suddenly reduced to a comparatively simple village level after the priests and rulers had been destroyed or made puppets by the Spaniards. In Asia, the Muslim peoples lost their central position as ocean routes became the carriers of trade rather than overland caravans. Only in China were the effects of the new world relationships at first unimportant.

From a Chinese viewpoint, it made little difference whether foreign trade, regulated within traditional forms, passed to Muslim or European merchants' hands. At the beginning, when the Europeans seemed to threaten their political integrity, first Japan and then China were strong enough to throw out the foreigners and they closed their borders against further meddling. Yet by 1850, even this chosen isolation could no longer be maintained; and China and Japan—along with the less developed cultures of central Africa—began to break down under the pressure of the newly industrialized Europe.

To realize the power of new developments in the West, it is enough to point out that as late as the mid 1920s there was only one territory on the whole inhabitable globe that was not controlled by Europeans or their descendants: Japan. Seven other non-European countries were considered independent; but even these had their economic life and political institutions run by Europeans or deeply influenced by them.

The key to world history from 1500 is the growing dominance first of western Europe, then of an enlarged European-type society, including the U.S., Canada and Russia. Even so, until about 1700, the ancient land borders of the Asian civilizations retained much of their old form. Only in Central America and western South America did Europeans succeed in establishing extensive land empires overseas during this period. So the years 1500-1700 may be regarded as a period of change between the old land-centered and the new ocean-centered pattern of world relationships—a time when European progress had modified, but not yet completely upset the balance of the old order.

The next major period, 1700–1850, saw a decisive change of this balance in favor of Europe. Two daughter cultures were added to the western world by the Europeanizing of Russia and by the colonization of North America, which we will discuss shortly. Less massive off-shoots of European society were at the same time being established in southernmost Africa, in the south American pampas (Argentina), and in Australia. India was conquered and became an English colony. The Muslim Middle East escaped a similar fate only because of intra-European rivalries; and the descendants of the conquering norsemen of Genghis Khan peoples of the Eurasian steppes, lost their last shreds of military and cultural significance with the progress of Russian and Chinese conquest and colonization.

After 1850, the rapid development of the industrial revolution, discussed in more depth later, enormously increased the political and cultural power of the West. China fell before the British naval power; and several European nations carved out large colonial empires in Asia and Africa. Even though these European empires have decayed since 1945, and the separate nation-states of Europe have been overshadowed by the now defunct USSR and the U.S., it is still true that, since the end of World War II, the desire to imitate and appropriate science, technology, and other aspects of western culture has continued to grow all around the world. So even the decline of western Europe from its brief political mastery of the globe, rapid cultural westernization of all the peoples of the earth goes on at an ever increasing pace.

Looking back from the end of the twentieth century, the expansion of western culture since 1500 appears as a vast explosion, far greater than any comparable phenomenon of the past both in its worldwide range and in deep change in the lives of ordinary people. Constant and ever increasing change, thrown together with a variety of conflicting ideas, institutions, aspirations, and inventions, has been a distinctive feature of modern European history. More recently, deliberate innovation in the form of industrial research laboratories, universities, military general staffs, and planning commissions of every sort, are accelerating the pace of technical and social change. Change appears to be built into the fabric of western culture.

The World Becomes One

Considering the thousands of years of human history, why should such a relatively recent date carry such significance?

One answer is that until 1500, humans had lived largely in regional isolation. The various racial groups and many cultures lived separately and quite unaware of each other. Not until about 1500 was there for the first time direct contact between most of mankind. Not until approximately that date were they finally all brought together, whether they were Australian or Chinese or American Indians. The degree of isolation, of course, varied from region to region. The peoples of Australia and of the Americas were on the fringes and were completely cut off on their respective continents, whereas those of Africa were only partly isolated. But with the European conquest of the oceans all were in direct contact by sea.

World history in the strict global sense did not begin until the voyages of Columbus to America, da Gama to India, and Magellan around the world. Before their trips, there were many histories of separate peoples developing in their own ways rather than one unified history of a world culture. During most of the pre-1500 period, northwest Europe was what today would be termed an underdeveloped area. Its peoples were looked down on as backward "natives." Greeks, Romans, Byzantines, and Muslims all assumed that the Europeans living to the north of the Mediterranean were stupid and couldn't be educated and were generally inferior. Yet it was the descendants of those inferior people who discovered continents unknown to the Greeks and Romans and who eventually became the masters of the entire globe.

Reasons Behind Europe's Rise

This surprising story raises a fundamental question. Why did the western Europeans become such leaders of the world? In view of their previous backwardness, why was it they, rather than the Chinese or Arabs, who brought together the continents of the world and thus began the global phase of world history? If Columbus had been a Muslim or Chinese, the world today would be very different from what it is. Was it just by chance he was a European?

During most of the period from roughly 500 BC to 1500 AD, western Europe was a relatively underdeveloped region. This underdevelopment proved an advantage by allowing change, in contrast to China's high development which acted as a break on change. Success tends to make one conservative. The Chinese enjoyed a sophisticated culture, advanced crafts, large-scale commerce, an efficient bureaucracy based on merit, and the creed of Confucianism that provided social harmony and intellectual purpose. Very naturally, the Chinese considered their civilization to be superior to any other. When the first westerners appeared on their coast, the Chinese assumed there was nothing important they could learn from those peculiar "long-nosed barbarians." Pride cometh before the fall.

This attitude, understandable though it was, left the Chinese as well as India and Islam unchanging during a time of great change in Europe. The western Europeans, precisely because of their relative backwardness, were ready and eager to learn and to adapt. They took Chinese inventions and developed them to their full potential. They were eager for new ideas and used them for overseas expansion. This expansion, in turn, triggered more

technological advances and institutional changes, as new ideas flowed in. The end result was the transition from medieval to modern civilization, characterized by change. The Europeans served as the pioneers and reaped the benefits.

Political

One further reason for the rise of Europe is political, the rise of the nation state. As compared with the many overlapping power centers that had prevailed in medieval times, power started to concentrate at relatively few centers. By 1500 the European continent came to be divided into a series of well-defined states, each controlled by a central and usually monarchical government. Within the borders of each successful state, the powers of government expanded rapidly. Matters which had once been strictly local came within the power of agents of the central government.

The ruler also acquired authority in matters of church administration and patronage, even in countries that remained Catholic and continued to recognize papal headship of the church. We spoke earlier of state domination of the church. Special privileges of both town and nobles suffered drastic curtailment. Every sort of local authority based on tradition fell before demands made in the name of the state by officials whose power depended on appointment by the king.

This process of political consolidation and dominance by the prince amounted to the application of techniques of government north of the Alps which had first been worked out during the Renaissance in the Italian city states, such as Florence. Nation-states north of the Alps proceeded on a much enlarged territorial scale containing many cities. With this much larger territory, the effective power controlled by many European governments increased enormously, and the whole scale of government increased with it.

When we look at the Americas we find four major languages spoken today: French, English, Spanish and Portuguese, a heritage of the four major leaders of European expansion. It is not a coincidence that these also represent the languages of the four first nation-states, France, England, Spain and Portugal, a new and very successful political organization.

Conquest of the Ocean

Another key to European expansion was their maritime supremacy. Supremacy at sea opened the entire world to European domination after 1500. But Europe's maritime superiority was itself the product of a deliberate use of science, especially applied science, which advanced seamanship in Portugal through the efforts of Prince Henry the Navigator and his successors. Not just science but applied science will prove the key to European success. With the introduction of the compass (thirteenth century), navigation beyond sight of land had become a regular practice in the Mediterranean; and the navigators' charts needed for such voyaging showed coasts, harbors, landmarks, and compass bearings between major ports.

In addition, the Portuguese devised a method of finding latitude by calculation so that sea captains could be out of sight of land for weeks and still feel confident of returning. At the same time, Portuguese naval experts attacked the problem of improving ship construction. They used a lot of trial and error; but soon deliberate experimentation, systematically pursued, rapidly increased the seaworthiness, maneuverability, and speed of Portuguese ships and presently (since improvements could not be kept secret) of those of other European countries. Some of the important changes were: a reduction of hull width in proportion to length; the introduction of multiple masts (usually three or four), and the substitution of several smaller, more manageable sails for the single sail per mast from which the evolution started. These innovations allowed a crew to trim the sails to suit varying conditions of wind and sea, thus making steering easier and protecting the vessel from disaster in sudden storms.

With these improvements, larger ships could be built; and increasing size and sturdiness of construction made it possible to transform seagoing vessels into gun platforms for heavy cannons, and this will prove to be key. By 1509, when the Portuguese fought for control of the Arabian Sea, their ships could deliver a heavy broadside at a range their Muslim enemies could not begin to match. Under such circumstances, the superior numbers of the opposing fleet simply provided the Portuguese with additional targets for their guns. The old tactics of sea fighting—ramming, grappling, and boarding—were almost useless against cannon fire effective at as much as 200 yards. All the navies of the world except the Europeans' were now obsolete.

Partly by reason of the new ideas that flowed into Europe from overseas, but primarily because of internal intellectual ferment, Europe entered upon a veritable social explosion of change in the period 1500-1650. While painful in itself, it nonetheless raised European power to a new level of effectiveness and for the first time gave Europeans a clear margin of superiority over the other great world cultures.

The Nation State

The ancient Greeks emphasized a political organization based on the city state, the polis. This traditional political organization remained the basis of Western civilization until 1500. When these local entities as well as the universal church broke down, they were succeeded by the national or nation-state. The consolidation of relatively large territories was achieved by using administrative techniques and ideas which had first developed in the smaller city-states of Italy between the thirteenth and fifteenth centuries, or the period of the Renaissance.

As nation-states grew, the rival governments of Europe became able to mobilize ever larger concentrations of power and wealth, both for warlike and (sometimes) for peaceable undertakings. The upshot was a greater increase in European power, particularly military power. The enormous variety of strictly local customs, laws, and institutions which governed the lives of most Europeans in the Middle Ages tended within each of the new nation-states to develop toward a national norm. The language of the Ile de France became the language of the French nation, for example.

With its well defined territories, the national state tended to mark off and divide the populations of Europe more sharply than had been the case in medieval times, when borders were ill defined. The retreat of Latin as a *lingua franca*, or common language, and the use of national languages for more and more purposes separated nations; but it was undoubtedly the religious divisions introduced by the Reformation and added to by the subsequent divisions within Protestantism that most powerfully supported the division of the Europeans into distinct, competing segments. The consequences of this division have been disastrous in this century and resulted in its great wars.

From the 1500s onward, the most successful and influential states of Europe were located along the Atlantic coast. Western Europe began to speed ahead of all rivals as the most active center of cultural innovation. Indeed, Europe's great transformation changed the medieval framework of western civilization into a new and vastly more powerful organization of society.

At no previous time in world history had the pace of social change been so rapid. The new contacts from around the world assured a continuance of idea exchange among the major cultures of mankind. The efforts to restrict foreign contacts and to withdraw from disturbing relationships with outsiders—especially the dominant and domineering westerners—were doomed to ultimate failure by the fact that the continuous changes in western European civilization, and especially in Western technology, rapidly improved the advantage Westerners were able to bring over the other peoples of the earth.

From one point of view, world history since 1500 may be thought of as a race between the West's growing power to dominate the rest of the world and the increasingly desperate efforts of other peoples to protect their cultural inheritance. If that failed, they have desperately borrowed from the West—especially technology—in the hope of thereby finding means to preserve their independence.

The early part of Europe's rise, from 1500 to 1700, represents a halfway point between the separated cultures of the preceding ages and the eventual European world domination achieved in the nineteenth century. Economically, the Europeans extended their trading operations to virtually all corners of the globe that were on oceans. At first they were not yet able to exploit the interiors of the great land masses, except in the Americas. Intercontinental trade reached new heights, though still small compared to what was to follow.

Culturally, it was a period of new horizons. Throughout the globe peoples were becoming aware of other peoples and other cultures. By and large, the Europeans were more impressed and affected by the ancient cultures of China and India than vice versa. They felt a sense of awe as they discovered new oceans and continents and civilizations. At the same time that they were greedy for gold and for trade. They sometimes underwent an occasional uneasy searching of conscience, as for example, during the cruel treatment of the Indians in Spanish America. But before this period had passed, Europe's attitude toward the rest of the world would harden and become more intolerant.

After 1750 the pace of European world dominance increased at a much faster pace due to the rapid advance of applied science and two great revolutions that continue to shape our world; the industrial revolution and the political revolution. These will be discussed in some depth in Chapter 11.

Focusing only on the world expansion of western culture would not give us a global point of view. A global perspective requires consideration not only of the expanding West but also of the regions into which the West expanded. The peoples of these regions, after all, continue to make up a considerable proportion of the human race, and their evolution must not be ignored. Moreover, the lands, peoples, and institutions of the non-European world were as significant in determining the outcome of western expansionism as were the Europeans themselves. There was an exchange.

Until 1500, for example, racial segregation existed on a global scale. All blacks, or Negroids, lived in Africa; all whites, or Caucasoids, lived in Europe and the Middle East; all Mongoloids, in east Asia and the Americas (Indians); and all Australoids, in Australia. This traditional regional autonomy began trends toward global unity when western overseas expansion began about 1500. Races no longer were isolated because millions of people moved, willingly or unwillingly, to new continents.

Since the Europeans took the lead in this global activity, they dominated the newly united world—both politically with their great empires and economically with their corporations. They also enjoyed cultural domination, so that western culture became the global model. It was equated with advanced civilization, and non-western cultures came to be regarded as backward and inferior. This western dominance was taken for granted by the nineteenth century, not only by Europeans but also by non-Europeans. It was assumed to be almost a part of the natural order of things.

It should not be thought that Europe in 1500 started out to dominate the world. It generally happened in the name of what we today would call "progress." Dominance from the new nation-states of Europe usually began in the military field. Non-Europeans were, at first, most impressed and alarmed by the West's superior military technology, and they tried to learn and copy its secrets as soon as possible. This happened wherever they went—in Russia, in the Middle East, in China, and in Japan. But up-to-date armies and navies required the development of industry, so that military objectives meant meeting new goals in economic organization.

For various reasons there was substantial industrialization in the nineteenth century in Russia and Japan but comparatively little in the Middle East, India, and China. Industrialization inevitably led to the westernization of values. Arms and factories required schools and science. One thing borrowed from the West always required the borrowing of something more. Military and economic change produced intellectual change. Social and political change followed. A new middle class appeared that challenged the traditional society and ruling groups. Eventually this same group also challenged western domination. The rise of this group explains the intellectual ferment and the revolutionary movements that opposed tsardom in Russia, British control in India, and Manchu rule in China.

Reaction to Western Domination

Western culture everywhere today is being directly challenged, and often rejected. Non-westerners often reject western ideas because they equate it with industry and advertising that reduces humans to producers and consumers, and results in a selfish, atomistic society. They feel because it emphasizes economic concerns, it leaves little to individual choice and destroys life's richness and diversity. This is the basis for the foreign intellectuals contempt of McDonald's and Coca-Cola.

Rejection of western global domination is not surprising. It was a special situation, produced by a peculiar combination of circumstances, and was bound to be temporary. Another surprise is that the forces of regional autonomy are also awakening today within many leading western states. National groups or subgroups, forgotten for centuries, are now stirring and demanding autonomy. In the United States, there are the minority groups: the

blacks, the Hispanics and the Native Americans. In neighboring Canada, unity is threatened by the separatist demands of French Quebeç. Britain likewise is coping with would-be secessionists in Scotland, Ireland, and Wales. France is facing the same challenge from Corsican, Breton, and Basque liberation fronts and Spain from Catalans and Basques. The break up of the USSR and Yugoslavia is part of this trend.

The demand for regional autonomy is not directed only against central authority in the West. In Iran, there have been uprisings by minorities such as the Kurds, Arabs, Baluchis, and Turkomen. Since these minorities comprise almost half of the total population of that country, Iran and Iraq are far more threatened by regional autonomy demands than is any western country.

Much of the turmoil of our age arises from the clash of two great contradictory forces. On the one hand, modern technology is uniting the globe as never before, thanks to modern communication media, multinational corporations, and world-encircling spaceships. On the other hand, the globe is being torn apart by the awakening of hitherto dormant masses who too are determined to create their own futures. McDonald's versus Holy war—the roots of this major modern conflict go back to the centuries after 1500 when western Europe for the first time brought together all the peoples of the world. The results of this unification, both positive and negative, are part of today's problem. Many cultural groups are frantically making a last ditch effort to preserve their future. This is well documented in the daily news by news of Armenians, Croats, Serbs, etc. struggling for independence.

Before leaving Western culture and moving to the eastern cultures of India and China, we will discuss three other areas, Russia, the Americas, and Africa. Both Russia and the Americas may be considered sub-groups of western culture. America is a direct descendent, having been colonized by the Europeans, and Russia is more a sister culture having similar Greco-Roman and Judeo-Christian roots, but having developed its own distinctive way due to location and history. Africa does not fit neatly anywhere. Africa north of the Sahara has always been a part of Mediterranian culture, while south of the Sahara it has only lately entered the world community and received the overwhelming problems of finding its way in a competitive, united world.

▶ RUSSIA

Russia is a part of Europe, and the Russian people are a European people. But Russia's history and culture have been distinct and cannot be included in the central theme of western culture. Russia lies on the fringes of Europe and has acted as a great meeting place between Asia and Europe. This has meant it has been an area of conflict. Also, while the Russians became Christian, they belonged to the Eastern Greek Orthodox Church rather than the Latin or Roman Church, which really defined western culture. A central issue of Russian history has been the influence or the impact of the Western Europeans on Russia and their reaction. Russia has a long history of feeling threatened by superior Western arms and organization. (See Figure 7-1.)

For a thousand years, the Russians have been members, not of our western culture, but of the Byzantine, which we discussed. They had the same Greco-Roman parentage as ours plus the Judeo-Christian, but developed a different civilization from our own, nevertheless. The Russian members of this Byzantine family have always put up a strong resistance against threats of being overwhelmed by our western world, and they are keeping up this resistance today. In order to save themselves from being conquered and overwhelmed by the West, they have repeatedly been forced to make themselves masters of European technology.

This has been partially achieved at least twice in Russian history: first by Peter the Great, and then again by the Bolsheviks. The effort has had to be repeated and we think of Gorbachav and Perestrioka, because western technology had continued to maintain a lead. Peter the Great had to master the arts of the seventeenth-century artisans and war methods. The Bolsheviks had to catch up with the western industrial revolution. And today again Russia finds itself hopelessly behind the West.

It has been only in the past 250 years that Russia has emerged from the Middle Ages. Long isolated from Western Europe, Russia grew up without participating in developments changing Western European society. Russia was never a part of the Roman Empire. She never recognized the temporal or spiritual authority of the Roman pope or was considered part of Christendom by Europe. The Renaissance and the Reformation both passed her by; the scientific revolution was in Russia only a feeble copy of the western model. When the great Bolshevik revolution did come in 1917, it seemed strange and frightening to western nations who had experienced their great upheavals in earlier centuries.

Russia's history is essentially that of a single people, the Eastern Slavs, the great Russians, Belorussians, and Ukranians. (See Figure 3-4.) Nature and geography have in many respects served Russia poorly. Seven eighths of modern Russia's vast bulk lies north of the United States-Canadian border. Because of Russia's climate, her agriculture has never flourished. Most of Russia is one enormous plain, once the floor of an ocean that stretched from the Arctic to the Black and Caspian Seas. This flatness helped tie the country together during its early development.

Russia did possess one great natural asset, a magnificent system of interlocking rivers. Slow-moving and meandering, these rivers make communication possible in almost any direction across the great plain. As early as the seventh century AD, traders and adventurers from Scandinavia, usually known as "Varangians," followed the western Dvina and the Volga southeast to the Caspian Sea, sailed across it and proceeded overland to Baghdad. In the eighth and ninth centuries active trade sprang up on the Dnieper, which empties into the Black Sea, and they made their way to Constantinople.

Not much is known about Russia before about 800 AD. It is known they were Slavs and in time they subdivided into three groups—the Great Russians, ordinarily called simply Russians; the Little Russians or Ukrainians; and the White Russians. Although the agriculture of the Slavs, because of the cold climate, was marginal, the forest provided things they could sell—furs, honey and beeswax. Trading centers, many of them fortified towns, were built along the waterways, and by 800 AD the Slavs were beginning to send fleets of small craft south to Byzantium.

It was natural that the Slavs would like to move out of their harsh forest environment to the fertile and open steppes to the south, but the open steppes were also an area of invasion by fierce tribes from central and eastern Asia, who had been pouring into it since the dawn of history. This was part of the steppes, a highway for Mongol horsemen.

The steppe nomads always drove off the Slavic attempts at invasion of the rich farmland. Perhaps

United States Superimposed on Europe

FIGURE 7-1 Remember that New York is on the same latitude as Madrid. For equal latitudes, Europe, on this map, must be placed much further north.

the Russian fear of foreigners is rooted in this experience. For centuries in the past, Russians never knew what new horror might come thundering down upon them across the steppes. Later they would have to look with equal anxiety toward the West. The latest example being its horrible invasion by the Germans under Hitler.

It was not until the mid 800s that the Slavs embarked on their long journey toward becoming Russia. The start came out of the far north in the form of wandering bands of Scandinavian warrior-traders. These Scandinavians—or "Varangians"—were brothers to the Vikings who ravaged England, France and Sicily. But instead of taking to the open ocean, they searched out the inland water routes. They were interested in whatever they could steal or trade. But above all, they wanted to get to the fabled riches of Byzantium, which, incidentally, had attacked several times.

As the Varangians proceeded southward along the Dnieper River, they passed through the heartland of the Russian Slavs, and gradually brought it under their domination. Traditionally, beginnings of the first Russian state are traced to the year 862, when the Varangians were "invited" to rule over the Slavs. These Varangians were also known as the Rus. The earliest histories record that the leader of the Varangian Rus was Rurik, a half-legendary figure who in 862 may have established himself at Novgorod and at the same time other leaders seized control of Kiev far to the south.

Kiev, because of its strategic location on the Dnieper, was the most important of all the towns of the Rus. It was the southernmost fortified point in the forest region. The ruler of Kiev, assuming leadership of the trading and military expeditions, also assumed a key political position; he took the title of Grand Prince while the chieftains of northern territories remained merely princes. The rule of Kiev continued to grow into a loosely knit empire based on tribute with nothing to hold it together but force. This Kievan Russia blossomed into a golden age.

In the year 980 Vladimir became grand prince. Vladimir was an excellent soldier and administrator who was able to devote great energy to the enlargement and consolidation of his state which eventually became one of the largest of European political units. Despite this success, Vladimir is primarily known because of his eventual acceptance of Christianity and his subsequent decree that all the people be baptized. Vladimir converted to the Christianity of Byzantium (Greek orthodox) with the most profound consequences for Russia, and indeed for all of Europe. The culture of Russia was strongly influenced by the Eastern church and the culture of Greek Byzantium.

Their new religion gave them a sense of belonging to the civilized world and they eagerly welcomed all that Byzantium had to offer. Most important to their cultural progress was the establishment of a standardized literary language—by Cyril and Methodius the "apostles to the Slavs." A modified form of Cyrillic based on Greek characters, one of the alphabets they devised, remains in use in present-day Russia. The establishment of a Russian church and scholarly language and alphabet was a great boon. It also had one unfortunate result. While it did away with the necessity of the Russian scholars' learning Greek or Latin, it cut them off from the classical heritage of the West.

The influence of Byzantine culture was dramatically evident in the arts, particularly icon-painting, religious frescoes and mosaics, and church architecture, which began to flourish in Kievan Russia after the year 1000. The Church also played a leading role in the widespread establishment of monasteries which were to have great importance in the colonization of the vast eastern frontier, serving as fortresses as well as religious centers. Kiev reached such a height that the family of the Grand Prince was bound by marriage to the great ruling Houses of Europe. In European eyes Kievan Russia was a great and enlightened state, already having a culture comparable to that of the West. There are no reliable population figures for the Kiev at its height, but historians believe it was as large as Paris, Europe's leading city, which had a population of about 80,000—twice as large as eleventh century London.

Kiev remained "the master of Russian cities." But its importance began a sharp decline. Byzantium, its principal trading partner, began trading with Western Europe. Kiev was no longer needed. As Kiev declined and the pressure of the steppe nomads increased, the population of the area around Kiev began to migrate. A large group—the "Great Russians"—found their way into the forests of the northeast, between the upper Volga and the Oka rivers where, one day, the state of Muscovy would arise.

Today Russians look back with nostalgia on the period of Kievan greatness, the era, the period of the conversion to Christianity and the development of a common language, law and art form. Kiev was the birthplace of Russian nationality. In their long and doomed fight against the invaders from the steppe—the Russian people underwent a great ordeal. It remains as a part of national pride.

In 1206 one of the most important figures in world history, a tribal leader named Genghis Khan, took all the Mongols under his rule. Five years later he broke through the Great Wall into China and, with an army of 100,000 conquered a nation of 100 million people. Genghis Khan then turned west with the intention of conquering the world. Nothing could stop the Mongol and they ravaged Russia, but then suddenly withdrew due to the death of Genghis Khan.

However, in 1237 they returned, led by Batu Khan, a grandson of Genghis, and the conquest of all Russia was soon effected. The one great city of Russia that was not overrun by the Mongols was Novgorod, in the north. And this was attacked not from the East but from the Christian West. Since the time of the split between the Roman and Byzantine Churches, the pope had regarded the "heretics" or "schismatics" of the Eastern Church as little better than infidels, and when it appeared that the Novgorodians were tied up with the Mongol threat, a crusade was organized against them. When the Swedes occupied the mouth of the Neva River and attempted to block Novgorod's access to the sea, the 21-year-old Prince of Novgorod, Alexander, met them beside the river and crushed them, winning for himself the title "of the Neva," which immortalized him in Russia history as Alexander Nevsky.

Nevsky knew that it was fruitless to take a stand against the Mongols, and so made peace with them, acknowledging their sovereignty, while he dealt with his Christian enemies.

The Mongols agreed to permit Alexander to remain as prince of Novgorod, on condition that he pay tribute. To the Russians, the action of their western fellow Christians in their time of great need was a stab in the back. Russia was now under the Mongol yoke that would bind the western part of the country for a century and the eastern part for two. The Mongols reduced the Russians to a state of numb terror and ruled from the lower Volga where their army remained poised in case of any uprising.

The Mongols were known as the Golden Horde because yellow was the imperial color. Although merciless in their exaction of tribute, the Mongols permitted the Russians to follow their own customs and laws, and were remarkably tolerant of the Church. Of great importance was the role of the Church as the preserver of what remained of the great Kievan legacy and as almost the sole unifying force among a demoralized people. It reminds one of the church's role in western Europe as a preserver of the Roman tradition.

As the Mongol yoke first began to lift in the west and southwest, the vacuum created was filled not by the Russians, but by their traditional enemies, the Latin Christian Poles and the Lithuanians. By 1350 the Poles had gained control of the rich principality of Galicia, and by 1400 the Lithuanians had carved out a huge area of what is now Russia that extended from the Baltic almost to the Black Sea including the Ukranian and White Russians. In the centuries to follow, this Russian-Lithuanian state would struggle with Moscow for ascendancy over the whole Russian land.

Great Russians remained under the Mongol yoke for many years thereafter, until Moscow—or Muscovy, as the entire state came to be called—became powerful enough to throw it off. Moscow was ideally situated as a center of communication and trade. Its location on the Moscow River gave it ready access to the headwaters of four greater rivers, the Dnieper, the Volga, the Don and the Oka. Under Ivan I, descendant of Alexander Nevsky, Moscow greatly expanded in power and prestige and led to one of the most important of all events in the early history of the city: the head of the Russian church, the Metropolitan, who had previously resided in Vladimir, transferred his see to Moscow in 1328. From that time forward the interests of the Church and the Muscovite state became closely intertwined, with the Metropolitans unfailingly supporting the princes' drive toward dominance in the Great-Russian area. The Metropolitans did not hesitate to employ the weapon of excommunication against the enemies of Moscow, and at times took an active part in the management of the state.

By 1378 Moscow had become strong enough to dare challenge the Mongols in battle; in that year Grand Prince Dimitry defeated a small Mongol army. When the Mongols organized to recoup their losses, the other Russian princes under Moscow leadership defeated the large Mongol army. Of great importance in rallying the Russians was the Church—Moscow was now the spiritual capital of the northeastern lands. Moscow gained great prestige and continued its momentum toward a center for the gathering of all the Russians. The Golden Horde went into decline and eventual disintegration.

The 250 years of Mongol domination in Russia left almost nothing of cultural value. Their heritage was mostly negative. The Mongols actively retarded the growth of Russian culture by blocking the stimulus from Byzantium and the West; conceivably, had it not been for the Mongols, Russia might have participated in the Renaissance. However, the Mongols did not permit them to develop their own culture.

The Mongol effect on the Russian social order was disastrous. The freedom and democracy and the fairness and mildness of the legal code that had marked the Kievan state were wiped out. Russian rulers gradually came to resemble the khans in their harshness and despotism, either through imitation or through the necessity of paying them tribute. Despotism and enserfment, the two key facts of all subsequent Russian history, began under Mongol rule.

The Rise of Moscow

Under Ivan III, called the Great, Moscow's growth proceeded at a remarkable pace. The largest acquisition was the city state of Novgorad which included thousands of square miles in the wilderness of the north and northeast, beyond the Volga. This occurred at the same time as a movement into the vast wilderness. The move to the wilderness had not been planned or directed by the state; it was simply a spontaneous surging of the people, who won an empire almost by without thinking. Moscow quickly acknowledged the movement, of course, and soon established a bureaucracy to collect taxes and administer law.

By the time of Ivan the Great's death, Moscow had all of Great Russia under its control.

To establish legitimacy, Ivan married Sophia Paleologus, a niece of Constantine XI, the last Byzantine emperor. The marriage made Ivan, or so he assumed, the rightful heir of empire. To his family crest he added a two-headed eagle, the Byzantine version of the Roman eagle, and to his several titles he added "czar" (i.e. Caesar) and "autocrat".

The church, interested in advancing and glorifying Muscovite absolutism, made some contributions of its own, tracing Ivan's lineage back to prove he was a brother to Augustus Caesar and therefore an heir to Rome. They also developed the Doctrine of the "Third Rome." It held that the first Rome had fallen into heresy, and as punishment had been overthrown by barbarians.

The second Rome, Byzantium, had also become heretical, and consequently had been overrun by the Turks. However, although "two Romes have fallen, a third stands, and a fourth there shall not be."

The third Rome was Moscow, the capital of the last truly Christian nation on earth, and the residence of a czar who in his power was "similar to God in Heaven." This doctrine further widened the splits between Russia and the West and the Church became even more closely identified with autocratic czardom and "Holy Russia."

Russia became the citadel of Orthodoxy and remained isolated from the Latin, Catholic West. It also tended to make Russians self-satisfied and isolated, and they ignored and scorned the great changes that were transforming the rest of Europe. By the sixteenth century, however, many far-seeing Russian leaders recognized that their economic and technological backwardness represented a threat to their national security. Thus it was that the Russians in the sixteenth century, like the Turks, the Japanese, and the Chinese in later centuries, began to borrow from the West as a measure of self-defense.

Under Czar Peter the Great (1682–1725), the process of westernization accelerated tremendously. He reorganized his administration and armed forces along western lines; established industries to support his armies; imported thousands of foreign experts of various types; sent young Russians to study abroad; and set up a number of schools, all of them utilitarian in character. He founded schools of mathematics and navigation, admiralty schools, war-department schools, ciphering schools, and an Academy of Sciences. Peter also shattered all precedent by traveling through Western Europe to study foreign institutions and practices. He defeated Sweden in a long and decisive war and acquired frontage on the Baltic Sea. Here he built his new capital, St. Petersburg—the symbol of the new Russia, as Moscow was of the old.

Peter's work was continued by the gifted and colorful Catherine the Great (reign, 1762–1796). She prided herself on being an enlightened despot. During her reign the higher Russian nobility became Europeanized. They had worn beards and flowing Oriental robes during Peter's reign, but under Catherine they copied the court of Versailles. Their children were brought up by French governesses, learned French as their mother tongue, and then picked up only enough Russian to manage the servants.

The Europeanization of Russia was no longer confined to technical matters, but it was still limited to the upper class. Indeed, the gulf between the Europeanized upper crust and the peasant masses who were bound to the estates as serfs was becoming wider and more dangerous. Catherine was aware of the division, but knowing that she depended on the nobles for her position, she never seriously challenged their interests and privileges.

Russia Moves East

During the years of Moscow's rise to become the center of a geographically vast state, contact with the West had been limited. And while the western nations, Spain, Portugal, France, Holland and England were exploring the world through their advanced technology and control of the Oceans, Russia was turning eastward and conquering northern Asia.

While the Russian's relationship to Western Europe was one of technical and economic inferiority, Russia's relationship to Asia was one of superiority. This superiority had enabled Russia between the sixteenth and eighteenth centuries to overcome the tribespeople of Siberia and to expand eastward to the Pacific. In the southeast the Russians had been halted by the strong Chinese Empire (1689). The drive east was carried on primarily by small bands of trappers organized as military bands seeking the great profit to be made from furs.

The Russian conquest of Siberia was a remarkable achievement. The Russians in Siberia won a great empire in a few years with incredibly small forces.

By the time of Catherine, the Russians resumed their advance to the east and the south, acquiring Alaska, and many of the Turkish people of central Asia who are now separated from the USSR. In central Asia they imposed their rule on ancient Muslim khanates that remained Muslim. Russia's technology, though inadequate against the West, was nonetheless sufficient to give the Russians a decisive advantage over the Chinese in east Asia and the Moslems in central Asia. Thus, the Russians continued to extend their imperial frontiers until they were stopped by powers that were technologically equal or superior—that is, by the Americans in Alaska, by the British in India and Persia, and by the Japanese in Manchuria.

Prior to the Bolshevik Revolution, the mass of Kazakhs, Kirghizes, Turkomans, Uzbeks, and Tajiks were little affected by the coming of the Russians. They continued in their own world separated by barriers of language, religion, and customs. Russia, a semi-western state with a painful relationship with Western Europe, was able to expand strongly into Asia and create a Russian empire to include more backward peoples of the forest and steppe zones of northern Asia.

In Russia, the great victory over Napoleon in 1812 and subsequent occupation of France by some Russian troops were to make a deep impression. Some of the liberal and radical ideas of France influenced their thinking, and the autocracy seemed very out of date. The contrast of life in Russia with that of the West was profound. Russia lacked the commerce, the industry, and the middle class that had played so decisive a role in the political evolution of the West. Instead, there were at the bottom the bound and inert serf masses and at the top the nobility, and while new ideas from West had some upper class followers, there was no mass support.

Worth mentioning is the Russian reaction to western ideas by the Slavophils. The Slavophils rejected the westerner's basic assumption of the unity of human civilization. They held that the differences between Russia and the West were fundamental and inherent and reflected profound dissimilarities in national spirit rather than degrees of advance. Far from considering western society superior, they rejected it as materialistic, irreligious, and torn by dissension and revolution.

A good example of Russia's weakness was illustrated by the Crimean War (1854–1856) between Russia and a number of western powers, of which the most important were Britain and France. The war was fought on Russian soil—and yet Russia was defeated and forced to accept a humiliating peace treaty. The Crimean defeat unveiled the corruption and backwardness of the old regime. Russia's soldiers had fought gallantly, but the odds were hopelessly against them. They had rifles that shot only a third as far as those of the western armies. They had only sailing ships to use against the steamships of the British and the French. They had no medical or food supply services that were worthy of the name. And the lack of railways in the Crimean peninsula forced them to haul military supplies in carts.

Some adjustments had to be made. One of the most dramatic was the Emancipation Decree of 1861 freeing the serfs and dividing the land that they tilled between themselves and the noble proprietors. This was a great turning point in Russian history. The freeing of the serfs involved an overwhelming majority of the population and led to further reforms of the law and local governments. Also further undermining the old regime was the start of the industrialization of the country.

On the eve of the World War in 1914 great strains and conflicts were showing within Russian society. The peasants had been far from satisfied with the terms of the Emancipation Decree, which they felt had left too large a proportion of the land to the nobles. Also they had real discontent over the intolerably heavy tax load. Peasant disaffection found political expression in the Socialist Revolutionary party.

The unrest of the peasants was matched by that of the urban proletariat, who had appeared with the growth of industry. The early days of industrialization in Russia involved gross exploitation of labor: sixteen-hour working days, low wages, child labor, and abominable working and living conditions. Under these circumstances the Russian workers, like those of central and western Europe, came under the influence of Marxist doctrines.

The Social Democratic party was organized in 1898 and later split into two parts: the Mensheviks and the Bolsheviks. Lenin was the leader of the Bolsheviks, who remained a small group until the outbreak of World War I. Then the disorder and misery produced by the Russian defeats at the front gave the Bolsheviks the opportunity to use their superior organization to mobilize and lead the disaffected masses.

Lenin maintained that his 240,000 Bolshevik party members could govern Russia in the interest of the poor against the rich as easily as 130,000 landlords previously had governed in the interest of the rich against the poor. Lenin persuaded the Central Committee of his party to vote for revolution, and the date was set for November 7. With almost no resistance, the Bolshevik forces seized key positions in Petrograd—railway stations, bridges, banks, and government buildings. Blood was shed only at the Winter Palace, and casualties there totaled one Red soldier and five Red sailors. The easy victory of the Bolsheviks did not mean that they commanded the support of all the Russian people, or even the majority. Nevertheless, they had the military power, which was crucial.

On March 3, 1918, the Bolshevik government signed the Brest-Litovsk Treaty with Germany, ending Russia's participation in the war. The treaty's severe terms required the surrender by Russia of Poland, the Baltic provinces, Finland, Ukraine, and parts of the Caucasus. The areas surrendered involved 62 million people and 1,250,000 million square miles of territory where, disastrously, three-fourths of Russia's iron and coal were produced. They also included half of its industrial plants and a third of its crop area. In this manner Russia dropped out of World War I, and the new Bolshevik rulers proceeded to organize the Union of Soviet Socialist Republics.

Communism and Russia

This brief history of Russia has pointed out that Russia was for many centuries separated, geographically and politically, from the development of western civilization and culture, and thus came late into what, for most of Europe, would be called the modern age. But the eighteenth and nineteenth centuries permitted a very considerable progress in the modernization of Russian society. By the time the country was overtaken by the First World War, its situation was not discouraging. Industrialization was proceeding at a level only two or three decades behind that of the United States. Under implementation was a program of education reform, and the first really promising program for the modernization of Russian agriculture was proceeding steadily and with good chances for ultimate success.

Still to be overcome as the war interceded were many archaic features in the system of government, among them the absolutism of the crown, the absence of any proper parliamentary institutions, and the inordinate powers of the secret police. Still to be overcome, too, was the problem of the non-Russian nationalities within the Russian Empire. This empire, like other multinational and multilingual political empires, was rapidly becoming an anachronism; the maintenance of it was beginning to come under considerable pressure. None of these problems, however, called for a violent revolution and there was hope Russia might proceed to a successful and reasonably peaceful advance into the modern age. This expectation, however, was shattered by the Revolution in the fall of 1917.

By mid-1917 the die was cast. The stresses of the first two and a half years of war with the collapse of the army and society led to the seizure of power by Lenin and his associates. This set up the communist dictatorship—which was to fasten itself on a defenseless and unprepared Russian society. It is difficult to summarize what this has meant to a long suffering Russia, but happily this period of Russian history has ended.

To begin with, the Bolsheviks destroyed the culturally important elements of society, to use their jargon word the "bourgeois" intelligentsia. Stalin later completed the process by doing the same to most of the Marxist intelligentsia that remained. Thus Lenin and Stalin managed, between the two of them, to eliminate a very large portion of the rather formidable cultural community that had come into being in the final decades of czardom.

Not content with these heavy blows to the country's intellectual and cultural substance, Stalin, as soon as his power was consolidated in 1928, turned to the peasantry and proceeded to inflict upon this great portion of the population (some 80 percent at that time) an even more terrible injury. In his sweeping campaign of collectivization, Stalin in 1929 set out to eliminate the most productive farmers by ruthless confiscation of what little property most of its members possessed, by deportation and by the punishment—in many cases the execution—of those who resisted.

The results were simply calamitous. They included a major famine in certain key agricultural regions of the country and the loss, within a short time, of some two-thirds of the country's livestock. A blow was dealt to Russian agriculture that set it back by decades, and from which it has not fully recovered to the present day. There was then unleashed upon Soviet society that terrible and almost incomprehensible series of events known historically as "the purges." Beginning with an obvious effort on Stalin's part to remove from office and destroy all those remnants from the Lenin leadership in whom he suspected even the slightest traces of resistance to his personal rule, these initial efforts, grew into a massive wave of reprisals against a great portion of those who at that time were taking any part in the governing of the country.

A frenzy overcoming millions of innocent but frightened people ensued who had been encouraged to see in the reckless denunciation of others, even others they knew to be as guiltless as themselves the only possible assurance of their own immunity to arrest and punishment. In the course of this hysteria, friend was set against friend, neighbor against neighbor, colleague against colleague, brother against brother, and child against parent, until most of Soviet society was reduced to a quivering mass of terror and panic.

It was then on a shaken, badly depleted, socially and spiritually weakened Russian people that there fell, in the first years of the 1940s, the even greater strains of the Second World War. The German attack was horror on a scale that put into shade all the sufferings of the previous decades: the sweeping destruction of physical installations—dwellings, office buildings, railways, everything—in great parts of European Russia; and a loss of life the exact amount of which is not easy to determine, but which must have run to close to thirty million souls. Not unnaturally, there was hope in all quarters, as the war neared its end, that victory would be followed by a change in the habits and methods of the regime—a change that would make possible something resembling a normal relationship between ruler and ruled, and would open up new possibilities for self-expression, cultural and political, on the part of a people long deprived of any at all.

However, Stalin continued the harsh regime as it was before the war. Even Stalin's death, in 1953, brought about no sudden or drastic change in the situation. Stalinism, as a governing system, was by now far too deeply planted in Russian life to be removed or basically changed in any short space of time. There was no organized alternative to it, and no organized opposition. It took four more years before Khrushchev and his associates succeeded in removing from power those in the leadership who had been most closely associated with Stalin in the worst excesses of his rule and who would have preferred to carry on in much the same manner.

However, the government rested upon an economy that, just at the time when the remainder of the industrialized world was recovering from the war and moving into the economic revolution of the computer age, was continuing to live in many respects in the conceptual and technological world of the nineteenth century, and was consequently becoming, on the international scene, increasingly uncompetitive.

The ideology as inherited from Lenin was no longer really there to support this system. It remained as a lifeless orthodoxy, and Soviet leaders would continue on all ceremonial occasions to take recourse to its rituals and vocabulary. But it had been killed in the hearts of the people: killed by the great abuses of earlier decades, killed by the circumstances of the great war for which Marxist doctrine offered no explanations, killed by the great disillusionment that followed that war.

It began to become evident, in short, in those years of the 1970s and early 1980s that time was running out on all that was left of the great structure of power Lenin and Stalin had created. It is difficult not to see the Communist takeover of Russia in 1917 in any light but a disaster of major proportions for the Russian people on whom it was imposed.

The postcommunist Russia we now have before us finds itself not only confronted with, but heavily involved in, the Herculean effort to carry out fundamental changes in the national life of the country. It must shift political power from the Communist party to a basically democratic government. It also must shift the economy from a centralized to a decentralized free enterprise system. And also it must change the Czarist empire into one comprised of national components. If successfully carried through, these changes would constitute the greatest watershed in Russian life since the Peter the Great's reforms of the early eighteenth century.

What is now emerging on the territory traditionally known as Russia will not be—cannot be—the Russia of the czars. Nor can it be the Russia of the communists. It can only be something essentially new, the contours of which are still, for us and for the Russians themselves, obscure. The collapse of Communism is a vast and historic transformation equal to the French Revolution for France and even the end of the Roman Empire in the West. What is more, this era of change is happening when the whole world is undergoing great change involving the new global economy and cultural interchange. The Soviet empire has been replaced with a Russian state; Communist dictatorship has given way to democratization, and the centralized state-controlled economy has been transformed into a market economy, however imperfect, with predominantly private ownership. Arbitrary repression has ended and has been followed by a struggle between rising crime and an emergent rule of law. Spiritually, Communist ideology has withered away. The question now is what will replace it, for the meeting of the new demands the Russian people are today poorly prepared. A great deal will have to be started from scratch. The road will be long, rough and perilous. The Russian people have made great efforts and contributions in the past. It has shown that they are a people of many talents, capable of rendering significant contributions, spiritual, intellectual and aesthetic to the development of world civilization. They have the potential for doing it again—in a better future. And we must make every effort to help them to a better future. *1st Test*

▶ AFRICA

The continent of Africa is effectively divided in two. The northern coast along the shores of the Mediterranean was a participant in the cultural developments of mankind throughout the days of the Greeks and Romans. And before the height of Greeks and Romans, there had developed along the Nile river one of the first of the great river civilizations. Throughout medieval history North Africa played an important role in the great European and Islamic cultures. We will not discuss further this part of Africa, which is included in western and Islamic culture sections.

South of the Mediterranian coastal regions stretches the Sahara desert which proved an effective barrier that restricted the influence of the Mediterranean cultures in the north from spreading south. In 641 AD Egypt fell to the Arabs and all of North Africa was Arab or Muslim by 711 AD. From then on, all of Africa received some Muslim influence. South of the Sahara in West Africa, Ghana was conquered by the Muslims and thereafter, West Africa was dominated by Muslim states.

Sub Sahara Africa (which from now on we'll refer to merely as Africa) had a history of contact with the European and Asian cultures. From Vasco da Gama's circumnavigation of Africa on his way to India in 1497–1498, the outline of the African continent was known by the Europeans.

However, the Europeans were much slower in influencing and colonizing Africa than they had been in America. Africa remained unexplored, and the "Dark Continent" centuries after the other newly discovered continents had been opened up and colonized. As late as 1865, when the Civil War was ending in the United States, only the coastal fringe of Africa was known, together with a few isolated sections of the interior. Even by 1900, about a fourth of the interior of Africa remained unexplored.

Why did Africa remain so isolated? One reason is that large portions of the continent's coasts have an inhospitable climate, and it was these portions that the Europeans first encountered.

The continent is also extraordinarily inaccessible. One reason is that the coastline, unbroken by bays, gulfs, or inland seas, is even shorter than Europe's, though Africa has three times the area. Africa's inaccessibility was increased by a formidable barrier in the north made up of the great Sahara Desert and the Nile marshes. Europeans set up some outposts on the West Coast of Africa in order to obtain slaves for the plantations of Brazil, the Caribbean and North America, but initially no great effort was made to go to the interior.

Geography, however, was not the only factor that hindered European penetration. At least as important was the fact that the African peoples' general level of social, political, and economic organization was high enough for them to effectively resist the Europeans for centuries. (See Figure 7-2.)

African Culture

The cultures of Africa were the outcome of a much greater degree of interaction with the outside world than had been possible in the Americas. For ex-

ample, the great majority of the plants that eventually were cultivated in Africa were from Mesopotamia and Egypt via the Nile—barley, wheat, peas, and lentils; from Southeast Asia—bananas, sugar cane, the Asian yam, and new forms of rice; and later from the New World—tobacco, corn, lima and string beans, pumpkins, and tomatoes.

As basic for Africa as the introduction of agriculture was that of iron metallurgy. Some archeologists believe that it came across the Sahara from Carthage or up the Nile valley from the Assyrians.

Agriculture and iron metallurgy had a profound influence on Africa. Population increased and those who were able to take the most advantage of these developments were the Negroes, rather than the Pygmies of the rain forest or the Bushmen of the inaccessible south. Shifting back and forth across the continent, colliding and mingling with each other, then moving off to form new groups, these migrants soon dominated the whole central and southern part of Africa. They ousted the less developed Bushmen and Pygmies, and united Africa in a huge family of related languages, the Bantu, which today are spoken over most of the continent south of the equator. In the process they created a complicated and diversified culture.

Leaders of this expansion were the Bantu, a Negroid linguistic group. Starting from their original center in the West African Highlands, they infiltrated around 100 AD into the Congo basin, where they developed a relationship with the sparse Pygmy hunters. From there some pushed southeast to the fertile, open Lakes country of central Africa, between AD 600 and 900. Then they continued southward across the savanna at the expense of the Bushmen. These migrations explain why the Negroes were the predominant ethnic group by the time the Europeans arrived in the 1500s, whereas a thousand years earlier they had shared Africa fairly evenly with the Bushmen and Pygmies.

Another basic influence on African culture was the faith of Islam. The many contributions came partly from the Muslim colonies along the East African coast, but much more from North Africa. Contacts with North Africa increased greatly when the Arabs overran North Africa in the seventh century AD Later the Muslims also extended their influence down Africa's east coast, first as merchants, and from the thirteenth century onward, as colonists.

FIGURE 7-2 Africa is very large—more than three times the area of the U.S. (including Alaska and Hawaii).

From their bases on the northern and eastern coasts of the continent, the Muslim Arabs exerted a profound influence on Africa. They used the camel, much more than did the Romans, and correspondingly expanded the trans-Saharan trade. Likewise on the east coast they traded with the interior for ivory, gold, slaves and later, iron ore.

Commercial contacts led to Muslim cultural penetration. Islam spread down the east coast as far as Zanzibar, and sometimes beyond. From the Mediterranean coast it spread south across the Sahara into the Sudan. As is usually the case with the diffusion of a new faith, Islam was adopted first by the ruling class and then seeped through to the people. In this manner, an important part of Negro Africa was Islamized and became part of the vast Muslim world.

The Islamization of Africa directly south of the Sahara is obvious to this day in such things as names, dress, household equipment, architectural styles, festivals, and the like. Islam also greatly stimulated the intellectual life of the Sudan. Literacy was spread with the establishment of schools for study of the Koran. State building also proceeded in the area just south of the Sahara in East Africa.

Three great empires emerged in that region: Ghana (700–1200), Mali (1200–1500), and Songhai (1350–1600). The Songhai empire stretched almost 1,500 miles from east to west, and in this expanse the rule of law and a common administrative system were given to many diverse subjects. Songhai's outstanding ruler, Askia the Great (1493–1528) was one of the foremost monarchs of his time—the equal of contemporary European kings and superior to many in humaneness, religious tolerance, and devotion to learning.

These empires, which at one point boasted a culture comparable to those of their European contemporaries, fell behind in modern times partly because of the invasions from the north. These invasions proved to be devastating and stunted cultural growth.

Largely because Africa was broken up into many parts, the level of general development varied greatly from region to region. Political units went from village communities that recognized only local chieftains to the great empires of the Sudan. Economically, the range was as great also: from the food-gathering Bushmen-Hottentot-Pygmies to the West Africans with their flourishing agriculture and extensive trade. When the Europeans first came to Africa, they traded with the West Africans, who being advanced, had the most to trade. And because they were advanced, the West Africans were able to hold their own against the Europeans much better than had the American Indians.

One great advantage the African had over the unfortunate Indians of the Americas was that, through frequent contacts, they had developed immunity to European diseases, (we will talk in the section on the Americas how disease wiped out the Indians) whereas the Europeans had developed none against the tropical diseases of the African coasts.

Thus for centuries the Africans were able to control the terms under which they traded with the Europeans. The coastal chieftains refused to allow the Europeans to go inland because they themselves wanted to monopolize their profitable position as middlemen between European buyers on the coasts and the producers in the interiors.

So Africa, apart from certain coastal regions, remained largely independent of Europe until the late 1800s. In the last two decades of that century, however, the European powers made up for lost time. They divided up virtually the entire continent and exploited its resources. By 1914 the African peoples had, in many respects, come under European influence even more than had the Asians, though many areas in the interior continued to live as before and were little influenced by European culture.

Slavery

For centuries the most valuable of African resources for Europeans were the slaves. Slavery had been an established and accepted institution in Africa prior to the Europeans. Prisoners of war had been enslaved, as were also debtors and individuals guilty of serious crimes. But these slaves usually were treated as part of the family. So slavery was not a western invention. And it cannot be denied that the wholesale shipment of Africans to the slave plantations of the Americas was made possible by the participation of African chiefs who rounded up their fellow Africans and sold them at a good profit to European ship captains waiting along the coasts.

Nevertheless, the Atlantic slave trade under the Europeans was on a scale of quantity and cruelty apart from that existing in Africa. The slavery of the Europeans was an economic institution, and they were quite willing to work their slaves to death if it was more profitable to do so rather than treat them humanely. This impersonal attitude was reinforced by racism when the Europeans became involved in the African slave trade on a large scale. Perhaps as a subconscious rationalization, they gradually came to look down on Negroes as inherently inferior, and therefore destined to serve their white masters.

The real stimulus to the rapid growth of the slave trade was the rise in the Americas of plantations. There was urgent need for labor, especially on the sugar plantations. The market for slaves was almost limitless, and several countries entered the slave trade to share in the rich profits. Portugal dominated the trade in the sixteenth century; Holland, during most of the seventeenth; and Britain, in the eighteenth.

The horrors of the slave trade are well documented. But just to underline the horrors, it is estimated of the 18 million slaves were imported to the Americas; many times that number were casualties due to mistreatment. This slave trade continued for four hundred years.

In England the Society for the Abolition of the Slave Trade was established in 1787. The movement was helped by the progress of the industrial revolution which was making slavery obsolete. Slaves were needed in labor intensive agriculture. The first success of the abolitionists was a law in 1807 prohibiting British ships from participating in the slave trade and banning the landing of slaves in British colonies. In 1833 Parliament passed a decree that completely abolished slavery on British territory. They further persuaded other European governments to follow its example in allowing British warships to seize slave ships flying other flags. Finally, slavery was abolished in the Americas, in the United States in 1863, Brazil in 1888, and the remaining states soon after.

The abolition of slavery helped open up Africa. Many Europeans hoped to develop "legitimate" or regular commerce that would replace the traffic in slaves. At the same time, a growing fad for geography and unexplored land combined to make Africa in late 1800s a center of European interest and exploration. With the termination of the European slave trade, most of the coastal footholds were abandoned. European leaders during this early period repeatedly stated their opposition to the acquisition of colonies.

After 1870 there was a sharp reversal of this anticolonial attitude. Colonies now were regarded as assets for the mother country, and the continent of Africa, being unoccupied and defenseless, became the focus of interest. The pattern was set by Leopold, King of the Belgians. His agents signed treaties with chiefs handing over 900,000 square miles to the International Association of the Congo, a new organization set up under Leopold's direction. The chiefs had no way of knowing that signing the pieces of paper and accepting token payments meant permanent loss of their tribal lands.

The immediate effect of Leopold's maneuvering was to jolt the other European leaders to action. The French already had sent their famous explorer Count de Brazza to the lower Congo, and he was able to acquire for his country the lands to the north of the river. The Germans also entered the race, obtaining in 1884 South-West Africa, Togoland, and the Cameroons. In the end, the entire continent was partitioned off into European control in the following 20 years. Except for the small republic of Liberia on the west coast, by 1914 Ethiopia was the only independent state on the whole continent. Even Liberia, set up in 1822 as a settlement for freed American Negroes, became a virtual U.S. protectorate in 1911 because of bankruptcy and internal disorders. The partitioning was carried out with little fighting. And where that was necessary, the conquering forces usually consisted of only one to two thousand men, mostly Africans, trained and led by European officers. Economic reasons drove the partitioning of Africa and drastic economic changes followed.

The industrialized west had need for raw materials and found them in the interior of Africa: first the diamonds and gold in South Africa, the gold and copper in Rhodesia and gold, copper and diamonds in the Congo. European and American companies bought vast plantations in such regions as the Congo, the Cameroons, and French Equatorial Africa. The Firestone Corporation in 1926 was given a ninety-year lease on 100,000 acres of land in Liberia.

Also, foreign settlers took over much of the good agricultural land. European settlers flocked in, particularly to Southern Rhodesia and East Africa. Before long they had gained possession of the most desirable agricultural properties in these regions.

To transport the minerals and the agricultural commodities now being produced, the Europeans proceeded to build a network of railways in Africa, as they already had done in Asia. All of these economic developments naturally had profound effects on the native peoples.

Forced to work for wages on the white man's plantation, or leave their families in order to work in the mines, their traditional economic independence was reduced. Africans were involved more and more in a money economy and the world economy. They were also everywhere working for the white "boss."

Cultural Impact of the Europeans

Together with the European traders, investors, and settlers came the European missionaries. Missionaries came with the avowed purpose of changing the African way of life. They used three instruments to carry this out: education, medicine, and religion. Schools offering a western education and western ideals were an integral part of every mission station. These schools were particularly influential since most colonial governments left the job of education to the missionaries. In many ways these schools were very constructive, teaching how to build better houses, improve agriculture and the rudiments of sanitation and personal hygiene. On the other hand, they often taught that the traditional way of life was primitive and wrong. In time the students listened less to their parents and elders and more to their European teachers, whom they learned to respect.

The missions also brought medical knowledge and facilities that saved the lives of many Africans. But besides saving lives, medicine also forced Africans to question their traditional ideas of what caused illness and death. Whites had the power to make people well even after the proper petitioning of spirits had not worked. So traditional religion no longer could be counted on to meet all emergencies and to provide all the answers, and to hold together the African way of life.

Politically, Europe left a mark that still haunts Africa today. When the boundaries of the various colonies were drawn, no attention was paid to the African people concerned. Hence single cultures often found themselves under the rule of two or even three European powers. Boundaries are still artificial and causing Africa problems today.

On the surface, the Africans retained their traditional political institutions. They still had their councils of elders, their laws, their courts, and their chiefs. But in practice this political structure was undermined. The chiefs could be appointed or removed by the local European administrators, and their decisions no longer had the force of law since tribespeople could go over their heads to the European officials, whose word was final.

Another factor undermining African traditions were their own people who earned money by working in cities or mines and acquired a status and independence that would have been inconceivable had they remained in their villages. In some cases, these newly rich people actually had more prestige and power than the old chiefs. Old ways were questioned.

Finally, a more serious threat to traditional tribal certainty and custom came from the class of European-educated Africans that gradually developed in almost all the colonies. They tended to challenge not only the native chiefs but also the European officials. They did so because they had learned in western schools certain political ideas such as individual liberty and political freedom, and they saw no reason why the principles of liberalism and nationalism should apply to Europe but not to Africa. They were also goaded into political agitation by the discrimination they frequently encountered in government and private employment. Usually they were not allowed to be more than poorly paid clerks in European firms or very minor officials in the colonial administration. Again, they could not see why, when they had the required education and experience, they should be kept in subordinate positions simply because their skins were dark.

The historical record is complex, but it is fair to say that when the Europeans first came to Africa there were coherent, functioning societies of varying degrees of sophistication, some of great political subtlety and artistic accomplishment, others simple hunting and gathering communities, some extremely cruel in their practices, but all possessing their own integrity and integrated into the natural environment of the continent. This was destroyed by colonialism.

What followed was exploitation on the one hand, including the atrocious trade in slaves, and on the other hand more or less sincere attempts at

Western-style education, "uplift," and religious salvation of "pagan" Africans so they could be remade culturally as European, assumed to be the most advanced form of civilization. Whatever the merits of the latter project (and it was also the project of the first generation of independent African leaders, all products of European education and politics), the colonizers did not stay in Africa long enough for it to have the faintest chance of succeeding. Colonialism lasted long enough to destroy the pre-existing social and political institutions, but not long enough to put anything solid and lasting in their place.

After the end of the second world war (1945), the colonial period came to an abrupt and dramatic end. Up until this time, national movements of liberation had a short history and were generally quite weak. Ten years after the end of the war, the liberation movements started. Thirty-one African countries won their independence. The few remaining colonies in turn got rid of foreign rule during the following years. The African saw other countries such as India gaining their independence and naturally asked why they, too, should not be rid of colonialism. The question became acute with the return of the war veterans, large numbers of whom had served the French in Europe and the British in Burma and the Middle East. All these factors combined to shake up and awaken tropical Africa.

Africa until recently has been surrounded by a lack of information. Often because of this lack of knowledge and the difficulty of understanding cultures different from their own, Africans have been judged inferior beings, and basically uncivilized. On the contrary, its people have had a long and lively history, and have made an impressive contribution to man's general mastery of the world. They have created cultures and civilizations, evolved systems of government and systems of thought, and pursued the inner life of the spirit with a dedication that has produced some of the finest art known to man.

The African Achievement

It is now clear from archeological studies and the piecing together of written records that Africa has had a long and fruitful record of achievement. Beneath its often primitive surface lay a profound and complicated cultural development. Far from being the helpless victims of their own ignorance, Africans had actually gone far toward taming their continent long before Europeans appeared on the scene. This achievement, so essential to survival, rested upon social and cultural advances of great antiquity. They depended upon spiritual values, and these spiritual values enabled Africans to build close-knit societies without which they might have perished. Thus Africa's evolution was inspired by forces comparable to those that inspire every other branch of the human family.

In a sense we are all Africans. It appears that Africa was in all likelihood the birthplace of mankind. From the evidence of fossil skulls and bone fragments found in the last few decades, some of man's most remote ancestors apparently inhabited the high inland plains of eastern Africa almost two million years ago.

North of the Sahara barrier emerged the high civilization of Egypt, nourishing and nourished by an interchange of ideas with the whole Mediterranean community. South of it people worked out their destiny alone. Much of the wide middle region of the continent has been infested since earliest times by the tsetse fly, a carrier of sleeping sickness among men and a comparable fever among their cattle. Riverbanks and plains alike are plagued by the malaria-carrying mosquito. And there is yellow fever.

Up to about 500 BC people south of the Sahara continued to live in primitive simplicity, few in number and always on the move in search of food. Then came a second phase, marked by a momentous discovery: how to mine, refine and work metals, especially iron. This occurred about the time of the birth of Christ.

With iron-tipped tools and weapons, rapid progress took place. Farming became easier, and hunting a less precarious operation. Larger and more dependable food supplies led to the growth of populations, and of more complex societies. Communities that became overpopulated in a given area left to start new communities.

In their contacts with Africa, westerners continue to misjudge it. Africans were different. They were a different color, they dressed differently and, probably most important of all, their values were different. To Europeans caught up in technology and science, it was easy to assume that Africa's technological simplicity was a sign of backwardness in everything else. Though far behind Europe in their technical knowledge, Africans are now known to have been skillfully inventive in many ways. They developed tropical farming techniques that have scarcely been bettered to this day. They were good miners and metal workers, producing, among other things, a steady supply of the gold that went into medieval European currencies, and without which those currencies might well have been impossible. They were sharp businessmen, as more than one non-African merchant had occasion to know. They operated political and social systems of considerable flexibility and sophistication. They were superb sculptors.

In community attitudes Africans joined people together as equals in moral rules that guided social behavior and in beliefs that exalted the spiritual aspects of life above the material. The African village achieved a kind of social harmony that often functioned without any need for centralized authority. This, in fact, was where Africa best displayed its real genius—in its capacity for social organization. It was a talent that operated at village level and in complex kingdoms. And it operated continuously, throughout a stubborn peoples' long, lonely and determined effort to tame their vast and inhospitable land. In its special way the achievement of Africa ranks with history's other examples of the greatness of man.

Where and how have Africans contributed to the sum of man's achievements? Of major importance was the African influence in the Americas. The history of the United States and Brazil would have been a very different one without the great contribution made by African labor, African arts and African skills. The African's role in the growth of the sugar and tobacco plantations is well known. Less familiar is the African contribution in other fields. At least until the early nineteenth century, the mines of Brazil were mainly worked by Africans who had learned their skill at home.

The African-Americans also lent something of the traditional African style to the many American crafts in which they engaged. If the slaves made many things that Africa had never known, they nevertheless created them with the artistry and skill that derived from their native culture. Few others dealt in the raw material of human nature with more subtlety or ease, or so successfully welded the

interests of the community and the individual. The Africans practiced the art of social happiness, and they practiced it brilliantly.

Out of this there came a number of attitudes, characteristics, and talents that the rest of the world has come to recognize as uniquely African. Among these are enduring gaiety of temperament (so often noted that it has become a cliche, but a true characteristic nonetheless), a certain indomitable optimism and tolerance, a joy in esthetic forms, colors, and sounds, and a genius for producing these.

These attitudes and characteristics have probably had more impact on the western world than those of any other non-western culture. They have influenced its painting and sculpture (as in the case of Picasso and his followers) its music (by way of American Negro jazz, blues and spirituals), and its way of looking at life (this also chiefly by way of the Negro American's intimate contact with white Americans).

Africa Today

For Africa, the last 25 years have been a period of unfortunate economic, social and environmental decline. Starting in 1980, depressed world commodity prices, declining agricultural production, ravaging drought and desertification, rising external debt, and both civil and interstate warfare indicated continent-wide disaster. Throughout the 1980s per capita income fell from a level already the lowest in two decades. From a continent with high hopes of recovery the reality has been that human conditions in Africa have continued to deteriorate.

Former U.N. Secretary-General Javier Perez de Cuellar lamented that the trend in Africa was "not to recovery and development but to drift and stagnation, if not a chronic state of crisis." Large parts of Africa are being reduced to chaos by drought, administrative incapacity, political instability and tribal confrontations. The Congolese author Ange Severin Malanda says, "From now on, the danger in several parts of the continent is of pure destruction or generalized destabilization. The destabilization is already evident in Somalia, Liberia, and Angola. The pure destruction began to be realized in Rwanda on the sixth of April 1994, annihilating every contemporary African standard of reference. Genocide there accomplished the unimaginable and the unlimited."

The unfolding tragedy in Africa must eventually cause Americans to pay attention to things African. In Africa accelerating deforestation and desertification, spreading malnutrition and disease (including AIDS), debilitating warfare in potentially rich agricultural countries such as Angola, Ethiopia and Sudan, deteriorating terms of trade and soaring international debt are combining to make Africa a human and environmental disaster area. The crisis is so complicated and of such magnitude that the United States and the world at large are avoiding getting involved.

▶ THE AMERICAS

I. Precolumbian—to 1500
II. Colonial—1500 to 1820
III. Modern—1820 to present

I. America before the Europeans
Chronology

25,000 BC	The arrival of man in the Americas
3,000 BC	The successful domestication of corn
1,000 BC	The beginning of Olmec culture
500 BC	The rise of Teotihuacan
0	The beginnings of the Mayas
700 AD	The fall of Teotihuacan to the Chichimecs, ancestors of the Toltecs and Aztecs
900 AD	Collapse of the Mayan culture
950 AD	The rise of the Toltecs
1000 AD	Toltecs overwhelm remaining Mayan culture
1160 AD	Toltecs destroyed by fellow Chichimecs, the Aztecs
1400 AD	The rise of the Incas in Peru
1519 AD	Cortez arrives in Mexico
1527 AD	Pizarro arrives in Peru

A world separated from the main developments in Europe, Asia and Africa developed independently in the Americas. Estimates of the population in the New World prior to Columbus vary today between 43 and 72 million in both North and South America. Most were concentrated in the three great civilizations of the Aztecs, Mayas and Incas, with the population outside these cultures spread thinly over large areas. The most remarkable thing about the ancient American civilizations was their independent development. All the European and Asian cultures, from Rome to Japan, developed in direct or indirect contact with each other. Ideas, inventions, knowledge and goods circulated among them for thousands of years, contributing to the growth of each culture.

The Americans, however, remained outside this cultural interchange. When in the early 1500s the Europeans arrived, the native American culture collapsed. Within a few years, millions died from famine, warfare, slavery and, above all, the European diseases to which they had never developed an immunity, living as they did isolated from the rest of the world.

The rise of the native Americans from savagery to sophisticated culture, to their ultimate downfall in the face of the Europeans is a fascinating story, although in many areas such as the Incas of Peru, no written records were left. Still today many Inca records remain undecipherable.

The earliest records of American history are vague, but one thing is certain: man is not native to the New World. There are no apes at all in the Americas. Anthropologists agree that the remote ancestors of the American Indians evolved in the Old World. They settled the New World during the last stage of the Ice Age, and they did so only after they acquired cultural equipment—clothing, shelter, tools—adequate to keep them alive in cold climates. They came in small bands from Siberia across the Bering Strait into Alaska. Perhaps they used boats or rafts of some sort, or crossed the water gap on the winter ice. Sometimes the strait was dry land because water withdrawn from the oceans by the Ice Age glaciers lowered the sea level by more than 200 feet.

These immigrants were generally of mongoloid stock. (See Figure 7-3.) The oldest traces of man in the Americas that can be definitely dated are about 23,000 years old. Early life must have been very primitive and dangerous for a very thinly spread population. The first progress toward agriculture was made in Mexico or slightly south, and many finds in once-inhabited caves tell step by step how it was done.

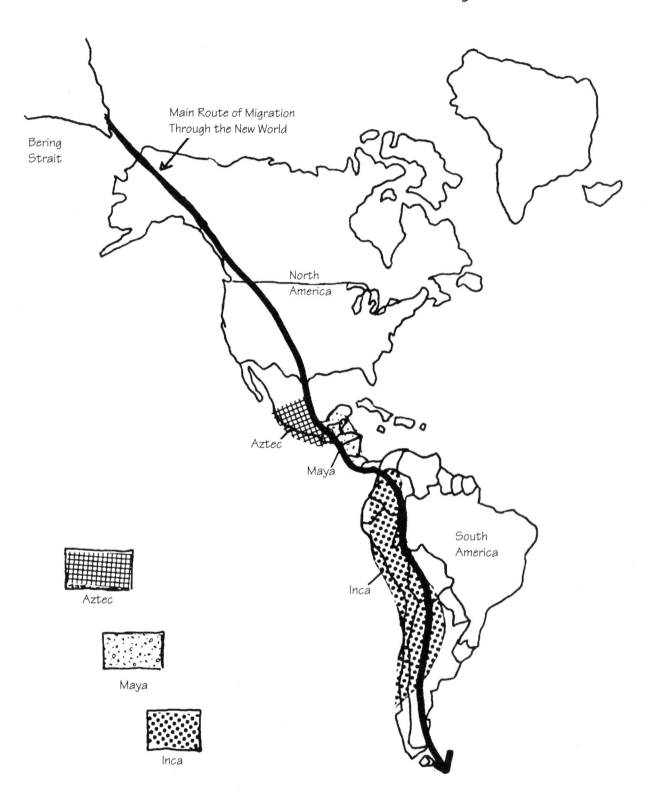

FIGURE 7-3 Main route of migration through the New World and the location of the three main pre-Colombian civilizations.

About 3000 BC a tiny primitive variety of cultivated corn (maize) made its first appearance, in various parts of Mexico, and steadily grew in size and cultivation. The origin of domesticated corn had been for years a favorite puzzle for botanists. Cultivated corn cannot seed itself; if the ears are left unharvested, the seeds or kernels do not scatter and grow; they remain wrapped in the tight husk and eventually die. No wild corn that could seed itself had ever been found. The explanation was found in mud layers 80,000 years old where wild corn had left its trace.

In layers dated about 5,000 BC cobs were found about an inch long, about 2900 BC. These had grown to two or three inches long, surely the result of cultivation. After 3,000 BC the cultivated corn was productive enough to support a considerable population on its cultivation. By 2,000 BC the magical crop was well established in most parts of Middle America and was moving across the Isthmus of Panama and on to South America.

The first plants domesticated in South America were different; root crops such as white and sweet potatoes. But it was not long before the best domesticated plants of each main region moved into favorable parts of the other region.

To follow the interchange of crops between the old and new worlds gives some idea of the value of cultural interchange. The crop plants domesticated by the ancient Indian farmers of Middle and South America now play a vital role in feeding the modern world. Corn is a primary food in most countries that are not too cold and sunless for its cultivation. It even competes with the native rice in parts of the Far East. White potatoes developed by the highland Indians of Peru have become such a firmly established staple in lands with coolish climates that it is hard to imagine life there without them. Sweet potatoes of the South American tropical forest are equally important in warm countries. Kidney beans (Mexican) are the poor man's source of protein nearly everywhere except the Far East. Peanuts (Peruvian) are not only an important industrial crop in many places, but they are an essential part of the diet in large parts of Africa. In addition, the long list of Indian contributions of the world's food includes lima beans, tomatoes, peppers, most kinds of squash and pumpkins, avocados, cocoa, pineapples and many lesser crops. Tobacco was widely cultivated in ancient America when the early explorers arrived, and they quickly introduced it into Europe.

For a thousand years, between 2000 and 1000 BC, the agricultural villages made progress slowly. They grew bigger and more numerous, fired better pottery, raised more and better crops and expanded into new territory. By 1000 BC, a firm agricultural base for civilization reached along a strip from central Mexico to southern Peru, more than 4,000 miles in all, but nothing that resembled true civilization had yet appeared. All of this changed rapidly around the year 1000 BC.

Until very recently no one knew when or where the first civilizations in Middle America (Mexico and northern Central America) got their start. Enormous pyramids and ruins were well scattered over central and southern Mexico which the Indians referred to as places where gods once came to earth.

Gradually archeologists have identified a mother culture that developed along the Gulf Coast of Mexico that existed for more than one thousand years without fundamental change. The creators of the ancient Gulf Coast culture, generally called Olmecs, are of uncertain origin. It is now believed the beginning of their culture dates from around 1000 BC—or 500 years before the height of Greece, discussed earlier.

Teotihuacan, Toltecs and Aztecs

The greatest achievement of the Olmecs was their invention of the system of religious leadership that was the basis of all Middle American civilization. The Middle American Indians were deeply religious, and remain so to this day. Most likely the peasants freely gave their corn to the great shrines and willingly pulled the great stone blocks on their way to building the huge monuments of the religious centers. Revolts were apparently rare and the idea of the ceremonial center as a social control mechanism spread to many parts of Middle America.

When Olmec influence began to expand, the mountain-isolated Valley of Mexico, where Mexico City now stands, was remote from the mainstream of cultural development. But here, the future home of the Toltecs and Aztecs, Olmec's influence penetrated. There is evidence Olmec missionaries reached the valley before 500 BC and established themselves as spiritual leaders.

From developments in the Valley of Mexico grew the great Teotihuacan civilization, one of the most splendid of ancient America. Teotihuacan included an enormous pyramid complex, 30 miles northeast of today's Mexico City. They can be visited today and are the most spectacular archeological sight in Mexico and one of the most impressive in the world.

Religious ceremonies in this setting must have been awe-inspiring. Crowds of pilgrims from distant places watched the solemn priests, all feather, gold and jewels, as they paraded across the courts to the the beat of drums and climbed in procession up the steep stairs of the pyramids. Around this great religious center stretched for miles more modest buildings and courtyards. These provided living space for at least 50,000 people. To support this way of life there must have been some great improvement in agriculture.

During its heyday Teotihuacan spread its influence to all civilized parts of Middle America, including the Mayas. Its building styles and methods were copied, many of its gods were worshiped, and its pottery and other manufactures were traded to distant places. Around 700 AD the great city fell. It was looted and burned, its people were massacred or dispersed, and its influence ceased suddenly. The city appears to have succumbed to an invasion of fierce barbarians from northern Mexico called the Chichimecs. Other civilized places held out for a while but a dark age fell gradually over most of Middle America. The Valley of Mexico itself went through a dark age and did not recover its cultural leadership for 300 years; when it did, it worshiped new and fiercer gods of the Toltecs and Aztecs.

Toltecs

A great change was taking place in the valley of Mexico brought about by the Chichimecs, the barbarians from the North who stormed over civilized Mexico for 500 years. Ancient Mexico's most celebrated and most dynamic people, the warlike Aztecs, who were at the height of their power when the Spaniards arrived, sprang from Chichimec ancestors. So did the vigorous Toltecs who preceded them—and who laid the foundations on which the Aztecs built the civilization whose savagery and splendor astonished its Spanish conquerors.

With the Toltecs, the recorded history of Mexico begins. Scraps of information about the Toltecs of Tula are preserved in the Aztec poems and legends that were memorized for many generations like the Homeric poems of the Greek Heroic Age. Around 950 AD the Toltec capital was placed at Tula beyond the Northern end of the Valley of Mexico. Their leader took the name of the old Teotihuacan god of fertility and peace, Quetzalcoatl. Tula was torn by religious conflict between devotees of the old civilized gods of Teotihuacan and those of the fierce war gods brought by the Toltecs from the savage north. The followers of the war god won, as symbolized by Quetzalcoatl's departure. Then he set out for the east coast. Before he left he promised to return from the direction of the rising sun, and he specified the date—a date corresponding to 1519 in the European calendar. This legend, known all over Middle America, was to have disastrous consequences for the Aztec civilization. By one of history's most remarkable coincidences, on the date of Quetzalcoatl's predicted reappearance the first conquistadors were to arrive in Mexico.

There are many signs that the cult of human sacrifice was widely practiced at Tula. Repeated over and over on the pyramid are carvings of an eagle, symbol of the sun, eating a human heart. Commonly the buildings were decorated with skulls and crossbones. Since skulls and crossbones are common on ancient ruins along parts of Mexico's Gulf Coast, they may well have been the inspiration for the black flag of the pirates who prowled the Caribbean in the seventeenth and eighteenth centuries.

Within a generation after Tula's founding around the middle of the tenth century, Toltec armies, probably a mixture of many different races and tribes, had spread over most of Mexico. They dominated both coasts and reached south to Guatemala and far into the country of their Chichimec ancestors in the north. About 1000 AD they achieved their most spectacular advance, sweeping into northern Yucatan and overwhelming centers where the late Maya civilization was still flourishing. The Toltecs, as ancient America's first clearly defined tribute state, set the governmental, economic and religious pattern that was to prevail throughout most of Middle America until the Spanish conquest. The Toltecs may have destroyed some Maya centers, but in return they built, with the help of

Maya artisans, a large part of the strikingly beautiful city of Chichen Itza that stands gleaming in the sun on a dry plain in northern Yucatan.

The architecture of Chichen Itza is Mayan, but there are many signs that Toltecs dominated the place, bringing with them their religion of death and human sacrifice, and their altars decorated with carved skulls. Tula was destroyed about 1160 AD, probably by another wave of the Chichimec barbarians. Warfare was continual for more than 200 years among the city-states, large and small, but none of them gained control of the whole rich valley, the key to mastery of all Middle America.

The group who finally gained dominance were a group of Chichimec descendants, the Aztecs who were destined to grow in a few centuries from a handful of savage outlaws into lords of the Valley of Mexico, with a large and gorgeous capital city and armies that exacted tribute from dozens of terrorized city-states. The Aztecs were the culmination of ancient Mexican civilization, and the climactic battle between them and the conquering Spaniards would mark the end of the native civilization.

Aztecs

Relatively secure in the water surrounding their city (Tenochtitlan) and stronghold built in Lake Texcoco of the valley of Mexico, the Aztecs, whose favorite occupation was war, could ally themselves with the city that offered the most for their help. They could not be easily reached and punished if a war went against them. The rise of the Aztecs was rapid. They built a tribute state ruthlessly. The system based on their religion worked in an unending cycle of conquest and human sacrifice. Their chief god, Huitzilopochtli, hungered for the fresh, bleeding hearts of human sacrificial victims. When the Aztecs gave them to him, he rewarded them with victories. Each victory gathered more captives, more hearts for Huitzilopochtli, more victories for the Aztecs. Decade after decade more and more captives taken in battle were led to the temple of the insatiable god. Each time Huitzilopochtli was gratified and duly scheduled for the Aztecs another success in war.

Besides taking captives from a defeated nation, the Aztecs exacted tribute in food, clothing, weapons and other things that their growing city needed. With these assets in hand, they could equip and maintain more soldiers, fight more wars and increase the flow of both captives and tribute from conquered cities. Their armies marched to the Pacific and Gulf Coasts and southward past the Isthmus of Tehuantepec, almost reaching the present boundary of Guatemala.

When the Spaniards invaded Mexico, the Aztec Empire was in the peak of its power and still expanding. Long files of captives marched toward Tenochtitlan, headed for their moments on the sacrificial stone, and armies of porters carried burdens of tribute to feed and adorn the Aztec capital.

It is helpful to put the Aztec achievement in perspective when we realize that in 1519 the time of the Spanish invasion, Tenochtitlan was five times as big as London at that time with an estimated 300,000 inhabitants. Each of the four main sections into which the city was divided had its local market, and two very large ones offered all the products of the Empire. Near the center of the city on wide canals were the palaces of the emperor, the great nobles and the high priests, and in the center itself stood the temple-pyramids and other ceremonial buildings which, in the eyes of the Aztecs, gave Tenochtitlan its reason for being.

In the center of the city was the sacred precinct, an active center whose principal product was human hearts for the gods. Nearly every enterprise of Aztec life, from crop planting to the launching of a trading expedition, called for the donation of at least one heart to win some god's favor, and during major ceremonies the great enclosure was densely crowded with priests, victims and worshippers.

The emperor in 1519 was Moctezuma II, who had ascended the throne in 1502. Basically, he was a religious intellectual dominated by doubts and worries about an Aztec culture based on war. He had deeply absorbed Toltec culture, especially those aspects that had come down to the Aztecs from the even more ancient and more peaceful era of Teotihuacan, and he knew that the gods had once been worshiped without human sacrifice and great floods of blood.

In particular he brooded about the exiled Quetzalcoatl, the giver of knowledge and all good things, who had sailed into the eastern sea and promised to return. That had been more than 500 years before, and the year when the god had said he would return was almost at hand. "What would happen then?" thought Moctezuma. Perhaps the beneficent god would vanquish the god of death and war. And then came rumors of strange men riding in white-winged ships on the eastern sea.

The rumors were correct; those were the ships of the Spaniards. In their leader, Hernan Cortez, the Emperor imagined he saw Quetzalcoatl fulfilling his promise to return. Dreading to offend a living god, Moctezuma hesitated to send his warriors to drive the invaders from Mexico. Instead, he allowed them to approach the Aztec capital of Tenochtitlan; and in so doing he opened the way to disaster and conquest.

The Mayas

At the time of Christ, the brilliant civilization of the Maya was taking shape far to the south. The Maya were a special breed with a distinctive language and the peculiar profile—sloping forehead, prominent curving nose and full lips—that is depicted on their ancient monuments and is still common among their descendants in modern Yucatan.

The Mayans appear to have drawn much from the ancient Olmec culture. The great Olmec social invention, the ceremonial center, was carried to its extreme by the Maya. Many of the Maya sites have been partially cleared and to a degree restored. If you had visited the land of the Maya around 200 AD you would have found footpaths leading to small groups of thatched houses surrounded by cornfields. Every few miles the well-trodden footpaths would lead to a minor ceremonial center with a small pyramid supporting a temple, a paved court and a few low stone buildings. At longer intervals the paths would converge and widen. We would be approaching a great city with tall pyramids with intricately carved temples painted in brilliant colors.

The Maya city-centers did not form an empire. There is no evidence of a dominant capital. They were a loose federation bound together by similarity of culture and the parallel interests of the high priests, whose power depended on their education and intellectual superiority over their peasant subjects. They had books on bark paper and other writings, most of which cannot now be read. They could count and calculate; they had invented the arithmetic concept of zero long before Europeans adopted it from the Arabs. By long-continued as-

tronomical observations they had learned to predict accurately the movements of the sun, the moon and the planet Venus. They knew the length of the year, including the final fractional day, with extraordinary precision. The calendar derived from this knowledge permitted them to carve accurate dates in stone on their major buildings.

In general, the Classic Maya period seems to have been peaceful and its people remarkably conservative. Their religious and social customs changed very little over the centuries and they accomplished their feats of building with primitive tools and techniques that show few improvements during the long life of their civilization. About 800 AD, their civilization began to decline; by 900 AD they had collapsed. All construction stopped; the great and small ceremonial centers were abandoned. The new civilization about to arise in Middle America would be even more vigorous, but harsher and in some ways less civilized. After the fall of Mexico's great city of Teotihuacan in about 700 AD came centuries of darkness and confusion for the Mayan and all Middle America.

The Incas

Another great civilization was facing European conquest as the Aztecs were falling, the Inca empire of Peru. It had developed independently and in nearly all ways was different than the civilizations of the Aztecs and Mayans. Piecing together the history of the Incas and of preconquest Peru is difficult. The Inca, in spite of their talent for government, had no written language with which to record events, and since they had risen to importance less than a century before the Spaniards overthrew them, their traditions revealed nothing about Peru's distant past.

We know that well before 1500 BC sedentary village life based on fishing, agriculture, or both, was solidly established in Peru. When cultivated corn was introduced from middle America or perhaps domesticated independently in the Peruvian highlands, it greatly increased the food supply; pottery arrived, probably from a northern source; and in the mountains the wild guanaco, a relative of the camel, was developed into the domesticated llama and alpaca.

When the Inca began their spectacular sweep along the Andes, Peruvian civilization had long been prospering. All its material technologies were far advanced. There were, naturally, many things lacking in isolated Peruvian culture that had long been commonplace in the Old World. As in Middle America, there was no knowledge of the wheel. There was no written language, only a system of keeping accounts with knotted strings called quipus—a very poor substitute. There was also no money or other convenient medium of exchange. One of the most striking things about Peruvian culture is that it developed so brilliantly without these elements, usually thought indispensable to the growth of civilization. The key was their extraordinary organizing power.

There are several versions of the origins of the Incas. The most popular recounts how the children of the Sun God came out of a cave near Cuzco and joined by a handful of followers they became the Inca, a word that originally identified a certain group of clans and that later referred to the emperor, "The Inca." Today the term is commonly used to signify all the people of the Inca Empire as well.

Like the Aztecs when they first entered civilized Mexico, the little band under Manco Capac, the first Inca leader, started out as landless wanderers, but they quickly overcame this handicap. Legends tell of colorful battles in which the early Inca were always victorious, but the fighting did not advance more than 25 miles from Cuzco. The Inca could well have fallen back into obscurity, but for the Inca Pachacuti, the actual founder of the Inca Empire. Under Pachacuti the expansion of the Empire was almost an explosion; wherever the Inca armies marched they met with victory. Though Pachacuti's armies fought ferocious battles when necessary, they often accomplished their objectives by bloodless diplomacy.

One of the most effective unifying devices employed by Pachacuti and later Inca rulers was the extension of Quechua, the language of the Cuzco region, as a common language. Just as English spread around the world with the expanding British Empire, Quechua marched with the Inca armies. It was made the formal medium of communication between the conquerors and the polyglot population and was taught to local chieftains and young people. (Refer to Chapter 3 on Language as Culture Element.)

As the empire expanded, its roads expanded with it. There had long been roads of varying qual-

ity in Peru, but the Inca improved them, linked them together and engineered them according to the terrain. On flat coastal deserts these routes might be no more than twin lines of guideposts while in settled districts they were often walled and bordered with shade trees. Swamps were crossed by earthen viaducts pierced with culverts for drainage, and in the rugged Andes the roads were carried across ravines on suspension bridges and either around high spurs or through them by means of tunnels. On steep slopes they zigzagged to reduce the grade, just as modern Peruvian highways climb in dizzy sequences of tight hairpin turns. In some of the steepest sections they became long stairways cut in the rocky mountainsides. Since they carried no wheeled traffic, only pack llamas and people on foot, the Inca roads were often no more than three feet wide, but they were frequently paved with stone and supported when necessary by solidly built retaining walls. The capital city Cuzco was completely rebuilt into a magnificent capital.

A great plaza occupied the city's center and about it stood imposing temples and other ceremonial buildings. Here, too, were the palaces of the Inca, the houses of the nobles, the offices of administrators and trained interpreters of the knotted-string quipus. The more important of the temples and royal edifices were plated with sheets of gold that gleamed in the bright Andean sunlight, and the first Spaniards who entered the city must have gasped in disbelief. The Incas spread their empire north, south, east to the jungle and west to the ocean, to the limit. When Topa Inca, the great conqueror, died in Cuzco in 1493 after a few peaceful years spent consolidating the Empire, he had no way of knowing that during the year before his death the three ships of Christopher Columbus, loaded with disease, had made their first landfall in the New World, and a few years later the mighty Inca empire would be conquered.

The Inca in 1525 was residing in Quito when he heard rumors that white-sailed ships from the north were exploring the coast of Peru. Shortly after, a great plague was raging through the empire. The plague may have been smallpox, measles or some other European disease deadly to Indians without natural resistance. It may have spread from the Spaniards in Panama or perhaps it traveled overland from forts built by Spanish explorers probing

South America's Atlantic Coast. Well before Pizarro and his audacious conquistadors attacked Peru, that great European helper, disease, had struck a crippling blow.

Three Civilizations

The three major American civilizations were the Mayan (in present-day Yucatan, Guatemala, and Belize), the Aztec (in present-day Mexico), and the Inca (stretching for 3,000 miles from mid-Ecuador to mid-Chile). (See Figure 7-3.)

The Mayan civilization was outstanding for its extraordinary development of the arts and sciences. Its accomplishments included a unique stone architecture, a sculpture that ranks among the great art of all times; an ideographic writing in which characters of signs were used as conventional symbols for ideas; and a knowledge of the movements of heavenly bodies, which showed the Mayans to be better astronomers than any in contemporary Europe and as competent mathematicians.

The Aztecs were brusque and warlike compared to the artistic and intellectual Mayans—a contrast reminiscent of that between the Romans and the Greeks in the Old World. The Aztecs paid more attention to the army, training all able-bodied men for war and holding them liable for military service. Their state also was better organized, including a well-developed judiciary and arrangements for the care of the needy.

The Incas were even more advanced than the Aztecs in their material accomplishments. Their remarkable roads, fortresses, and temples were built of great blocks of stone so perfectly joined that eve now, nearly 500 years later, a knife cannot be inserted between them. An extensive irrigation system, parts of which are still in use, made the Inca Empire a flourishing agricultural area. Above all the Incas organized the only integrated and dynamic state in the Americas—a state geared for indefinite expansion outside and for regimentation and paternalism inside. The instruments of control included state ownership of land, mineral wealth, and herds; obligatory adherence to the official Sun religion; careful census compilations for tax and military purposes; deposition of local hereditary chieftains; forced population resettlement for the assimilation of conquered peoples; and mass marriages under state auspices. The Inca Empire probably was the most successful totalitarian state the world has ever seen.

Impressive as these attainments are, the fact remains that a comparative handful of Spanish adventurers were able to overthrow and ruthlessly destroy all three of these civilizations. And this despite the fact that these civilizations had dense populations numbering tens of millions. The explanation is to be found ultimately in the isolation of the Americas, which left the Indians too far behind in technology. It is generally felt that by AD 1500, the New World had reached the stage of civilization that western Europe had attained in 1500 BC and the Middle East in 3500 BC.

The Conquests

1521 AD	The Aztec capital falls to Cortez
1535 AD	The Incas fall to Pizarro
1549 AD	The first Portuguese Governor of Brazil is installed

The year 1519 was the date of Cortez's arrival in Mexico and his expedition against the Aztecs. This is the beginning of the age of the conquest and the conquistadors. In the 30 years that follow, the arrival of Cortez and a few thousand European adventurers will conquer the Americas and begin the first big surge of European expansion.

It is difficult to imagine the great Indian empires of the Aztecs and the Incas falling so rapidly to a handful of Europeans. When Cortez landed in Mexico he had 600 men, a few small cannons, thirteen muskets and sixteen horses. After some fighting, he reached agreements with various tribes that were hostile to their Aztec overlords. Without the help of these Indians, Cortez could not have won the victories he did. By also playing on the superstitions of the Montezuma, he was able to march peacefully into the capitol. (See previous reference of the return of Quetzecoatl.)

Once in the Aztec capital, Tenochtitlan, the Spaniards captured Moctezuma and started destroying native temples. The priests led a revolt which forced Cortez and his men from the city. Cortez lost a third of all his men and all of his belongings. He recovered with help from his Indian allies and reinforcements from Cuba.

A few months later Cortez returned and laid siege to the capital with a force of 800 Spanish soldiers and at least 25,000 Indians. The fighting dragged on for four months. Finally, in August 1521 the surviving defenders surrendered their city. Today, Mexico City stands in its place, with hardly a trace left of the original Aztec city.

In Peru, Francisco Pizarro, illiterate drifter, would lead the conquest of the Inca empire. He arrived like Cortez with a ridiculously small force comprising 180 men, 27 horses, and 2 cannons. He set forth with his four brothers in 1531 on the great adventure. After some delays they finally entered a deserted Inca city. Having heard immediately of the strangers, the following day the Inca ruler, Atahualpa, who was curious about these "men with beards," paid a formal visit to Pizarro. In imitation of Cortez, Pizarro captured the unarmed and unsuspecting emperor and massacred many of his followers. The emperor paid an enormous ransom for his freedom—a room twenty-two feet by seventeen feet piled seven feet deep with gold and silver articles. Pizarro seized the booty and executed Atahualpa. The Inca Empire was now left leaderless, and the Indian population, used to unquestioning rule from the top, offered little resistance. A few weeks later Pizarro entered and looted the capital, Cuzco. The next year, 1535, he left for the coast, where he founded Lima, still the capital of Peru. The Inca empire without the leader fell apart.

The triumphs of Cortez and Pizarro inspired other conquistadors to march through the huge areas of both the American continents in search of more booty. They found nothing comparable to the Aztec and Inca treasure, but they did explore all of South America and of a large part of North America. By the middle of the 1500s they had followed the Amazon from Peru to its mouth. By the end of the century they were familiar with the entire coastline of South America, from the Gulf of California south to Tierra del Fuego and north to the West Indies.

In North America, Francisco de Coronado, in his search for the fabled Seven Cities of Cibola, traversed thousands of miles and discovered the Grand Canyon and the Colorado River. Hernando de Soto explored widely in the southeast of what was to become the United States. He landed in Florida in 1539, made his way north to the Carolinas and west to the Mississippi, and followed that river from its junction with the Arkansas River to its mouth. These men, and many others like them, opened the New World for the Spaniards in the same way that La Salle and Lewis and Clark opened it for the French- and English-speaking peoples.

In the greater part of the Americas the population was not very dense and additionally the Indian population would be decimated by European disease, so that it was possible for Europeans to settle in large numbers in the New World and to impose their culture. In the Americas was built a true colonial empire as opposed to the trading empires in Africa and Asia. The invasion of the Europeans would simply overwhelm the Indian cultures and basically change the lives of the people. The isolated American cultures, which had developed without contact with the rest of the world, were forced to compete with vigorous Europe, whose technologies and institutions were superior in most respects to the Indians.

Before the Indian countries could become adjusted to living with European culture, nearly all their inhabitants would be reduced to serfdom and great numbers of them would have an early death. Cities would shrink to villages, and villages would disappear. Waves of disease took a shocking toll among the susceptible Indian population. Some of these devastating epidemics were smallpox, others probably measles and influenza. The Gulf and Pacific coasts of Mexico were swept almost clear of people. The Valley of Mexico lost about 80 percent of its Indians by 1600. The same happened in Peru, where the dense populations of the coastal oases practically disappeared.

Regardless of where they lived, whether in the great empires of the Aztecs and Incas or scattered north and south of them all Indians died at an appalling rate on first contact with the Europeans. This is why the first settlers often found abandoned fields and deserted villages, which they simply took over. Mexico's population in 1492 is estimated at 25 million. By 1608 it had shrunk to 1,069,255. The decline was equally steep in other regions. A whole people was almost wiped out. Later, when the immigration from Europe was under way, the Indians were hopelessly overwhelmed.

To further the Europeanization of the Americas, the Indians became Christian. The missionaries who set out to Christianize the Indians met little resistance. Converts pressed around them for baptism, which was often done in mass ceremonies. Some of Mexico's oldest churches have balconies from which the officiating priests baptized crowds of Indians packed into walled courtyards. One Franciscan friar claimed to have baptized 400,000 Indians during his lifetime. Another baptized 14,000 in a single day.

Few European women came in the early years. The conquerors had no race exclusiveness and out of the unions between the conquerors and the Indians came a new class of mixed blood. While some entered into the hierarchy, most adopted a mode of life partway between the European and the Indian. The civilizations of the ancient Americans will never rise again. Developed in isolation, they could not compete with the dynamic world culture they met with the arrival of the European. Mexicans will never revert to human sacrifice; Peruvians will never again keep their accounts with knotted strings. But in Mexico and Peru—and in Guatemala, Ecuador and Bolivia—Indian tradition are still very much alive and are even extending their influence. For the foreseeable future the Indian countries of Middle America and the Andes will continue to bear the distinctive marks of their Indian cultural pasts.

Colonial America 1500 AD to 1820 AD

During the 300 years of colonial rule in the Americas, European or Western culture became dominant. Today the Americas are correctly included in the European cultural realm. The discovery of America initiated a long-term program of exploration, conquest, and colonization in the new land.

Colonial America/Spanish America

The first wave of immigration to America created a copy of European society, culture and economy. The second stage depended primarily on support, financing and equipment provided from American bases. The Spanish conquest, designed to capture and control regional centers, moved from Indian town to Indian town, leaving the pacification of the rural areas for another time. Through this process, a small force conquered large areas in a short time by dominating strategic centers, thereby acquired nominal control over the surrounding countryside.

Throughout the campaigns, the Spanish conquerors inserted European city forms and functions onto the Amerindian structure. Everywhere they founded towns with church, plaza, and council, after the classic Mediterranean pattern. This careful attention to city organization and the bureaucratic town structure, Spanish America would never have come into existence so quickly. The Spanish system of government for the Americas before 1700 had two major bureaucracies, one in Spain and one in America. The king ruled, and all other officials governed in his name and by his authority. Nevertheless, he governed not as an absolute monarch, but in consultation with a number of councils. The Council of the Indies, located in Spain, provided advice on American affairs.

The viceroy served as the king's substitute in America with responsibility for the organization and control of the area included in his viceroyalty. Always Spanish born, he received a high salary and usually came from the upper nobility, frequently the second son of an important family. Viceroys reported mostly to the Council of the Indies, and on special occasions or in times of crisis directly to the king. They were expected to maintain the majesty of royal law and custom in America. In the early years of the conquest of America, town councils had extensive powers as the sole representatives of royal government in America. They handed out Indian labor and legitimized conquests.

The production of food became a major source of prosperity for many Spanish colonists. Commerce involved primarily the importation of Spanish and European goods, the sale of cattle and grain, and the transportation of gold and silver.

Traffic to and from America had to be on Spanish ships. Commerce, essentially finished goods to America, went through Spain and Spanish ports. Gold shipments, whether private or state-owned, also went through Spain, specifically Seville. To keep the system working correctly Americans were not supposed to develop local manufactures that would compete with Spanish industry. By the beginning of the eighteenth century, any rational observer could have seen that the Spanish imperial economic system did not work. America had developed an economic life independent of Spanish control, and Americans had come to depend on supplies and trade that came from outside Spain. Once this process was well under way, the subsequent independence movement provided the political readjustment needed to complement the economic realities.

Colonial Brazil

In the beginning the Portuguese showed little interest in America. This was largely due to the large rewards reaped by the Portuguese from trade in Asia. Most of the profit in the Portuguese empire was based on quick exploitation and trade, not long-term colonization and control, and in Brazil about the only product of interest was brazilwood, an exotic tropical tree used to make dye. This neglect was filled by French interests who almost drove the small Portuguese trading ports for brazilwood from Brazil. The Portuguese crown decided to expand its commitment in Brazil by introducing the captaincy system, designed to settle and control the coast through a series of fifteen large land grants. The captain or donatario who received this grant accepted an obligation to find colonists, bring them to the New World and establish a colony.

The conquest and settlement of Brazil differed considerably from the Spanish pattern in the Americas. Rather than undertaking a planned expansion of permanent colonies, the Portuguese moved from trading stations to more permanent settlements only in the face of outside competition. Additionally, the very nature of the Indian population of Brazil differed. The Portuguese did not find a large civilized and controllable Indian population, but rather a somewhat fierce, seminomadic hunting-and-gathering people. As far as they were concerned, slavery was the only means of exploiting the labor of these Indians. Disappointment with their early colonial arrangement led the Portuguese to establish a central government in Brazil in 1549. The progress of Portuguese expansion was greatly hindered by the lack of labor for plantations, and continuing Indian raids. To resolve these problems the royal government introduced institutions not previously very important: the Jesuits, an irregular military force, and black slavery. Thus emerged, almost by accident, three of the most powerful and enduring influences on Brazilian history.

The Portuguese plan used the Jesuits, a new and zealous religious order, as the crown's agents for Indian affairs. Their task was to pacify, Christianize, and concentrate the Indians in towns, where their labor could be most readily exploited. The second element of the plan called for an irregular militia made up of Portuguese settlers and their retainers. These irregulars supplemented the efforts of royal troops against French rivals and any rebellious Indians. The large landowners, as a result, organized impressive private armies to protect themselves, and on occasion, to assist in the common defense. The third element in the plan helped eliminate the critical shortage of plantation labor. Slave traders brought black slaves into Brazil in large numbers to provide workers for the sugar plantations. Black slaves from Africa entered in significant numbers (by 1600, slaves equaled perhaps a quarter of the population), and a category of mixed races, combinations of European, American Indian, and African, appeared in substantial numbers.

At the beginning of the seventeenth century, Brazil was settled only along the coast, and only a small portion of its territory had been thoroughly explored. The pattern of plantation society and Portuguese-dominated culture and government institutions had been firmly established, however. From 1650 on, the future of Brazil was closely tied to Portugal's course as a colonial power.

A mining boom took place in the late 1600s that had a big influence on the future of Brazil. Before mining grew, Brazil had been tied into an economic system based on a few large sugar mills. Emigration from Portugal was not attractive to poor people, for only individuals with enough money to finance some large scale enterprise could prosper in Brazil's plantation economy.

The mining boom started a new cycle of migration dominated by men of limited wealth. The number of Portuguese who decided to migrate to Brazil is unknown. But many came, so many that the Portuguese authorities worried about a possible depopulation of Portugal and imposed restrictions on migration to Brazil. A tenfold increase in the European population of Brazil during the eighteenth century would probably be a close estimate.

As the American colonies matured and because of French control of Spain and Portugal (The French under Napoleon conquered both Portugal and Spain in 1810, radical members of some local upper classes pushed toward a declaration of independence. The American thirteen colonies' successful separation from England also offered an exciting example. Some of the interest in independence may have come from the common people, but not much. Independence was essentially the work of American-born elites. It took a civil war to establish freedom from Spain. None of the Spanish-American areas had the institutions, national organization, or experience to create viable governments. All had strong royalist parties to contend with. Many Spanish-Americans had long-established interests that linked them to Spain. Many competent royal officials, and in some places the royal army, resisted a break with Spain. Under these circumstances, wars of liberation broke out. In some areas a short war sufficed; elsewhere the wars lasted over a decade, causing great destruction and loss of life.

The political systems that emerged in Spanish America after independence tended to be highly unstable, based on temporary alliances between powerful local leaders, with changes in government. Although we can trace the evolution of Spanish and Portuguese America from the first days of conquest and settlement through imperial organization and economic life to the emergence of politically independent nations, the history of Latin America's dependence did not come to an abrupt halt in 1810 or 1820 with independence. Instead, the economic, political, social, and cultural dependency of the area shifted during the late eighteenth and early nineteenth centuries from a system of Spanish and Portuguese control and domination to a more complex arrangement of industrial nation control, the United States being the most prominent.

Within the dramatic changes that have subsequently occurred in the Americas, especially the rapidly accelerating pace of change in the twentieth century, many patterns of colonial society, colonial economy, and colonial politics remain virtually untouched. Contemporary Latin America bears a surprising resemblance to the Latin America of the 1700s.

The Americas Become European in Culture

More far reaching than Europe's impact on Asia and Africa during the nineteenth century were its effects on the Americas. In fact, this "impact" was so extensive and dramatic that it is more appropriate to refer to it as outright Europeanization. In the Americas the scanty Indian populations were either wiped out or pushed aside, and tens of millions of European emigrants swarmed in and occupied the lands of the native peoples. With them the Europeans brought their political institutions, their ways of earning a living and their cultural traditions.

Thus the ethnic Europeanization of the Americas was followed inevitably by political, economic, and cultural Europeanization. Although the first European settlements were in Central and South America, North America was the goal of most of the European immigrants.

The fundamentally different character of the Spanish and Portuguese colonies, compared to the English, explains the greater immigrant population in North America. The Spaniards and the Portuguese settled in territories with relatively dense Indian populations. The Indian populations were concentrated in what came to be Latin America. These native peoples supplied all the labor that was needed (excepting Brazil), so European settlers were not required for that purpose. Accordingly, emigrants to the Spanish and Portuguese colonies in the Americas were mostly soldiers, members of the clergy, government officials, and a few necessary craftspeople.

North of the Rio Grande, by contrast, the Indian population was relatively sparse and provided no reservoir of labor. The English along the Atlantic seaboard and the French on the banks of the St. Lawrence had to do their own work, whether it was cutting the forests, plowing the cleared land, or fishing the coastal waters. Under these circumstances North America wanted all the settlers it could get, and so the British North American colonies were open to immigrants of all races, languages, and faiths. By 1835 there were 4.8 million European settlers in all of Central and South America as against 13.8 million in North America.

In the second half of the nineteenth century European emigration steadily increased, reaching its height between 1900 and 1910 when almost one million people left each year. This unprecedented flood poured into every continent, so that Australia, South Africa, and South America now were peopled by substantial numbers of Europeans, although North America continued to be the main beneficiary.

As far as the specific sources of immigration were concerned, the Latin American countries were peopled, as might be expected, mostly by emigrants from Spain and Portugal, although considerable numbers also came in the late Nineteenth Century from Italy and Germany. The great majority of the emigrants to North America were, until 1890, from northwestern Europe. After that date, approximately one-third came from northwestern Europe, and the remaining two-thirds came from eastern and southern Europe.

The net result of these migrations has been the ethnic Europeanization of the Americas. The substantial Negro element introduced into the Americas as a result of the slave trade is an exception to ethnic Europeanization. It is estimated that approximately 10 to 14 million slaves reached the New World. Their descendants today comprise about 12 percent of the total population of the United States, and 21 percent in Brazil.

European population of North America was also accompanied by political Europeanization. The Americas adopted constitutional governments of various forms. They also had European-derived law codes—English common law in the United States and Canada, Roman law in Latin America and Quebec. The political forms adopted reflected the different mother countries. For example, Latin America and The United States won their political independence through armed revolution. By contrast, Canada gained self-government in the late nineteenth century by acts of the British Parliament and remained loyal to Great Britain. You will recall we subdivided western culture into four segments; Latin Europe, Northern or German Europe, Latin America and North America. While all are in the great western tradition, Latin America received its main cultural roots from the Latin countries of Spain and Portugal. The United States and Canada,except Quebec, got their cultural traditions from Northern Europe or more specifically from Britain. I would like to expand on the British legacy of the United States.

Professor Schlesinger points out that America's language and political purposes and institutions are derived from Britain: "To pretend otherwise is to falsify history. To teach otherwise is to mislead our students." But he adds that "the British legacy has been modified, enriched, and reconstituted by the absorption of non-Anglo cultures and traditions as well as by the distinctive experiences of American life."

✸In four major fashions—the British mind and British experience for more than a dozen generations, have shaped the American culture.

The first of these four ways is the English language and the wealth of great literature in that language. The English language should be of even greater advantage to Americans today than it has been in the past as it becomes the world's common language.

The second of these ways is the rule of law, American common law and positive law being derived chiefly from English law. This body of laws gives fuller protection to the individual person than does the legal system of any other country.

The third of these ways is representative government, patterned upon British institutions that began to develop in medieval times, and patterned especially upon "the mother of parliaments," at Westmnster.

The fourth of these ways is a body of moral habits and beliefs and conventions and customs. These compose an ethical heritage. According to Tocqueville, Americans' *mores* have been the cause of the success of the American Republic.

In yet other ways, the United States benefits from a British patrimony: the American economy, for instance, developed out of British experience and precedent; and American patterns of community and of family life are British in considerable part. American culture still today is predominantly British in its mixture.

While the political unification of the original Thirteen British colonies led to the United States of America and eventual expansion from the Atlantic to the Pacific, Latin America experienced political fragmentation. The original eight Spanish colonies in Latin America ended up as eighteen separate countries. Whereas the United States has kept its 1787 Constitution to the present day, the Latin American states have adopted an average of nearly ten different constitutions each. Almost all the "revolutions" responsible for these constitutions have been revolutions in name only. A true revolution is one that produces a fundamental change in a system, a basic reorganization of the social and political order. Most of the so-called "revolutions" in Latin America simply involve the replacement of one military dictator by another without fundamental changes in the existing order. A procession of military and civilian leaders have succeeded each other, with little attention being paid to the wishes of the people or to the needs of the countries involved.

Europeanization prevailed in the economic field. As far as the European powers were concerned, all believed in the mercantilist doctrine of subordinating colonial economies to those of the mother countries. Latin America never achieved balanced economic growth. Instead there was chronic subservience to northwestern Europe and later to the United States.

The economic history of the British thirteen colonies was fundamentally different. Strengthened by the fact that land was more plentiful than labor, the English colonists worked out their own economic institutions and practices. In the warm, rich, southern colonies, settlers found their best crops were cotton, tobacco, rice, and indigo. In the middle colonies—Pennsylvania, New Jersey, Delaware—grain grew well, and this area quickly became the breadbasket of the colonies. Most of New England also turned to agriculture, but the long winters and rocky soil were a severe handicap. So they also resorted to other occupations, mainly fishing, shipping, and manufacturing, opening the West and building of transcontinental railroads.

Great quantities of foodstuffs and various raw materials were hauled by railroads and steamships to the rapidly growing urban centers of eastern United States and western Europe. At the same time, the millions of immigrants provided an abundant supply of cheap labor and further expanded the domestic market for American industrialists and farmers. The net result was that the U.S. economy spurted ahead in the second half of the nineteenth century at a rate unequaled in that time: In 1860 the United States was ranked fourth in the industrial nations of the world; by 1894 it was the first.

By contrast the European countries flooded Latin America with their manufactures, and in return received coffee, cocoa, sugar, rubber, and minerals. But it was foreigners who gained most of the profits from all this exporting and importing because they owned the mines, plantations, banks, railways, and shipping lines. Thus Latin America had won political independence in the nineteenth century but had remained economically dependent on Europe, and later on the United States. Precisely the opposite was the outcome in the United States, where protectionists rather than free traders determined national policy. (After becoming the dominant economic power following World War II, the United States changed its policies and became a champion of free trade.)

Cultural Europeanization in the U.S. continued along with political and economic Europeanization. Despite substantial Indian and African populations, American culture is overwhelmingly northern European in origin, even though its European characteristics were drastically modified during the process of transplantation and adaptation. In Latin America the predominant cultural pattern is Spanish, with the exception of Portuguese Brazil; this pattern is evident in the Spanish language spoken by the majority of the people and in their Roman Catholicism. One sees it also in architectural forms such as the patio or courtyard, the barred window, and the house front that is flush with the sidewalk. Town planning, based on the central plaza rather than on the main street, is equally revealing. Much of the clothing is Spanish, including the men's broad-rimmed hats of felt or straw and the women's cloth head coverings—mantilla, head shawl, or decorative scarf. In family organization the typical Spanish pattern of male dominance and close supervision of young women had been followed, as has the tendency to regard physical labor as undignified and unsuitable for gentlemen.

Although Latin American culture is basically Spanish or Portuguese, a strong Indian influence prevails, especially in Mexico, Central America, and the northwestern part of South America, where the Indians still make up a majority of the total population. This influence is evident in cooking, clothing, building materials, and religious practices. Latin American culture also has a considerable African element, brought over by the millions of slaves imported to work on plantations. This African influence is strongest in the Caribbean and Brazil, where most of the slaves settled.

The culture that developed in the United States was less influenced by the native Indian population than was Latin American culture. The main reason is that the Indians were fewer in number and less advanced. Nevertheless, Indian influence was not altogether negligible: 25 states bear Indian names; at least 300 Indian words are now part of the English language; and many Indian inventions such as moccasins, canoes, toboggans, and snowshoes are in common use.

Likewise, the United States has been less influenced by African culture than have Brazil and certain Caribbean states. Still, the influence here has been considerable; blacks make up nearly 12 percent of the total U.S. population compared to the one-half of one percent that is Indian. Europe's cultural influence was stronger longer in Canada than in the United States or Latin America. One reason was the preservation ties to England, which caused more interaction with the mother country. Also, a much larger percentage of the peoples of Canada were of European origin than were those of the United States and Latin America, with their substantial black and Indian elements. The Europeanization of the Americas has been enduring, as a traveler need only confirm by a visit to Chicago, Buenos Aires or Montreal and compare it to Cairo, Tokyo, Bombay.

Latin America and the United States

Trends in Latin America today are having a significant impact on the United States, and will have even more in the years to come. Latin America could become increasingly important for the United States in a new global context that will force this country to look inward, turning greater attention to domestic problems—creating jobs, increasing U.S. economic competitiveness, fighting drug consumption and improving schools. All these issues will be influenced by Latin America because the region is so close and large, with large potential for growth, and its future is tightly intertwined with the United States. Today Latin America's significance for the United States derives from its economic impact, the influence of migration, shared regional problems and from its importance for core values at the heart of U.S. society.

Latin America could become a major export market for the United States in the 1990s. The newly conceived North American Free Trade Act could be extended to all of the Americas. In the thirty years following the Second World War, Latin America's production of steel multiplied twenty times, and its output of electric energy, metals and machinery each expanded more than tenfold. Latin America's population growth has also been very rapid; starting with approximately the same population as the United States in 1950, the region will have nearly twice as many inhabitants as the United States by the end of the century.

An important impact of Latin America on the United States comes from massive and sustained migration to this country, especially from Mexico, the Caribbean and Central America.

—More than 20 million persons of Hispanic-American descent now live in the United States, and Latinos are this country's fastest growing ethnic or cultural group.

—Half the public school students in Los Angeles County and in four southwestern states are of Latino origin.

—Some ten percent of Central America's population fled the region during the war-torn 1980s, mostly to come to the United States.

—The influx from the Caribbean has been relentless; since the end of World War II, more than five million people from the Caribbean islands have come to the U.S. mainland, almost one of every eight persons born in the region during this period.

The United States will need even more immigrant workers in the years to come. Without them, U.S. manufacturers, service industries and agriculture could face shortages of unskilled labor, rising real wages and a loss of international competitiveness. These massive migrations are affecting the United States in myriad ways—shaping education, employment, public health, business, politics, culture and more. The immigrant communities are bound to influence how the United States sees its stake in the hemisphere's social, economic and political conditions and how it relates to the countries of origin. In California, Texas and Florida, increasingly important in electoral terms, voters of Latino origin are already affecting U.S. perceptions and policies.

Shared Problems

As U.S. interests and energies turn inward to domestic challenges, Latin America may well be increasingly pertinent. Far from becoming irrelevant, Latin America's problems and opportunities will increasingly be our own. President Bush had held out a long-term vision of region-wide free trade, promised that Washington stood ready to negotiate agreements with individual nations or regional subgroups, pledged cooperation with Latin American nations in the General Agreement on Tariffs and Trade's Uruguary Round, and indicated he would seek deep tariff cuts on products of special interest to Latin American exporters.

Because of the growing interchange between the U.S. and Mexico, I offer a short glossary of words often left untranslated:

Alcalde—A major or municipal judge.

Audiencia—An administrative-judicial court; a supreme court.

Bracero—A field hand or farm worker.

Caballero—A mounted horseman, hence a Spanish knight or gentleman.

Cacique—An Indian chieftain or leader; a local or political boss.

Camino Real—The royal highway.

Campesino—A farm worker; one who lives in a rural area.

Caudillo—A military chieftain, political leader, or dictator.

Criollo—A person of European ancestry who was born in the New World.

Curandero—A folk medicine healer.

Ejido—A communal or village landholding; a cooperative farm.

Encomienda—An allotment of Indian tribute to principal conquistadors.

Estancia—A ranch or grazing rights for live stock.

Fiesta—A celebration of a public or religious holiday.

Gringo—A term, usually derogatory, applied to a foreigner.

Grito—A cry, especially the *Grito de Dolores* heralding independence.

Hacendado—An owner of an hacienda or large estate.

Hacienda—A large landed estate; also the government treasury.

Hidalgo—A nobleman; he was called *Don* and his womenfolk *Dona*.

Licenciado—A licentiate, an academic degree normally used by lawyers.

Machismo—An exaggerated sense of virility or maleness.

Mestizo—A person of mixed ancestry, usually Spanish and Indian.

Mordida—A "bite"; slang word for a bribe to an official.

Noche triste—The "Sad Night" when Cortez's men fled Tenochtitlan.

Pemex—Petroleos Mexicanos, the nationally-owned petroleum industry.

Peninsulares—Spaniards born in Spain, or the Iberian Peninsula.

Peones—Manual laborers or daily wage workers, especially farm workers.

Peso—A colonial silver coin; Mexico's monetary unit.

Pueblo—A town or people; also a group of New Mexico Indians.

Pulque—A mildly alcoholic beverage made from Agave plants.

Reales—Spanish coins valued eight to a peso; "pieces of eight."

Rurales—A rural police force created to suppress highwaymen and bandits.

Tortilla—A thin unleavened cake of cornmeal, the Mexican bread.

Vaquero—A cowboy or herdsman.

Zapatista—Named after its revolutionary leader Emiliano Zapeta it is now applied to the insurgents in Chiapos, south Mexico.

Zocalo—A marketplace; the central plaza of Mexico City.

► Canada

A few special words about the neighbor of the United States, Canada. While most Americans can go to Canada without experiencing great cultural shock, Canadians don't care to be patronized or to have Americans ignore their separate history and values.

In 1997 Canadians will mark the 500th anniversary of the first officially recorded European sighting of Canadian territory. Five centuries of explorers, traders, farmers, shopkeepers and financiers have created with a territory still largely wilderness a vital, wealthy and influential nation.

Through it all, some principal aspects of Canadian development emerge repeatedly as significant for understanding the still young nation's character.

The first is that Canadians have always lived in or on the doorstep of a demanding wilderness filled with riches. The second is that while embracing this new and difficult land, Canadians have maintained strong political ties with the founding nation, Great Britain. And finally throughout its history, Canada has had a large French speaking and essentially unassimilated people in Quebec.

The first official sighting of present day Canada has long been identified as John Cabot's on 24 June 1497; it is unknown whether he saw Labrador, Newfoundland or Cape Breton Island. It is known that European explorers, and even European settlers, had already made their way to Canada. Archaeologists have identified the remains of Viking farm buildings. In addition to the Vikings, whose recollections of the New World were passed down as legends long after the settlement was abandoned, English fishermen may have been regular visitors to North America. Only 37 years after Cabot laid claim to Newfoundland for King Henry VII of England, Jacques Cartier claimed the territory surrounding the mouth of the St. Lawrence River for France. Thus began an almost 250 year struggle between the two European powers for control of the territory that would one day form Canada.

The French were the first to found a permanent settlement. In 1605 Sieur de Monts and Samuel de Champlain established the colony of Port Royal in present-day Nova Scotia. The climate, hostile Indians and lack of supplies constantly threatened the small company of settlers from France, whom Champlain envisioned as forming the basis for a permanent colony supported by farming rather than trapping and hunting. In 1663, the first census of New France revealed that there were only 3,215 settlers living in the French centers along the St. Lawrence and in Acadia (Nova Scotia). The seventeenth century brought the institution of royal government for the colony, and New France promised a rich future.

But the agricultural and trading colony of New France was soon surrounded by a growing British presence in North America. To the south were the Thirteen colonies which, like Champlain's followers, were determined to make the New World the site of a permanent farming settlement. To the north and west was the Hudson's Bay Company, founded in 1670 and concerned only with fur trading. To expand the Thirteen colonies and the work of the company, Britain wished to control North America. In the Treaty of Utrecht (1713), it acquired France's territory of Acadia, some of eastern Canada's richest farmland.

Greater French losses soon followed. Increasing numbers of French and British colonists were seeking new territories, and both groups claimed the Ohio valley region, one of the principal battlegrounds and prizes in the Seven Years' War. The decisive moment was the battle for Quebec City fought on 13 September 1759 by the Marquis de Montcalm and the British General James Wolfe. In this action, called the Battle of the Plains of Abraham, Quebec fell to the British. By 1760, Montreal too had surrendered and the whole of the colony was in the hands of the British; the Treaty of Paris (1763) made the transfer official. Thus Britain became the master of North America, but within twenty years would lose the Ohio valley and the Thirteen colonies.

Between the British defeat of the French in America and the British North America Act creating the Dominion of Canada, 104 years elapsed. Agitation over the troubles in the colonies led Britain to accommodate its French holdings in Quebec with the Quebec Act of 1774, which provided for the continuation of French civil law, the seigneurial system of land ownership and the Roman Catholic religion; this ended a brief period of British attempts to replace these traditional aspects of Quebec society with British institutions.

The Quebec Act itself was a contributing factor to the American War of Independence, during which Montreal was briefly occupied by rebel forces. The War of Independence also brought an infusion of settlers from the south. The United Empire Loyalists came primarily to Nova Scotia (later forming a separate province in New Brunswick) and to the land north of Lake Ontario.

During the War of 1812, fighting along the border between the U.S. and the British colonies in Canada was an important front. After the war, border disputes continued to flare up for many years. At the time of the American Civil War, there was another invasion scare which had much to do with influencing Canadians to unite in Confederation.

✗ The British North America Act of 1867 was proclaimed, creating the new Dominion of Canada from the union (Confederation) of the former provinces of Canada, Nova Scotia and New Brunswick. There were actually four provinces in Confederation, because the BNA Act created two provinces, Ontario and Quebec, from the Province of Canada. The two new provinces corresponded to the old provinces of Upper and Lower Canada, which had been combined into the united province in 1841. Assemblies were modeled on the one that had existed in Nova Scotia since 1749. These were in a perpetual state of evolution, particularly in Upper and Lower Canada, where disputes brought about short-lived rebellions in 1837–1938. Socially, there was much chaffing between established, monied interests and newly arrived immigrants, as well as long-time colonists who feared that the evolving social order left little room for them.

There was a growing conviction that Britain could not administer properly from overseas. From 1864 to 1867 the chief political figures of all the provinces were involved in a series of conferences aimed at determining the character of federal union. Under the British North American Act, passed by the British Parliament early in 1867, powers were divided between the provinces and the new government of Canada, with authority in foreign affairs still held in Britain. On 1 July 1867, the new nation of Canada was proclaimed. In 1871, the first Dominion census revealed a population of 3,689,257.

The latter half of the nineteenth century saw the emergence of the National Policy announced on 15 May 1879 by Canada's first prime minister, Sir John A. Macdonald, and followed by his principal successor before World War I, Sir Wilfrid Laurier. Under their leadership, Canada gained five new provinces and vast territories. Two provinces, British Columbia (BC) and Prince Edward Island, joined the Confederation in 1871 and 1873 respectively, and Manitoba (1870), Alberta and Saskatchewan (both 1905) were created from the territory Canada purchased from the Hudson's Bay Company. (Newfoundland did not enter Confederation until 1949.) Principal inducements for joining Confederation were the promise of the railway, government protection of local industry through tariffs, and plans to develop new territories by encouraging immigration.

The first large waves of European immigration had begun to transform the prairies into rich farming country, and mineral wealth was rewarding northern explorers, especially in the Klondike Gold Rush of 1898. At the same time, the deep-seated cultural and economic divisions surfaced again in the Manitoba Separate School dispute of the 1890s. French Catholics in Manitoba fought the provincial government's refusal to finance the dual system of both nonsectarian and religious schools that already existed in eastern provinces. The issue of the federal government's role in this dispute brought Sir Wilfrid Laurier to office in 1896.

Laurier's government fell in 1911 over the question of Canada's ties with the U.S. and Great Britain. Laurier's proposal for a reciprocity treaty with the U.S. was defeated in the House of Commons, although Laurier's desire for better relations with Canada's southern neighbor reflected the growing importance of U.S. markets and companies to the Canadian economy during this period. At the same time, Canada's role in the British Empire continued to trouble the nation. Canadian troops were called upon to serve in Britain's colonial wars and in World War I.

The wars of the twentieth century have cost Canada a great deal: 60,000 Canadians were killed in World War I, 40,000 in World War II. During both conflicts, heated debates arose over conscription, Canada's limited role in making the policies that affected Canadian soldiers, and Canadian financial contributions to the war effort. Yet there was also a widespread willingness in English Canada to support the Allies.

The wars brought Canada into the twentieth century, but it was not the twentieth century envisioned by a hopeful Laurier. By 1945, the wars and the intervening years of economic turmoil had transformed Canada from a rural, agricultural dependent of Britain to the world's fourth greatest industrialized power. Canada had gained new autonomy in foreign affairs through the Statute of Westminster in 1931. The demands of war production propelled the country into the 1950s with an advanced industrial economy. At the same time, the sorrows of the war and the Depression had taught many Canadians to doubt some features of the constitutional framework of Confederation.

The Royal Commission on Dominion-Provincial Relations which reported in 1940 was one of a series of attempts to create a new form of constitutional accord among the provinces. The assertion of Canadian identity grew stronger with evidence that economic prosperity and alliance with the U.S. had come at the price of a dependency that was replacing the old bond with Britain. Internally, the search for national identify was mirrored by a movement in the 1960s for Quebec separation and independence, a movement which created the October Crisis of 1970 and which has returned in force with the Parti Quebecois, a separatist party that now forms the Quebec provincial government.

In 1981, Prime Minister Pierre Trudeau's Liberal government succeeded in winning Canadian parliamentary approval for a revised Canadian constitution which will form the basis for a new age in Canadian government. But the achievement of the constitution in itself will not resolve the cultural, economic and political problems of modern Canada. The province of Quebec is only the leading voice in a large chorus that has been raised to challenge the relevance of the new constitution to the fundamental issues facing Canada:

— the settlement of native land claims with the federal government, particularly as they relate to northern resource development

— a mutually acceptable balance of powers between the federal and provincial governments

— resolution of the strong movement for protection of French Canadian rights, which has often taken as its rallying point Quebec's separation from Canada.

Most Canadians are friendly and get along well with Americans. They are, however, proud of their cultural heritage, which includes French, British, and other European influences. The people in general are proud of being Canadian, and despite many similarities between their nation and the United States, they emphasize they are not U.S. citizens and not U.S.-type people just living in Canada. The preservation of Canadian culture, even against influence from the United States, is very important in Canada. Quebec's seven million people account for 27 percent of Canada's total population (26.3 million). About 82 percent of the people are of French origin, while 12 percent have a British heritage.

Although both French and English are official languages in Canada, French is used almost exclusively in some parts of Quebec. A recent law requiring only French usage in Quebec has been changed to allow for bilingual street signs and business transactions. While a separate English-language school system exists, most children go to schools where French is used to teach all subjects.

Religious beliefs in Canada follow traditional lines. The French are generally Roman Catholic; those of British-descent are mostly Protestant. Before Quebec was controlled by Great Britain, it was largely ruled by the Catholic Church through French civil law. Although there is an official separation of church and state in Canada, religion is publicly recognized and private religious schools are often subsidized by the state. Religious organizations have played a greater role in politics in Canada than in the United States.

Canada is the second largest country in the world, after Russia. However, much of the north is uninhabitable because of the arctic climate and permanently frozen ground. Therefore, most of the people live within one hundred miles of the U.S border. Quebec is the largest province and is one-sixth the size of the United States. The Canadian Shield—a vast, U-shaped, rocky expanse surrounding the Hudson Bay—covers most of the province and includes 470,000 square miles of rocky, coniferous forest.

The total population of Canada is about 28 million people. Of this, approximately 36 percent live in Ontario, making it the most heavily populated province in the country. Twenty-seven percent live in the combined region of the prairie provinces, British Columbia, Yukon, and Northwest Territories. Ontario is not only populated by those of British and French descent but also by sizable German, Italian, Ukrainian, Chinese, and Japanese communities. Immigration from Asia has increased over the last few years. Most European nations are represented. Most Canadians are Christians, but the beliefs and doctrines of the different Christian churches are diverse, and society is highly secularized. Ontario plays the leading role in Canada's economy as the industrial heart of the nation.

A special footnote on the province of Quebec is in order. Within their province, Quebeckers enjoy wide control of their own affairs, with exclusive responsibility over social matters, education, culture, health, housing, natural resources, training and municipal affairs; and joint responsibility in eleven other areas, including energy, immigration, industry, language and so on. Quebec has its own legal system, based on the French civil code. French is spoken by a higher proportion of Quebeckers than ever before. Recently the collapse of the Meech Lake Accord which was designed to knit Quebec into the Canadian federation was not approved by the other provinces. This has led to much discussion of separatism and the question of the future form of Canada is in doubt.

To understand the situation it helps to review a little Canadian history. Bear in mind above all that the French got to this part of North America (in 1534) before the British. Having established New France, they lost it in 1759 on the Plains of Abraham, when Wolfe defeated Montcalm. Four years later France ceded Canada to Britain, and New France became Quebec. Anxious above all to keep the Americans out, Britain chose not to impose its values on Quebec but instead allowed it to maintain its French laws and land-tenure system and granted it, in 1774, "the free exercise of religions of the Church of Rome."

After the American civil war, refugees by the thousands came north to settle in Quebec. Not wanting to be part of a French-speaking Catholic society, they persuaded the British Parliament, in 1791, to split Quebec into two provinces: English-speaking Upper Canada (now Ontario) and French-speaking Lower Canada (now Quebec). Canada's first separatists were thus English-speakers.

The two groups did not get on. When the Earl of Durham was sent from London to Canada in 1838 to investigate grievances after a series of disturbances, he "expected to find a contest between a government and a people"; instead, he found "two nations warring in the bosom of a single state." His advice was to anglicize the French.

The 1840 Act of Union made an effort at this, by rejoining the two Canadas i a single province, each having equal representation in the legislature.

But the French-speakers were not to be assimilated by the English, and soon won recognition for the use of French in debates. Harmony, never mind assimilation, proved elusive.

The response was the British North America Act of 1867. Usually regarded as a pulling-together measure—the act joined the provinces of Canada, Nova Scotia and New Brunswick into one dominion, the core of today's Canada—it was also an act of division: Upper and Lower Canada were once again "severed," to form two separate provinces, Ontario and Quebec. Quebec's civil code was left intact and the use of French in Parliament, in Quebec's legislature and in both federal and Quebec courts was explicitly protected. Thus was the Quebeckers' concern for *la survivance* satisfied—for awhile.

There is no doubt Quebec is a distinct society. Quebec has a cohesiveness, embodied not just in its use of French and its affection for its culture but in its *projet de societe*—the common enterprise on which the whole society is embarked—that Canada as a whole markedly lacks.

Canada is today threatened by secession of Quebec after 128 years of confederation and many Canadians, both English and French, are becoming exasperated with the uncertainties. A question arises whether Canada will remain a united great country or will it break down into a number of smaller states perhaps affiliated with the United States. This break up seems like an odd outcome in a country that is prosperous. Polls taken indicate 90 percent of both English and French speaking Canadians believe they live in the world's most pleasantly habitable country, and the United Nations has recognized Canada's quality of life as the highest of any country in the world (1994–1995). The world will be watching the Canadian future with interest.

The issues are complex, but I hope the reader will recall the discussion of the role of language as a source of cultural values and also the theme of Professor Huntington that cultural conflicts will be of growing importance.

Worksheet ▶

CHAPTER SEVEN

Discuss:

- Why would historians divide the world into pre-1500 and after 1500?

- Applied science and its role in the rise of the West.

- The new role of sea power.

- The reaction to European domination.

- Latin Europe—Greek Russia.

- The role of the Mongols in isolating Russia.

- Russia's expansion to the East.

- The African slave trade.

- The challenge to Africa today.

- Why do we put the Americas in the European cultural realm today?

- What are some American crops that have become staples throughout the world?

- What has been some of the long-term significance of Vladimir of Kiev converting to the Greek Orthodox branch of Christianity?

- Why Chapter 11 is called The West and the Rest.

- There are two historical cultural fault lines in Europe, one along the Rhine and one separating the Greek and Latin churches.

Define or identify:

- Nation state—City state

- Vasco da Gama

- Slav

- Varangian—Rus

- Cyrillic alphabet

- Czar

- The Third Rome and "Holy Russia"

- Pre-Columbian, colonial and modern American periods

- Aztec, Maya, Inca

- Hernan Cortez, Pizzaro

- Conquistador

- Quetzalcoatl

- Moctezuma

- Virgin of Guadelupe

- Teotihuacan

- Mestizo, Creole, Penninsulare, and Indio

- Who were three conquerors of Mexico that entered through Vera Cruz?

- The British North American Act of 1867.

Explain:

- What are the reasons behind Europe's rise to predominance in the world?

- Why is Russia not a part of the mainstream of European culture and history?

- What are the two Africas?

- What was the principal cause of Indian deaths by the Europeans?

- What horrified the Spanish about Aztec religion?

- Why is Brazil's history distinct from the rest of Latin America?

- How long was the colonial period in the Americas?

- What is the special place of Quebec in Canada?

- The Marine Corp hymn, "From the Halls of Montezuma" commemorates the U.S. victory over what nation?

- The Virgin of Guadelupe is a symbol of faith to Mexicans. Can you recount the story of her appearance to Juan Diego? She is called the "Virgen Morena"—the dark virgin. Why is this significant?

- What did the Monroe Doctrine say about colonization in the Americas?

- What is the dominant province of Canada?

- What basis of law does both the U.S. and Canada share?

- The scientific method was key to the rise of Europe. Explain hypothesis, testing and law; "I don't know" versus "see what the authorities say."

- What four countries were the first nation states.

- Mexico is our neighbor to the south and its culture is playing an increasing role in American culture. Outline the story of Mexico, dividing your discussion into pre-Columbian, colonial and modern periods.

Chapter 8 ▶ ▶

Indian Culture

One of the earliest civilizations of man developed along the Indus River in India. It reached its maturity around 2500 BC and remained virtually unchanged for another 1000 years. Like the great cultures of Sumer and the Nile, that of the Indus was primarily agricultural. The causes of its decline aren't clear, but it was in decline when, about 1500 BC, invaders came down from central Asia. It was overrun by tribes people who, with the military advantage of iron weapons and horse-drawn chariots, easily overwhelmed the copper weapons and ox-drawn carts of the natives.

The invaders called themselves Aryans and the land in which they settled, Aryavarta, or land of the Aryans. They were of the Indo- European family of peoples we talked about when we described the beginnings of Greece in Chapter 4. Infiltrating in small groups, the Aryans easily overthrew the decaying Indus Valley civilization, so that, as in Greece, a primitive new society emerged around 1500 BC. They left few remains because they built of wood and had no cities, but they did leave a wealth of literature in the form of Vedas. Again, this has a correlation with the epic poems of Homer in Greece.

The word *veda* means knowledge, and for the Hindus, the Vedas are a primary source of religious belief, as the Bible is for Christians and the Koran for Muslims. There were originally four Vedas, but the most important is the oldest, the Rig Veda. In the course of time, other works were added to the four Vedas and acquired a similar sacred status. As Homer's epics are to Mycenaean Greece, the Rig Veda is a primary source for study of the early Aryans. It is, in essence, a collection of 1,028 hymns arranged in ten books, making it about the length of the Iliad and *Odyssey* combined.

This early Aryan society was basically different from later Hinduism. Cows were worshiped but eaten. Intoxicating spirits were not forsaken but joyously consumed. There were classes but no castes, and the priests were subordinate to the nobles rather than dominating the social pyramid. In short, Aryan society resembled much more the other Indo-European societies, such as early Greece, than it did the classical Indian Hinduism that was to develop in later centuries.

India developed into a culture different in many fundamental ways from the West. There was nothing developing in the West remotely resembling basic Indian concepts and institutions such as caste, ahimsa (nonviolence), reincarnation, and karma (the law of moral consequences). These were not just eccentric or abstract ideas. They constituted the bedrock of Indian beliefs or culture, molding the thought and daily lives of all Indians. The pattern that resulted was so distinctive and so enduring that Indian culture to the present day has many distinctive characteristics that mark it off from all other Western, Far Eastern, and Islamic cultures.

▶ Caste

One distinctive feature unique to India is the caste system. Originally the Indo- Aryans, like other Aryans, were divided into three classes: the warrior nobles, the priests, and the common people. They had none of the restrictions associated with caste, such as hereditary professions, rules limiting marriages to people of the same caste, and taboos about whom you can eat with. But, by 500 BC the caste system was functioning with all its essential features. Although many theories have been advanced concerning its origins, it is generally agreed that color was a basic factor. In fact, the Sanskrit word for caste, *varna*, means color.

The Aryan newcomers were very conscious of the difference in complexion between themselves and the dark natives, and dubbed them *Dasas*, or slaves. With their strong sense of racial superiority, the Aryans strove to prevent mixture with their despised subjects. For this reason, they evolved a system of four hereditary castes. The first three comprised their own already defined classes, the priests *(Brahmans)*, the warrior nobles *(Kshatrtyas)*, and the farmers *(Vaishyas)*. The fourth caste *(Shudras)* was reserved for the conquered Dasas, who were excluded from the religious ceremonies and social rights enjoyed by their conquerors.

Literally thousands of castes have grown up within these four broad divisions. Each caste has four basic features. One is characteristic employment, so that bankers and merchants, for example, would belong to the Vaishya caste. Another feature of caste is the hereditary principle, expressed in detailed marriage regulations and restrictions. Caste also involves further do's and don't's concerning food, water, touch, and ceremonial purity. Finally, each caste has its *dharma*, or moral code, which defines such duties as family responsibility and the ceremonies at marriage, birth, and death.

Outside this system are the outcasts, or untouchables, comprising today about a seventh of the Indian population. They are restricted to trades or crafts regarded as unclean because their function involves some ritual defilement or the taking of human or animal life forbidden to Hindus. These occupations include hunters, fishermen, butchers, executioners, gravediggers, undertakers, tanners, leather workers, sweepers, and scavengers.

Working in these occupations has led in turn to social segregation. Untouchables live apart in isolated villages or in quarters outside town limits and are required to use their own temples and wells. They have to be most careful to avoid polluting members of the castes by any kind of physical contact or, in extreme cases, by even coming within their sight. For this reason, until recent decades

they never moved outside their quarters or villages without striking a pair of clappers together to warn others of their approach, much as lepers did in medieval Europe.

The untouchables are further subjected to psychological pressures that are as crippling and degrading as the physical. The doctrine of *karma* holds that one's status in present life has been determined by the deeds of previous lives. The untouchables therefore deserve their low position because of past sins, and their only hope for improved status in future lives is the dutiful performance of their present duties.

This combination of social and religious sanctions has enabled caste to function to the present day. Of course, with its many provisions for mutual aid, caste does provide security as long as one follows its rules. So it continues to serve as the rigid framework of Hindu society. And, although it has been attacked by reformers, such as the Buddha and Ghandi, and undermined by the pressures of modern westernized industrial society, caste nevertheless still operates in rural India, where three-fourths of the total population continues to live. Most Americans find the caste system repugnant. It is contrary to all our values of personal freedom, individual responsibility, and social position based on merit.

▶ Hinduism

The religion of most Indians today is Hinduism. Its origins go back to the Vedas invaders and it continues to exert an overwhelming influence on the daily life and values of present-day India. Hinduism has, however, remained localized in India. Hindus have never tried to spread their beliefs and the rest of the world has not felt sympathetic with many of its beliefs.

This does not mean we should look on it as unimportant. The great historian, Arnold Toynbee, in 1952 predicted that in fifty years the world would be under the leadership of the United States, but that in the twenty-first century as religion captures the place of technology, it is possible that the Indian philosophy of Hinduism will dominate the world. And today many leading western intellectuals are serious students of the Vedas and Indian religious thought. We should consider seriously a philosophy and religion that can interest so many keen minds of the western world while inspiring a life like Mahatma Gandhi.

⚹ The basic principle of Hinduism is that the ultimate reality is *Brahman* which is described as good—truth—mercy. But man has problems seeing this reality because maya clouds knowledge of Brahman.

The key questions asked and answered by Hinduism are:

What am I?
Answer: In your inner self you are part of Brahman.

What is life? Answer: A search to find Brahman in yourself.

How can I know Brahman?
Answer: By knowing yourself—(and Brahman).

So the Hindu sees Brahman in several forms of which the most important are:

Creator = Brahma
Sustainer = Vishnu
Destroyer = Shiva

The world is continuously destroyed and recreated. Vishnu is most often worshiped. He has elements of a savior.

The goal of Hinduism is to escape maya by union with Brahman, and there are many ways, including:

1. seeking sensuous, aesthetic pleasure

2. participating in economic activity and public welfare

3. doing what is ethical and moral

4. aspiring to high goals

5. becoming one with Brahman through Yoga

6. practicing *ahimsa* (non-violence) to persons and animals

Becoming one with Brahman through the study of yoga means to join or yoke (yoke oxen) with Brahman through self-discipline based on self-contemplation.

Much yoga is based on sound physiological principles of good physical and mental health.

Reincarnation—Called the Pilgrimage

The soul (Java) passes through various states until it reaches the highest goal of a human being. The individual's actions build up merits and demerits (law of *Karma*). The soul ascends or descends with each reincarnation until it reaches an eternal, timeless state of Nirvana and becomes one with Brahman.

The Sources of Wisdom for Hinduism are the oral and written epics of:

The Vedas
The Upanishads
The Bhagavad-Gita
Karma za

Karma

Karma is the Hindu doctrine of cause and effect. Every action in life in which a participant is emotionally involved produces karma. We might talk of someone's chickens coming home to roost. We also have a saying that those who live by the sword, die by the sword. These thoughts are close to the concept of karma, with the difference that the idea of karma is intimately linked to a belief in reincarnation. In Hinduism, actions of a past life can come home to roost in this life.

Westerners often define karma as fatalism, plain and simple. This is a misconception. Karma is used to explain why a person is born rich or poor, strong or weak, whole or crippled, male or female. Nonetheless, Hinduism emphasizes that this supposed fate was earned. The karma idea stresses that our past thoughts and actions alone determined our present condition. Correspondingly, our future situation depends upon our choices now. The person who obeys his dharma, or duties in life, will generate new karma that will bear good fruit in the future. This cause and effect is hardly fatalism.

Hinduism has endured. Even though its origins are 3–4,000 years old, contemporary with Egypt and Sumer, Hinduism is alive and being practiced in India.

Hinduism says to man: You can have what you want. So—What do you want? Of course, common answers would include:

Pleasure
Wealth
Fame
Power

It might surprise you to learn that Hinduism says go after it, if that's what you want.

Hinduism is not other-worldly. It believes that worldly desires are legitimate, but there is a big warning: you must be intelligent.

If you are intelligent you:

I. Don't hurt other people.

If you raise other passions against you, it won't pay off.

Practice basic decency, fair play.

II. Find your proper place, your capacity and endowment. If you go against your nature, you will not be successful. The basis of the caste system is this finding of your place.

There are four kinds of people in the Hindu analysis:

1. The intellectual or spiritual

2. Temporal leaders, administrators

3. Artisans (merchants)

4. Laborer

III. A person should evolve and pass through the four stages of life.

1. As a Student:—learn, marry and acquire skills

2. As a Householder—family care, raise children

3. When you are 50+ having given to society and as strength ebbs—you retire and begin adult education

4. Contemplative—begin the spiritual pilgrimage. "Atman" is your inner self striving to reach Brahman

Hinduism asks the question: Is a life focused on this world worthwhile?

And they answered that there are four limitations to earthly desires:

1. Desires are unattainable in most cases.

2. We often get them and find they don't satisfy.

3. If we make them the main objective, (i.e., wealth) they become insatiable, never enough, even though we have millions.

4. Many are fleeting and, often, after all the effort, vanish overnight.

Hindus say, "Man can never get enough of what he does not want."

Is there then anything more in life than earthly satisfaction? The Hindu reply is, "Man is only truly satisfied with the infinite, when he becomes one with Brahman."

Nothing less than the infinite will satisfy the spirit of man. Union with Brahman gives utter awareness—utter joy.

In summary, the Hindus taught that the supreme spirit permeating the universe was Brahman, a being capable of all knowledge and feeling. He was the universal soul and the all-pervading breath, all else was illusion. The individual soul—Atman—was a spark of the supreme being. By transmigration, it passed from state to state until it attained release by reabsorption into Brahman, the soul of the universe.

This identification of the individual soul and the Soul of the universe was the ultimate goal that holy men sought to reach by discipline, meditation, and withdrawal from the world of the senses. Seekers after truth could abandon the world and rest within the fold of Hinduism.

As Hinduism and the caste system evolved in early India, the upper class priestly Brahman exclusiveness and emphasis on ritual were a factor in the religious reformation in India in the sixth and fifth centuries BC.

One sign of the unrest was a trend toward asceticism. Some of the most active minds, alienated by the society about them, concentrated on pure introspection. They developed techniques for disciplining or "yoking" (yoga) the senses to an inward focus, ending in a state of trance or ecstasy, which mystics describe as "enlightenment" and skeptics call "self-hypnotism."

Out of this inward searching and speculating came many reforms, of which the most important was Buddhism. The new religion had no place for caste or for Brahmans and their special religious role. It required that the scriptures should be understood by all believers and not merely by a few at the top. Buddhism also banned all magic, sacrifices, and obscure writings that had been growing in Hindu practice.

▶ Buddhism

Hinduism remained isolated in India. But, out of India came a great religion that would become a moral ethical system adopted by most of Asia. Buddhism, in its Mahayana form, spread to Mongolia, Tibet, China, Korea and Japan while the Hinayana or Theravada branch dominated in Burma, Thailand and Cambodia.

How does Buddhism differ from Hinduism? Remember it was a reform movement.

1.   No caste system based on separation of nobility, priests, common people, slaves. Man's goodness is not based on economic or social status.

2.   Emphasis on individual—not on supernatural or on social reform.

3.   Emphasis on labor, discipline, compassion —not on tradition, ritual, metaphysical speculation.

4.   No interest in origin of world or in a personal god.

5.   Revolution against idea of a continuous series of reincarnations—Persons do not transmigrate, the past only influences.

The story of Buddhism began with a man. While the rest of the world was dreaming as in sleep yet calling it life, one man roused himself. Buddhism began with a man who shook off the dream-like nature of ordinary living. It began with the man who woke up. When they asked the Buddha who are you? Buddha answered "I am awake."

Buddha means the "Enlightened One" or the "Awakened One."

The historical facts of his life are roughly these: He was born around 560 BC (note that significant date 500 BC) in northern India. His father was a king. His full name was Siddhartha Gautama of the Sakyas; Siddhartha was his given name, Gautama his family name, the Sakya the name of the clan to which his family belonged.

He was a man who had everything—handsome appearance, wealth, a beautiful wife, prestige.

Despite all this, as he entered his twenties, a discontent came to him which was to lead to a complete break with his worldly way of life.

He came to see the real world and didn't like what he saw. For the teachings of Buddha show unmistakably that it was the body's inescapable involvement with disease, old age, and death that made him give up hope of finding happiness in the physical pleasures. "Life is subject to age and death. Where is the realm of life in which there is neither age nor death?"

Once he came to this conclusion, he could not return to his sensual life. One night when he was 29, he made the break, his "Great Going Forth." Making his way in the early morning hours to where his wife and son were sleeping, he said a silent goodbye, then ordered the gatekeeper to bridle his great white horse. The two got on their horses and rode off toward the forest. Reaching its edge by daybreak, Gautama changed clothes with the servant who returned with the horse to break the news, while Gautama shaved his head and "clothed in ragged raiment" went into the forest in search of enlightenment.

Years followed in which all his energies were concentrated toward the great search for enlightenment. He practiced extreme asceticism but found it did not bring enlightenment. He settled and taught the middle way between the extremities of asceticism and indulgence. He felt the body should be given precisely what it needs in the way of food and rest for optimum functioning but no more.

One evening after years of prayer and fasting in northeast India, south of the current town of Patna, he sat beneath a fig tree which has since come to be known popularly as the Bo tree (short for *Bodhi* or enlightenment). The place was later named the Immovable Spot for tradition reports that the Buddha, sensing that he was on the brink of enlightenment, seated himself that epoch- making evening with the vow not to rise until illumination was his.

The great awakening had arrived. Gautama was being transformed and he emerged the enlightened one or "the Buddha."

Following the enlightenment, Buddha spent the rest of his life preaching his message until his hair was white, and his body exhausted. He spread his ego- shattering, life-enhancing message. He founded an order of monks, challenged the deadness of ritualistic Brahmin society, and as other prophets received the resentment, queries, and bewilderment his words caused.

After a very strenuous ministry of 45 years at the age of 80 and around 480 BC, Buddha died.

What was the message of the man who awoke? Buddha revealed four Noble Truths:

1.   Life means suffering.

2.   Suffering is caused by desire.

3.   Suffering is cured by restraining desire.

4. The means of restraining is desire and thus eliminating suffering is via the Eightfold Path.

The Eightfold Path

"Happiness he who seeks may win" Buddha said, "if he practices": The Eightfold Path is a discipline and a way of life.

1. Right Knowledge

A way of life always involves more than beliefs, but it can never bypass belief completely, for man, in addition to being a social animal, is also a rational one. Not entirely, but partly, we all need some blueprint, some map the mind can trust if we are to move ahead. Whether or not man's reason has the power to pull his life in the direction it wants, it certainly holds the power to say no; let it not believe something and it will be impossible for the individual to move wholeheartedly in that direction.

Some convictions, therefore, are necessary if one is to take up the Path. What convictions? There are the Four Noble Truths; that suffering abounds, that it is caused ego and desire for self-fulfillment, that by suffering can be avoided by the Eightfold Path.

2. Right Aspiration

Whereas the first step asks us to ascertain life's problem, his second asks us to follow with our hearts. It is really enlightenment we should look for. If there is to be significant progress on the Path, regular effort is indispensable; our determination to rise above our separateness and identify ourselves with the welfare of all must be by conviction. Men who achieve greatness are almost invariably passionately interested in some one thing.

3. Right Speech

Now we get to those daily practices that run our lives. Language is the first. Language does two things: it furnishes both an indication of our character and a means for changing it. We will do well to begin with language to know our character. Our first move is to become aware of our speech patterns and what they tell us about ourselves. We could start by counting how many times during the day we bend the truth and then ask why we did so. The same with the lack of charity or other elements in our speech.

Why do we make up stories? Behind the arguments and defenses we use, the motive is almost always a fear of revealing to others or to ourselves what we really are. Each time we give in to this fear, we are protecting our ego and in so doing, we remove ourselves further from life and the long-range prospects of happiness (per the Second Noble Truth).

The second direction in which our speech should move is toward charity. Lying, idle chatter, abuse, and slander are to be avoided not only in their obvious forms, but also in their less obvious ones. For these subtle innuendoes are often more vicious precisely because their evil intention is concealed.

4. Right Behavior

Here, a call to understand one's self is a prerequisite to improvement. Reflect on the things done, with special eye to the motives which prompted them. In the end, how much kindliness was involved and how much self-seeking? The direction we should be going is toward more selflessness and charity. This general directive is sharpened up in the Five Precepts, the Buddhist equivalent of the ethical part of the Ten Commandments:

> Do not kill. Most Buddhists extend this prescription to animals; the strict ones, and as a consequence, are vegetarians.
> Do not steal.
> Do not lie.
> Do not be unchaste. For monks and the unmarried this means chastity: for the married, it meant restraint in proportion to one's interest in and distance along the Path.
> Do not drink intoxicants.

5. Right Livelihood

Our work occupies most of our waking attention. Buddha considered spiritual progress to be impossible if work pulls in the opposite direction.

For those who are so intent upon liberation as to wish to give their complete lives to it, right livelihood demands joining a monastic order and partaking of its discipline. For the layman it means, simply, engaging in occupations that promote life instead of destroying it. Buddhists believe that if Buddha were living today, he would be less concerned with which occupations men enter than with the many who have made their jobs the center of their lives rather than simply a part of life.

6. Right Effort

Buddha laid tremendous stress on the will. People serious about making the grade will have to exert themselves enormously. There are virtues that must be developed, passions to be curbed, and evil mind states to be transcended if love and detachment are to have a chance. "'He robbed me, he beat me, he abused me'—in the minds of those who think like this, hatred will never cease."

The only way to overcome life's temptations and ties is through effort. "Those who follow the way," said Buddha, "might well follow the example of an ox that marches through the deep mire carrying a heavy load. He is tired, but his steady gaze, looking forward, will never relax until he comes out of the mire, and it is only then he takes a respite. O monks, remember that passion and sin are more than the filthy mire, and that you can escape misery only by earnestly and steadily thinking of the Way."

7. Right Mindfulness

No teacher has credited the mind with more influence over life than did Buddha. The best loved of all Buddhist texts. the Dammapada, opens with the words, "All we are is the result of what we have thought." It is also quoted at the beginning of this book.

If we could really understand life, if we could really understand ourselves, we would find neither a problem. It is ignorance, not sin, that struck Buddha as the offender. When sin is at fault, it is caused by a more fundamental ignorance.

The greatness of man is the one with greatest self-knowledge.

Buddha insisted that everything be seen "as it really is." Thoughts and feelings are to be seen as swimming in and out of our minds but do not form a permanent part of us; they are to be taken intellectually, not emotionally. Everything we witness, especially our moods and emotions, is to be traced to its cause. This agrees with modern psychoanalysis.

8. Right Absorption

This path involves basically the techniques of meditation.

Something happened to Buddha under that Bo tree, and something has happened to every Buddhist since who has persevered in meditation. Meditation is needed to see reality, to be awake. Through meditation the mind comes to rest and with it comes enlightenment.

The Big Raft and the Little Raft

Religions are always splitting. In the section on early Christendom, we saw it split into the Eastern and Western Churches, and later the Western Church into Roman Catholicism and Protestantism, and Protestantism has continued to splinter into its many denominations. The same happens in Buddhism. Buddha dies, and before another 100 years, the beginnings of division are starting to show.

Buddhism divided over the questions people always seem to divide over.

Some see people as individuals; whatever progress they makes will be through their own doing. Some say the opposite; our future is always tied to others, and we progress together or not at all.

This difference is expressed in the divisions of Buddhism. Each called itself a *yana*, a raft or ferry, for each proposed to carry man across the sea of life to the shore of enlightenment. One group, looking to progress together, claimed to be the larger vehicle of the two. It took the name *Mahayana*, the Big Raft, Maha meaning "great" as in Mahatma (The Great Souled) Gandhi. As the name caught on, the group that saw progress as individual effort came to be known by contrast as *Hinayana* or the Little Raft. Not exactly pleased with this name, they have preferred to speak of their brand of Buddhism as *Theravada*, or the Way of the Elders. In doing so, they voice their claim to represent the original Buddhism as taught by Gautama himself.

Some of the different emphasis between the two branches of Buddhism include:

Hinayana—Theravada

vs

Mahayana

Man as an individual

vs

Man as involved with others

Man is on his own in the universe—
(emancipation by self-effort)

vs

Man not alone—(salvation by grace)

Key virtue: wisdom

vs

Key virtue: Koruna, compassion

Religion a full-time job—(primarily for monks)

vs

Religion relevant to life in the world— (for laymen as well)

Ideal: the Arhat

vs

Ideal: the Bodhisattva

Buddha a saint

vs

Buddha a savior

Avoids metaphysics

vs

Elaborates metaphysics

Avoids ritual

vs

Includes ritual

Confines prayer to meditation

vs

Includes petitionary prayer

Conservative

vs

Liberal

For the Theravadans the ideal was the Arhat, the perfected disciple who, wandering lonely like a rhinoceros, strikes out on his own for Nirvana and with prodigious concentration, on his own, makes his own way unswervingly toward that pinpointed goal.

The Mahayana ideal, on the contrary, was the Bodhisattva, "one whose essence is perfected wisdom (bodhi)," a being who, having brought himself to the brink of Nirvana, voluntarily renounces his prize that he may return to the world to make it accessible to others. He deliberately sentences himself to age-long servitude that others, drawing on his acts for others, may enter Nirvana before him.

The difference between the two types is illustrated in the story of four men who, travelling across an immense desert, come upon a compound surrounded with high walls. One of the four determines to find out what is inside. He scales the wall and on reaching the top, gives a whoop of delight and jumps over. The second and third do likewise. When the fourth man gets to the top of the wall, he sees below him an enchanted garden with sparkling streams, pleasant groves and delicious fruit.

Though longing to jump over, he resists the impulse. Remembering other travelers who are trudging the burning deserts, he climbs back down and devotes himself to directing them to the oasis. This last man was a Bodhisattva, one who vows not to desert this world "until the grass itself be enlightened."

Mahayana Buddhism is called the religion of infinite compassion, or concern for one's fellow man.

The Mahayana branch becomes the one with the most followers. Part of the explanation lies in the fact that it converted one of the greatest kings the world has ever known. In the history of the world's kings, the figure of Asoka (c. 272–232 BC) stands out, though not that well-known in the West. If we are not all Buddhists today, it was not Asoka's fault. Not content with his personal conversion, he made every effort to extend it over three continents. When he was converted, Buddhism was an Indian sect. When he died, it was a world religion.

There is a deeper reason for Mahayana Buddhism's success. There is nothing in the Hina-yana outlook which, for general appeal, can rival the inspiration of the Bodhisattvas who, full of mercy and compassion, create an atmosphere of trust and love. Mahayana Buddhism provided a devotional and personal religion which the Far East was lacking. China in particular was to find in Mahayana Buddhism a new world of the spirit that appealed to all levels of her society.

Today, Buddhism is strongly represented in every Asian land but India. In India, Buddhism came to be not so much defeated by Hinduism as absorbed by it. It's as if Catholics and Protestants were to work out their differences and merge once again into one Christian community.

Buddhism became a powerful force in central Asia and East and Southeast Asia. After AD 600, however, it lost ground within India. One reason for the decline of Buddhism at home was that it failed to provide for the usual crises of life. It offered no ceremonies for birth, marriage, death, and other critical turns in the lives of the people. By contrast the Brahmans were ready with their rites, and their survival was assured despite the attacks of the reformers. More important, the Brahmans themselves embraced reform and absorbed the Buddhist teachings.

Buddhism has survived to the present in India because its basic tenets have been incorporated in the Hindu reaction to the Buddhist challenge. India has had a cultural unity through the years because of its shared religious beliefs.*

► Indian Science

Indian science has made a large impact on the world, and the Gupta period 300–900 AD was outstanding. Contact with Greeks resulted in mutually beneficial exchanges of ideas. Aryabhata, born in India in AD 476, is one of the greatest figures in the history of astronomy. He taught that the earth is a sphere, that it rotates on its own axis, that lunar eclipses are caused by the shadow of the earth falling on the moon, and that the length of the solar year is 365.3586805 days—a calculation with a remarkably slight margin of error.

The greatest achievement doubtless was the formulation of the theory of zero and the consequent evolution of the decimal system. The base could have been any number; the Hindus probably chose ten because they counted on their fingers. With this system, individual numbers were needed only for 0, 1, 2 . . . 9. By contrast, for the ancient Greeks each 8 in 888 was different. And for the Romans, 888 was DCCCLXXXVIII. The difficulty of division and multiplication with these systems is apparent.

The simple Hindu numerals were carried westward by Arab merchants and scholars, and so became known to us as "Arabic numerals." Despite their obvious advantage they were long scorned in the West as pagan and as too vulnerable to forgery; one stroke could turn 0 into 6 or 9. It was not until the late fifteenth century that Hindu-Arabic numerals were common in the West and the door was opened to modern mathematics and science. Looking back, this Indian contribution stands out as comparable to the invention of the wheel, the lever, or the alphabet.

►The Moguls

India absorbed numerous invaders in its history. However, in 1500 Hindu India was struck by Muslim Turks we know as the Moguls. In 1524, Babur, with a small force of 12,000 men armed with matchlock muskets and artillery, defeated an Indian army of 100,000, After his victory, Babur occupied Delhi, his new capital. Four years later he died, but his sons followed in his path, and the empire grew rapidly. It reached its height during the reign of Babur's grandson, the famous Akbar, who ruled from 1556 to 1605. The invaders brought with them a culture that was based on ideas and attitudes very different from those of Hinduism.

Muslims devoted their lives to Islam, which we will discuss in the chapter on Islamic cultures. The religion of Islam preached a rigid monotheism: there is no God but God, and Muhammed is His Prophet, quite different than the Gods of Hinduism. Also, Islam held that all Muslims were brothers and that all men were equal before God regardless of their class or their color, in contrast to the Hindu caste system.

Hindus felt that the search for religious truth was each man's private affair, and whether he found it in God, gods or a godless intellectual concept was no concern of anybody else. Hinduism, then, was flexible in theology, the one area in which Islam was not.

On the other hand, Hinduism insisted that social inequality was the law of the universe and that if there was such a thing as blasphemy, it was to be found in the act of tampering with the social order; the belief that brahmans were superior to all other created beings was as sacred to Hindus as it was repugnant to the Muslims.

For 200 years Mogul rule dominated India. Under the Mogul ruler, Akbar made concessions to the Hindus and also opened the top state positions to Hindus, who now ceased to look on the Mogul empire as an enemy organization. A new India was beginning to emerge, as Akbar had hoped—a united state rather than a divided land of Muslim masters and a Hindu subject maiority. Akbar opened his bureaucracy to all his subjects. Ability rather than religion became the test for appointment and advancement.

Mogul India flourished in a way that dazzled the world. The Mogul rulers brought their adopted

Persian ideal of elegance to its flower in India. This new emphasis on material as opposed to spiritual values was to exert lasting influences on India, permanently affecting the style of life for both Muslims and upper-class Hindus.

With the Maharajas, Persian manners and styles became the model for all fashionable India, just as French manners and styles in the seventeenth and eighteenth centuries became the model for all fashionable Europe. Persian became the court language and the language of upper-class society. The rough Persian of the troops, intermixed with Indian languages, became Urdu, which remains today the popular language of the Punjab and northern India and an official language of India.

Hindus of good family wore Persian clothes and gave their children Persian names (the Indian Prime Minister Nehru was an example of the Persianization of highly placed Hindus: his familiar high-necked jacket, leg-hugging churidar trousers and small cap were all Muslim; he spoke the Urdu language in his home; and his given name, Jawaharlal, is Persian.)

However, more noteworthy than any effect on fashion was Persian penetration of the arts. A graceful mingling of Persian-Muslim styles, on the one hand, with Hindu traditions, on the other, led to a distinctive Indo-Islamic style and the creation of some of the world's most beautiful paintings, music and buildings.

The new style quickly proved itself in painting. The Hindus adapted the delicate brushwork and other techniques of the Persians to produce miniatures, for example, that are considered by many authorities to be unsurpassed in the art of East or West; they raised portraiture to extremely high levels; and they also used their new technique to paint classic Hindu subjects—the mythology of Vishnu and Shiva, the heroes of the great epics, the Ramayana and the Mahabharata.

Somewhat the same thing happened to music. Hindu music changed its tune. Borrowing from Persian, Arabic and central Asian music, it turned from Hindu spiritual themes to the sensuous use of constantly repeated words and musical phrases.

The greatest of the Indo-Islamic arts to bloom at the Mogul court was architecture, and it was Shah Jahan who was the great builder. His treasury apparently was full, for he lavished money not only on music and painting, but also on enormously expensive structures, some of which still stand to awe tourists with their magnificence. The best known monument, and one of the greatest achievements of world architecture, was no public building but a tomb—the famous Taj Mahal in Agra.

Such outstanding achievements in the arts made the Mogul Empire one of the greatest the world has ever seen. But the refined Indo-Islamic culture of the Moguls did not change daily routine of Indian life. In the villages, where then as now the vast majority of Indians lived, the Mogul culture was remote and the Hindu tradition remained in full force. Governments in Delhi hardly disturbed Indian villagers; most saw Hindus and the great Moguls as one group of tax collectors taking the place of another. Even at the height of Mogul rule, village government stayed completely in the hands of Hindu headmen who maintained traditional caste life. In India, two worlds were living side by side. It was not a question of ruler and ruled. It was not the matter of customs and habits. It was not even the obvious difference between Muslim and Hindu attitudes toward God. When the Mogul empire fell, the two cultures were still separate and less than a fifth of the Indian population had become Muslim.

As the Mogul empire weakened, still another group of invaders was waiting to enter with another strange culture. This time they wouldn't come through the mountain passes of the Hindu Kush, but on ships; their purpose would be trade and not conquest of land. The new conquerors are Europeans; they would come in waves: first the Portuguese, and later and more importantly, the British. They would have their centuries of rule. But once again Hinduism, which seems to patiently absorb or passively resist any culture that comes in contact with it, would keep the Indian culture intact.

Prior to the appearance of the British, India had been invaded many times—by the Aryans, Greeks, Scythians, Turks, and Moguls. Each of these invaders left its mark on local culture, contributing in varying degrees to the evolution of India's traditional society. The impact of the British was more disruptive to this traditional society. The other invaders wrought changes at the top, and most were unaffected, but the British presence was felt down to the level of the village. The reason for this difference is to be found in the dynamic and expansive nature of western culture, which challenged the comparatively static and self-sufficient society of India.

▶ British Rule

For 250 years after the Portuguese had first come to India, the Europeans stayed in a few trading posts along the coasts. Then around 1350 the balance of power shifted decisively, and the whole of the Indian subcontinent fell under British rule. The British came to India in search of markets and commodities. They brought with them the new Western ideas of the industrial and political revolutions and they would profoundly change India's economy.

There was a strong demand in Europe in the 1800s for Indian raw materials such as jute, oil, seeds, wheat, and cotton. These commodities were transported to the seaports by a British-built railroad network totalling 4,000 miles by 1870 and 41,000 miles by 1939. The opening of the Suez Canal also facilitated the export of Indian raw materials by reducing the shipping distance between London and India from 10,800 to 6,100 miles. Thus India became one of industrial Europe's important sources of raw materials. And because of the high prices commanded by these materials, India was left with a favorable balance of trade.

The resulting capital surplus could have been used to invest in Indian industry. The fact that this was not done left India an underdeveloped agricultural economy. Britain made no attempt to encourage manufacturing in India, and in some competitive areas, such as textiles, actively discouraged it. There would be no tariffs to protect infant industries against British competition.

Meanwhile, thanks to western medical science, health measures, and famine-relief arrangements, India's population grew rapidly. Similar population growth had occurred earlier in Europe with the innovations, but had been absorbed by new factories in the cities. Since no such industrialization occurred in India, the new extra millions could only fall back on agriculture. They naturally put a terrible overpressure on the land. And this remains to the present day one of the major problems of the Indian economy—and indeed of most of the world's poor agricultural economies.

British rule profoundly affected India intellec-tually as well. A national system of education was put in place, made up of universities, training colleges for teachers, high schools, and elementary schools designed for villagers. At the same time, the introduction of the printing press greatly stimulated intellectual life in India, as it had previously in Europe. Sanskrit works became public instead of being the exclusive property of the Brahmins. Newspapers appeared in modern Indian languages as well as in English.

These developments changed the general intellectual climate. Most of the masses, however, remained completely illiterate, and the Muslims generally remained hostile to the new schools and books. In this way, English education became almost the exclusive possession of a small Hindu upper class, familiar with English language and culture and exposed to liberal western ideologies. This western-educated class used European ideas of political organization to attack British rule and would eventually lead to an independent India. When the British opened their schools, the Hindus used them to get the education they needed to fill the posts in the new bureaucracy, and this gave them further contact with western ideas.

This new contact with western culture provoked different reactions. One saw it as the wave of the future and accepted it all, seeing it superior in every way to their traditional culture. There was also complete rejection. Western culture was seen as subversive and its customs repugnant. The most common reaction was a compromise between worship and outright rejection. This view accepted the essence of Western views on the individual and learning, but it also sought to reform Hinduism from within and to preserve its basic truths while ridding it of corruptions and grossly inhuman practices. The outstanding leader of this school of thought was Ram Mohan Roy, widely venerated as the "father of modern India."

Ram Mohan Roy was the pioneer leader not only of India's religious renaissance but also of its political awakening, or nationalist movement. This was a new phenomenon in India. For the first time a leader spoke of India as a unity and was the beginning of a feeling of national patriotism. Nationalism developed for several reasons. One was the English conviction that they were a racial elite and divinely ordained to rule India permanently.

This racism was found in the army and the bureaucracy, where Indians could not rise above certain ranks regardless of their qualifications, and in social life, where Indians were excluded from certain hotels, clubs, and parks. Under these circumstances it was inevitable that the Indians should react with the gradual development of a sense of cultural and national consciousness.

The British also helped nationalism by creating a united Indian peninsula. For the first time, the whole of India was under one rule. The British also tied this together with railroads, telegraphs, and mail service. And on top of all, they created a peninsula-wide elite who all spoke English and shared a western education experience including western ideas about liberalism and nationalism, personal freedom and self-determination. The Indian leaders used not only western political principles but also western political techniques. Newspapers, campaign slogans, mass meetings, and monster petitions—all were used to promote Indian nationalism.

At first the attacks were moderate and full of cooperation. But after 1890 the demands became more extreme.

It should be noted that the early nationalist movement was confined largely to the intellectuals. There was little contact between the nationalist leaders and the illiterate peasants. The gulf existed until bridged by Mohandas Gandhi. Gandhi succeeded because he sensed the essentially religious outlook of the Indian people and preached, not political abstractions in Western terms, but religious concepts they understood and to which he gave a political meaning.

We have outlined the story of three great invasions of India, each of which has left a significant impact on traditional India. First, the Aryans bringing the Vedas out of which grew the religious practices and values we call Hinduism. Then came the Moguls whose empire lasted in India from the early 1500s to the 1700s. This period left in India a strong artistic tradition, but very important for understanding India today, they left Islam. Finally, we have the overlay of the British Raj. British rule lasted for nearly two centuries in many areas. Here we see carried out a central theme of this book, the meeting of western culture with the world's other cultures. This meeting with the West introduced by the British continues on today and is a central feature of the religious and political life of present-day India.

► India's Traditional Society

The basic unit of traditional Indian society was the village, as it was in most of the rest of the world, including Europe, in the preindustrial period. Within the village it was not the individual that mattered, but rather, the joint family and the caste. This group form of organization was a source of social stability, but it did not lead to a national awareness.

The land was regarded by ancient custom as the property of the ruler, who was entitled to a share of the production. This land tax was the main source of state revenue. Transportation and communication facilities were primitive, so the villages tended to become self-sufficient units.

Each village had:

- its potter, who made the simple 'utensils needed by the peasants

- its carpenter, who constructed and repaired the buildings and equipment

- its blacksmith, who made axes and other necessary tools

- its clerk, who attended to legal documents and wrote correspondence between people of different villages

- its town herdsman, who looked after the cattle

- its priest and its teacher, often the same person

- its astrologer, who indicated the time for planting, for halvesting, for marriages, and other important events.

These specialists served their villages on something akin to a barter basis. They were paid for their services with grain from farmers or with tax-free village land for their own use. These heredltary and traditional divisions of occupation and function were turned into obligations by the caste system.

The village had little contact with the outside world. The combination of agriculture and local crafts made each village largely independent of the rest of the country except for a few specialties like salt and iron. The large towns that did exist in traditional India were not manufacturing and trading centers. Rather, they were religious centers such as Benares, Puri, and Allahabad or political centers such as Poona, Tanjore, and Delhi. The Indian village remained relatively unchanging and self-sufficient, despite invaders, until the coming of the British and wesern ideas.

Hinduism is the backbone, the heart and the soul of Indian civilization. It is entirely Indian, never having sought to extend its sway by proselytizing. Its strange gods, its outlandish legends, its lack of authoritative scriptures, of church and canon law, make Hinduism almost impossible to understand for those brought up in the comparative certainties of the Judeo-Christian tradition. But some effort must be made to understand Hinduism if we are to get anywhere near to understanding India itself.

While Hinduism is not normally thought of as monotheistic, they do believe all things are manifestations of one God. All idols, for example, are just manifestations of that one God.

One of the principles of Indian thought has been that all ideas are only an approximation to the truth. Therefore, no idea represents the whole truth. As a consequence, Indians developed an attitude towards other opinions and ideas which was very accepting.

Everything was valid; so that the question was not between truth and untruth, or what was right and wrong, but between incomplete perceptions and, relatively speaking, more complete perceptions. This may account for the Indian tolerance, hospitality, and understanding of other people's problems. They do not take a very rigid stand on ideas. Because of this unique tolerance, Islam and Christianity still flourish in India, though both have been deeply influenced by Hinduism.

Despite these traditions of tolerance, there are two very important areas of strain and friction in present day India and they revolve around caste and the Hindu-Muslim relationship.

Into India modern western ideas are coming through communications such as the movies and through the globalization of the world's businesses. It is one of the many paradoxes of modern India that although discrimination by caste has been outlawed, most politicians admit that caste, not ideology, continues to dominate Indian politics.

Important changes have already taken place in the caste system, and they have affected politics. Since independence, Harijans (Untouchables) have been guaranteed certain seats in state assemblies and Parliament and a percentage of government jobs and educational opportunities. These reserved opportunities, or "reservations" as they are known, have produced a new harijan leadership, and a new party has been formed to represent their interests. One of its goals is to try to unite the Harijans with other castes he believes are still oppressed by those at the top of the caste tree.

But the caste system still counts for much in India. It is natural that everyone would retreat to the group they know. Still, if we look back, we can see the progress that is being made.

Fifty years ago, if an untouchable's shadow fell on a south Indian Brahmin, he would go and bathe six times. Now in an overcrowded bus, does anyone verify who is the person who is crushing him? Many people also go to restaurants now. Everybody takes water from the municipal tap. And what multinational company can organize along caste lines? It seems certain that modern technology and ideals will eventually break down the caste systems.

Muslim leaders also have raised real concerns about a growing militant Hinduism, as they find themselves living in a Hindu state. Hindu's reply is that their fears are baseless. Hindus by nature are tolerant. Their outlook is catholic. They want equal treatment for all, but not special privileges for any community.

Nevertheless, communal riots are flaring up more frequently and Hinduism's traditional tolerance is breaking down. Muslims are becoming more militant too as they react to what they see as real grievances. The Muslims, of course, are not the only restless community in India. Until the 1980s, communal tension between Hindus and Sikhs was almost unthinkable. The Sikhs had their demands and pursued them vigorously; but they also emerged as one of the most prosperous communities, spread throughout India and well integrated wherever they lived. Yet, in 1984 Delhi was to be the scene of anti-Sikh riots which were more violent than anything India had seen since the massacres of partition; and they were to be sparked off by the assassination of Prime Minister Indira Gandhi by two Sikh members of her bodyguard.

▶ Independent India

Gandhi was by all odds the outstanding figure in this postwar anti-British movement. The Indian Congress Party, organized in 1885, did not seriously threaten the British before 1914. It had remained essentially a middleclass movement with little support from village masses.

Gandhi's great contribution was that he managed to break through to the villagers, establish rapport with them, and involve them in the struggle for independence. His message was simple and appealing. He pointed out that in 1914 the British were ruling 300 million Indians with a mere 4,000 administrators and 69,000 soldiers. This was possible only because all classes of the population were cooperating with the British in one way or another. If this cooperation were withdrawn British rule inevitably would collapse. What must be done then, was to educate and prepare the people for nonviolent passive resistance.

He had developed these ideas from his reading of the American Henry David Thoreau's essay "On Civil Disobedience" (also key in the thinking of Martin Luther King). Gandhi called on the people to boycott British goods. In place of imported machine-made goods, Gandhi preached the wearing of homemade cloth. This would undermine the economic basis of British rule and also revive village industries. He himself wore a loin cloth he made himself and publicly set the example by working at his spinning wheel. Gandhi's example made Indian home rule possible. Once India's villagers understood his teachings and acted on them, the days of British rule would be numbered.

Another nationalist leader, Jawaharlal Nehru, was now coming to the fore alongside Gandhi. The son of a wealthy lawyer, Nehru had been educated at Harrow and Cambridge in England. On his return, he got involved in the nationalist movement and became a follower and admirer of Gandhi. Nehru, however, was very different from the religious Ghandi. He was a socialist and a firm believer in science and technology as the means for liberating humanity from its age-old misery and ignorance, ideas he had learned in England. Nehru nevertheless recognized Gandhi's extraordinary service in arousing India's peasantry.

A problem for a united front against the British, however, was the increasing dissension between warring Hindu and Muslim blocs. The All-India Muslim League was becoming significant under the leadership of a Bombay lawyer, Mohammed Ali Jinnah. Many Indian Muslims felt they had more in common with the rest of the Muslim world than with their Hindu neighbors. Many centuries old sores were opened. Jinnah's Muslim support made possible the future establishment of the independent Muslim Pakistan. The subcontinent of India would be divided into three states, one Hindu and the other two Bangledesh and Pakistan, Muslim.

When Britain declared war on Germany on September 3, 1939, the viceroy, the same day, proclaimed India also to be at war. Leaders of the Indian Congress protested that they were not consulted on this key decision. But were snubbed by the viceroy. When Japan proceeded to conquer Southeast Asia in early 1942, the Indian situation became critical. With Japanese armies poised on India's border, Churchill sent Sir Stafford Cripps to India with a message:

Stay with us during the war and when it is over, India can become fully autonomous, with the right to secede from the Commonwealth.

The truth was that Britain could no longer rule the country against the wishes of its people. Nor was there much desire any longer to try to do so.

In March 1946 a three-man cabinet mission went to India to make arrangements for self-government. Two months later a plan was made public, but it failed to reconcile the demands of the feuding Congress party and Muslim League. The Labour government in England then sent out Admiral Lord Louis Mountbatten as the new viceroy. He concluded that no plan for preserving Indian political unity was feasible and recommended partition, with the two governments each to have dominion status. By this time the Congress leaders had realized that partition was inevitable, so they accepted the plan. In July 1947, the British Parliament passed the Indian Independence Act, and on August 15, both Pakistan and the Union of India became free nations.

▶ Challenges

India is about one-third the size of the Unites States, but has three and one-half times as many people. The 903 million people who live there represent about one-sixth of the entire population of the world. And their numbers are increasing at a rate of 1.86 percent per year. India is a very crowded country, and getting more so every day. The country is also very diverse. It is a nation clearly divided by geographic regions; by languages, religions, and cultures; by cities and villages; and by poverty and wealth. India is a land of many contrasts.

The differences between the geographic regions of India and between urban and rural life within these regions are not the only sources of contrast in this diverse country. Even within a single region, people may be divided in many other ways—by language, by religion and by castes. The differences in environment from region to region contribute to, but do not account for, the complex mingling of distinct languages and religions and communities that are found in such wide array throughout India today.

The Constitution of the Republic of India recognizes 15 different Indo-European and Dravidian languages in the country. This list does not include English, which is still the language of higher education, the professions, and national business and government. Nor does it include the many tongues spoken by the mountain and tribal peoples who live in the remote regions of north, east, and peninsular India.

India is also divided by religions. Hindus comprise 83 percent of the total population and command a majority in every region of the country. Islam is the largest of the minority religions. There are 100 million Muslims in India, the second largest Muslim population in the world. But Muslims nevertheless are only 11 percent of the total population of the country. All other religious minorities—Sikhs, Jains, Christians, Buddhists, and others, together add up to only 6 percent. These religious groups tend, however, to concentrate in specific regions of the country in large enough numbers to become politically significant. Muslims are an overwhelming majority in and are a sizable minority in the north-central state of Uttar Pradesh. Sikhs comprise 62 percent of the population in Punjab.

And the Jains are in sufficient numbers in Gujurat, and Christians along the southwest Malabar Coast, to have an impact on the cultural, educational, and political dimensions of life in those areas.

So India as a nation has to deal with a multi-ethnic, multi-religious, multi-linguistic country. In addition to these challenges is the extent, especially in the urban areas, of poverty. It is estimated that about 20 percent of India's urban population live in slums. And in Calcutta, India's largest city, it is estimated that beyond the slum dwellers, some 700,000 people sleep on the streets each night

Without some reduction in India's birth rate and an increase in urban planning and control, it is hard to imagine how the nation's considerable economic progress will be able to reduce the anguish of poverty and environmental decay for an increasing number of its population. All the gains now have to be distributed among too many additional needy people.

Remarkable in this context has been the emergence during the past decade of a significant middle class, of households that are earning more than is necessary for simple survival. A recent survey identified nearly 300 million people or about a third of the total population with household incomes that allowed them to live comfortably. This is a population bigger than the entire population of the United States.

As eager consumers, they are creating a vast new market, new opportunities, and new objectives for a population long characterized as austere and protected by very restrictive economic planning and import controls. National economic policy began to change in 1985, before the collapse of the socialist economy in the Soviet Union, so that today India is already well on its way to being a consumer- driven economy. Change is in the air.

Another significant change in India today—comparable to the emergence of a middle class—is the growth of the urban population. The villagers are continuing to be lured by the opportunities of the city. This dramatic increase, the pressure on urban lands and services is staggering, the ability to cope is near—some would say past—its limit. Already rioting that expresses social unrest and its accompanying violence has appeared.

The future of urban development in India is extremely challenging. The average projected increase in population of India's 5 largest cities, from the year 1980 to 2000, is more than 103 percent. At that rate, it is projected that by the year 2001, India's urban population will number from 340 million to 350 million. India will then have the largest urban population in the world. Yet even with this staggering urban growth, the cities are projected to hold only 35 percent of the total population of the country. India will be for the foreseeable future primarily a rural country, a nation of villages.

So we see an India faced with severe challenges, many with cultural origins. As in the religious challenge of integrating the Muslim and Hindu population. The return to cultural militantism confirms Professor Huntington's view of the growing role of culture discussed in Chapter One. On the other hand, the rising urban middle class and the entering of India into the global commercial scene would seem to confirm the prediction of one world growing out of the adaptation of Western technology. Still, we see a stubborn caste system and vast poverty that appear resistant to change. Will India be a society where we have both a strong return to cultural separatism while espousing McWorld?

▶ History Summary: India

Early Indus Valley Civilization
The Coming of the Aryans   1500 BC
The Mogul Empire   1526–707
The British Raj   1785–1947
Independent India   1947–present day

Note

*The most lucid and concise of the many books on world religions that I have found is *The Religions of Man* by Huston Smith, published by Harper and Row. Dr. Smith takes complex philosophical concepts and makes them understandable to the average reader. I have drawn principally from Dr. Smith in the short outline of the basics of Buddhism, Confucius, Taosim, and Islam.

Worksheet ▶

CHAPTER EIGHT

Define or identify:

- Aryan—Indo-European

- Vedas and the Rig Veda

- Reincarnation

- Union with Brahman

- Caste

- Untouchable

- Ahimsa

- Karma

- The Buddha

- The Bo Tree

- The "Great Going Forth"

- The Eightfold Path

- Mogul

- Raj—Rajah—Maha raja

- Mahayana—Hinayana

- Congress Party

- Passive Resistance

- Namaste

- Emperor Asoka

- "On Civil Disobedience"—Thoreau

Explain:

• Why are the languages of Europe related to the language of India?

• The Hindu attitude toward time.

• The four noble truths of Buddhism.

• Why would a practicing Buddhist have reservations about American advertising?

• What invasion of India was the cause of two major religions in India today?

• Why is the Taj Mahal in India Persian in its inspiration?

• What is the connection between the American Thoreau and Gandhi? And Martin Luther King, Jr.?

• The partition of India.

• Why in India would English be used in a newspaper and taught in the schools?

• Time is circular, time is linear. How does Hindu attitudes to time relate to re-incarnation?

Discuss:

- The four castes of India and the Untouchables.

- How does the concept of caste run counter to American concepts of justice?

- How in America do you see desire or attachment causing suffering?

- What did the Buddha mean by "right livelihood?"

- The Indian contribution of the concept of zero.

- What would you list as some of the Western cultural ideas the British brought to India?

- Name some principal legacies of the three invaders of India: Aryan, Mogul, British.

- In your opinion, why would Arnold Toynbee predict that in the next century Hinduism will dominate the world?

Chapter 9 ▶ ▶
Far Eastern Culture___

▶ China

Another of the very earliest civilizations arose along the Yellow or Huang Ho River in China. Chinese history begins with the Shang Dynasty in about 1600 BC and its culture was different from the other earliest cultures in Egypt, Sumer and the Indus. To the present day, Chinese civilization remains different, and the main reason is its geographic isolation. China is located at the eastern end of Eurasia, separated from the rest of the continent by great mountains, deserts, and steppes. To the east China faces the vast Pacific Ocean, and to the north, the frozen Siberian steppes.

Although China was isolated, it was not completely cut off from outside influences. The early Shang civilization started along the Yellow River precisely because that area was a cultural meeting place, influenced by nomadic peoples to the northwest, by agricultural peoples to the east, and by forest dwellers to the south. Even the far away Middle East influenced early China; by contributing wheat cultivation, bronze weapons and the horse-drawn chariots used by the invaders who established the Shang dynasty about 1500 BC. These invaders became the rulers of many scattered communities of north China.

What happens throughout Chinese history happened to the Shang: the Shang were simply assimilated into Chinese culture, and the general populace remained distinctively Chinese. Although China was enriched by elements from the early Middle East such as barley, wheat, sheep, cattle, horses, bronze, and the wheel, these innovations did not change China fundamentally. Whereas the other ancient civilizations have long since disappeared, Egypt, Mesopotamia and the Indus, China's civilization has continued uninterrupted. Today China can boast the oldest continuous civilization in the world.

Not only the oldest, China's civilization is also unique. Just to mention a few differences, it was the first to raise silkworms and to weave delicate fibers into silk. It was the only major civilization that did not use animal milk and milk products for human consumption. Even today, the Chinese have the same reaction toward drinking milk we might have about eating grasshoppers. Also, ancestor worship was a prominent and important feature of Chinese religion from the beginning.

Related to this was the importance attached to one's family name, which is always ahead of the personal name instead of following it, as we do. This custom reflects the traditional strong emphasis in Chinese society on the importance of the family, instead of the individual, the state, or the church.

The familiar Chinese style of building, with the fancy roof supported by rows of wooden pillars, also goes back to earliest times, and they used chopsticks rather than forks and spoons.

Very important for the later history of China and all east Asia was the complex form of writing found in Shang ruins. Chinese writing is descended from this early style, again illustrating the continuity of Chinese civilization. Long ago the ancient writings of the Mid-East became unintelligible to the inhabitants, but the ancient Shang script is still recognizable to modern Chinese.

As with the other early civilizations, the peasants were required to yield a portion of their crops to support the officials gathered in the towns. Also they had to serve under their rulers in time of war as lightly armed warriors. Only the ruling military class, all bronze age armies, could afford the two-horse chariots and the bronze helmets and armor that they wore into battle. The ruling elite's monopoly of bronze metallurgy sharpened class differentiation within Shang society, just as it had in the Greek.

As for the role of women, the same inequity existed in Chinese civilization as in all others. The discrimination began at infancy, for baby girls were more likely than baby boys to suffer from infanticide. During childhood, girls were subjected to the practice of footbinding, which left them crippled and kept them from venturing far beyond their households.

Chinese sex inequality was supported by the uniquely Chinese view of the world as the product of two interacting complementary elements, yin and yang. Yin was the attribute of all things female, dark, weak, passive. Yang was the attribute of all things male, bright, strong and active. Although male and female were both necessary and complementary, one was by nature passive and subordinate. Woman's role was defined by thousands of years of elaborated behavior patterns by which Chinese women were to be properly obedient and passive.

Chinese culture is characterized by cohesion and continuity. There were numerous nomadic invasions of China, and even a few conquerors. But it was not the Chinese who were forced to adopt the culture of the invader. Rather it was the invader who invariably became Chinese, quickly and completely. As has always been true in China, these invasions did not create a complete break with the Chinese culture's past, as they did in Greece and India. Hence the distinctively Chinese civilization has continued uninterrupted from the early Shang period to the present, sometimes modified but never destroyed or transformed.

One reason for this was the greater isolation of China, as we mentioned. It was invaded only by the nomads of the northwest, all its other borders being too remote. It did not have to cope with the succession of peoples we listed in the previous chapter who invaded India and who, with their relatively advanced cultures, were able to keep in varying degrees their own cultural identity. The Chinese were all Mongoloids to begin with, as were their nomadic invaders, and these relatively primitive tribes were easily absorbed. For this reason the Chinese enjoyed racial and cultural cohesiveness throughout their history. This similarity was further cemented, by the standardization of the writing system, which enabled speakers of widely differing dialects to communicate with each other. In India, there are today fourteen "national languages," one of which, English, serves, in Nehru's words, as "the link" among the other thirteen. In China one writing system was the link. Throughout Chinese history the writing of Chinese in all dialects was uniform. Chinese writing is based on pictograms and ideograms or the combination of pictures into an idea. For example, a picture of one tree is a tree while two trees is a forest. So if we write 4 we all understand what this means even though we may call it four, quatre or vier. Thus, all Chinese whatever they spoke could understand the writing and the literature of a common culture.

The remarkable political unity that has existed through the ages in China has been as important as its cultural homogeneity. This unity results in large part from the unique worldliness of Chinese civilization—the only great civilization that has at no time produced a priestly ruling class. It is true that the emperor was also a priest who made sacrifices to heaven for all of his subjects, but his religious function was always secondary to his real function, that of governing. As a result, there was never in China any great struggle between church and state, which existed in the other civilizations.

The Chinese classics outlined in detail the life of human beings in society, and particularly the relations between the members of a family and between a king and his subjects. This strong secular characteristic provided a firm underlying foundation for political organization and stability. Stability was further encouraged by a unique Chinese institution—a civil service recruited on the basis of public competitive examinations. It was 2,000 years before anything comparable appeared in the West, or anywhere else for that matter.

Because of the secular, this worldly nature of Chinese culture, its outstanding thinkers tended to be practical men who were mainly interested in winning over to their views the rulers of the various states by persuasion. In the course of their travels and teachings, they attracted disciples and gradually formed various schools of philosophy. So intense was this intellectual activity at one time that the Chinese call this period the time of the "Hundred Schools." Although the founders of the various schools often were original thinkers, almost all of them looked for inspiration to a supposedly golden age in the distant past. A similar tendency is found in most cultures, but special veneration of the past was always exceptionally strong among the Chinese. They carefully preserved and studied the writings of earlier ages and considered knowing them necessary for the proper conduct of both private and public affairs.

The most important of these ancient works were the Five Classics, made up of poems, popular traditions, and historical documents. The Classics were studied and used by philosopher-teachers, of which the most outstanding by far was Confucius. His influence has been so overwhelming and lasting that the Chinese way of life during the past 2,000 years can well be called Confucian.

In the second century BC Confucianism was declared the official dogma or faith of the empire. The Classics became the principal study of scholars and statesmen. Until the fall of the last emperor more than 2,000 years later, in 1911, the teachings of Confucius were unchallenged in China. While in many ways Confucianism was to remain dominant in forming distinct Chinese culture, two other moral ethical systems Buddhism and Taoism also contributed strongly. In the chapter on India we discussed Buddhism. The Mahayana branch (see Big Raft, Little Raft) was the imported religion of China. We will now discuss the basic ideas of Confucius and Taoism.

▶ Confucianism

The man whose ideas have formed Chinese culture more than any other is Confucius—Kung Fu-Tzu or Kung the master. He is called the first teacher because he stands above all other teachers in rank. The culture he so influenced has remained remarkably distinct for 25 centuries. For over two thousand years, every Chinese school child has raised his clasped hands each morning to a tablet in the corner bearing Confucius' name. Every Chinese student has poured over his sayings for hours with the result that these have become a part of the Chinese mind, trickling down even to the illiterate in spoken proverbs. Chinese government, too, has been influenced more deeply by Confucius than by any other thinker. Since the start of the Christian era a large number of governmental offices, including some of the highest, have required a knowledge of the thinking of Confucius.

Confucius was born about 551 BC. Note, the Buddha and Lao Tzu are almost contemporaries. In Europe, Greece is entering its Golden Age. His early home life was modest; he wrote, "On reaching the age of 15, I bent my mind to learning." In his twenties he worked as a tutor or teacher, and he was was obviously good. His reputation for practical wisdom spread rapidly and he attracted a circle of enthusiastic disciples. Despite this success, he considered himself a failure. His goal was public office, because he believed that his theories, which he sincerely believed, would not take hold unless they were put into practice by some government. He had supreme confidence in his ability to reorder society if given a chance. When he was told of the growth of population in the state of Wei and asked what should be done, he answered, "Enrich them." "And what after that?" "Educate them," was his famous reply, adding with a sigh, "Were a prince to employ me, in a twelve-month period something could be done, but in three years the work could be completed!"

Though he failed in his ambition to practice what he taught, Confucius was without doubt one of the world's greatest teachers. To the end he remained faithful to his goal of remaking society through educating his students. Power and wealth could probably have been his if he had been willing to compromise his principles with those in authority. He preferred his integrity.

Like other great religious leaders, Confucius looked out and saw a world full of suffering. Confucius lived at a time of undiluted horror known as the "Period of the Warring States." Generals put prisoners to death in mass executions. Soldiers were paid upon presenting the severed hands of their enemies. In the midst of such an age the one question that was most important was: *How can we learn to live together?*

Answers differed but the question was always the same. (This is a question, of course, for all of us today with the potential we have for destroying each other.)

The heart of the message of Confucius lies in his answer to how people can live peaceably together. What sort of social glue will keep society from falling into anarchy?

The answer Confucius came up with was *tradition*; values transmitted from generation to generation which over centuries eliminate destructive values and move toward a peaceable way of living together in societies that don't simply pass out of existence by destroying each other.

Let's examine what Confucius was saying and relate it to some of our experiences. For example, we know there are tribes among the Eskimos and Australian aborigines that do not even have a word for disobedience, so unknown is the phenomenon among them—because tradition does not tolerate disobedience.

"In the old days there were no fights about hunting grounds or fishing territories, There was no law then . . . everybody did what was right." An American Indian recalls a past based on tradition.

When tradition is no longer adequate to hold society together, man faces the hardest test. It is a crisis that the West should have no difficulty in understanding, for in recent years it has been a major American problem. While we have absorbed peoples of varying nationalities and traditions, we have not been successful in replacing them with other well defined traditions. America has become one of the most traditionless societies in history. As substitutes for tradition we have proposed reason and education.

Has reason worked? With more education than almost any other nation, America leads the world in rising crime rates, divorce, drug use and delinquency rates.

Another approach we have favored to solve the problems of society is through police and law. This approach seems the only way to avoid universal violence in a society composed of self-seeking individuals, by maintaining a large and effective police force to bat the people back in line when they misbehave. There must be laws that allow people to know what is and is not permitted; the penalties for violation must be so heavy that no one will dare incur them. In short, laws with teeth in them. People

left on their own act like savages so we must restrain them.

Does this work? We tried this approach in our war on drugs with very little success.

Society, Confucius was convinced, needs more than an efficient police force to make it good.

As for reliance on love, Confucius dismissed this as unrealistic. Love requires agreed-on social structures to come into being. To call for it alone he said was to call for the end without building the means that might bring it into being. When Confucius was asked, "Should one . . . love one's enemy, those who do us harm?" he replied, "By no means. Answer hatred with justice and love with benevolence. Otherwise you would waste your benevolence." (Compare this with Christ's "I tell you love your enemy. If someone hits you on one cheek, turn the other.")

Confucius found himself intrigued by tradition as the answer to the social problem. As most thinkers of his day, he believed that there had been in China's past a period of Grand Harmony. It was tradition that had created this golden age; because the traditions were powerful, people lived by them; and these traditions allowed the people to live well. The decisive difference between his age and the age of Grand Harmony was that men had become individuals, self-conscious and reflective. This being so, accepted tradition—a tradition that had emerged unconsciously out of the trial and error or innumerable generations and that held its power because men felt completely identified with their society—could no longer be accepted. The way to overcome this was to create a deliberate tradition. When tradition can no longer hold its own because of all the doubting and attacks, it must be supported by giving it deliberate attention and reinforcement.

Therefore every means of education, formal and informal, should be used to seeing that these values are made second nature as far as possible by everyone. As one Chinese describes the process: "Moral ideas were driven into the people by every possible means—temples, theaters, homes, toys, proverbs, schools, history, and stories—until they became habits in daily life. . . . Even festivals and parades were always religious in character." By these means even a society composed of individuals can, if it puts itself to the task, create an enveloping tradition, a power of suggestion, which its members will unconsciously follow and which will prompt them to behave properly even when out of sight of the law.

For nearly 2000 years, the first sentence a Chinese child learned to read was "Man is by nature good." Tradition was meant to bring out the goodness in people.

▶ Jen, Chun-tzu, Li, Te and Wan

What were some of the elements of the deliberate tradition Confucius set about creating?

Jen

Jen was the virtue of virtues in Confucius' view of life. Jen involves simultaneously a feeling of humanity toward others and respect for oneself, a sense of the dignity of human life wherever it appears. Other attitudes will follow automatically: magnanimity, good faith, and charity. In the direction of Jen lies the perfection of everything that separates man from the beasts and makes him distinctively human. In public life the man of Jen is untiringly diligent. In private life he is courteous, unselfish, and gifted with empathy, "able to measure the feelings of others by his own." "The man who possesses Jen, *wishing to be established himself, seeks also to enlarge others.*" Such an attitude recognizes no national boundaries for the man of Jen knows that *"within the four seas all men are brothers."*

Chun-tzu

If Jen is the ideal relationship between human beings, Chun-tzu refers to the ideal term of such relations. It has been translated True Manhood, the Superior Man, and Manhood-at-its-Best.

The person possessing Chun-tzu is the opposite of the petty person, the mean person, the little person. Fully adequate, poised, they have toward life, as a whole, the approach of the ideal host who is so at home in his surroundings that he is completely relaxed and, being so, can turn his full attention to putting others at their ease. As he needs nothing himself, he is wholly at the disposal of others. Having come to the point where he is at home in the universe at large, the virtue of Chun-tzu carries these qualities of the ideal host with him through life generally. His approach to others is in terms not of what he can get but of what he can do to help.

The Chinese ideal of the gentleman is part of Chun-tzu. Poised, confident, and competent, the gentleman is a man of perfect ease. His movements are free of brusqueness and violence; his expression is open, his speech free of lewdness and vulgarity. The gentleman does not talk too much. He does not boast, push himself forward, or in any way display his superiority except perhaps at sports. Holding always to his own standards however others may forget theirs, he is never at a loss as to how to behave and can keep things going smoothly where others are at a loss. Schooled to meet any contingency "without fret or fear," his head is not turned by success nor his temper soured by adversity.

Li

There are two meanings to Li. The first is propriety, the way things should be done. Confucius believed in the search for precedence. Confucius wanted to lift to everyone's attention the finest precedents for social life that had been discovered, so everyone might gaze and memorize and copy. Behind the concept of Li stands the presumption that the various roles and relationships of life will have been formally delineated and defined.

The Five Relationships

1. *Father* must be kind, the *Son* obedient.
2. *Husband* must be just, the *Wife* obedient.
3. *Older Brother* must be courteous, *Younger* humble.
4. *Older Friend* must have wisdom, *Younger* respect.
5. *Rulers* must be just and benevolent, *Subjects* loyal.

In effect Confucius is saying: You are never alone when you act. Every action affects someone else. Here in these five relationships is a frame within which you may achieve as much as is possible of individuality without doing damage or creating a bitter conflict with any other individual in the pattern of life. The goal is harmony.

That three of the Five Relationships are concerned with the family is indicative of how important Confucius believed the family to be. He was not inventing but continuing the Chinese assumption that the family is the basic unit of society.

Also note the Confucians show great respect for age. The West, accenting the physical, has praised youth as the best years of our lives. For the Chinese there is a sense of wonder that only time can give. Age gives to all things, objects, institutions, and individual lives, their value, their dignity, their worth. As a consequence, esteem should always turn upward to those who have gone ahead and stand before us. Three of the Five Relationships prescribe that the bulk of respect should flow from young to the old.

Te

The word means power, specifically the power by which men are ruled. What is this power? "Scholars," Confucius said, "remember this: oppressive rule is more cruel than a tiger."

No state, Confucius was convinced, can rule by force all its citizens all the time nor even any large fraction of them a large part of the time. It must depend on widespread acceptance of its will, which in turn requires a certain positive fund of faith in its integrity. Observing that the three essentials of government were economic sufficiency, military sufficiency, and the confidence of the people, he added that popular trust is by far the most important since "if the people have no confidence in their government, it cannot stand."

Wen

Wen refers to the arts of peace as contrasted to the arts of war; to music, art, poetry, culture.

Confucius valued the arts tremendously. He saw them as an instrument for moral education. Confucius contended that the ultimate victory goes to the state that develops the highest Wen, the most exalted culture—the state that has the finest art, the noblest philosophy, the grandest poetry, and gives evidence of realizing that "it is the moral character of a neighborhood that constitutes its excellence." For in the end it is these things that elicit the spontaneous admiration of men and women everywhere. The Gauls were fierce fighters and so crude of culture that they were considered barbarians; but once they experienced what Roman civilization meant, its superiority was so evident they never, after Caesar's conquest, had any general uprising against Roman rule. Confucius would not have been surprised.

Jen, Chun-tze, Li, Te and Wen—goodness, the gentleman, propriety, government by virtue—these are the values set forth by Confucius. They are the deliberate tradition by which men could live a full life together in peace.

▶ Chinese Culture and the Tradition of Confucius

To summarize some Confucian traditions:

Nowhere has family solidarity been greater than in China.

Age in China has always been treated with respect, even veneration.

In social prestige the scholar has traditionally ranked at the top of the scale, the soldier at the bottom.

Legal action is regarded as something of a disgrace, reflecting an incapacity to work things out by sensitive compromise.

Acute social sensitivity is reflected in the concern with "saving face." In the Orient, suicide is involved to escape the loss of self respect, for falling short of expectations. It enables relatives to face society without humiliation.

China has a reputation for having the most peaceful people in the world.

Some of the sayings of Confucius:

If there be righteousness in the heart, there will be beauty in the character.

If there be beauty in the character, there will be harmony in the home.

If there be harmony in the home, there will be order in the nation.

If there be order in the nation, there will be peace in the world.

The true gentleman is friendly but not familiar; the inferior man is familiar but not friendly.

Tzu King asked: "What would you say of the man who is liked by all his fellow townsmen?" "That is not sufficient," was the reply. "What is better is that the good among his fellow townsmen like him, and the bad hate him."

The well-bred are dignified but not pompous. The ill-bred are pompous, but not dignified.

Is not he a true philosopher who, though he be unrecognized of men, cherishes not resentment?

What you do not wish done to yourself, do not do to others. (The Golden Rule)

I will not grieve that men do not know me; I will grieve that I do not know men.

Do not wish for quick results, nor look for small advantages. If you seek quick results, you will not attain the ultimate goal. If you are led astray by small advantages, you will never accomplish great things.

The nobler man first practices what he preaches and afterwards preaches according to his practice.

If, when you look into your own heart, you find nothing wrong there, what is there to worry about, what is there to fear?

When you know a thing to recognize that you know it; and when you do not, to know that you do not know—that is knowledge.

To go too far is as bad as to fall short.

A man without virtue cannot long abide in adversity, nor can he long abide in happiness.

When you see a man of worth, think of how you may emulate him. When you see one who is unworthy, examine your own character.

Wealth and rank are what men desire, but unless they be obtained in the right way they may not be possessed.

Feel kindly toward everyone, but be intimate only with the virtuous.

Maids and servants are hardest to keep in your house. If you are friendly with them, they lose their deference; if you are reserved with them, they resent it.

After Confucianism, the most influential Chinese philosophy was Taoism. The two doctrines supplement each other neatly. Between them they satisfy both the intellectual and emotional needs of the Chinese people. Whereas Confucianism emphasized decorum, conformity, and social responsibility, Taoism stressed individual whim and fancy and conformity to the great pattern of nature. This pattern was defined as Tao (the "road" or "way"), and its disciples were known as Taoists. The key to conforming with Tao was abandonment of ambi-tion, rejection of honors and responsibilities, and a meditative return to nature.

▶ Taoism

In China, the classical and rather formal teachings of Confucius have been balanced by the spirituality of Buddhism and the romanticism of Taoism (pronounced Dowism). Taoism is difficult to define.

Tao is *not* a god

— it is a *Source*
— it is *Reality*
— it is a *"Way"* or *"Path"*

Taoism teaches life is not a struggle between good and evil, light and darkness, as it is portrayed in many religions, rather they are joined and one of the whole.

Taoism originated with a man named Lao Tzu (also written Lao Tze) who was born in China between 600 and 500 BC. Lao Tzu can be translated "The Old Boy" or "The Old Fellow," being a term of endearment and respect.

Discouraged by men's disinclination to seek the goodness he preached, and looking for more time alone in his closing years, Lao Tzu is said to have climbed on a water buffalo and headed westward toward what is now Tibet, the wilderness. At the Chinese border a gatekeeper sensing that this was someone unusual tried to persuade him to turn back. Failing this, he asked the "Old Boy" if he would not at least write down some of his beliefs for the future generations he was deserting. This Lao Tzu consented to do. He withdrew for three days and returned with a slim volume of 5000 characters titled *Tao Te Ching*, or "The Way and Its Power." a testament to man's oneness with the universe. It can be read, at many levels, in an hour, a week, or a lifetime. It is the basic text of all Taoist thought.

Lao Tzu didn't preach; he didn't organize a church. He wrote a few pages, rode off on his water buffalo, and that (as far as he was concerned) was the end of the matter. It's a short life history and we're not even sure Lao Tzu isn't all legend.

The main idea of Taoism revolves around the concept of Tao itself. Literally this word means the path or the way. Tao is the way of ultimate reality. It cannot be known, for it exceeds the reach of the senses. *"The Tao which can be conceived is not the real Tao."* This ultimate, unknowable Tao is the ground of all existence. There is a famous Taoist saying: "Those who know don't say, and those who say don't know." Taoism is the way of the universe; the norm, the rhythm, the driving power in all nature, the ordering principle behind all life, but likewise in the midst of all life.

Basically spirit rather than matter the Tao cannot be used up; the more it is used the more it is present.

Graceful instead of abrupt, flowing rather than hesitant, it is always giving. Giving as it does without holding back, it may be called "the Mother of the World;" Tao guides the way man should order his life to be in harmony with the way the universe operates.

What are some of the principles of conduct advocated by Taoism?

Wu Wei—A possible translation is creative quietude, combining supreme activity and supreme relaxation. The conscious mind must relax, stop standing self-consciously and let go. Only by letting go is it possible to break through the law that the more we try, the more we fail.

Wu wei is the supreme action, the rare suppleness, simplicity, and freedom that flows from us, or rather through us, when our private egos and conscious effort yield to a higher power. Actions follow being; new action, wiser action, stronger action will follow new being, wiser being, stronger being. The *Tao Te Ching* puts this point without wasting a word. It simply says "strive to be."

One simply lets Tao flow in and flow out again until all life becomes a flow in which there is neither imbalance no effort. *Wu wei* is life lived without tension:

"In stretching a bow
You repent of the pull,
A whetted saw
Goes thin and dull."

Far from inaction, however, it is the pure embodiment of gracefulness, simplicity, and freedom—a kind of pure effectiveness in which nothing is wasted on outward show.

One may move so well that a foot-print never shows, speak so well that the tongue never slips, calculate so well that no counter is needed."

There is a Taoist story of a fisherman who was able to land enormous fish with a thread because it was so delicately and precisely made that it had no

weakest point at which to break. Taoist skill should not be noticed. Viewed by others wu wei is never forcing, never under strain and seems effortless. The secret lies in the way it seeks out the empty spaces in life and nature and moves through these it does not force.

Chuang Tzu, the greatest popularizer of Taoism, makes this point with his story of a butcher whose cleaver did not get dull for twenty years. When asked for his secret, the butcher replied, "Between the bones of every joint there is always some space, otherwise there could be no movement. By seeking out this space and passing through it my cleaver lays wide the bones without touching them."

"Those who flow as life flows know
They need no other force:
They feel no wear, they feel no tear,
They need no mending, no repair."

Water was the closest parallel to Tao in the natural world. It was also the model of wu wei.

The Taoists were struck by the way water adapts itself to its surroundings and seeks out the lowest places. So too,

"Man at his best, like water,
Serves as he goes along:
Like water he seeks his own level,
The common level of life."

Yet despite its yielding, water holds a power greater than hard and brittle things. In a stream it wears the stones' sharp edges into smooth pebbles, rounded to conform to water's streamlined flow. It works its way past barriers put in its way. Its gentle current erodes rock and levels hills that seem to be there forever.

"A leader is best
When people barely know that he exists.
. . . Of a good leader, who talks little,
When his work is done, his aim fulfilled,
They will all say, "We did this ourselves."

Still following the analogy of water, the Taoists rejected all forms of self-promotion and competition. The world is full of people who are determined to be somebody. They want to get ahead, to stand out. Taoism has little use for such ambition. "The ax falls first on the tallest tree."

"Standing on tiptoe a man loses balance,
Admiring himself he does so alone. . . ."
"At no time in the world will a man who is sane

Over-reach himself,
Over-spend himself,
Over-rate himself."

What is the point of competition or assertiveness? Tao seems to get along very well without them.

"Nature does not have to insist."

On the whole the modern western tradition has been to regard nature as an enemy, something to be dominated, controlled, conquered. Taoism's attitude toward nature tends to be just the opposite of this. Nature is to be made a friend.

"Those who would take over the earth
And shape it to their will
Never, I notice, succeed."
"The earth is like a vessel so sacred
That at the mere approach of the profane
It is marred
And when they reach out their fingers it is gone."

This idea of blending with nature has been an inspiration of famous American architects Frank Lloyd Wright and Alden B. Dow. Taoist temples do not stand out from the landscape. They should blend in with nature. western man "conquers" Mount Everest. The Taoist might ask, "Why were they fighting?" This idea of blending with nature can be seen on the Michigan Northwood campus designed by Dow.

This Taoist approach to nature has made a deep impression on Chinese art. Painters took nature as their subject, and before painting anything would go out to nature, and become one with it. They would sit until they felt a part of nature before making a stroke. Man's part in nature is small, so he does not dominate the picture as in wesern art. Usually he is pictured climbing with his bundle, riding a buffalo, or poling a boat—man on a journey with a burden to carry, a hill to climb, and we see beauty through the parting mists. Man is not as big as a mountain; and his life is short, but he too belongs in the scheme of nature as much as the birds and the clouds. And through him as through the rest of nature flows the movement of Tao.

Do these concepts seem compatible with today's concern for the environment? There is a renewed interest in Taoism because of our environmental concerns.

Another feature of Taoism is its notion of the relativity of all values and, their idea of the identity of contraries. Here Taoism tied in with the traditional Chinese symbolism of yang and yin, pictured as follows:

This polarity sums up all life's basic oppositions: good-evil, active-passive, positive-negative, light-dark, summer-winter, male-female, etc. But though its principles are in tension, they are not flatly opposed. They complement and counterbalance each other. Each invades the other's hemisphere and establishes itself in the very center of its opposites territory. In the end both are resolved in an all-embracing circle, symbol of the final unity of Tao.

In Taoist perspective even good and evil lose their absolute character. We in the United States tend to be very black and white and unyielding in our distinctions. Schools give true and false tests and students are right or wrong.

Indian Buddhism combined with Chinese Taoism formed Japanese Zen, a major influence on their culture, as will be discussed later.

It should be no surprise to find an outlook as opposed to violence as Taoism to be opposed to war. That in traditional China the scholar ranked at the top of the social scale may be the doing of Confucius, but Taoism is fully as responsible for placing the soldier at the bottom. "*The way for a vital man to go is not the way of a soldier.*" Only the man "who recognizes all men as members of his own body is a sound man to guard them. . . . Heaven arms with compassion those whom she would not see destroyed."

Taoism's approach to every problem is lighthearted, yet it is sophisticated and charming. "*He who feels punctured must once have been a bubble,"* epitomizes much of Taoist thought.

Taoists liked having fun. Confucius tended to be stuffy and pompous, according to Taoists.

Blending like yang and yin themselves, Taoism and Confucianism represent two parts of the Chinese outlook. Confucius represents the classical, Lao Tzu the romantic. Confucius stresses social responsibility, Lao Tzu praises spontaneity and naturalness. Confucius' focus is always on man, Lao Tzu's beyond man, to nature.

The *Tao Te Ching* written by Lao Tzu has been translated more frequently than any other work except the Bible.

The philosophy of Lao Tzu is simple: Accept what is in front of you without wanting the situation to be other than it is. Study the natural order of things and work with it rather than against it, for to try to change what *is* only *sets* up resistance. Nature provides everything without requiring payment or thanks, and also provides for all without discrimination; therefore let us present the same face to everyone and treat all men as equals, however they may behave. If we watch carefully, we will see that work proceeds more quickly and easily if we stop "trying," if we stop putting in so much extra effort, if we stop looking for results. In the clarity of a still and open mind, truth will be reflected. *Te*—(which may be translated as "virtue" or "strength")—lies always in *Tao*, or "natural law." In other words: Simply be.

Here are some selected quotes from the Tao Te Ching.

"The Tao that can be told is not the eternal Tao. The name that can be named is not the eternal name."

"The highest good is like water. Water gives life to the ten thousand things and does not strive. It flows in places men reject and so is like the Tao."

"Thirty spokes share the wheel's hub; it is the center hole that makes it useful. Shape clay into a vessel; It is the space within that makes it useful. Cut doors and windows for a room; it is the holes which make it useful. Therefore profit comes from what is there; usefulness from what is not there."

"Accept disgrace willingly. Accept misfortune as the human condition. What do you mean by 'Accept disgrace willingly'? Accept being unimportant. Do not be concerned with loss or gain. This is called 'accepting disgrace willingly.'"

"Give up sainthood, renounce wisdom, and it will be a hundred times better for everyone. Give up kindness, renounce morality, and men will rediscover filial piety and love. Give up ingenuity, renounce profit, and bandits and thieves will disappear."

"Yield and overcome; bend and bestraight; empty and be full; wear out and be new; have little and gain; have much and be confused."

"Those who know do not talk. Those who talk do not know."

"Practice non-action. Work without doing. Taste the tasteless. Magnify the small, increase the few. Reward bitterness with care."

"Under heaven nothing is softer and, yes, more yielding than water. Yet for attacking the solid and strong, nothing is better; it has no equal. The weak can overcome the strong; the supple can overcome the stiff. Under heaven everyone knows this, yet no one puts it into practice."

▶ Outline of Chinese History

China's long history has been marked by three great revolutions that fundamentally changed its political and social structure. The first in 221 BC ended the feudal system and created a centralized empire; the second in AD 1911 ended the empire and established a republic; and the third in 1949 put the present Communist regime in power.

The first of these revolutions was the work of the leaders of the northwest state of Ch'in in the Wei River valley. This location contributed to the victory, for the valley is largely inaccessible and easy to defend. With these advantages, the Ch'in leaders extended their possessions steadily, overcoming the surrounding states one by one. By 221 BC the Ch'in ruler was master of all China, and he adopted the title of Shih Huangti, or "First Emperor." His successor would be "Second Emperor," and so on down the generations for "ten thousand years," meaning forever. The new emperor abolished all other Chinese kingdoms. He reorganized this united China into administrative areas, and sent officials to run them who were responsible to the central government. To consolidate his position he disarmed all soldiers except his own, and made the old aristocratic families live in his capital where he could keep an eye on them. The new emperor also organized the economy by standardizing weights, measures, and the currency; in other words, he created a united China.

One of the most important innovations for the unification of China was the scrapping of the numerous ways of writing that had been developed in the separate kingdoms. In their place a standardized script was required that was used and understood from one end of China to the other. This proved to be a most effective and lasting bond throughout China because of the nature of Chinese writing. It is not based on twenty-six signs expressing sound like our alphabet. Rather, it consists of a large number of symbols or characters, each one of which is a picture or symbol of an object or a concept.

The system is precisely that used in the West for numbers. We all know what the symbol "5" means, whatever we may call it. So it is with Chinese characters, or ideographs, which have meaning but no sound. They are ideas, like numerals, which every reader can sound according to his own dialect.

Thus the new Ch'in standardized script, which has continued with modifications to the present, could be read and understood by all educated Chinese, even though they spoke different languages and couldn't understand each other. For the same reason, their writing was equally comprehensible to foreign peoples, so that educated Japanese, Koreans, or Vietnamese can read Chinese without being able to speak a word of it. It is easy to see how important this system was for uniting Chinese culture and spreading it throughout Asia.

It was during the Ch'in Dynasty that the famous Great Wall of China was built to keep out the nomads from the north. Although Ch'in rule was very short, it left a deep and permanent imprint on China. The country we call China had been changed from a group of small countries into a centralized empire, which it remains down to today. It is only appropriate that our name for China comes from from the Ch'in.

The Han Dynasty followed the Ch'in. It prospered for four hundred years, about the same length of time as the Roman Empire. And during the same time, the Han Empire also resembled the Roman Empire in its great size. During the first sixty years of their reign, the Han rulers concentrated on building up the country and consolidating their power. But under the "Martial Emperor," Wu Ti (141-87 BC), the country's borders were greatly expanded in all directions. Tribal territories in the south were conquered, though it took several centuries of Chinese immigration and influence before this part of the empire could be called Chinese in culture. The greatest growth was toward the west, where Chinese expeditions drove across central Asia, establishing contact with India and greatly increasing the volume of trade along the Silk Road.

The Han Empire was comparable to the Roman Empire in population as well as territorial extent. A census taken in the year AD 1, and believed to be reasonably accurate, showed the empire to have 12.2 million households with a total of 59.6 million people. By contrast the population of the Roman Empire at the same time is thought to have been around 120 million. The Han Empire had an efficient bureaucracy that was responsible for the physical well being and prosperity of the people.

In the first century BC the Chinese bureaucracy is said to have numbered 130,000 officials, or only one for every 400 or 500 inhabitants. This small number in relation to the total population was typical throughout Chinese history and is to be explained by the tradition of small central government. "Governing a country," according to a Chinese proverb, *is like cooking a small fish: neither should be overdone."*

Consequently Chinese governments did not feel responsible for all the social services that we take for granted. They saw the main roles of government as collection of taxes and defense of the country against foreign enemies and also the protection of the dynasty against internal subversion. The bureaucracy was a privileged, but not hereditary, elite. During the Han period, the unique system was started for the selection of civil-service personnel by means of competitive public examinations.

Since the examinations were based on the Confucian Classics, the empire in effect was run by Confucians and according to Confucian principles. Each official was assigned to a post outside his home province to be sure that he would not use his position to build up local family power. The result was an administrative system that was far more efficient and responsive than any other until modern times.

Indeed this civil service based on merit was a major factor in the long continuity of the Chinese imperial system from the time of the First Emperor to our time. There was another side, however, to this examination system. Since it was based on total acceptance of a single body of doctrine, it produced a rigid orthodoxy and an intellectual arrogance that was to hurt China centuries later when the Europeans arrived with another set of values.

Although China was to suffer deeply in modern times because it fell behind the West in science and industry, during the Han period it was a very different story. China then took a lead in technology that it was to keep until just recently. Some of the more important Chinese inventions of these centuries were the water-powered mill, the shoulder collar for horses—which greatly increased their efficiency—and the techniques for casting iron, making paper, and glazing pottery. Rag paper, dating from about AD 100, soon replaced cumbersome wooden and bamboo slips for writing. But paper is not as durable as wood, and since it was developed by the Chinese long before printing, we must, oddly enough, blame the use of paper for the loss of certain books. Pottery glazes, which were eventually developed into porcelain, or china, were a blessing to mankind. They not only were beautiful, but they also represented a major advance in hygiene, since smooth porcelain was more sanitary than the rough pottery or wooden utensils used before.

▶ Dynasties

In political theory the Chinese thinkers shared a belief in the idea of the "Mandate of Heaven." They held that a king ruled under the blessing of Heaven only as long as he possessed the virtues of justice, benevolence, and sincerity. When he no longer had these virtues and misruled his kingdom, he was automatically deprived of the Mandate of Heaven, and rebellion against him was, therefore, not a crime but a just punishment from Heaven brought on by the rebels. Thus Chinese thinkers, although often aware of the social and economic factor behind dynastic decline, held them secondary to what they thought to be a more basic underlying consideration—the moral qualifications of the ruler. The rise and fall of dynasties was seen as the workings of the Mandate of Heaven.

Chinese history records the succession of dynasties. Rather than the Mandate of Heaven, we could look to economic reasons: a combination of personal ambitions, family influences, and institutional pressures inevitably led the emperors sooner or later to overextend themselves. They squandered their human and financial resources on roads, canals, fortifications, palaces, court extravagances, and frontier wars. Thus each dynasty began to experience financial difficulties about a century after its founding.

A vicious circle was set in motion—rising taxes, falling revenues, neglected roads and dikes, and declining productivity. Eventually this development resulted in famines, breakdown of law, and full-scale peasant uprisings. Meanwhile frontier defenses were likely to be neglected, inviting raids across the borders by nomads. Often it was the combination of internal revolt and external invasion that brought down the tottering dynasty and cleared the way for a new beginning.

Thus in AD 222 the Han Dynasty disappeared, in a swirl of peasant revolts, warlord coups, and nomadic raids. China then entered a prolonged period of disunity and disorder similar to the Dark Ages in Europe following the collapse of the Roman Empire.

The Han Dynasty was followed, in time, by the T'ang and Sung dynasties (618–907 and 960–1279), which represented a continuation of the traditional civilization, although with certain refinements and modifications.

The Yuan Dynasty that followed (1279–1368) was unique in that it was Mongol rather than Chinese. The Mongols, under Genghis Khan, had overrun most of Eurasia, so that China was now part of a huge empire extending from the Pacific to Europe. But these Mongol rulers were few in number compared to their millions of Chinese subjects, and they failed to win the support of the Chinese gentry and peasants. They ruled as conquerors, making few concessions to Chinese institutions or to the Chinese way of life. When their military power declined, their regime was swept away by rebellious peasants and hostile scholar-bureaucrats, leaving little behind.

Following the expulsion of the Mongols, China was ruled by two more dynasties, the Chinese Ming (1368–1644) and the Manchu Ch'ing (1644–1911). Although the Manchus from Manchuria were foreigners like the Mongols, they were successful in ruling China because they gave prestige and opportunity to Chinese scholar-bureaucrats and Chinese culture while maintaining administrative control. They respected and utilized Chinese institutions but created a system of checks to protect their own position. While ruling at the top, local government remained largely in Chinese hands.

This entire period, from the mid-fourteenth century to the nineteenth, when the European intrusion in China began in earnest, is one of the great eras of orderly government and social stability in human history. The traditional institutions and practices continued smoothly and effectively—the agricultural economy, the Confucian way of life, the examination system for the selection of public officials, and the revered rule of the Son of Heaven in Peking. The idea of continual change and "progress," which now was taken for granted in Europe, remained foreign to the Chinese mind.

▶ The Coming of the Europeans

China began to feel the direct impact of an expanding new Europe when Portuguese merchants began trading with Canton in 1514 and established a permanent trading post at Macao in 1557. The Portuguese bought Chinese silks, wood carvings, porcelain, lacquerware, and gold, and in return they sold nutmeg, cloves, and mace which they brought in from the East Indies; sandalwood from Timor; drugs and dyes from Java; and cinnamon, pepper, and ginger from India. No European goods were involved for the simple reason that there was no market for them in China. The Portuguese were functioning only as middlemen for a purely intra-Asian trade. European impact on Chinese culture at this point was minimal.

The Dutch and the British arrived in the early seventeenth century to challenge Portugal's monopoly in the China trade. Neither was given permission by the Chinese to trade, so for years the Dutch and English preyed on Portuguese shipping and traded haphazardly along the south China coast.

By the mid-eighteenth century the Chinese opened up the trade to all countries, though limiting it to Canton and Macao. The English soon won the lion's share of this trade, partly because of their growing commercial and industrial superiority and also because of their convenient base of operations in India.

Meanwhile the Russians in Siberia had been trying to open trade relations with China, and the Chinese had reacted by restricting and regulating the commerce closely. The Chinese remained supremely self-confident and self-centered following their first contacts with Europe. They had kept European traders confined to a few seaports and frontier trading posts; and they had shown only a passing interest in Jesuit teachings about science and theology. Never in history had a people faced the future with so much self-assurance and with so little reason for it.

By the mid-nineteenth century the situation changed suddenly and drastically. Europe had grown dramatically more powerful, while China remained conservative and self-satisfied. First China and then Japan were forced to open their doors and to accept western merchants, missionaries, consuls, and gunboats.

Both Japan and China were fundamentally affected, though with very different results. Japan adopted and used the instruments of western power. It was able to use them for self-defense and, later, for growth. China, by contrast, was unable to reorganize itself to meet the western challenge. Being too large and united to be conquered outright like we saw in India, China was never to be a European colony. Yet, China remained uneasy and off balance in its relationship with the West until World War I, and even for some decades thereafter.

The Chinese were forcefully jarred out of their seclusion and complacency by three disastrous wars: the first with Britain in 1839–1842, the second with Britain and France in 1856–1858, and the third with Japan in 1895. The humiliating defeats suffered in these wars forced the Chinese to throw open the gates, to end their superior attitude toward the West, and to reappraise their own traditional values. The outcome has been the launching of a new China that is still being defined and will certainly be a major part of a new global society.

Britain was able to take the lead in opening up China because it had a powerful base in India as well as control of the seas. Britain's main goal was to open up China to trade. The first cause of a big problem was the English trade in opium. European sailors had introduced opium smoking in China in the seventeenth century, and the habit had spread rapidly from the ports. The demand for opium solved the British balance of payments problem. At first the British had been forced to pay mostly in gold and silver, because the Chinese were little interested in English goods. But now the market for opium reversed the balance of trade in favor of the British. The Chinese government issued decrees in 1729 and 1799 prohibiting the importation of opium, but the trade was so profitable that Chinese officials could be bribed to permit smuggling.

The Opium War broke out when the Chinese attempted to enforce their prohibition of the opium traffic. During the fighting that followed, the hopeless military inferiority of the Chinese became obvious. With a squadron of ships and a few thousand men, the British were able to seize port after port at will. The Chinese fought bravely. Their garrisons often resisted to the last man. But the odds against the non-Europeans were even worse now than they had been between the conquistadors and the Aztecs in Mexico.

European warships and artillery had improved immeasurably since Cortez, whereas Chinese military technology had stagnated at a level little above that of Aztec capabilities. In 1842, the Chinese government surrendered and accepted the Treaty of Nanking, the first of a long series of unequal treaties that were to eat away much of China's sovereignty.

Fighting began again in 1856. The occasion this time was the imprisonment by Chinese officials of the Chinese crew on board a Chinese ship flying the British flag. When the Chinese government refused to release the crew, the British bombed Canton. The French entered the war, using the murder of a French priest as a pretext. The Anglo-French forces proved irresistible. They captured the capitol and forced China to sign a humiliating treaty. It opened several more ports on the coast to Europeans. In the interior, they redefined and extended extraterritoriality and permitted the establishment of foreign legations to Peking and of Christian missions throughout the country.

The third defeat suffered by China was the most humiliating, for it was at the hands of the small neighboring kingdom of Japan. The Japanese, in contrast to the Chinese, had been able to adapt western technology to their needs and to build an efficient military establishment. Thus they accomplished what no other oriental state had been able to do. Japan now pressed certain shadowy claims in Korea. Traditionally, the Koreans had recognized the leadership of China, but they had also periodically paid tribute to Japan.

So when China sent a small force to Korea in 1894 in response to an appeal for aid in suppressing a revolt, the Japanese also landed a detachment of marines. The two forces clashed, and war was formally declared by China and Japan in August 1894. The Chinese armies again were easily routed, and, in April 1895, Peking was forced to accept yet another humiliating treaty.

The loss to Japan was a shattering blow to the pride and complacency of China. The great empire had been shown to be completely helpless at the hands of a neighbor they looked down on. Furthermore, the European powers during the preceding years had been taking advantage of China's weakness and annexing outlying territories that traditionally had recognized China's rule. Russia took territory in the north; France seized Indochina; Britain took Burma; and Japan, by defeating China, annexed Korea in 1910. Further, the western states divided up China itself. They set up "spheres of influence" in which the political and economic primacy of each European power was recognized.

The humiliations and disasters that China experienced in the later half of the nineteenth century forced the traditionally self-centered Middle Kingdom, as they called themselves, to undertake a painful self-assessment and reorganization. The Chinese slowly and with reservations tried to follow the western model. The failures at reform demonstrated the futility of trying to modernize China within the existing order. The alternative was revolution from below, and this did take place in 1911, when the Manchu Dynasty finally was overthrown and its place taken by a republic.

The leader and ideologist of the revolutionaries was Dr. Sun Yat-sen (1866–1925). Compared to previous reform leaders, Sun was very different. He was not one of the upper-class intellectuals. In fact, his training was as much western as Chinese. He was born near Canton, which had been subject to foreign influence longer than any other area in

China. At the age of thirteen he joined his brother in Honolulu, where he remained five years and completed a high school course in a Church of England boarding school. Then he went to Queen's College in Hong Kong, and after graduation he enrolled in the Hong Kong Medical College, where he received his medical degree in 1892.

Sun Yat-sen derived his main support from Chinese merchants outside China. Within the country only a few students and merchants were influenced by his ideas, and the mass of the people remained as always illiterate and apathetic. In any case, the revolutionists exploited the general discontent and worked effectively among students and soldiers. Despite lack of coordination, the revolutionary movement spread rapidly throughout the country. Sun Yat-sen, who was in the United States at the time, hurried back, and on December 30, 1911, a provisional revolutionary assembly elected him president of the United Provinces of China.

The weakness and failure of this new republic forced real government into the hands of local warlords. These warlords paid little attention to the republican government that was supposed to be ruling from Peking. Instead, they pillaged the countryside mercilessly and dragged China down to a brutal anarchy. These early years of the republic marked one of the worst periods in the long history of China.

Sun Yat-sen died in 1925, at the very time when the instruments were in place to fulfill his ambitions of reforming China. Although he did not live to see the warlords humbled and the country united, he is today recognized as one of the creators of modern China. With Dr. Sun's death, Chiang Kai-shek became the leading figure in the Kuomintang. In May 1926 he assumed command of the "Northern Expedition," a campaign to unify China by crushing the warlords in the north. The Kuomintang forces, preceded by propaganda corps that included Chinese Communists, swept everything before them.

During the following years, China made appreciable progress under Chiang's guidance. Railway mileage almost doubled, and that of modern roads quadrupled. Internal tariff barriers were abolished in 1932, and a unified currency was created for the first time. Significant progress was also made in governmental procedures, public health, education, and industrialization. Equally striking were the government's successes in the diplomatic field. Control of the tariff was regained, some of the territories ceded to foreign nations were recovered, and many of the special privileges wrested by the western powers were returned.

But there were serious gaps in Chiang's reform program, and these ultimately proved fatal. Badly needed land reform was neglected because the Kuomintang party in the rural areas was dominated by landlords who opposed any change. And Chiang's authoritarian, one-party government prevented the growth of democracy, so that opposition groups could not assert themselves by constitutional means; revolution was the sole alternative. Finally, the Kuomintang failed to develop ideas that could attract the support of the people. Nationalist appeals had little attraction for land-hungry peasants and poverty-stricken city workers.

These weaknesses of the Kuomintang regime might have been gradually overcome if it had been given a long period of peace. But it did not have this opportunity because of two mortal enemies, the Communists at home and the Japanese abroad.

The Chinese Communist party was organized in Shanghai in July 1921, and in the following years branches appeared in all parts of the country. Many students and intellectuals joined the ranks, attracted by the call for action and the assurances of a classless and equitable society for the future. The Communists first cooperated with Sun Yat-sen and then broke with Chiang Kai-shek in 1927. Most of the Communist leaders were killed off by Chiang, but a number managed to escape to the mountainous interior of south China.

One of their leaders was Mao Zedong, who now worked out a new revolutionary strategy in defiance of the Communist International in Moscow. He rejected the traditional Marxist doctrine that only the urban proletariat could be depended on to carry through a revolution. From firsthand observation in the countryside he concluded that the poor peasants, who made up 70 percent of the population, were "the vanguard of the revolution. . . . Without the poor peasant there can be no revolution." This was pure heresy in Moscow, but Mao went his way, organizing the peasants and building up a separate army and government in the south.

Chiang responded by launching a campaign of extermination of Communists. He did succeed in completely surrounding the Communists with his armies. However, 90,000 managed to break through, and, of those, fewer than 7,000 survived a 6,000-mile trek of incredible hardship. During this historic "Long March" of 368 days (October 16, 1934 to October 25, 1935) they fought an average of almost a skirmish a day with Kuomintang forces totaling more than 300,000.

Finally the Communist survivors reached the northwest provinces, where they dug in and established a base. Their land-reform policies again won peasant support, so that they were able to build up their strength to the point where they became serious rivals of the Kuomintang regime. The "Long March" is the great epic of modern China, and all the leaders until recently were part of it.

While Chiang was involved in this domestic struggle with the Communists, he was being attacked from the outside by the Japanese. This aggression began with the occupation of Manchuria in 1931 and continued until, by the beginning of World War II, the Japanese were in control of the entire east coast. The combination of Communist Japanese attack ended in 1949 with Chiang's flight to Taiwan (Formosa), leaving Mao and the communists to rule China from his new capital in Peking.

When the victorious Chinese Communists established the People's Republic in 1949, they were promptly recognized by the Soviet Union. A score of other countries, including Britain and India, did likewise. The United States, however, continued to treat Chiang Kai-shek's exiled regime in Taiwan as the legal government of China. Peking therefore turned to Moscow and, in 1950, signed a thirty-year treaty of "friendship, alliance, and mutual assistance." Under the terms of the treaty, the Soviet Union helped China to build a large modern army and to begin an ambitious program of industrialization.

The Russo-Chinese alliance began to show signs of disruption in the late 1950s. Peking criticized Soviet Premier Khrushchev and Moscow retaliated. The quarrel between the two Communist giants grew to an outright schism, including name calling and open rivalry all over the globe.

As an alternative to Russian five-year plans, Chairman Mao launched two great reform movements, the Great Leap Forward of 1958 and the Cultural Revolution of 1966, with their slogans such as "organization without bureaucracy" and "serve the people." The Russians regarded these plans as doomed to failure, which was one reason why they stopped their aid to China.

Mao's successors have had to launch new measures to undo the disaster caused by Mao's initiatives. These measures included restoring family farms in place of communes; substituting individual managers for revolutionary committees in factories; rewarding good workers and penalizing poor ones; and moving away from industrial self-reliance and toward mass importation of factories and technologies.

This "modernization" brought prosperity to at least some Chinese citizens, whose aspirations have grown from the original "three big pieces"—a wristwatch, a bicycle, and a foot-powered sewing machine—to three bigger pieces—a color television set, a refrigerator, and a tape-cassette player. The lure of western consumerism is at work in modern China.

▶ China Today

China seems to bring out in Americans an irresistible desire to serve as China's teachers in the ways of the modern industrial world, and thereby presumably help China improve itself. Yet China seems driven to reject our help and to act in ways that seem to us to be damaging to China's well-being.

It is of course understandable that cultural differences should arise in relations among people with different traditions, such as the U.S. and China.

Unfortunately, the differences are not superficial; their roots extend deep into China's historical experience. Any true understanding of these problems, therefore, calls for an analysis of the complex and unique ways in which the Chinese state and society have evolved. The starting point for understanding the problem is to recognize that China is not just another nation-state in the family of nations. *China is a civilization, not just a state.* The story of modern China could be described as the effort by both Chinese and foreigners to fit a very old civilization into the form of a modern nation state, an institutional invention that came out of the the West's own experience. Viewed from another perspective, the miracle of China has been its astonishing unity.

Chinese civilization has produced a distinctive and enduring pattern of relations between the state and society. Although the affairs of the state were always secret and tainted with the suspicion of scandal, the realm of government projected grandeur and thus gave all Chinese a right to pride and dignity. Chinese society remained peculiarly passive toward its government. And we spoke earlier of how the government remained small and unobtrusive. It has always been a society composed of inward-looking groupings, and thus grouped in its structure. Society in China existed only at the local level; there were no national institutions of society, such as the church in Europe. The state existed alone at the very highest level. (See the three functions described earlier.)

In traditional China, as in present-day China, the clash of politics occurred among the upper-most rulers and their bureaucracies. The people as a whole had almost nothing to say or do about public affairs, even though the fiction might be that all policies were executed in their name. The Confucian mandarins understood that the purpose of bureaucratic government was to uphold the ideal of stability, which is best achieved when bureaucrats bend all their wits and energies toward blunting each other's new ideas. This distinctively Chinese relationship between the state and society was sustained by a shared belief in a moral order, the upholding of which gave the government legitimacy, and the existence of which gave the people security and peace.

With modern western ideas, the balance of power shifts in favor of society and the emerging interests of the people (We the people of the United States). The authority of government comes to de-

United States Superimposed on China

FIGURE 9-1 China is a continent-size country, as is the U.S.A. Generalities about climate or vegetation are not meaningful.

pend on the outcome of political processes. Instead of legitimacy being derived from an orthodox moral order, it comes alive by the play of politics as agreed in a system of laws.

Marxism-Leninism in its Maoist form became the new moral order that reenergized rulers' pretensions of moral superiority and invincibility. The result is a distinctive system, which could be called Confucian Communism, in which rulers, especially under Mao Zedong, claims to have a monopoly on virtue. Society is guided by a moralistic ideology, and the hierarchy of officialdom is supposedly composed of exemplary people skilled in doctrinal matters like the Mandarins. This continuing Chinese emphasis on a moral order explains the exaggerated importance of ideology in the Maoist years, the current tendency to revert to orthodoxy at every sign of political difficulties, and the generally erratic behavior of the state.

The great importance of a moral order for political legitimacy has made Chinese leaders, both Confucian and Communist, dogmatic believers that values can be vividly categorized into those that are at the core or essence of the moral order; those that are foreign but useful, such as western science and technology; and those that are an abomination because they contaminate the purity of the core values. The last must be vigilantly guarded against and denounced.

Panic grows at the thought that the purity of the core values is being contaminted by Chinese who are supposed to be learning only practical matters from alien cultures. The Chinese have elevated science and technology to the ranks of their core values and have come to revere science in much the same spirit as the earlier mandarins did Confucianism. Thus, instead of science having the liberating effect it did in the West, in China it has become a new orthodoxy for a state-supported technocratic elite.

The stunted growth of special interest groups in China is rooted in part in the nature of traditional Chinese society, which was essentially agrarian, and in which the only established channel for upward mobility was the government bureaucracy. China did not have the diversities that emerged in Europe with the rise of cities, the development of a merchant class, the growth of professions and occupations, and all of the other social changes that contributed to the pluralism basic to modern western politics.

In the West the rise of interest groups in society was also fueled by religious beliefs that valued the individual and gave legitimacy to individualism and the search for self-realization. In China the society was community oriented; individuals were expected to find their identities as members of the collectivity.

The fact that all Chinese derived their identities from being members of a group, starting most importantly with the family and the clan, gave stability to China's unique structure of state-society relations, making it relatively easy for the government to rule.

In the Ming Dynasty as few as 100,000 officials managed an empire of 100 million people, and a single magistrate was responsible for a county averaging 50,000 people. Apply this ratio to your town to see how it compares. Collectivities governed themselves and the state could rely on the principle of collective responsibility.

Society also benefitted from this system in that individuals could derive a strong sense of security from being a part of a group that provided mutual support. An individual could thus become a part of a complex network of associations extending outward from the family to people from the same town, province, school or other institutions. People who shared any commonly recognized identity could count on each other. For both the mandarins of the past and the Communist groups of today, these networks of personal relationships have provided the basic elements of Chinese politics.

Just as individuals are not supposed to assert their identities, likewise all subordinate interests in China's hierarchical society are expected to defer to higher interests. China never openly acknowledged that political power might be harnessed to advance economic interests. Although China has great regional differences, ranging from the rice economy of the south to the millet and wheat economies of the north, and from its cosmopolitan coast to this provincial interior, these differences have never been openly acknowledged. Everyone has simply gone along with the pretense that whatever the central authorities advocated is in the interest of all Chinese. The rule against asserting one's own material interest has made selfishness China's ultimate political sin.

China never had the clash of church and state, of religion and science, that established the western intellectual as a legitimate outside critic of authority. As a result the Chinese governmental process has rarely had the benefit of effective sharp criticism.

The overriding duty to defend a great civilization by upholding a moral order seems to cause today's Chinese leaders to discount the risks of irritating other governments. Other governments should simply do what is "right" and be thankful to China for providing moral instruction and guidance.

Chinese society, in spite of current repression, continues to have surprising dynamism. The coastal provinces have fought back the forces of political repression and economic recession and, consequently, economic progress at the local level continues. The modernizing elements in the society seek to expand their international contracts as best they can. The unshakable idea that China remains a great civilization fuels a comfortable superiority complex and makes the vast majority of Chinese optimists, for they must believe that it is only an anomaly that things are as bad as they currently are, and in the future greatness will inevitably return.

In dealing with China, the outside world has every reason to follow its own optimistic instincts and try to build ties with elements of China's distinctive society. There is no reason not to believe that in the not too distant future China will be an active member of a world economy and society.*

The issue of Far Eastern culture and the West is discussed in further detail at the close of this chapter. The main thesis is that East and West will be moving toward a fusion of cultures by borrowing from each other.

▶ History Summary: China

The Shang Dynasty	1600 BC
The Centralized Empire	221 BC
The Collapse of the Empire	1842–1911
The Republic of China	1911–1949
The People's Republic of China	1949–Present

Note

*About the best explanation of the conflict between present Chinese aims and their misunderstanding by the United States and the rest of the world I have found is an article in *Foreign Affairs*, Fall, 1990, entitled *"China: Erratic State, Frustrated Society"* by Lucian W. Pye. I have used his insights in describing "China Today."

▶ KOREA

Koreans are one ethnic family speaking one language. Culturally they are within the Far Eastern cultural realm and over the centuries have been strongly influenced by China. Confucianism permeates all aspects of Korean society, it encourages correct social behavior, righteousness, ancestral worship, and filial piety—especially between father and son. Because of its remarkable recent rise from one of the world's poorest nations to at least middle class status and its growing role in the world economy, we should know in at least outline form some of its distinctive features.

Early history of the Koreans is full of legends and myths of their origins and takes them back to an original founding father Tan-gun. The kingdom he founded is said to have lasted until the second century BC.

Korea's earliest recorded history is characterized by clan communities which combined to form small city-states. The city-states gradually united into tribal leagues with increasingly complex political structures. This state of affairs prevailed throughout the peninsula and southern Manchuria until roughly the beginning of the Christian era.

Among various tribal leagues, Koguryo (37 BC–AD 668), along the middle course of the Amnokkang River (Yalu), was the first to mature into a kingdom. Its belligerent troops conquered neighboring tribes one after another. They finally drove the Chinese out of Nangnang in 313 AD and expanded their territory deep into Manchuria.

These developments in the north had repercussions in the politically and culturally less advanced southern part of the peninsula. A group of refugees from Koguryo founded a new kingdom named Paekche (18 BC–AD 660) south of the Hangang River in the vicinity of present-day Seoul.

The people of Paekche were evidently more peaceful than the ferocious warriors of Koguryo, so they kept moving south to avoid the threats of their northern rival. By the fourth century, they completely dominated the southwestern part of the peninsula. Paekche was firmly established as a prosperous and civilized state, trading extensively with China across the sea.

Shilla (57 BC–AD 668), which was geographically removed from Chinese influence, was at first the weakest and most underdeveloped of the three kingdoms. The last to adopt foreign creeds and ideas, its society was markedly class-oriented and developed remarkable power, drawing resources from its unique Hwarang (Flower of Youth) Corps and Buddhist teaching.

By the mid-sixth century, Shilla had brought under its control all of the neighboring Kaya kingdoms, a group of fortified town-states that developed in the southeastern region from the mid-first century to the mid-sixth century. It effected a military alliance with T'ang China to subjugate both Koguryo and Paekche. But China was a dangerous ally. Shilla had to take up arms against China when the Chinese exposed their own ambition to incorporate the territories of Koguryo and Paekche into their own empire.

Shilla's victory over China in 676 was a triumphant turning point in Korean history. Shilla succeeded in repelling the Chinese from the peninsula and achieved its first territorial unification. Following this, the people of Koguryo repulsed T'ang forces in Manchuria and the northern part of the peninsula, and established the Kingdom of Parhae in 698. This period has been referred to as that of the Northern and Southern Kingdoms.

Although politically separate, the three kingdoms of Koguryo, Paekche and Shilla were related ethnically and linguistically. Each of them developed a sophisticated political structure and legal system and adopted Confucian ethics and Buddhist faith. Over the centuries, however, conflicts among them continued to grow with various and changing alliances between two against the other or against China or with China against the others.

Buddhism spread rapidly among the upper classes of these kingdoms after it was introduced in the fourth century through China. Rulers of all three kingdoms patronized Buddhism and used it to bolster their power. Korean monks traveled to China and India to study the scriptures and transmitted Buddhist literature and arts to Japan, playing a decisive role in the development of that country's ancient civilization.

The date Confucianism was introduced in Korea was around the beginning of the Christian era, almost at the same time as the earliest written Chinese material entered the peninsula.

Confucianism became a powerful instrument for reorganizing the state and society and for infusing new discipline into intellectual life in the fourteenth century with the inception of the Choson Dynasty (1392–1910), which is better known in the West as the Yi Dynasty.

The early rulers of Choson replaced Buddhism with Confucianism in order to counter the dominant Buddhist influence and to appropriate the great wealth accumulated by monasteries during the Koryo period. Neo-Confucian theories of state and society provided the ideological basis for wide-reaching reforms in the hands of the elite of the new dynasty. Confucian ethics and values came to dominate social structure and behavior through the following centuries.

The Choson rulers governed with a well-balanced, sophisticated political system. The civil service examination system was firmly established as the main avenue of recruitment for government office. The examinations formed the backbone of social mobility and intellectual activity during the period.

The society in general valued academic learning while disdaining commerce and manufacturing. You will recall how this mimics the Chinese system and attitude. Confucianism is the religion of the "gentleman scholar."

In the late sixteenth century, however, Korea experienced the trauma of a seven-year war with Japan. After the court of Choson rejected a request by the Japanese warlord Toyotomi Hideyoshi to make way for his invasion of China, Hideyoshi launched a Korean campaign. Most of the peninsula was devastated, and numerous Korean artisans and technicians were forcibly taken to Japan. The war ended at last in 1598, having left a disastrous impact upon Korea. Following this shock there was a movement to bring in some progressive ideas as a way to build a modern nation state capable of resisting Japanese and western threats, but the government of conservative aristocrats, however, was not ready to accommodate their ideas.

Korea remained a "hermit kingdom" adamantly opposed to the western demands for diplomatic and trade relations in the nineteenth century. Korea adhered to its alliance with China, which was fighting for its own life against western encroachment and could not help Korea. Japan, which had risen as a new industrial power, eventually stepped into the power vacuum and annexed Korea in 1910.

The Japanese rule was repressive and stimulated the growth of nationalism among Koreans. Korean intellectuals were infuriated by Japan's official assimilation policy. They asserted their differences and struggled to distance themselves culturally from their colonial masters. In 1919, Koreans staged nationwide protests at the cost of thousands of lives. This independence movement failed to depose the Japanese, but gave Koreans strong bonds of national identity and patriotism, and led to the establishment of the Provisional Government in Shanghai and to an organized armed struggle against the Japanese colonialists in Manchuria.

Japan implemented a policy to assimilate Koreans into Japanese culture. The Japanese language was used in Korean schools and Korean-language newspapers were closed down. The Japanese conducted quasi-historical and archaeological research to prove that Korea was closely related but inferior to Japan. Koreans reacted vehemently against this type of cultural and psychological aggression.

Koreans welcomed the defeat of Japan in World War II with great joy and relief. However, their joy was shortlived. Liberation did not bring the independence for which the Koreans had fought so hard, but the inception of ideological conflict in a partitioned country.

On June 25, 1950, North Korea launched an unprovoked full scale invasion of the South and started a war that lasted three years. As the Communist North Koreans campaigned to unify the country by force, the entire land was devastated and millions of people were left homeless and separated from their families. A cease-fire was signed in July 1953, and both sides have since gone through enormous changes in their efforts at rehabilitation.

Reunification remains the long-cherished but elusive goal of all Koreans on both sides of the vigilantly guarded Military Demarcation Line. The fall of Communism in the Soviet Union and Eastern Europe and the unification of Germany raised expectations in Korea that unification could be achieved in the not very distant future. Some apparent progress in promoting trust and cooperation between the two halves of the peninsula was made in 1991 and 1992, but the threat of North

Korea's suspected nuclear weapons development program has stood in the way of real forward movement. If and when this issue is solved, it is more than likely that substantial progress will be made toward reestablishing a sense of belonging to one national community, eventually leading to full unification.

▶ Some Notes on Culture

Koreans have been strongly impacted by Chinese, Japanese and western culture. Despite its thorough integration of Chinese culture over many centuries and despite the traumatic inroads of Japan and the West, Korea keeps its own distinct culture.

Fitting western values and behavior patterns into Korean tradition is an ongoing process, which began only a hundred years ago. This process, often painful, is an unavoidable part of Korean modernization and industrialization. The Koreans must therefore be understood in terms of both a relatively fixed tradition and a rapidly changing present. Here is a vivid illustration of a society that cherishes its traditions but finds itself moving away from these traditions toward a new cultural synthesis. Contemporary Korean culture is assimilating western culture as it did the Chinese, and Korean authors and artists are gaining recognition in the West. But the assimilation is not without some pain and although it is the Koreans themselves who have accepted U.S. movies, jazz, blue jeans, English vocabulary, and the rest, all this is part of the painful process of cultural accommodation.

▶ Family

The family is basic to the life of every Korean. Its importance has for centuries been greatly reinforced by the Confucian philosophy, received from China, and fully accepted into Korean culture by the fifteenth century. This philosophy emphasized family relationships as fundamental to the entire social fabric and includes relatives far beyond the simple parent-children household. Although the nuclear family (father, mother, children) as a living unit is becoming the norm in the big cities, the traditional Confucian view of family relationships and responsibilities continues as a strong influence on individual attitudes and behavior.

▶ Community Life

The rural community was the center of social activity for most Koreans for thousands of years. By the first century of the Choson Dynasty, the community also was guided by Confucian principles; a sixteenth-century scholar, Cho Kwang-cho (1482–1519) institutionalized them in the form of a "village code." Except for taxes, labor on public works, military service, and occasionally the control of major disputes, the villages managed their own affairs. They were largely self-sufficient, with a simple barter economy. Markets held every five days in local centers and itinerant peddlers supplemented village handicrafts. As late as 1960, over 70 percent of the South Korean population lived in centers of fewer than 50,000 people.

Village affairs, including maintenance of social order and propriety, were traditionally governed by an informal council of elders from the constituent families; one of them might be recognized by the central government as village chief, but his authority (except in actions ordered by the state) was subject to the elders' consensus. The process did not originally involve elections or voting.

Industrialization and urbanization began to affect Korean community life in a significant way only in the twentieth century. The Japanese occupation, World War II, the division of Korea, and the Korean War all combined with the industrialization process to uproot traditional agrarian communities. Yet traditions persist to a considerable extent in the shrinking agricultural population and even in the urban consciousness.

▶ Individual and Interpersonal Relations

The Korean individual's view of himself and his place in society traditionally centered on his family, of which he considered himself a part. In the Confucian tradition the dominance of men was unquestioned in form, although not infrequently the facts were otherwise. The henpecked husband is very much a part of Korean folklore. Male children were preferred because only they could carry on the family line.

It was the man's duty before his parents and his ancestors to assure continuity and prosperity of the family; his success was their success, his failure their shame. Social responsibility beyond the family extended to the community, and in some measure to the person of the ruler and his officials, but not to society as a whole. Anyone outside the established circles and lines of relationship was viewed as a "non-person," to whom only the universal courtesy for strangers was due.

The status of women in Korean society has greatly advanced and is still rapidly evolving in both South and North Korea. Christianity from its beginnings in Korea emphasized the equality of all persons under God. A U.S. missionary funded the first girls' school in Korea in 1886—the nucleus for the noted Ewha Woman's University. This influence, together with the example of modernized societies elsewhere, has had great effect. Women's access to education is virtually the same as for men. Women in considerable numbers pursue high-prestige occupations; there have been women cabinet members, women members of the legislature, and women presidents of universities. many women leaders are interested in advancing the status of their sex.

Despite women's progress, male dominance continues. Male babies are still preferred; women workers largely fill low-paid factory and household jobs—often to earn a dowry for marriage—and women still do most of the household work. The family law is still based on male superiority in marriage, divorce, household administration, and inheritance. However, revision of the law is under discussion.

In interpersonal relations, age and relative status still carry some of their traditional importance: The junior owes respect to the senior, and the senior carries the obligation to look out for the junior. It is still impolite to smoke or cross one's legs before a senior without permission. Koreans bow to superiors; they also shake hands with acquaintances. Calling cards are usually exchanged when introductions are made, partly to establish social relationship. It is still customary for people to call upon their parent, senior relatives, and office or factory superiors, at New Year's and at other occasions, such as a death in the family. It is usual in such calls to bring a present—a pleasant custom, but one that has sometimes deteriorated into bribery. Koreans are alert to one another's state of mind, and respect for others' personal dignity and social status ("face") has high priority in social intercourse. Outspokenness, therefore, is not ordinarily a Korean virtue.

▶ Attitudes and World View

Korean behavior is the result of three main factors: the traditional Confucian ethic; and underlying individualism that is somewhat at odds with that ethic; and an overlay of western ideas.

In the traditional Confucian order, harmony among men was the supreme goal. Lack of harmony might disrupt the order of nature; thus a linkage was perceived between social disorder and natural calamities, such as floods or earthquakes. It was the ruler's duty to maintain social order by his benevolence and superior wisdom and that of his ministers. It was the people's duty to obey the benevolent ruler's commands. Similar relationships applied to each family.

Within tradition, the individual's attitude toward the self and the self's future was in terms of cultivation rather than improvement: that is, realizing one's innate capacities, rather than transcending them. The ideal to be achieved was true wisdom or sageness. Mastery of the classics, and self-discipline and right conduct, could bring full realization of one's inherent capabilities. For some, self-cultivation might include solitary contemplation and esoteric practices of various kinds, such as breathing exercises—akin to the ideas of Zen Buddhism, but not inherently religious. In seeking to fulfill oneself, of course, each person was conscious of responsibility to the family collective. The Koreans accommodated themselves to Chinese cultural and military superiority, accepting younger-brother status to China's world family. The collapse of China, source of so much of their culture and political institutions, had a traumatic effect, adding to Korea's own internal difficulties and external challenges.

Although the Koreans have not accepted the cultural superiority of any other nation in the way they did China's, the relationship of South Korea to the United States after liberation in 1945, or of North Korea to the Soviet Union, was a transference from China of the older-brother-younger-brother relationship. Koreans, both North and South, criticize themselves for their obeisance to power, or over-respect for greatness.

Today's South Koreans have discarded some of their traditional Confucian intellectual baggage because as a whole it has not shown itself capable of guiding the nation into the modern world. Nevertheless, there has been renewed recent attention to the positive elements of the Confucian tradition, along with growing nationalist sentiment. The survival of Confucian values makes Korean behavior sometimes incomprehensible and frustrating to Americans.

To statistically illustrate the cultural interplay, especially growing Christianity, in the Republic of Korea consider the status of practiced religions. According to 1991 statistics 54 percent of Koreans follow a specific religious faith, of the 54 percent:

11,962,000 are Buddhists (51.2%)
8,038,000 are Protestant Christian (39.4%)
2,523,000 are Roman Catholic (10.6%)
421,000 are Confucian (1.8%)
The eastern and western traditions joined.

▶ Summary History: Korea

The beginnings	
The Three Kindoms	
Unified Shilla	668–935
Koryo	918–1392
Choson	1392–1910
Japanese Colony	1910–1945
Republic of Korea	1945
The Korean War	1950–1953

▶ JAPAN

Although today Japan is a major world power because of its rise as a world economic power, it was traditionally on the perimeter of the Chinese cultural center. The Japanese are basically a Mongoloid people who migrated from northeast Asia displacing the local Ainu people. Early Japan was organized in a large number of clans, each ruled by a hereditary priest-chieftain. Toward the end of the first century AD, the Yamato clan established a loose political and religious control over the others. Its chief was the emperor, and its clan goddess, the Sun Goddess, was made the national god.

This clan organization was undermined by the importation of Chinese civilization, which began on a large scale in the 500s. Buddhism, introduced from Korea, was the medium for cultural change, fulfilling the same function here as Christianity did

United States Superimposed on Japan

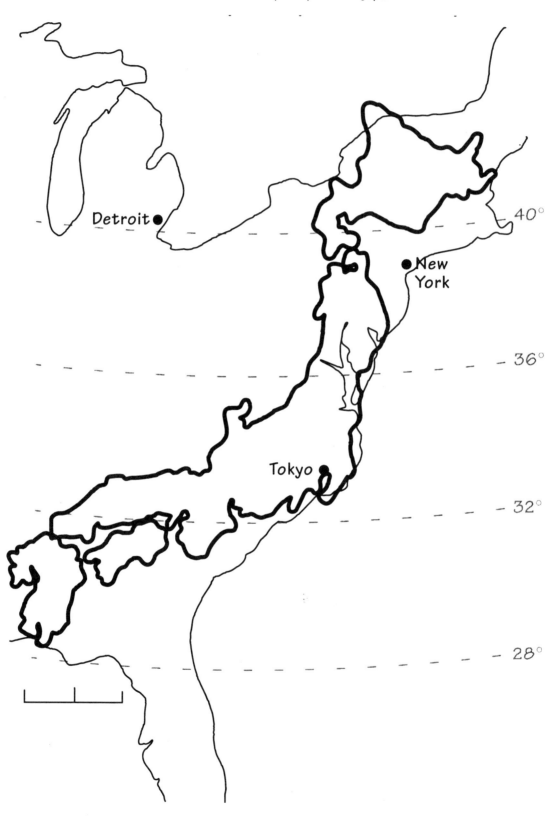

FIGURE 9-2 Japan has a vareity of climates from north to south.

among the Germans and Slavs in Europe. And at about the same time students, teachers, craftsmen, and monks crossed over from the mainland, bringing with them a whole new culture as well as a new religion. The drive for change culminated in the Taika Reform, which began in 645 and sought to transform Japan into a centralized state on the model of the T'ang dynasty in China. Following the Chinese model, the country was divided into provinces and districts ruled by governors and magistrates who got their power from the emperor and his council of state.

These and other changes were designed to strengthen central authority, and they did so in comparison with the preceding clan structure. But in practice, the Japanese changed and adapted everything they borrowed from China and made it Japanese. They limited the power of their emperor by allowing the hereditary aristocracy to keep their large landholdings. They borrowed Chinese writing figures but developed their own system of writing. They borrowed Confucianism, but modified its ethics and adjusted its political doctrines to satisfy their own spiritual needs to fit their native Shintoism. They built new imperial capitals, first at Nara and then at Kyoto, that were modeled after the T'ang capital. But there was no mistaking the Japanese character of the temples, pavilions, shrines, and gardens.

The importance of being an island is particularly apparent in the case of Japanese history. In this respect there is a close parallel with the British Isles at the other end of the Eurasian continent. The Japanese islands, however, are more isolated than the British. One hundred and fifteen miles separate them from the mainland compared to the twenty-one miles of the English Channel. Thus until their World War II defeat by the United States, the Japanese had only once before been seriously threatened by foreign invasion, and that was in the thirteenth century by the Mongols.

The Japanese, therefore, have been close enough to the mainland to benefit from the great Chinese civilization, but distant enough to be able to select and reject as they wished. The Chinese system of imperial organization introduced by the Taika Reform of 645 worked effectively for a long period. By the twelfth century, however, it had been undermined and replaced by a Japanese variety of feudalism.

The net result of this process was that by the end of the twelfth century, local power had been taken over by the new rural aristocracy. At the same time, this aristocracy had become the dominant military force because of the disintegration of the imperial armed forces. They became mounted warriors and gradually increased their military effectiveness until they completely overshadowed the imperial forces. A feudal relationship now developed between these rural lords and their retainers, or samurai (literally "one who serves"). This relationship was based on a code of ethics not too different than the medieval knight's ideal of chivalry, known as *bushido*, or "way of the warrior." The samurai enjoyed special legal and ceremonial rights, and in return they were expected to give unquestioning service to their lords. The samurai also found the beliefs of Zen Buddhism congenial to their ideals and were instrumental in making Zen an important part of Japanese culture.

▶ Zen Buddhism

I want to discuss Zen briefly because it is an important element of Japanese tradition, but also because I would like to expose you to a completely different way of thinking. A branch of Mahayana Buddhism's intuitive school took hold in Japan and is still today very much alive, playing an influential role in forming Japanese values as it has through the centuries. This Buddhism called Zen from the Chinese Ch'an has its origins in the Sanskrit word meaning *meditation that leads to insight*. In addition to its influence on Japanese thinking, it is having a strong influence on a number of leading philosophers, psychotherapists, writers and artists throughout the world, including the United States.

The great Zen insights were carried to China in 520 AD by Bodhidharma who may be considered the founder of Zen. From China it spread to Japan in the twelfth century.

Trying to enter the world of Zen is to enter a world completely foreign to our normal thought patterns, full of bewildering statements, contradictions and non-sequiturs. For example:

A monk approaches a master saying, "I have just come to this monastery. Would you kindly give me some instruction?" The master answers, "Have you eaten your breakfast yet?" "I have," is the reply. "Then go wash your bowls." It is said that this conversation accomplished its purpose. The inquirer was brought to the understanding of Zen.

Is it possible to make any sense out of this? Our first reaction is they must be joking. The answer is they are completely serious. Zen realizes the limitations of words. Words often build up a false world full of stereotypes. They can also hide our real or true feelings. Words are never an accurate description of experience. Can you describe the taste of an orange? Different from our Christian tradition rooted in the words of the Bible, Judaism in the Torah and Confucianism in the Classics, Zen is without scriptures.

Account after account will depict disciples interrogating their masters about Zen, only to have their minds turned back by a roared "Ho!" for answer. For the master sees that through these questions the seekers are trying to fill the lack in their lives with *words* and *concepts* instead of *experience*.

Zen insists that the map of a territory is not the territory and would have understood immediately Magritte's realistic painting of a pipe titled "This is not a pipe." (Of course it is not a pipe. It is a *painting* of a pipe. A crucial difference.)

Zen is basically interested only in living experience. Zen wants to plunge into experience, to startle the mind out of its rut of conventional thinking.

And what is the method for achieving the Zen goal of experienced reality?

There are four key terms: *zazen, koan, sanzen,* and *satori.*

Zazen means seated meditation. Zen monks spend hours sitting, silently in their meditation halls facing the center. Eyes are half open, the gaze unfocused on the floor a few feet in front of them. They are seeking to develop their intuitive powers and relate this to their daily lives. To aid them they use a very strange device called the *koan.*

Koan means problem. But a koan is not a normal problem.

Here are some examples:

Question: If I have nothing, what should I do!

Answer: Throw it away!

You are not allowed to travel at night, but you must arrive before day-break.

The bridge flows, the water does not.

What is the sound of one hand clapping?

If you run away from the void, you can never be free of it.

If you search for the void, you can never reach it.

Question: What is the pure dharmakaya?

Answer: The blossoming hedge around the privy.

What is the meaning of Bodhidharma's coming from the west?

Answer: The cypress tree in the garden.

A master, Wu Tsu, says, "Let me take an illustration from a fable. A cow passes by a window. Its head, horns, and the four legs all pass by. Why did not the tail pass by?"

One more: Li-ku, a high government officer of the T'ang Dynasty, asked a famous Ch'an master: "A long time ago a man kept a goose in a bottle. It grew larger and larger until it could not get out of the bottle anymore. He did not want to break the bottle, nor did he wish to hurt the goose; how would you get it out?"

The master called out, "O Officer!"

"Yes," was the response.

"There, it's out!"

We in the West trust reason so fully that we must remind ourselves that in Zen we are dealing with a perspective that is convinced above everything else that reason is by its very nature limited and in the end must yield to another method of knowing that can grasp reality far more accurately.

The koans are designed to raise the mind above its limitation by reason. By paradox and puzzle it will stimulate, excite, baffle, and exhaust the mind until it sees that thinking is never more than thinking *about* things, or feeling more than feeling *about* things.

Then having brought the subject to an intellectual and emotional impasse, it counts on a flash of sudden insight to bridge the gap between knowing about-to firsthand experience. Reason collapses entirely, clearing the way for sudden intuition. (Robert Pirsig, in his *Zen and The Art of Motorcycle Maintenance,* might call such a moment "stuckness.")

In his struggle with the koan the monk generally confronts his master twice daily in a private audience known as *sanzen*. The meeting is brief. The koan is stated and the answer to which the trainee has arrived. The answer the master may accept or in most cases asks for further work.

All this leads on intuitive experience called *satori*, the flash of experience that makes everything ever after look different.

We find in Zen a feeling that the divine is in ordinary things "Have you eaten? Then wash the bowls" A simple act of doing the dishes can be the justification of existence. The experiencer passes beyond good and evil, pleasure and pain. Each has its place. As self disappears, so does the difference between finite and infinite, life and death.

Zen's influence on the cultural life of Japan has been enormous. The samurai, seeing in Zen's code a clear statement of their warrior ideals of indifference to pain and death, made it a part of their code. In *sumi* or black ink landscape painting, Zen monks, living their simple lives close to the earth, have rivaled the skill and depth of feeling of their Chinese masters. In landscape gardening, Zen temple gardens surpassed those of their Chinese teachers and raised the art to a perfection unrivaled anywhere else in the world. Flower arrangement began by placing floral offerings before the Buddha, but developed into an art which today is a part of the training of every refined Japanese girl. Finally there is the celebrated tea ceremony in which a simple but beautiful setting, a few fine pieces of old pottery, a slow, graceful ritual and a spirit of utter tranquility combine to epitomize the harmony, respect, clarity, and calm that characterize Zen at its best. The tea ceremony epitomizes the Japanese ideal.

► Outline of Modern Japanese History

By the twelfth century, Japan was controlled by competing groups of feudal lords. In the end, one of these lords emerged victorious. He was appointed by the emperor as *"shogun."* Henceforth Japan was controlled by a succession of shogun families, called *shogunates*. They commanded the military forces while the emperor lived in seclusion in Kyoto, the capital.

The most important recently was the 250 year Tokugawa shogunate. The Tokugawa rule came after a century of chaos and was intended above all to establish and maintain peace and staticity. It was based quite consciously on Confucian principles. Society was held to consist of four main categories ranked in order of precedence and usefulness—warriors, farmers, craftsmen and merchants. Beggars, bandits and other riffraff put themselves outside the security of the law. There were substantial outcast groups such as the ETA who were regarded as ritually unclean and Hinin (non-humans) degraded to such tasks as handling dead bodies or diseased persons (recall the discussion of caste in India). Even today in Japan there are some three million ETA clustered into some six thousand segregated communities.

The material basis of Tokugawa power lay in their territory, which comprised between a fourth to a third of the total arable land and consisted of estates scattered strategically throughout the country. These estates provided control points against potentially hostile *daimyo*, or local landholding families. Top government posts were filled by members of the Tokugawa family or friends. The emperor was provided with revenues for his own support as well as that of a small group of court nobles, but he had no political function or authority—something like Queen Elizabeth of England.

As part of their effort to prevent any change that might undermine their rule, the Tokugawa perpetuated a rigid, hereditary class structure. At the top was the aristocracy, comprising about six percent of the population. This included the court nobles, who had social priority but no power or property and were therefore dependent on the shogun for support. Much more important was the feudal aristocracy headed by the shogun and including the local squires as well as the samurai retainers.

The vast majority of Japanese were farmers, the second-ranking class, which included landless tenants as well as landholders with plots ranging from an acre and a quarter to as many as eighty-five acres. Whatever their status, these peasants produced the rice that, in the final analysis, supported the aristocracy and society.

The last two classes recognized by the Tokugawa were, in order of rank, the artisans and the merchants. The long period of peace and security during this shogunate allowed these townspeople to grow enormously in numbers and wealth. The wealth of the country flowed increasingly into the pockets of the merchants. In large cities such as Edo and Osaka, they lived on a lavish scale and generated their own cultural forms, such as the Kabuki drama, the woodblock print, and the novel.

The Tokugawa created an ideological basis for their regime by sponsoring the Chu Hsi school of Confucianism, which stressed the virtues of filial piety and of loyalty to one's superior in any social grouping. Paternal power was absolute and unquestioned in the ideal Japanese family, and even more specifically spelled out than in China.

Particularly appealing to the Tokugawa was the Confucian emphasis on the moral basis of political legitimacy and on all the conservative virtues. In *Laws for the Military Houses,* a code of conduct is prescribed for samurai that stressed personal loyalty, sobriety, frugality, and the acceptance of class distinctions.

One effect of this ideology was that the Japanese family system, especially that of the samurai, was closely integrated into Tokugawan society because of its subordination to the interests of the shogun or the aristocracy. This harmony between the family and the state, much stronger than in China, facilitated the modernization of Japan in the nineteenth century by providing a grassroots basis for national unity and action.

▶ The Arrival of the Europeans

The first Europeans to arrive in Japan were Portuguese traders in the mid-sixteenth century, who discovered that rich profits could be made carrying goods between China and Japan. Because of raids by Japanese pirates, the Ming emperors had banned all trade with Japan. The Portuguese quickly stepped into the void and prospered, handsomely, exchanging Chinese gold and silk for Japanese silver and copper. These merchants combined missionary enterprise with their commercial activities, as both the Portuguese and Spanish always did. Francis Xavier, a famous saint of the church, and other Jesuit fathers landed in 1549 and were allowed to preach among the masses of the people. They were unusually successful, apparently because their revivalist methods satisfied the emotional needs of the downtrodden peasantry.

By 1600 Dutch traders, and a few British, were active in Japan alongside the Portuguese. The intense rivalry among these Europeans gave the Japanese a new freedom of action. They could now move against the missionaries, who they felt had gained too much power, without fear of losing the commerce they now needed. And they did want to curb the missionaries, whose success they feared was undermining traditional Japanese society with foreign ideas. Accordingly, the Shogun decreed in 1614 that all missionaries must leave, and their converts, who by now numbered 300,000, must renounce their faith. This order was ruthlessly enforced, and many died. Missionaries also were martyred.

The Japanese went a step further and in 1624 banned all Spaniards. In 1637 all Portuguese also were forced to depart, leaving only the Dutch, who had never shown any interest in propagating Christianity. Henceforth the Dutch were the only Europeans allowed to carry on trade, but only under severely restricted conditions on a small island in Nagasaki harbor. The isolationist policy was extended in 1636 to Japanese subjects, who were prohibited from going abroad on penalty of death. A wall was built around Japan and over two centuries of seclusion had begun.

The policy of excluding all foreign influences and freezing the internal status quo was designed to perpetuate the Tokugawa dominance. In practice it proved extraordinarily effective. Japan was united and subjected to a centralized political control. But a heavy price was paid for this security and stability. Japan did not have the change and growth that western Europe did during this period. There was no ending of feudalism, no Renaissance or Reformation—no breakthroughs in science—and no overseas expansion. For the Japanese, as for the Chinese, the price of two centuries of conservative self-satisfaction was organizational and technological backwardness. This became apparent, more quickly to the Japanese than to the Chinese, when their hermit world was forced open in 1853.

▶ The Opening of Japan

The challenge of western culture was met quite differently by the Japanese from what we just read was the Chinese reaction. What were the reasons

Japan was able to maintain its independence and became a major industrial power while China was completely overrun? There are several explanations.

The fact Japan was small and an island made national unity easier to maintain. It also made the country quickly aware of the foreign threat, unlike the vast interior spaces of China, which remained unaware and untouched by the foreign presence. Furthermore, Japan's long tradition of borrowing from the great Chinese cultural world made similar borrowing from the western world in the nineteenth century less of a problem. Japan had for centuries selected aspects of Chinese culture with the slogan "Japanese spirit and Chinese knowledge." Now it borrowed what it wished from the West with the slogan "Eastern morale and western arts."

Also, Japanese government and the people were closely knit in structure in comparison with the aloofness of Chinese government. The merchant class in Japan had more independence and economic strength. The military elements in Japan were at the top of the social ladder, rather than at the bottom, as was the case in China. This meant that Japan had a ruling class that was much more sensitive and responsive to western military technology than were the Chinese intellectuals.

In all, geography, cultural traditions, and social organization combined to make Japan more vulnerable to western intrusion that China, and more able to respond quickly to that intrusion.

On July 8, 1853, Commodore Matthew Perry led American warships into Tokyo Bay and delivered a letter from President Fillmore asking for trading privileges, coaling stations, and protection for shipwrecked Americans. Within a week he sailed away after warning that he would be back for an answer the following spring. When he returned in February 1854, he made it clear that the alternative to a treaty was war. The Japanese yielded and on March 31 signed the Treaty of Kanagawa. The treaty in effect opened Japan and granted most-favored-nation treatment for the United States.

The United States later negotiated the Commercial Treaty of 1858. Soon after signing with the United States, Japan concluded similar pacts with Holland, Russia, Britain, and France. Thus Japan, like China now was open to western influence. But its response to that influence was altogether different from that of China.

The Meiji Restoration

The shogunate officials knew that their antiquated shore batteries were no match for Perry's cannons. They had no recourse but to give way, choosing to do so as little as they could. In so doing, they set in motion a nationwide debate between advocates of continued isolation and reformers who wanted to open up the country. The debate lasted 15 years—a period of great turmoil, ending only with the collapse of the Shogunate, the abolition of feudalism, and the establishment of a reform-minded central government under the direct rule of the Emperor Meiji. This series of events is known today as the first opening of Japan.

The Meiji era, which lasted for nearly half a century, was a heady time for Japan. The young reformers gathered around the emperor knew that for Japan's survival, they had to make drastic changes in the political, economic and social institutions of their country. One of the five pledges with which Meiji inaugurated his reign was to "seek knowledge throughout the world." His reformers created a modern army and navy, introduced capitalism, universal education, and a limited form of constitutional democracy, including the concept of equality under the law.

The Tokugawa group was kicked out, and their place was taken by the Satcho Hito clans, which henceforth controlled the government in the name of the new Meiji emperor. It was the young samurai class in the service of these clans who provided Japan with the outstanding leadership that made Japan successful in keeping their independence. In contrast to China's Mandarins, Japan's new leaders realized that they were behind in certain fields, and they were willing and able to do something about it.

Japan's new leaders were interested only in those features of western civilization that they felt would help Japan. In the field of religion, for example, the Meiji leaders supported Shinto as the state religion because it identified the national leadership with the emperor, whom they held was descended from the Sun Goddess. In other words, Shinto stimulated national unity and patriotism, and these attributes were deemed necessary if Japan was to hold its own in the modern world. In education, it was specifically stated that the objective to further Japan's interests rather than the development of the individual.

▶ Shinto—The Way of the Gods

The native religion of Japan was that promoted by the Meiji Restoration deserves some attention.

Shinto emphasizes that *patriotism* and loyalty to homeland are important. It also holds that:

- *No idols or statues are to be used* (names of gods written on slips of paper during worship).

- *Spirits of dead ancestors help* protect the country.

- *Divine and human* have *no* dividing line.

- In worship there is nothing too small to ignore or revere. (There should be an emphasis on thanks, not correction of shortcomings.)

- It is *Polytheistic* and many nature deities are worshiped.

- In its *Attitude toward sin* there are no commandments—people make mistakes but are not full of sin. (Japanese feel a shared guilt for everyone's shortcomings.)

- *Big question in Shinto is* not—"What is MY life?" but—"What IS life?"

- *Beauty is in all things* in the world and should be cultivated in the home.

Shinto has no founder; rather, Shinto is the traditions of the Japanese dating from their early history. It is a way of devotion to the guardians of life and custom; for example, local spirits, ancestral powers, heroes, the divine being, one's living parents and one's living children. Since the Deity is present in all things, all things should be looked on as divine, from the pots and pans of the kitchen to the Mikado: this is Shinto, "The Way of the Gods."

The Shinto way of worship is primarily that of preserving and cultivating purity of wants. Emphasis is placed on following the Right and Moral Way.

Here are some examples of Shinto sayings:

What pleases the Deity is virtue and sincerity, not any number of material offerings.

The Eight Hundred Myriads of Gods are but differing manifestations of one unique Deity, Junitokatachi-no-Kami, The Eternally Standing Divine Being of the Earth, The Great Unity of All Things in the Universe, The Primordial Being of Heaven and Earth, eternally existing from the beginning to the end of the world.

The awe-inspiring Deity manifests Itself, even in the single leaf of a tree or a delicate blade of grass.

With the unseen God who seeth all secret things in the silence, the heart of the sincere man communes from the earth below.

The function of reverence in Shinto is to honor that Deity in all things; the function of purity to sustain Its manifestation in oneself.

Because of its native roots, it has stood in opposition to another great religious tradition of Japan—imported Buddhism or Butsudo "the way of the Buddha." During the Meiji period from 1868 onward, Shintoism with its strong emphasis on patriotism and the primacy of the God-emperor was strongly encouraged by the government. It developed into a sort of state sponsored patriotism, much as if our pledge of allegiance were considered a religious statement of solidarity.

Consider the patriotism, one might say chauvinism, of the following statement:

The true way is one and the same, in every country and throughout heaven and earth. This way, however, has been correctly transmitted only in our imperial land . . . the "special dispensation of our imperial land" means that ours is the native land of the heaven-shining goddess who casts her light over all countries in the four seas. Thus our country is the source of the fountainhead of all other countries, and in all matters it excels all the others.

—Motoori, Precious Comb-box 6

As a result of Japan's defeat in the Second World War, state Shinto was removed. Nevertheless, Shinto remains a living belief in Japan. The Association of Shinto Shrines has a membership of some 80,000 shrines, and it is thought that there are about 60 million believers in Japan. Being Japanese in spirit, it has not spread to other countries.

Compulsory elementary education was required by the Meiji because the state needed a literate citizenry. Large numbers of foreign educators were brought to Japan to found schools and universities, and thousands of Japanese studied abroad and returned to teach in the new institutions. But the entire educational system was kept under close state supervision to ensure uniformity of thought as well as of administration.

In military affairs the Japanese abolished the old feudal armies and organized modern armed forces based on the latest European models. They built a conscript army with the aid of a German military mission and a small navy under the guidance of the British. The Meiji leaders could see that the new military forces required a modern economy to supply their needs. Accordingly, they secured the establishment of the needed industries by granting subsidies, purchasing stock, or forming government corporations.

The government leaders were careful to support not only light industries such as textiles but also heavy industries such as mining, steel, and shipbuilding, which were necessary to fill military needs. Once these enterprises were founded, the government generally sold them to various favored private interests at extremely low prices. In this way a few wealthy families, collectively known as the Zaibatsu, gained a stranglehold on the national economy that still exists.

The Japanese also overhauled their legal system. The laws were disorganized and harsh, individual rights were disregarded, the police were arbitrary and all powerful, and prison conditions were primitive. In 1871 a judicial department was organized, and in the following years new codes were adopted that were more along western lines.

At the same time various political innovations were made to provide Japan with at least the appearance of parliamentary government. A cabinet and a privy council were first established, and then, in 1889, a constitution was adopted. This document promised citizens freedom from arbitrary arrest; protection of property rights; and freedom of religion, speech, and association. But in each instance the government was given authority to curb these rights when it so desired.

The constitution provided Japan with a parliamentary structure while preserving rule by a few and emperor worship. Indeed, the first article of the constitution provided that "The Empire of Japan shall be reigned over and governed by a line of emperors unbroken for ages eternal," and the third article likewise stipulated that "The Emperor is sacred and inviolable."

With the adoption of the constitution and of the legal reforms, the Japanese could fairly argue that Japan now had taken its place in the ranks of the advanced nations.

▶ The Russo–Japanese War

In 1894 the Japanese won the unexpected and spectacular victory over the Chinese empire mentioned earlier and, henceforth, there could be no more question of treating Japan as a backward country, and the other powers soon followed Britain and the United States in yielding them special privileges. By 1899, Japan had gained legal control over all foreigners on its soil, and in doing so, it became the first Asian nation to break western domination. After its self-modernization, Japan embarked on a career of expansion on the Asian mainland. This is not surprising in view of Japan's warlike tradition and the immense prestige that its military leaders enjoyed from earliest times.

Furthermore, the Far East was then a hotbed of international rivalry, and the practical-minded leaders of Japan drew the obvious conclusion: Each people must grab for themselves. Their first expansionist move was in Korea where, as noted earlier in this chapter, the Japanese defeated the Chinese and then annexed Korea in 1910.

After their victory over China, the Japanese were faced by the much more powerful Russians, who were advancing southward into Manchuria and Korea. In the 1890s Russia was showing more interest in the Far East. The Trans-Siberian railway, which was slowly nearing completion, presented new opportunities for Russian economic and political expansion. The Russians saw their role as arbitrator between Asia and the western world.

Russia succeeded in signing a treaty with China providing for mutual assistance in case of Japanese aggression, received a concession to build a railway across Manchuria to Vladivostok and negotiated a 25-year lease of the Liaotung peninsula, including strategic Port Arthur. Two years later the Russians took advantage of the disturbances caused by the Boxer Rebellion to occupy the entire province of Manchuria. This steady Russian encroachment alarmed the Japanese, who had ambitions of their own on the mainland of Asia.

In July 1903, the Japanese proposed that Russia should recognize Japan's "preponderant interests" in Korea, and in return they would recognize Russia's "special interests in railway enterprises in Manchuria." While the Russians were divided about acceptance of the offer, eventually they favored a little victorious war that would take pressure off popular unrest at home. There was no doubt in their minds, or in those of the military, that Russia would win in a war with Japan.

The Russians rejected the offer and the Japanese struck promptly and decisively. On February 5, 1904, they broke off negotiations, and three days later they attacked the Russian fleet at Port Arthur without a formal declaration of war. In the campaigns that followed, the Japanese consistently defeated the Russians.

After a siege of 148 days they captured Port Arthur and defeated Russian armies in Manchuria. Finally in 1905 the entire Russian Baltic fleet which had sailed almost two-thirds the distance of the total circumference of the world arrived in the straits between Korea and Japan. It was attacked by the Japanese. Within a few hours virtually all the Russian units had been sunk or captured. The Japanese merely lost a few destroyers.

The Russians were forced to sue for peace. The subsequent Treaty of Portsmouth acknowledged Japan's "paramount political, military, and economic interests" in Korea; Russia surrendered all preferential or exclusive concessions in Manchuria; and ceded to Japan the southern half of Sakhalin Island and the lease of the Liaotung peninsula. Japan had stopped Russia's expansion in the Far East.

Looking back, the Russo–Japanese War stands out as a major turning point in the history of the Far East, and even of the world. Certainly it established Japan as a major power and altered the balance of power in the Far East. But more significant is the fact that for the first time an Asian state defeated a European state, and a great empire at that.

This had an electrifying effect on all Asia. It demonstrated to millions of colonial peoples that European domination could be overturned. For the first time since the days of Columbus, a white race nation had been beaten, and a thrill of hope ran through the non-white people of the globe. The victory of an Asian power over a European one encouraged leaders of the move to independence in other Asian countries. Ironically, Japan responded by becoming itself a colonial power by annexing

Korea in 1910. This aggravated a continuing antagonism between the two nations. Japan may have been influenced by the desire to be on a par with western powers who all possessed empires. In this sense, the Russo-Japanese War stands out as a landmark in modern history; it represents the beginning to the great awakening of the non-European peoples. Today that awakening is transforming the entire world, and is a central feature of world politics.

Japan's modern development, that is to say from the Meiji Restoration in 1864, has been a story of western influence being adapted and modified to suit Japanese cultural values. They have shown a strong tradition of group cohesiveness while using western ideas to catch up and surpass the western powers. The Japanese are an astoundingly homogeneous people. To be Japanese is to be a Japanese citizen, born in Japan, living there and speaking Japanese. State, people, and language coincide to a degree unknown in the modern world. Ninety-nine percent of all the Japanese live in Japan itself. Japan has no minority greater than one percent which is different by virtue of religion or ethnicity. Japanese values have for centuries been principally centered on the maintenance and furtherance of the group. One adaptation was the use of the western idea of the nation state to shift group loyalties to the state during the Meiji Restoration.

The Japanese traditions of ancestor worship and subordination of branch families to the main family were integrated to achieve loyalty on a national scale. The imperial family was regarded as the main family of the entire Japanese people, and the nation regarded as an extended family: The emperor occupied the position of patriarch of the common main family.

The American ships that forced Japan to open its doors forced Japan to seek national goals. "Maintain independence," "Catch up with and surpass the West," and "A rich nation and a strong military" reflected such national goals, and Japan commenced rapid modern development based on a broad national consensus. The goal to catch up with and surpass the West was considered so important that anything which was useful for the achievement of this goal was used without hesitation. With the goals set, Japan proved very flexible in accepting western ideas.

Among the various western ideas important in the context of this chapter was Social Darwinism, which began to spread rapidly in Japan form the 1880s. This was an ideology that justified the domination of the weak by the strong. While they did not wish to disturb the highly regarded value of harmony internally, they did see its application in international relations. The actual world in which Japan would have to compete to survive was seen as one of dog-eat-dog.

After Japan's defeat in 1945 and the new Constitution of 1947—pacifism, democracy, and respect for fundamental human rights began to take root.

When Japanese conservatism attempted to amend the Constitution, the Japanese people resisted any tampering with these "imported" concepts. As time has passed, many people have become accustomed to enjoying these freedoms and their rights. In fact, the attempted revision in 1958 of the Policy Duty Law was thwarted by the people's deep concern over their right of privacy. They now considered the "imported" ideals to be their own, and the Constitution to be one in which they had a vested interest.

Despite radical changes on the surface from changes of the occupation, both group-orientedness and the goal of catching up with and surpassing the West remained, but with a necessary modification. Postwar group orientation did not center on the state nor on the Emperor. Instead, it became more directly a form of group belonging, as an identification with their own family and with their company. Incidentally, in Japan "lifetime employment" is the norm, a worker stays with the same company until his retirement. In fact, the disintegration of Imperial ideology did not necessarily mean the emergence of individualism. At least in the first stage, it resulted in competition among various groups with differing goals (such as labor unions, agricultural cooperatives), released from the monolithic Imperial Rule Assistance Association.

The aim of catching up with and surpassing the West also underwent a metamorphosis, because the option of becoming a great military power was blocked by the Constitution, which made pacifism a national policy. It came to focus primarily on competition with the western powers in the field of economic development. Instead of conflict by means of warships and other in armaments, conflict became competition, centered on the volume of Japan's gross national product and growth rate.

The military gained control of government policy which became expansionist with the goal of a Japanese dominance of East Asia. In the year 1931 Japan occupied Manchuria (their Manchuko) and from there proceeded to overwhelm China, the Malaysian Peninsula all the way to Guadalcanal in the Solomon Islands where their expansion was finally stopped by the United States Marine Corps. Of course, all Americans know the date, December 7, 1941, the day the Japanese bombed Pearl Harbor and brought the United States to declare war. This hard-fought war ended on a controversial note with the Americans dropping atom bombs on the virtually undefended cities of Hiroshima and Nagasaki. The United States had achieved its goal of unconditional surrender.

The news of the defeat of Japan in 1945 came as a shock. Japan had never been defeated, much less occupied. Would the occupying army pillage, rape? The war had cost Japan 1,855,000 dead, the loss of her overseas empire. Eighty percent of her shipping fleet had been sunk, a third of all industrial machinery had been destroyed by bombing and a quarter of all buildings. All major cities had been devastated. When the U.S. occupying troops saw the extent of the destruction, they had no wish to add revenge. The U.S. policy was one of reform and rebuild.

▶ Cultural Gaps

What about the future? Will the uniquely homogeneous Japanese maintain this uniqueness under the pressure of modern communications and world straddling business? Several decades of (refer back to the discussion of Jihad and the world and put the Japanese fears into this context) ever rising affluence have raised concern about the war of traditional values by young generations so unlike its parents as to be called by their elders "a new generation." Older Japanese look on this generation as "semi-Americanized." They grew up with cars giving mobility, they have money to spend, they are learning English and now American music and movie stars; and they are familiar with computers, technology and critical thinking. They are generally more open, more optimistic and more flexible than their parents. What concerns older generations is whether the young will have the spirit of unselfishness and dedication to the group which have preserved the Japanese in times of challenge. Incidentally, those who thought that the United States ought to be the model for Japan were greatly disillusioned by Vietnam and Watergate.

To a very great extent the issue of Japan's internationalization has revolved around the nature of Japan's relations with the United States—its chief ally, major customer and most important source of foreign ideas and technology. This has and will continue to mean some friction and misunderstanding, as for instance, the famous gaffe by Japanese prime Minister Nakasone in a visit to the U.S. when he suggested that, after all, Americans couldn't really be expected to compete effectively with the Japanese because the Japanese were so much better educated and more intelligent. The insult was further compounded by his attempted "explanation" that Americans as such weren't actually less intelligent but that, having so many blacks, Hispanics and other ethnic minorities, the United States was intrinsically disadvantaged compared to homogeneous Japan.

The popular attitude has become more and more realistic and less and less ideological as the economic recovery has continued. The principles of the Constitution have become something in which the Japanese people have a stake, although not many people are aware of them as universal principles. Most people are eager to maintain a peaceful family life; in order to do so they must keep the company for which they are working prosperous. Usually they are not particularly interested in promoting world peace or improving democratic participation, but when they have felt that their peaceful daily life and democratic procedures were in danger, they have protested.

Japan illustrates very well the blending of western science, technology, and communication with local tradition. Men wear western suits to the office but slip into a comfortable *yukata* at home. Executives may take a weekend in the country to meet clients over golf and stay overnight in one of the country's 80,000 *ryokan* (traditional inns). Over 95 percent of Japanese companies have word processors and fax machines, but every year more than a million people take the official examination for proficiency in the use of the *soroban* (Japanese abacus). Japan adopted the metric system over 30 years ago, but rooms are still measured in terms of the number of *tatami* (straw mats) they will hold. And there are still 30,000 traditional fortune tellers in gainful self-employment.

To sum up, one of the most important characteristics in the postwar value system is fragmentation. In one sense this means the disappearance of monolithic ultranationalism and the emphasis on a loyalty focused on the immediate group, such as the company or the family - nuclear family rather than the extended family. In another sense, as a result of privatization in mass society, people's interests are limited to immediate concerns rather than ideological causes.

▶ History Summary: Japan

500–800 AD	Chinese cultural influence
1543–1639	The arrival of the Europeans
1639–1853	The closing of Japan
1853–1912	The opening of Japan—the Meiji Restoration and Russo–Japanese War
1941–Present	Pearl Harbor, American occupation and resurgence

▶ Far Eastern Culture and the West

We have discussed the three principal countries of the Far Eastern cultural realm China, Korea and Japan. In that discussion, we have emphasized some distinctive features of the culture and contrasted these with some of our western values. For centuries Europe set the course of world history and we emphasized the year 1500 AD as a pivotal date when the world started on the road to becoming one world. Europe colonized the world, it shook up empires and societies including China, India, Japan and Islam and occupied relatively empty places like North America and Australia. While there may be an element of anti-western feeling in former colonies and charged societies, all must admit they are greatly indebted to Europe. The huge creative burst that started in Europe around 500 years ago has carried the world to where it is today. However, this period of European dominance is ending and it appears there will be three power centers—Europe, North America and East Asia.

For proof that the role of East Asia has changed we need only look at its new economic weight. As recently as 1960, Japan and East Asia together accounted for 4 percent of world GNP, while the United States, Canada, and Mexico represented 37 percent. Today both groups have about the same share of the world's GNP (some 24 percent each), but, with more than half the world's economic growth taking place in Asia in the 1990s, the economies of North America and Europe will progressively become relatively smaller.

It is difficult for Americans and Europeans to think of the new non-western power centers without assuming they are becoming more like western societies. This would be the pattern described of the world becoming one because of western technology. Or will there be the "clash of civilizations" we described espoused by Professor Huntington. Neither may take place. What we seem to be witnessing is a fusion of western and Far Eastern cultures. It is this fusion that explains the explosive growth of the Pacific and provides the possibility of continued peace and prosperity in the region.

It is common for us to assume that for the Far East to progress it must model their societies on the pattern of western society, becoming more liberal capitalist and democratic. But it is more probable East Asia will go its own way, and will develop its own sense of community. The reason East Asia has emerged as the dynamic region of the world is because it has drawn on the best practice and values from both eastern and western culture. Japan is a good example. Culturally it remains distinctly Japanese while its westernized bureaucracy, business, science, and technology are among the best. It has modernized and is no longer a feudal society. But there is no doubt that the Japanese remain Japanese. Their homes are Japanese. Their souls are Japanese. Although many Japanese teenagers look like their European or American counterparts, their value systems, though changing, remain fundamentally Japanese. They bow deeply and behave reverentially toward their elders. There is relatively little juvenile delinquency or crime. The glue that holds Asian societies and families together has not been weakened by modernization. To many, this is an economic and industrial miracle. But this success is due neither to Japanese culture nor western methods; it is the result of the combination of both. In the long run, American society may well improve if it undergoes a similar osmosis, absorbing the best of Asian civilization.

Across the Pacific, the traffic on trade, investment, information, aviation, cultural, and educational highways is increasing by leaps and bounds. History teaches us that trade and investment bring not just money and goods, but also ideas. The explosion of two-way trade and investment cannot leave the two cultural universes across the Pacific intact. So far, it is mainly East Asians who are experiencing the fruits of the cultural fusion of East and West, while North Americans and Australians are being drawn to the region by sheer economic logic. But the explosion of contacts must eventually lead to a two-way process of cultural osmosis. Over time a fusion will take place.

Worksheet ▶

CHAPTER NINE

Define or Identify:

- Huang Ho River

- Dynasty

- Pictogram, ideogram

- The Middle Kingdom

- Mandate of heaven

- Gentleman-scholar

- The meaning of Lao Tsu, the Buddha, Christ

- Tao Te Ching

- Yin and Yang

- Wu Wei

- Shogun

- Samurai

- Ainu

- Kamikase

- Bushido

- Zen-zazen, koan

- Meiji Restoration

- St. Francis Xavier

- Shinto

- December 7, 1941

- The three principal countries of the Far Eastern culture

Explain:

- Why even though conquered, we can still call China the world's oldest continuous civilization.

- What was the main reason Confucius felt society was falling apart?

- Why would the social prestige of an elderly scholar be high in China?

- Why would Confucius recommend an appreciation of music?

- Why would Confucius emphasize courtesy?

- What is a gentleman?

- Why is Taoism often referring to water?

- Why do Confucianism and Taoism blend together in China?

- How does Taoism relate to the martial arts, impressionist painting and the architecture of Frank Lloyd Wright?

- Why would a rabid environmentalist be comfortable with the teaching of Taoism?

- What is the sound of one hand clapping?

- What was Takugawa's reaction to the European presence in Japan?

- What was the shock to the world of the Japanese victory in the Russo-Japanese War?

Explain:

- What is the place of the Japanese in the Shinto religion's view of the world?

- Why might Koreans feel a strong animosity against the Japanese?

- In China when we find a man is 50 years old, we compliment him by saying he is at least 60. Why?

- What is the approximate date in history of Confucius, Lao Tzu, the Buddha, and the height of Greece?

Discuss:

- What was the fate of the barbarian conquerors of China?

- What was the situation in China at the time of Confucius that he set out to remedy?

- What are the five relationships? How does this differ from the American idea of rights?

- What is the role of family in the Confucian system?

- "Study the arts of peace, not of war." What did Confucius mean? Is he right?

- "He who says doesn't know. He who knows doesn't say." "He who feels punctured must have once been a bubble."

- How do you see the forces of Jihad and McWorld working in China today?

- The role of China in Japanese culture.

- Why does the book refer to Confucianism as a "moral ethical" system rather than a religion?

- A) Taoism (B) Buddhism (C) Confucianism—How do they relate to the following:
  The inferior owes loving obedience and loyalty to the superior, and the superior owes loving responsibility to the inferior.
  The best way to live is the natural way. People's fears, suffering is to crush desire and sever earthly attachments.
  Desire is the course of suffering. The way to avoid suffering is to crush desire and sever earthly attachments.

- How did the Japanese reaction to the threat from the West differ from that of China and India?

- The impact Perry had on Japan in 1853.

- The Japanese slogan "Eastern morale and western arts."

- Why during the Meiji Restoration would the Shinto religion be emphasized?

- As you see Japan today, discuss the play of force of Jihad and McWorld.

- What are some common behaviors and attitudes you might find among Chinese, Koreans, and Japanese today?

- What do you think will happen to future relationships between the U.S. and China?

· Describe what you feel to be the essential teachings of Buddhism, Confucianism and Taoism. Mention something about the founder, the principal beliefs and how those beliefs are being expressed in today's oriental culture.

· Which of the above teachings is the most appealing to you? Why?

Chapter 10 ▶▶

Islam

In the time when Europe had not yet recovered from the fall of the Roman Empire and was still in its Dark Age, the world saw the rise of Islam. The years 600 to 1000 and the rise of Islam were a turning point in world history.

Muslim warriors united the entire Middle East. The Middle East before the Muslim was dominated by two great empires: the Byzantine, which we described in some detail, and the Sassanian. The Byzantine heirs of Rome, from its great city, Constantinople, controlled the lands of the eastern Mediterranean; and the Sassanian heirs to Persia, with its capital at Ctesiphon, ruled the Tigris-Euphrates valleys and the Iranian Plateau.

The two were constantly at war and one reason was a cultural clash, for one was Christian with the Greco-Roman culture, and the other Zoroastrian with Persian-Mesopotamian traditions. Their exhausting wars left both of them weakened and unprepared for new warriors who were gathering in the Arabian deserts.

The Islamic conquests of the seventh and eighth centuries united under Islam all the territories from the Pyrenees to India and from Morocco to central Asia, one of the world's great empires and cultural groups.

More remarkable than the great military victories were the cultural achievements of Islam. Although the conquered territories were the centers of some of humanity's oldest civilizations, nevertheless, by the eleventh century, the conquering Arabs had made dominant both their language and their culture. Arabic became the language of everyday use from Persia to the Atlantic. And a new Islamic culture emerged that was an original blending of the preceding Judaic, Persian-Mesopotamian, and Greco-Roman cultures. This cultural change has been going on to the present day, so that Iraquis and Moroccans now have as much linguistic and cultural unity as do the English, Australians, and Canadians.

Arabia, before the rise of Islam, was regarded as a backward place populated by nomadic barbarians. Apart from in the far south, where there was agriculture and central government, the rest of Arabia was very thinly populated by wandering tribes. The sheikhs, or elective tribal leaders, were merely the first among equals and were bound by the same traditional custom that governed all. Their principal functions were to lead in time of war and to serve as caretakers of holy places.

Most of the tribes were pagan and worshiped trees, fountains, and stones that were regarded as the dwelling places of vaguely defined powers. There was also a belief in more personal gods, which were beneath a higher deity called Allah. Both Judaism and Christianity had entered Arabia from the north, occasionally converting entire tribes in the border region and some isolated groups in the remainder of the peninsula.

Compared to these religions, the idolatry and polytheism, the tribal warfare, and the political disunity of Arabia must have seemed shamefully primitive to many thinking Arabs. One reason for Mohammed's success was that his teachings satisfied the needs and longings of his people, who were looking for a higher religion they could all unite behind.

▶ Islam

Islam: the name comes from the word *salaam* or peace, "the perfect peace that comes when one's life is surrendered to God." One who surrenders is a Muslim (Also spelled Moslem; we use Muslim throughout the book as today's most acceptable spelling). Mohammedanism is not an acceptable term to a Muslim because from his point of view, Mohammed is not the founder of his religion; God is the founder, Mohammed is His prophet.

Islam emerged with a man, the prophet Mohammed. He was born in Mecca (Arabia) in approximately 571 AD. The world into which he was born was barbaric. Mecca was full of vice, gambling leading to fighting and bloodshed was commonplace. The prevailing religion provided no help. It was centered on jinns or demons that represented the terrors of the desert. Blood feuds that lasted for years were common.

Mohammed grew up among all this fighting and general immorality and he thought deeply about it. As a young man, he married a wealthy widow named Khadija. Though she was 15 years older, the marriage proved happy in every respect. In the difficult days when no one was believing his message, Khadija consoled him and kept alive his faith and hope.

After his marriage, Mohammed developed the habit of withdrawing from Mecca to meditate. He thought and prayed in a cave outside Mecca, on the mysteries of good and evil. He longed for insights on God's plan. After years of prayer (about 15) one night known as "The Night of Power and Excellence," the message came. As he lay on the floor of the cave, his mind locked in deepest contemplation, a voice commanded Mohammed to cry. Twice the voice commanded but Mohammed resisted, wishing nothing so much as to escape from the overwhelming Presence. "Cry!" commanded the voice for the third time.

"What shall I cry?" answered Mohammed in terror. The answer came back:

> Cry—in the name of thy Lord!
> Who created man from blood coagulated.
> Cry! Thy Lord is wondrous kind
> Who by the pen has taught mankind
> Things they knew not (being blind).

Getting up from his trance he rushed home and told Khadija who, on hearing his full story, believed he was chosen by God and became his first convert.

Returning to the cave he heard the voice return again and again, and always it told Mohammed to go forth and preach. After great spiritual struggle, Mohammed surrendered to the will of Allah. From that time he preached with unswerving purpose in face of persecution, insult and threats the words which God was to give to him over a period of 23 more years.

The reaction to his message in Mecca was at first violently hostile. Its monotheism threatened Mecca's revenue coming from Bedouin pilgrimages, its moral teachings demanded an end to a lifestyle the people did not want to give up, and its reorganization of society would put an end to an unjust economic order. Mohammed was preaching to a people who were very conscious of class, that in the sight of God all men were equal.

At first he made few converts. After three long years of complete dedication, he had fewer than 40 converts. But slowly the convincing words of Mohammed started to get results until by the end of ten years several hundred families were acknowledging Mohammed as God's true prophet. In the face of this threat to their very existence, the Meccan leaders decided to kill Mohammed.

As he faced this severe crisis Mohammed received a delegation from Yathrib, a town about 200 miles north of Mecca. They invited him to come to their city and become their leader. After having the delegation agree that the city would worship one God and accept the precepts of Islam, Mohammed agreed to come.

Even though the Meccans did everything to prevent his departure along with many of his followers, Mohammed made his escape. The year of 622 AD marks the date of this escape or flight known as the Hegira. It is regarded by Muslims as the turning point in world history and is the year from which they date their calendar. The city of Yathrib, where Mohammed is buried, became known as the city of the prophet or simply "the city," Medina.

In Medina, Mohammed moved from religion to political leadership. Tradition tells us his administration was an ideal blend of justice and mercy. As the leader of his people, he exercised the justice necessary for order, never hesitating to punish those who were guilty. When the injury was toward himself, on the other hand, he was gentle and merciful even to his enemies.

Exercising superb diplomacy, he blended the five different and conflicting tribes of the city, two of which were Jewish, into an orderly unit. His reputation spread and people came from every part of Arabia to see the man who had done this remarkable thing.

His success led to conflict with Mecca, who still felt threatened by his message. After both victory and defeat, the Meccans made a desperate last effort to force the followers of Mohammed to capitulate. The failure of their effort turned the tide permanently in Mohammed's favor and, eight years after his forced flight from Mecca he returned as a conqueror.

The city that had treated him cruelly now lay at his feet with his old persecutors at his mercy. He refused, however, to press his victory; in the hour of his triumph the past was forgotten. Making his way to the famous Kaaba stone which had been the religious focus of Mecca since time immemorial and which he now rededicated to Allah, he accepted the almost mass conversion of the city.

The entire work, Muslims say, was the work of God.

The Koran

Despite their respect for the Prophet, Muslims never confuse him with the cornerstone of their faith. This place is reserved for Islam's bible, the Koran. The only proof Mohammed ever offered that he was God's prophet was the fact that even though uneducated and, in fact, illiterate, without God how could he have written a book embodying all wisdom and theology essential to human life; which, in addition, is grammatically perfect and a poetic masterpiece. The Koran is perhaps the most widely read book in the world. Certainly it is the most often memorized and possibly it exerts the most influence on those who read it.

According to the strict believer's view, the Koran's every letter was directly dictated by God. Its words came to Mohammed in manageable segments over twenty-three years through voices that seemed at first to vary and sometimes sounded like "the reverberating of bells" but gradually focused in a single voice that became identified as the angel Gabriel's. No orthodox Muslim doubts the divine origin of the words themselves. Fixed on Mohammed's mind, they were recorded by his followers on whatever they had, bones and bark and leaves and scraps of parchment, with God preserving their accuracy throughout.

Islam assumes that the Bible of Jews and Christians too is originally authentic revelation from God, which entitles those who hold them sacred, Jews and Christians, to be classed with Muslims as "People of the Book." Nevertheless, the Old and New Testaments share two defects from which the Koran is free. Having been revealed at earlier stages in man's spiritual development when, as with a child, he was incapable of receiving the full truth, they are incomplete. Beyond this, the Jewish and Christian Bibles have in the process of being written become partially corrupted, a fact that explains the discrepancies that occasionally appear between their accounts and parallel ones in the Koran. Because it is free of error the Koran is the final and infallible revelation of God's will.

Despite its poetry and theology, the Koran is a book which emphasizes action rather than ideas. Islam teaches man how to walk the straight path. And in detail the phrase from the Koran that is repeated by every Muslim each day:

> Guide us in the straight path,
> The path of those whom Thou hast favored,
> Not the path of those who incur Thine anger
> nor of those who go astray.

Compared with other religions, Islam spells out the way of life it proposes; it pinpoints it, nailing it down through clear instructions. The result is a definiteness about this religion that makes it special. A Muslim knows where he stands. He knows who he is and who God is. He knows his obligations and, if he disobeys, the punishment.

The Five Pillars of Islam

The instructions for following the straight path that spells out man's duties in his daily life are contained in the Five Pillars of Islam.

The first pillar states Islam's belief briefly, simply and in a single sentence. *"There is no God but Allah and Mohammed is his Prophet."* At least once during his lifetime a Muslim must say this belief correctly, slowly, thoughtfully, aloud, with full understanding, and with heartfelt conviction in its truth. In actuality, practicing Muslims repeat it many times each day, but at least once during one's lifetime is required.

The first part states the belief in one God. "There is no God but Allah." There is no God but God. Once and for all, it throws out the many idols the Bedouin had worshiped since the dawn of history, and in the Muslim's view pointed out to Judaism and Christianity as well to be aware of their near-idolatry of the Torah and Christ.

The second part—that "Mohammed is God's prophet"—states the Muslim's faith in God's choosing Mohammed and in the truthfulness of the book he transmitted, the Koran. Although there was some attempt to deify Mohammed after his death, this was squashed by his appointed successor in a famous speech. "If there are any among you who worshiped Mohammed, he is dead. But if it is God you worship, He lives forever."

The second pillar of Islam is *prayer*, in which Muslims are told to be constant. The basic reason is to keep man's life in perspective. Man must learn and continuously relearn that he is not God. Man has a tendency to put himself in the center of the universe and live as a law to himself. When man tries to play God, everything goes wrong.

When should a Muslim pray? Five times a day—upon getting up, at noon, in mid-afternoon, after sunset, and before going to bed. The times are not absolutely binding. Muslims kneel and put their forehead to the ground facing Mecca. While in Islam no day of the week is as sharply set apart from others as is the Sabbath for the Jews or Sunday for the Christians, Friday is their holy day.

Formality is not a pronounced feature in Islam but the closest that Muslims come to a formal service of worship is when they gather on Fridays for noon prayers and collective recital of the Koran. These gatherings are usually in mosques.

The exact answer to where the Muslim should pray, however, is anywhere. Every corner of Allah's universe being equally pure, the faithful are encouraged to spread their prayer rug wherever they find themselves at the appointed hour.

The third pillar of Islam is *charity*. Material things are important in life, but some people have more than others. Why? Islam is not concerned with this theoretical problem. Instead, it turns to the practical question of what should be done about the situation. Its answer is simple. Those who have much should help lift those who have little. The figure Mohammed set was two and one-half percent of worth. Poorer people owe nothing, but those in the middle and upper-income brackets must annually distribute among the poor one-fortieth of the value of all they possess. And to whom among the poor should this money be given? This too, characteristically, is spelled out: to those in the most need; to slaves in the process of buying their freedom; to debtors unable to meet their obligations; to strangers and wayfarers; and to those who collect and distribute the alms.

The fourth pillar of Islam is the *observance of Ramadan*. Ramadan is a month in the Arabian calendar, Islam's holy month, because during it Mohammed received his initial call from God and ten years later made his historic Hegira from Mecca to Medina. To commemorate these two great occasions, able-bodied Muslims not involved in crises like war or unavoidable travelling fast during Ramadan. From daybreak to the setting of the sun, the Muslim must not eat or drink; after sundown they may eat in moderation. Being a month in a lunar calendar or 28 days, Ramadan falls in different seasons. When it falls in the winter its demands are not too difficult. When, on the other hand, it falls during the scorching summers, to remain active during the long days without so much as a drop of water is a real trial.

Why, then, does the Koran require it? For one thing, fasting makes one think. For another thing, fasting teaches self-discipline. If you can do without, you will have less difficulty controlling your desires at other times. Fasting reminds us of our dependence on God. Fasting reminds us vividly of our essential frailty and dependence. Finally, fasting helps us feel sympathy for others. Only those who have been hungry can know what hunger means. If you have fasted for thirty days within the year, you will be apt to listen more carefully the next time you are approached by someone in need.

Islam's fifth pillar is *pilgrimage*. Once during his lifetime every Muslim who is physically and economically in a position to do so is expected to make the trip to Mecca, where God's great revelation was first given to Mohammed. The basic purpose of the pilgrimage is to heighten the pilgrim's devotion to God and to his revealed will, but the practice has some beneficial side effects as well. It is, for example, a reminder of the equality between all humans.

Upon reaching Mecca pilgrims remove their usual clothes, which tend to carry clear indications of their social status, and put on two simple sheet-like garments. Everyone as he nears Islam's center on earth wears the same thing. All distinctions of rank and hierarchy are removed; prince and pauper stand before God as equal human beings.

Pilgrimage also provides a useful service in international relations. It brings together people from various countries demonstrating that they have in common a loyalty that goes beyond the loyalties of separate countries. Pilgrims pick up information about their brothers in other lands and return to their own with better understanding of one another. The pilgrimage to Mecca is called the *Haj.* One who makes the pilgrimage is henceforth deemed worthy of the title *Haji.*

Islamic Values

In addition to respecting the five pillars, Muslims have traditionally been expected to abstain from gambling, alcohol, and pork. The proscription against gambling continues in force but liberal Muslims tend to relax the other two. The rule against drinking, they say, was directed against the wild excesses of Mohammed's day; not drinking but intoxication is the true target of this rule. The prohibition against pork was for hygienic reasons which need continue only as long as the disease connected with that meat remains.

In looking at Islam, we should realize Islam is not a theory or theology so much as a clear and precise plan for achieving its ideals. Islam speaks out on social issues and while other religions emphasize personal religious experience, Muslims are called to establish a very explicit kind of social order. In trying to understand modern Islamic countries' actions, we should remember faith and politics, religion and society are inseparable in Islam. Separation of church and state is not a belief of Islam.

Let's survey Muslim thinking in some important areas of society.

Islam is aware of the physical basis of man's life. The needs and care of the body are essential to rise to higher spiritual and social maturity. Society's health requires that goods be equally distributed and wealth not be concentrated and frozen within a small group. Muslim economics are based on this principle. Mohammed himself in his administration broke up vested interests and enormously reduced the injustices of special privilege. Islam does not oppose profit or economic competition or discourage a man to work hard and improve his position. But it insists on the need for fairness and compassion. (Note the third pillar mentioned above with its requirement of 2.5% of total worth marked for annual distribution to the poor.) Mohammed also ruled against primogeniture which restricts inheritance to the oldest son. He required the inheritance be divided among all children, daughters as well as sons. This assures a more even distribution of wealth.

While Islam allows interest, it is against usury and believes interest rates should be kept low. More difficult for the modern American might be the Islamic principle that unearned money is not one's own. For all of life's gifts the good Muslim should be able to answer "yes" to the question: "Have I contributed to the society enough to deserve what I am now receiving?"

Certainly a great deal of ignorance and prejudice exists regarding Islamic attitudes on the status of women. One chief reason is that because of its permission of several wives it is seen as degrading women.

If, however, we see this permission historically it looks different. In Mohammed's time women were regarded as little more than another of man's possessions. Daughters had no inheritance rights, and marriage arrangements were very loose and easily changed. The birth of a daughter was regarded as a calamity and many were buried alive.

Mohammed improved the status of women enormously. He forbade infanticide. He required that daughters be included in inheritance. In her rights as a citizen—education, suffrage, and vocation—the Koran opens the way to woman's full equality with man, an equality which should be realized as the customs of Muslim nations become modernized. It sanctified marriage, and made it the only place for the sexual act.

Islam demands a woman's full consent before she is wed; not even a sultan may marry her without her express approval. Purdah, woman's practice of secluding herself generally and veiling her face when outside the home, Mohammed saw as an advantage as a check on the widespread promiscuity of his day. He would never have sanctioned the extremes to which this is carried today in some Muslim societies.

There's no reason to assume that as the Islamic countries become industrialized and democracy and general education grow that Muslim women will hold any lower position than women in Europe or America.

Islam stresses absolute racial equality. As the ultimate test of this is willingness to intermarry. According to the Muslim view, Abraham's second wife, Hagar, was a Negro. Mohammed himself married a Negro as one of his wives and gave his daughter in marriage to a Negro. Today Muslims are drawn from all colors—black men from Africa, brown men from Malaya, yellow men from China, white men from Turkey. The spectacular advances Islam is making in color-conscious Asia and Africa today are no doubt helped by the explicit way in which the principle of absolute racial equality is emphasized in Islam's teachings.

An outstanding general himself, Mohammed left a tradition regarding war. Agreements are to be settled; treachery avoided; the wounded are not to be mutilated, nor the dead disfigured. Women, children, and the old are not to be slain; orchards, crops, and sacred objects are to be spared. According to the Koran a righteous war must be defensive or to right a wrong. This call to righteous wars for justice leads to the idea of the *jihad*, the Muslim concept of a holy war in which those who die for the cause of Islam are assured of heaven. The sword is not to be used for convincing people. Two verses from the Koran are short and explicit.

> Let there be no compulsion in religion (ii:257).
> Unto you your religion, and unto me my religion (cix:6).

or consider the words of Mohammed:

> "Wilt thou then force men to believe when belief can come only from God?" Once when a deputy of Christians visited him, Mo-

hammed invited them to conduct their service in his mosque, adding, "It is a place consecrated to God."

► Islam Today

There are strong indications that at precisely the present, when history seems to be focusing around the Near and Middle East, Islam is emerging from the partial stagnation which followed in the wake of its once mighty empire. Youngest of the major religions of the world, it is again stirring with some of the strength and vigor or youth. From Morocco on the Atlantic, eastward by way of Egypt through the entire Middle East, Pakistan and Indonesia, the former Soviet Union to the Philippines in the Pacific, Islam is a vital force in the modern world. In the vicinity of one out of every five persons in today's world, belongs to this religion which guides both thought and deed to a detail not often paralleled in the West. Nor is Islam merely consolidating its position; it is expanding and expanding rapidly.

Today Islam is spreading not only in Africa, Southeast Asia and the former USSR ,but even to some extent in China, England, and the United States. It is the fastest growing religion in the world. As recently as 1947, a new Muslim state has been born, Pakistan, with a population of 70 million. In some areas where Islam and Christianity are competing for converts, Islam is gaining at a rate of ten to one.

Around the world, day or night, the faithful will be called to prayer in these words:

> God is most great!
> God is most great!
> I testify that there is no God but Allah.
> I testify that Mohammed is the prophet of Allah.
> Arise and pray; arise and pray.
> God is great;
> There is no God but Allah!

► From the Koran

Generosity and Love

> Allah is All-Embracing, All-Knowing. Those who spend their wealth for the cause of Allah and afterward make no reproach nor let injury follow that which they have spent, their reward is with their Lord, and there shall no

fear come upon them, neither shall they grieve. A kind word with forgiveness is better than almsgiving followed by injury. Allah is Absolute, Merciful! O ye who believe! Do not render your almsgiving vain by injury and reproach, like him who spends his wealth only to be seen and believes not in Allah and the Last Day.

The Pilgrimage to Mecca

Performing the pilgrimage and the visit for Allah. . . .Observe your duty to Allah, and know that Allah is severe in punishment . . . and whoever is minded to perform the pilgrimage . . . (let him remember that) there is (to be) no lewdness nor abuse nor angry conversation on the pilgrimage. And whatsoever good ye do, Allah knows it. . . .

Charity

Whatever alms ye spend or vow ye vow, lo! Allah knoweth it. Wrongdoers have no helpers. If ye publish your almsgiving, it is well, but if you hide it and give it to the poor, it will be better for you, and will atone for some of your ill-deeds. Allah is informed of what ye do. . . .

The Unity

In the name of Allah, the Beneficent,the Merciful! Say: He is Allah, the One!
Allah, the eternally Besought of all!
He begetteth not nor was begotten.
And there is none comparable unto him.

(Mohammed said "The Unity" was equal in value to a third part of the entire Koran.)

The Lord's Prayer of Islam

In the name of Allah, the Beneficent, the Merciful!
Praise be to Allah, Lord of the Worlds, the Beneficent, the Merciful, Ruler of the Day of Judgment,
Thee alone we worship; Thee alone we ask for help. Show us the straight path,
The path of those whom Thou hast favored;
Not of those who have earned Thine anger nor of those who go astray.

Women

And they (women) have rights similar to those (of men) over them in kindness, and men are a degree above them. . . .When ye have divorced women, and they have reached their term, then retain them in kindness or release them in kindness. Retain them not to their hurt so that ye transgress (the limits). He who doeth that hath wronged his soul.

▶ The Expansion of Islam

Mohammed had found Arabia divided with many local idolatrous practices. He left it with a religion and a book of revelation, and with a community and a state sufficiently well organized and armed to dominate the entire peninsula. Within a century his followers were to march from victory to victory, building an imposing empire across the breadth of Eurasia and spreading his creed throughout the world.

With the death of Mohammed the tribal sheikhs, who considered their submission to him ended with his death, stopped their tribute and went back to their old ways. The ideal appeal to this group, the Muslim leaders knew, would be to initiate some foreign raids that would promise the booty beloved by every Bedouin, as the desert nomads are called.

The leader of the raids was the caliph, or deputy, who was chosen to represent the Prophet. There was no possibility, of course, of a successor to Mohammed as Prophet, but a chief of the community was essential. So when Abu Bakr, Mohammed's father-in-law, was selected as caliph, it meant that he was the defender of the faith rather than religious leader.

It was under Abu Bakr the earliest foreign raids began. The great conquests that followed represented the expansion not only of Islam but of the Arab tribes, who on many occasions in earlier centuries had pushed northward into the Fertile Crescent. The size and success of the expansion at this time can be explained by the exceptional weakness of the Byzantine and Sassanian empires we mentioned and by the unity and vigor generated by the new Islamic faith.

In 636 the Arabs won a decisive victory over the Byzantines. Attacking in the midst of a blinding sandstorm they almost annihilated a mixed force of Greek, Armenian, and Syrian Christians. Emperor Heraclius fled to Constantinople, abandoning all of Syria to the victors. The Muslims now turned against the neighboring Sassanian province of Iraq. Its Semitic, partly Christian, population was alienated from its Persian and Zoroastrian masters. This split contributed to the great victory won by the Arabs in the summer of 637. The Persian emperor hastily evacuated his nearby capital, Ctesiphon, and fled eastward. (See Figure 10-1.)

The astonishing triumphs over Byzantines and Persians left the Muslims with unheard of riches, which further swelled the flood of Bedouin tribes from the southern deserts. Their pressure on the frontiers was irresistible, and the Arab armies rolled onward, westward into Egypt and eastward into Persia. Within two years (639–641) they had overrun the whole of Egypt.

The successors to the great Abu Bakr and Omar in the caliphate bore the banners of Islam still further afield, driven on by the momentum of victory, of religious enthusiasm, and of nomadic greed. In North Africa the Arab forces, supplemented by native Berber converts, fought their way right to the Atlantic and then crossed the Straits of Gibraltar into Spain. In 711 they defeated Roderick, the last Visigothic king of Spain, and crossed the Pyrenees into France. There they were finally stopped by the Frank Charles Martel at Tours in 732. This battle is often described as a major turning point in the history of western Europe.

What had started out as a simple desert religion had grown in little more than one century into a great Asian, African, and European empire. With the first phase of expansion completed, the Arabs now settled down to enjoy the fruits of victory. Virtually an army of occupation in their conquered lands, they lived mostly in strategically located camp

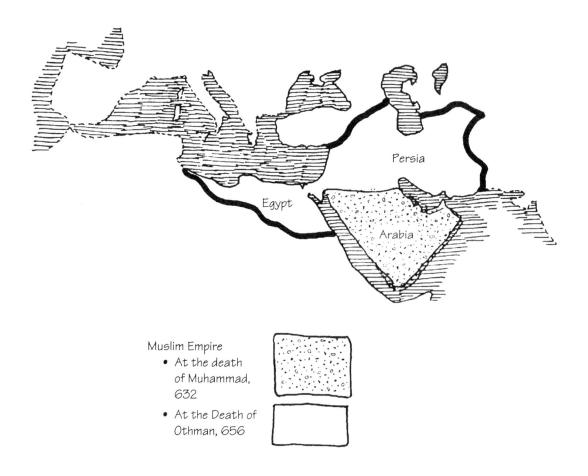

Muslim Empire
- At the death of Muhammad, 632
- At the Death of Othman, 656

FIGURE 10-1 Early Growth of Muslim Power

cities, from where they controlled the surrounding countryside.

To run an empire is different than conquering one. Among other things many of the conquered became Muslims. The caliphs moved the capital to Damascus as a more useful home for Arab rule. Non-Arab Muslims began to outnumber the Arab aristocracy and regard it as a parasite clique. The imperial structure changed radically with the shift of the capital from Damascus eastward to Baghdad in 762. This will mean that Islam will absorb a great deal of the high culture of Persia. The caliph no longer was a simple Arab sheik but a divinely ordained autocrat—the "Shadow of God upon earth." His authority rested not on tribal support but on the salaried bureaucracy and standing army. Thus the caliphate became an oriental monarchy similar to the many that had preceded it in ancient Mesopotamia.

Under stability of this monarchy, a culture that was a mixture of Judaic, Greco-Roman, and Persian traditions evolved during the following centuries. Islam ceased to be merely an Arab tribal power but became instead a new and distinctive culture. Within a century Baghdad numbered about a million people, the greatest city in the world.

In the center was a citadel some two miles in diameter in which were the caliph's residence and the quarters of his officials and guards. Beyond the citadel walls a great commercial metropolis sprang up, supported by the productive farms of the fertile Mesopotamian valley.

Industry also flourished, textiles being the most important in the number of workers employed and the value of the output. Linen, cotton, and silk goods were produced in many parts of the empire, both for local consumption and for export. Carpets were made almost everywhere. The art of paper making, learned from Chinese prisoners, spread rapidly across the Islamic world, reaching Spain by 900. Other industries including pottery, metalwork, soap, and perfumes flourished.

Muslim merchants traded overland through central Asia and overseas with India, Ceylon, Southeast Asia, and China. A flourishing trade was carried on also with Africa, in gold, ivory, ebony, and slaves. We know about trade with northern Europe from the discovery in Scandinavia of large hoards of Muslim coins dating from the seventh to the eleventh centuries.

The two goals of Therus, who founded Russia, were Constantinople and Baghdad. In exchange for these coins, the Muslims received furs, amber, honey, and cattle. Such large-scale trade stimulated a highly developed banking system with branches in all leading cities, so that a check could be drawn in Baghdad and cashed in Morocco.

With this solid economic base, caliphs were able to enjoy themselves in their luxurious palaces. The Thousand and One Nights describes Harun al-Rashid (786–809), the best known of these caliphs, as a gay and cultured ruler surrounded by poets, musicians, singers, dancers, scholars, and wits. Among the popular indoor games were chess, dice, and backgammon; and outdoor sports included hunting, falconry, hawking, polo, archery, fencing, javelin throwing, and horse racing. Harun lived at the same time as Charlemagne, but their respective capitals, Baghdad and Achen, were quite incomparable—Islamic Baghdad was a sophisticated great city, while European Achen was a provincial village.

▶ Muslim Cultural Contributions

The caliphate should be remembered also for its relative tolerance in religious matters at a time when this quality was markedly absent in Europe. The explanation is to be found partly in the religious law of Islam. The sacred law recognized the Christians and Jews as being, like the Muslims, People of the Book. Both had a scripture—a written word of revelation. Their faith was accepted as true, though incomplete, since Mohammed had superseded Moses and Jesus Christ. Islam therefore tolerated the Christians and Jews. It permitted them to practice their faith, with certain restrictions and penalties.

The caliphate also was noteworthy for its achievements in the field of science. It is true that the tendency here was to preserve and to pass on rather than to create something new. On the other hand, its contacts with literally all regions of Eurasia, and its rich legacy from the great centers of civilization that it ruled over all contributed to the very real achievements of Islamic science that contributed greatly to the rise of Western science. Baghdad, for example, boasted a "House of Wisdom" that had a school of translators, a library, an observatory, and an academy. The scholars associated with it translated and studied the works of Greek scientists and philosophers, as well as scientific works from Persia and India.

In astronomy, the Muslims generally accepted the basic discoveries of the Greeks. But they did continue without interruption the astronomical observations of the ancients, so that the later European astronomers had available some nine hundred years of records, which provided the basis for their breakthrough discoveries.

Mathematics was of great interest to Muslims because it was needed both in astronomy and in commerce. Thanks to Babylonian and Indian contributions, the Muslims made important advances, especially in popularizing the Hindu number system based on decimals. Misleadingly called Arabic numerals (see "Indian Culture"), this system did for arithmetic what the discovery of the alphabet had done earlier for writing. It made mathematics available for everyday use by non-specialists.

Algebra was a Muslim invention and a great gift to world science. In geography, as in astronomy, the Muslims made little original contribution, but the extent of their empire and of their commerce enabled them to accumulate reliable and systematic data about Africa, Asia, and Europe.

Islamic medicine also was based on that of the Greeks, but the greater geographical spread of Islam made it possible to learn of new diseases and drugs. To the ancient list of drugs the Muslims added ambergris, camphor, cassia, cloves, mercury, senna, myrrh; and they also introduced new pharmaceutical preparations such as syrups, juleps, and rose water.

Indeed, Arab drugs were an important part of the cargoes that Italian captains brought from the Middle East. Muslims established the first apothecary shops and dispensaries; founded the first medieval school of pharmacy; required state examinations and certification for the practice of medicine; and operated well-equipped hospitals, of which some thirty are known.

The great Islamic doctors, such as Mohammed al-Rasi (844–926) and Abu Ali al-Husein ibn Sina (980–1037), famous in Europe as "Rhazes" and "Avicenna," were brilliant men of wide knowledge ranging from astronomy through botany to chemistry and their texts that were used in European medical schools until the seventeenth century.

Besides their own original achievements, the Muslims made an invaluable contribution to Europe by translating and transmitting Greek works. The "House of Wisdom" in Baghdad included a large staff of translators. Their translation included works of Hippocrates, Galen, Euclid, Ptolemy, Plato, and Aristotle. Another great translation center was in the city of Toledo in Muslim Spain, where the translators during the Twelfth and Thirteenth Centuries included Jews, Spaniards, and foreign scholars from all over Europe. This activity was of utmost significance, for western Europeans had lost direct acquaintance with Greek learning and for long were unaware even of its existence. Greek science reenters Europe thanks to the Muslims. Muslim scholarship preserved the Greek works until western Europe was past the Dark Ages and was once more ready to pick up where it had left off.

▶ One Culture

What was emerging was a genuine Islamic culture. Two basic bonds held together the diverse peoples: the Arabic language and the Islamic religion. It could be said that much more important than the Arab conquests was the spread of the Arabic language (recall the chapter on language as an element of culture). By the Eleventh Century Arabic had taken the place of the old Greek, Latin, Coptic, and Aramaic languages and was used from Morocco to Persia, as it is to the present day. This common language explains the feeling of common identity prevailing in this region, even though it includes many races and nations. Even beyond this vast area that was permanently Arabized, Arabic exerted a profound influence on other Muslim languages. Arabic words are as common in these other languages as Greek and Latin words in English.

The Islamic religion also is a powerful bond—much more powerful as a bond than Christianity because it is not only a religion but also a social and political system and a general way of life. Religion is the basis of Islamic culture.

▶ Decline

The Caliphate at Damascus reached its height during the reign of Harun al-Rashid and then declined in much the same way as we described the decline of the Roman Empire. There was first the matter of sheer size. The outlying provinces broke away: Spain in 756, Morocco in 788, and Tunisia in 800.

Further, as in the case of Rome, there was the problem of government expenses, which were excessive and unsupportable by the prevailing economy and technology. The luxury of the Baghdad court and the heavy weight of the huge bureaucracy were not matched by increased revenues. Government weakness, as usual, invited barbarian attacks.

Just as the Roman Empire had been invaded across the Rhine and the Danube, so the caliphate now was assaulted from the north, south, and east. European Christians permanently got back Spain and Sicily. Christian crusaders established themselves in Palestine and Syria. The most important and far reaching for world history, however, were the conquests of the Turks and Mongols from the East.

▶ The Seljuk Turks

Nomadic movements through the great Eurasian landmass have affected deeply world history. Many of these nomads converted to Islam, and they then further spread their new religion. During their centuries of glory after Genghis Khan they overran all Eurasia except for edges such as Japan, Southeast Asia, southern India, and western Europe. The nomadic Turks were a linguistic group. Their common bond was that they all spoke one form or another of a Turkish family of languages. Although a racially mixed people, they are generally Caucasoid in appearance rather than Mongoloid.

About 970, a branch of the Turkish people known as the Seljuks crossed over unopposed into Muslim territory and soon started gaining power. This new power was formally recognized in 1055 when the caliph, in Baghdad, proclaimed the Seljuk leader, a "sultan," or "he who had authority." Although the caliphs remained the supposed heads of the empire, the real rulers from then on were the Turkish sultans.

Under their vigorous leadership, the frontiers of Islam now were extended into two regions. Asia Minor had remained for centuries a center of the Christian Byzantine power despite attacks by the Arabs. But in 1071 the Seljuks won an overwhelming victory at Manzikert in eastern Asia Minor, even taking the Byzantine Emperor prisoner. This proved to be a turning point in Middle Eastern history.

The Asia Minor peasants, who had been exploited by corrupt Byzantine officials in Constantinople, now welcomed the Turks with relief. So between the eleventh and the thirteenth centuries the larger part of Asia Minor, now Turkey, was changed from being Greek and Christian to a Turkish and Muslim region, and it remains so today. Furthermore, Byzantium was so weakened by the loss of Asia Minor, that had always provided the bulk of the army manpower that they never recovered. Constantinople, a big city, was like a huge head with a very small body. This was the beginning of events that would lead to the fall of Constantinople in 1453.

To the east the Turks conquered India. Fired by their new faith, the Turks came to India not only in search of plunder but also to convert the infidels. They also brought social conflict—the clash between two different cultures, one believing that all men are brothers and the other based on caste. It was at this time, then, that the struggle of the fundamentally different cultures of Islam and Hinduism began. After World War II this struggle ended in the division of the peninsula into Hindu India and Muslim Pakistan. (See "Indian Culture.")

The relative ease with which the Turks conquered a land in which they were hopelessly outnumbered was due partly to the outdated Indian military tactics. They hadn't changed much since they were defeated by Alexander 1,500 years earlier. The infantry was an undisciplined mob, and their main weapon, the elephants, was useless against the Muslim cavalry.

Equally damaging, and a more fundamental weakness, was the Hindu caste system, which left the fighting to only the Kshatriya, or warrior caste. The rest of the population was untrained and largely indifferent, particularly because caste separated one group from another. So the masses either remained neutral or else welcomed the invaders.

This pattern was to be repeated frequently in the future and explains why, as we saw in Chapter 8, the British ruled from Delhi just as the Turkish sultans had before.

▶ Genghis Khan's Conquests

While the Turks were becoming the masters of the Muslim world, an obscure chieftain in far off

Mongolia was beginning his conquests that would create the greatest empire of history. (See Figure 10-2.) Genghis Khan (spelled also Chinggis, Chingis, Jenghiz, etc.) whose personal name was Temujin, was born about 1167, the son of a minor clan leader. After turning against his overlord and eliminating various rivals he finally was able to combine the various Mongol-speaking tribes into a single unit. An assembly of Mongol chieftains, held in 1206, proclaimed him the supreme head of his people with the title Genghis Khan, meaning "ruler of the universe."

Genghis Khan began with the built-in advantage enjoyed by all nomad warriors—their daily life prepared them for war. Dressed in leather and furs, leading extra horses as spares, and capable of riding several days and nights in succession with very little rest and food, these warriors introduced the German idea of blitzkrieg in the 1200s.

During operations on open plains, they could cover 270 miles in three days. They carried leather bags for water, which when empty could be inflated for swimming across rivers. Normally they lived off what they could find, but if needed they drank the blood of their horses and the milk of their mares. Their skills in hunting, learned in boyhood, taught them to coordinate the operations of widely spread horse columns over long distances.

Their favorite tactic was to pretend defeat, letting the enemy follow them for days. Then they would turn and destroy them. Other tricks included the tying of branches to the tails of horses to stir up

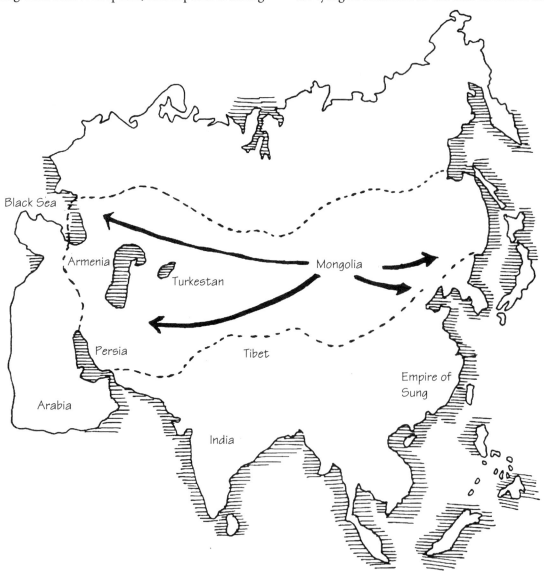

FIGURE 10-2 The empire of the Genghis Khan at his death (1227).

dust in order to give the impression of large forces on the march, and also the mounting of dummies on spare horses for the same purpose.

The basic Mongol weapon was the compound long bow, more powerful than the English longbow and capable of killing at 600 feet with its armor-piercing arrows. This was a deadly weapon in the hands of Mongol horsemen, who were able to carry a supply of thirty arrows and shoot them all at full gallop.

Other equipment included a steel helmet, light body armor made of hide, a saber, and sometimes a lance with a hook and a mace. The tough Mongol horses grazed only on the open range, and needed no shelter during the long, bitter winter and no hay or grain. They were somewhat small but very tough and adaptable.

In 1211 Genghis Khan attacked north China, first overrunning the region north of the Great Wall and then in 1213 piercing the wall and reaching the Yellow River plain. By 1215 he had captured and pillaged Peking and also gained the services of educated Chinese who knew how to besiege cities and how to run an empire.

Turning west, rich and ancient cities such as Bokhara and Samarkand, in central Asia, were pillaged and everyone massacred. The only exceptions were a few skilled artisans, who were sent to Mongolia. Not content with these spectacular triumphs in the Far East and Middle East, the Mongols swung north to the Caucasus where they defeated the Georgians. Advancing on the Ukraine, they crushed a numerically superior army of 80,000 Russians in 1223. (See section on Russia where this is discussed.) Meanwhile Genghis Khan had returned to Mongolia to direct another victorious campaign against the Chinese, who had revolted against his rule. This was his final campaign, for he died soon after in 1227.

After a two-year interval, Genghis Khan's son Ogodai was selected as successor. During his reign from 1229 to 1241 the campaigning was resumed in the two ends of Eurasia—China and Europe—some 5,000 miles apart. Genghis Khan's grandson Batu was sent with a force of 150,000 Mongols and Turks to Russia. Crossing the middle Volga in the fall of 1237 he fell upon the towns of central Russia.

Town after town was captured, including the then comparatively unimportant town of Moscow.

The Mongols pressed on into Poland and Hungary, defeated a German army of 30,000 in Silesia, crossed the frozen Danube, captured Zagreb in Yugoslavia, and reached the Adriatic coast. Thus Mongol armies now were in control across the whole of Eurasian continent from Europe to Japan.

Meanwhile, other Mongol armies were devastating the Muslim Middle East. After capturing Baghdad in 1258, most of its 800,000 inhabitants are reported to have been massacred. In 1260, however, the Egyptian Mamelukes unexpectedly defeated the advancing Mongols in Palestine. The defeat marked the high-water mark of the Mongol Empire. Unable to expand further, the Mongol Empire fell apart almost as rapidly as it had been built up. The Mongols adopted the languages, religions, and cultures of their more-advanced subjects and were absorbed by the higher culture.

In Persia the Mongol's adoption of Islam in 1295 as their official religion made them part of Islamic culture. With the breakup of the Mongol empire the Muslim Turks quickly came to the front. The most noteworthy of the new Turkish conquerors was Tamerlane. He seized Samarkand in 1369, and from there he struck out in all directions.

First he destroyed the rulers in Persia and Mesopotamia, then defeated the Golden Horde in Russia and the Ottoman Turks in Asia Minor, and he even invaded India and sacked Delhi. At its height, his empire extended from the Mediterranean to China. When he died in 1405, his empire fell apart even more rapidly than that of the Mongols.

▶ The Ottoman Turks

After Timur, the outstanding development was the extension of Muslim Turkish power in India and in Byzantium. In the Middle East Islam was being extended into Byzantium by the Ottoman Turks. These newcomers from central Asia settled in the corner of what is now Turkey, less than fifty miles from the strategic straits from the Black Sea that separates Asia from Europe. In 1299 the leader of these Turks, Uthman, declared his independence from his Seljuk overlord, and from these small beginnings grew the great Ottoman Empire, named after Uthman.

The Turks' first step was the conquest of the remaining Byzantine portion of Asia Minor. This was accomplished by 1340, thanks to the dissatisfaction of the Christian peasantry and extra ghazis, or warriors of the faith, who came in from all parts of the Middle East to battle against the Christian infidels. Next the Turks crossed the straits, into Europe. They hardly could have selected a more favorable moment for their advance into Europe.

The Balkan peninsula was divided by war between rival Christian churches and the Byzantine, Serbian, and Bulgarian states, all past their prime. Also the Christian peasants of the Balkans were as dissatisfied as the peasants in Asia Minor. And Western Christendom would not help, because of the age old division between Roman Catholic and Greek Orthodox Christians. Thus the way was clear in Europe for the Ottoman Turks, and they took full advantage of the opportunity.

In 1453 they took the second Rome, Constantinople, and with this the Ottomans were the masters of the entire Balkan Peninsula to the Danube River, with the exception of a few Venetian-held coastal fortresses. (See Figure 10-3.)

In India the Muslims established a national dynasty—the Mogul rulers, a very remarkable achievement in a predominantly Hindu country. This chapter in Indian history and its profound effects on Indian history and culture were explained in Chapter 8 on Indian Culture.

The Turkish conversion to Islam between 1000 and 1500 then greatly expanded Muslim influence and power. When the West began its world expansion in the 1500s, Islam still was expanding overland in all directions. The Ottomans were crossing the Danube into central Europe; central Asia was completely won over; and the Mongols were about to begin their conquest of virtually the entire Indian peninsula.

Also, Islam was spreading steadily into the interior of the continent of Africa from two centers.

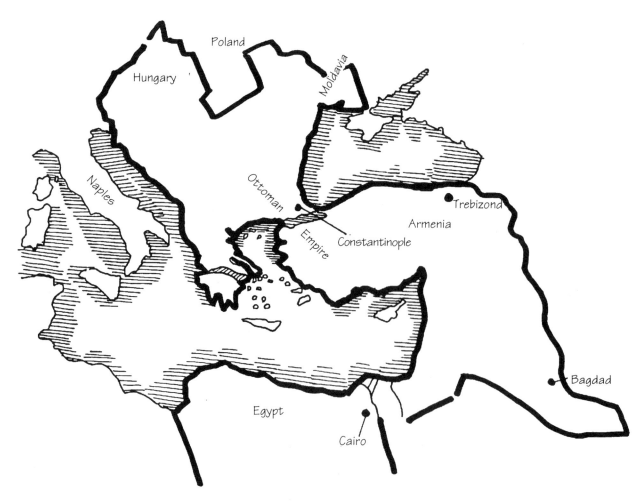

FIGURE 10-3 The Ottoman Empire at the death of Suleiman 1566 AD.

From the North African coast it advanced across the Sahara to West Africa, where a succession of large Negro Muslim kingdoms flourished. Likewise from the Arab colonies such as Zanzibar on the East African coast, Islam spread inland.

Islam also was carried by Arab and Indian merchants to Southeast Asia. Here, as in Africa and other regions, conversion was helped by the simplicity and adaptability of the new faith. All one had to do to become a Muslim was to repeat the words "I bear witness that there is no God but Allah and that Mohammed is the Messenger of Allah." Local practices and traditions usually were accepted and made holy simply by the addition of Islamic ritual.

Thus the faith was spread, not only by the sword, but by the work of traders who won over the populace by learning their language, adopting their customs, marrying their women, and converting their new relatives and business associates. By the end of the fifteenth century, Islam had spread as far east as the Philippines. Today the country with the largest Muslim population is Indonesia.

This spread of Islam during five centuries almost tripled the area that accepted the Muslim faith, with important effects on the course of world history. The continued expansion of the Muslim faith made Islam by 1500 a world force rather than simply a Middle Eastern power. It explains why today the Indian peninsula is divided into two parts, why Muslim political parties are so influential in Southeast Asia, why Islam is a powerful and rapidly growing force in Africa, and why it is now the faith of one-fifth to one-sixth of the people of the world.

The Turkish invasions are significant also because of the intercultural contact they made. In the technological field it was responsible for giving a number of Chinese inventions to the world, including gunpowder, silk, machinery, printing, and the blast furnace for cast iron. The opportunities offered by this cross-fertilization were really fully used only by the new changing Europe. All the other world cultures were too set in their ways.

▶ Islam and the West

At first it seemed as though the Islamic world would have no difficulty in adapting and changing. Islam had been willing to borrow from the great established civilizations and succeeded in making a culture that was new and impressive. But in the end there was too great a gulf between the dogma of the Islamic faith and the rationalist philosophy and science of the Greeks. They supported conservative theologians who rejected all scientific and philosophical speculation as heresy and atheism.

This had also been true in Europe when the church stood alone against the barbarians. Theology was the accepted queen of the sciences. People turned to religion for support and consolation in the face of material disaster. But in the West old assumptions were eventually challenged and replaced.

In the Muslim world they remained dominant through the nineteenth century. Intellectual growth and innovation in the Muslim world ceased, and at a time when Europe's universities were full of new ideas, the Islamic schools were content with rote memorization of the Koran.

Whereas the Muslim world had been far ahead of the West between 800 and 1200, by the year 1500 the gap had disappeared, and thereafter it was the West that boomed ahead while Islam stood still and even went backward.

A similar difference developed between the West and Chinese and Indian cultures, for the simple reason that only the West made the big jump to modern science. India was conquered by Islam and was affected by its attitude. China, reacting against the Mongols, who were expelled in 1368, developed a strong fear of foreigners—an almost instinctive hostility and scorn for all things non-Chinese and therefore barbarian. Russia also succeeded in 1480 in throwing off the Mongol role, but permanent scars remained. The country had been closed to fresh winds from Europe for 250 years, and both Mongol ideas and usages had paved the way for the absolutism of the czars and of the Orthodox Church.

Western Europe alone was the exception to this general pattern of stagnation. Only there occurred the great change—the emergence of modern culture with a new technological base that quickly proved a superiority that would spread it throughout the entire globe. This uniqueness stems from the Greco-Roman and Judeo-Christian traditions which allowed new concepts and institutions to take root and flourish.

▶ Islam in 1500

An observer looking at the earth about 1500 would have been more impressed by the Muslim than by the Christian world. The observer would have been impressed first by the extent of the Muslim world and then by its unceasing expansion.

Not only was the Muslim world the largest about 1500, but it also continued to expand after that date. Contrary to our assumption, western Europe was not the only part of the world that was extending its frontiers at that time. The Muslim world was still expanding, but by land, whereas the Christian world was reaching out by sea.

The Portuguese in the early sixteenth century were gaining footholds in India and the East Indies, and the Spaniards were conquering the Americas. But at the same time, the Ottoman Turks were pushing into central Europe. They overran Hungary, and in 1529 they besieged Vienna, the Hapsburg capital in the heart of Europe. Likewise, in India the great Mogul emperors were steadily extending their empire southward.

Elsewhere the Muslim faith continued to spread in Africa, central Asia, and Southeast Asia. The Muslim world of 1500 then was most impressive. Muslims ruled empires that were at least the equals of those in other parts of the globe, and yet these empires were soon destined to go downhill. Islam was to fall far behind western Europe, and they have remained behind to the present day.

One explanation for the misfortunes of the Muslim world was that it lacked the dynamism of Europe. It did not have those far-reaching changes that were revolutionizing European society during these centuries. In the Muslim economic field, for example, there were no basic changes in agriculture, in industry, in financial methods, or in commercial organization. A traveler in the Muslim lands in the seventeenth or eighteenth centuries would have observed essentially the same economic practices and institutions as the crusaders saw five hundred years earlier.

As long as the rulers were strong and enlightened, the autocratic empires functioned smoothly and effectively. But when central authority weakened, the courtiers, bureaucratic officials, and army officers all combined to fleece the productive classes of society, whether peasants or artisans or merchants. Their uncontrollable exploitation stifled private enterprise and incentive. Any subject who showed signs of wealth was fair game for arbitrary confiscation. Consequently, merchants hid their wealth rather than openly investing it to expand their operations.

Another cause and symptom of decline was the blind superiority complex of the Muslims, with their attitude of invincibility vis-a-vis the West. It never occurred to them at this time that they might conceivably learn anything from non-Muslims. Their attitude stemmed partly from the history of religious prejudice and partly from the spectacular successes of Islam in the past.

Islam had grown from an obscure sect to the world's largest and most rapidly growing religion. Consequently, Muslim officials and scholars looked down with arrogance of anything relating to Christian Europe as second rate.

One of the most damaging results of this self-centeredness was that it let down an intellectual iron curtain between the Muslim world and the West, especially in the increasingly important field of science. Muslim scholars knew virtually nothing of the great new European achievements of advances in medicine, anatomy, and astronomy. Not only were they ignorant of these scientific advances, but Muslim science itself had grown rigid, with little challenge and debate.

A final factor explaining Muslim decline is that the three great Muslim empires were all land empires. They were built by the Turks, the Persians, and the Monguls, all peoples with no seafaring traditions. Their empires faced inward toward central Asia rather than outward toward the oceans. This situation was significant, because it allowed the Europeans to become the masters of the world trade routes with little opposition from the Muslims, who before had controlled most of the trade between Asia and Europe.

The control of world trade enriched the Europeans tremendously and further fed their economic, social, and political development. For Islam a vicious circle developed, with worldwide trade making Western Europe increasingly wealthy, productive, dynamic, and growing, while the once great Muslim empires, left out of the world economy, fell further and further behind.

▶ The Mideast

The West's dominating impact on the modern Arab world may be said to begin on the day in 1798 when Napoleon landed in Egypt with his army of invasion. Napoleon's real objective was to strike at Britain's position in the East, but after Admiral Nelson destroyed his fleet near Alexandria, Napoleon gave up his objective and returned home. Yet his expedition had a lasting effect on Egypt, for it was more than a military affair. It was also a cultural incursion by the West into the heart of the Arab world. Napoleon brought with him the first printing press to reach Egypt, and he was accompanied by scientists, who deciphered the ancient hieroglyphic writing, and by engineers, who prepared plans for a Suez Canal joining the Mediterranean and Red Sea.

Napoleon also smashed the power of the established ruling class in Egypt during his brief campaign in that country.

Thanks to Napoleon's expedition and the adaptation of western ideas by Egypt's rulers, Egypt became by far the most significant entry point for westernism in the Arab world. Later, Syria would also become a center for Western influence. One reason was the flourishing trade between Syria and Europe and the large number of Syrian merchants who engaged in business activities abroad. Another reason was the extensive missionary-educational activity carried on mostly by French Jesuits and American Presbyterians, who established schools in Syria that trained Arab students and printed and distributed Arab books. In this manner the Syrian Arabs rediscovered their past and learned about Western literature, ideology, and technology.

This stimulus from the outside was responsible for the earliest stirring of Arab nationalism. The leaders at the beginning were mostly Christian Arabs, since the Muslims did not enroll in the missionary schools until a later date. Nationalism was further aroused by the growing western domination. This resulted in strong anti-western sentiment among the intellectuals. The Muslim mass remained largely apathetic.

The tide of recent history has continued to run against Islam. The strength of Islam vis-a-vis the West diminished until most Muslim states in one degree or other adapted western political and industrial principles. By 1907, all Muslim territory had been made either colonies or protectorates of European powers, all conquering the Ottoman empire itself—traditional guardian of the Muslim world against Christendom—had become a stooge of the European great powers, and World War I gave the empire its death blow. Not until World War II and after did such countries as Morocco, Tunis, Egypt, Pakistan, and Indonesia achieve independence.

With their recent history it is understandable that Muslims have a profound nostalgia for an irrecoverable past. The Muslim peoples have in the recent years been simultaneously exposed to the force of the western political, scientific and industrial revolutions. (These revolutions are covered in Chapter 11.) This was not accidental. At the beginning of Europe's modern age, the Muslim peoples as we pointed out rejected change, preferring the shelter of authoritative doctrine and established institutions. Muslims were forced to pay the price of their earlier backwardness by confronting within a single century all the advances which Europe had developed in the course of some four hundred years. Small wonder there was shock and confusion.

While not repudiating their religion, most educated Muslims felt uneasy within the rigid framework of traditional Islam. Industrialism made very few inroads upon the Muslim world and the political and scientific revolutions only slightly more so. Western machine-made goods disrupted old handicraft and ways of life almost everywhere; and on top of all would be the discovery of oil that would further focus western business and political attention on Islam.

▶ Muslim Resentment of the West

If you will recall Professor Huntington's thesis (Chapter 1) that culture will play an increasingly important role and will be a source of future conflicts as the nation state withers, Islam and the West stand out as a prime example. In fact Benjamin Barber when he talks of Jihad and McWorld borrows the holy war concept of the Islamic Jihad as his prototype.

What are the root causes of the conflict with the increasing westernization of the world and a more specific target of anger and resentment, the United States? Let me summarize what I consider the best presentation of the problem published in the September issue of *The Atlantic* under the title "The Roots of Muslim Rage" by Bernard Lewis.

We can start with the idea of the separation of church and state, which most of us recognize as being essentially American. This idea was not entirely new; it had some precedents in the writings of Spinoza, Locke, and the philosophers of the European enlightenment. It was in the United States, however, that the principle was first given the force of law and gradually, in the course of two centuries, became a reality.

Even before that Christianity recognized two authorities and referred to often quoted saying of Christ, "render . . . unto Caesar the things which are Caesar's and unto God the things which are God's." Since they are two, they may be joined or separated, subordinate or independent, and conflicts may arise between them over questions of demarcation and jurisdiction.

Islam is one of the world's great religions. Islam has brought comfort and peace of mind to countless millions of men and women. It has given dignity and meaning to drab and impoverished lives. It has taught people of different races to love in brotherhood and people of different creeds to live side by side in reasonable tolerance. It inspired a great civilization in which others besides Muslims lived creative and useful lives and which, by its achievement, enriched the whole world.

But at times all religions seem to go through periods when hatred is directed against others. Now Islam, though far from unanimous in its rejection of western culture, has in certain places such as Libya, Iran and the Near East, seen a surge of hate. It can reach more than just a rejection of American values, and see them as basically evil and those who accept them as "enemies of God."

In Islam there is a dualistic conception of a struggle in human hearts between good and evil, between light and darkness, order and chaos, and truth and falsehood. The duty of God's soldiers is to dispatch God's enemies as quickly as possible to the place where God will chastise them—that is to say, the afterlife.

In the classical Islamic view, to which many Muslims are beginning to return, the world and all mankind are divided into two: the House of Islam, where the Muslim law and faith prevail, and the rest, known as the House of Unbelief or the House

of War, which it is the duty of Muslims ultimately to bring to Islam. The Muslims in their heyday saw themselves as the center of truth and enlightenment in a world they would enlighten and civilize.

The barbarians to the east and the south were polytheists and idolaters, offering no serious threat and no competition at all to Islam. In the north and west, in contrast, Muslims from an early date recognized a genuine rival—a competing world religion, a distinctive civilization inspired by that religion, and an empire that, though much smaller than theirs, was no less ambitious in its claims and aspirations. This was the entity known to itself and others as Christendom, a term that was long almost identical with Europe.

The relationship between Christendom and Islam was a series of jihads and crusades, attacks and counterattacks. For the first thousand years Islam was advancing; Christendom, in retreat and under threat. They conquered the old Christian lands of the Near East and North Africa, and invaded Europe, ruling for a while in Sicily, Spain, Portugal, and even parts of France. The attempt by the Crusaders to recover the lost lands of Christendom in the east was held and thrown back, and even the Muslims' loss of Spain to the Reconquista was amply compensated by the Islamic advance into southeastern Europe, which twice reached as far as Vienna. For the past three hundred years, since the failure of the second Turkish siege of Vienna in 1683 and the rise of the European colonial empires in Asia and Africa, Islam has been on the defensive, and the Christian and post-Christian civilization of Europe and her daughters has brought the whole world, including Islam, within its orbit.

This rise of the West has long fostered a desire to reassert Muslim values and greatness. It was just too much to endure this incomprehensible force that had subverted their dominance, disrupted their society, and finally violated the sanctuary of their home with films, music and consumerism. It was also natural that their rage should be directed primarily against the thousand year enemy and should draw its strength from ancient beliefs and loyalties.

For some, America represented freedom and justice and opportunity. For many more, it represented wealth and power and success, at a time when these qualities were not regarded as sins or crimes. And then came the great change, when the leaders of a widespread and widening religious revival sought out and identified their enemies as the enemies of God, and gave them "a local habitation and a name" in the Western Hemisphere. Suddenly, or so it seemed, America had become the great enemy and opponent of all that was good. The U.S. was accused of racism, sexism, imperialism and exploitation of the poor. But what Mr. Lewis suggests may be at the heart of the problem and is evil and unacceptable is the domination of infidels over true believers is, "for misbelievers to rule over true believers is blasphemous and unnatural, since it leads to the corruption of religion and morality in society, and to the flouting or even the abrogation of God's law."

More and more traditional Islam feels threatened. More than ever American technology, capitalism and democracy are seen as an authentic and attractive alternative to traditional way of thought and life. Fundamentalist leaders are not mistaken in seeing in Western civilization the greatest challenge to the way of life that they wish to retain or restore for their people.

And surely some of the hostility and rejection must come from a feeling of humiliation, a recognition that their long dominant civilization has been overwhelmed by those they long regarded as inferiors.

Overriding all may be the fear of many religious fundamentalists regarding secularism and modernism. And of course Islam is correct in locating the center of this threat to their way of life in the United States as representing these evils in their most advanced stages. Again to quote Bernard Lewis, "It should by now be clear that we are facing a mood and a movement far transcending the level of issues and policies and the governments that pursue them. This is no less than a clash of civilizations—the perhaps irrational but surely historic reaction of an ancient rival against our Judeo-Christian heritage, our secular present, and the worldwide expansion of both. It is crucially important that we on our side should not be provoked into an equally historic but also equally irrational reaction against that rival."

The conflict with Islam will continue. We should never forget that there are many members of Islam who are open and tolerant, looking for a way to resolve their problems consistent with the Islamic tradition but recognizing that adaptation must be made to the new forces that are shaping the modern world.

Some of the university-educated radicals of the Islamic revivalist movement now say that the interpretation of God's will should not be the monopoly of a more or less self-selected minority; every good Muslim's voice should be heard. If they say that about God's will, they can hardly insist that day-to-day government should be left in the hands of a minority.

On our side it would help if we search to achieve better appreciation of their religious culture, their history and achievements. We must be very careful that we don't start a new era of religious wars based on perceived differences and ancient prejudices.

▶ The Vocabulary of Islam

Ali—Son-in-law of Muhammad and fourth caliph, whose rule precipitated a crisis over succession in the caliphate; those siding with "Ali were known as shiat Ali or, subsequently, as Shiite Muslims.

Allah—The Islamic term derived from Arabic and meaning God.

Ayah—A verse of the Koran. Each chapter contains one or more of these verses.

Caliph—Term deriving from the Arabic term *khalifah*. It was the title used by the rulers of the Islamic Empire. It can also mean representative or deputy.

Dervish—Turkish; Persian refers to Sufi practitioners who may employ whirling in religious performance to produce a religiously ecstatic state; *Darwish* in Arabic.

Haj—Pilgrimage, specifically to Mecca.

Hegirah—"Emigration." The term used to refer to the journey by the Prophet Mohammed and his companions form Mecca to Medina in 622.

Imam—Used by Muslims to refer to the leader of a session of prayer or a religious teacher. The shi'ah use the term for special individuals viewed as the religious and political leaders of the community.

Islam—The peace that comes from submission to the one God, Allah.

Jihad—"Struggle" or great effort of Muslims, which can be either internal, as in the struggle within oneself to live an upright life, or external, as in the better-known "holy war" to defend the religion.

Kaaba—Sacred enclosure at the center of the Great Mosque in Mecca; the focal point of Muslim prayer.

Koran—"Discourse" or "recitation," the immutable body of revelations received by Mohammed.

Muezzin—The individual who makes the call to prayer five times daily from the minaret of a mosque.

Muslim—A believer of Islam; anything pertaining to the religion, law or culture of Islam.

Ramadan—Lunar month of fasting; at the end of Ramadan comes the great holiday, the Id al-Fitr, when the fast is broken.

Shari'ah—The system of law in Islam based on the Koran and Mohammed's Sunnah. Often translated as "holy law."

Sufi—The mystical path in Islam, derived from the Arabic *suf* (wool), garments worn by some Sufis and symbolizing a lack of regard for the material world; the Sufi Way is characterized by the performance of *dhikrs*, rituals which emphasize music and dance and a populist approach to religion.

Sunni Islam—The majority branch (90 percent) of the world's Muslim population, as contrasted with the minority Shia branch of Islam.

Sura—A chapter of the Koran.

Ulama—Official interpreters of the Sharia and holy sources of the religion; often associated with the power of the state.

Ummah—Community, specifically a religious community. Most often used in Islam to refer to the Islamic community.

Worksheet ▶

CHAPTER TEN

Define or identify:

- Islam—Salaam

- Muslim—Moslem

- Semite

- Arab

- Yathrib—Medina

- Khadija

- "The night of power and excellence"

- Purdah

- The five pillars of Islam

- People of the Book

- The vocabulary of Islam listed

Explain:

- Theistic religion—humanistic religion. What are the three great and related Theistic religions? What is the common source?

- List the five pillars of Islam and for each give the Christian equivalent.

- What is Islam's position on alcohol, pork, Jesus Christ?

- Which day of the week is specially set aside for prayer by Muslims, Jews, Christians?

- Which country in the world is predominantly Shiite?

- Which country in the world has the largest Muslim population?

- What was the only proof Mohammed offered as proof he was God's prophet?

- What did Mohammed do to dramatically set an example of his attitude on race?

- In what major ways has Islam contributed ot the rise of Europe?

- What was the effect of the Mongols on Islam?

- Which European country had a Muslim presence for 800 years?

- In which part of Europe is there still a strong Muslim presence? Why is it there?

Discuss:

- What is the Muslim attitude toward the Koran?

- Today Islam is growing increasingly militant against the West and all western culture stands for. Why do you think this is so? Can you discuss reasons some characterize the U.S. as the "Great Satan"?

- Since ancient time it was realized that a canal across the Suez Peninsula would be a great accomplishment. In the nineteenth century the French built it. Why didn't the Egyptians?

- Islamic law is swift, public and punishing. How does Islamic law differ from the western tradition of Roman law?

- Why are there so many similarities between Islamic and Christian doctrine?

- What was the situation in Arabia at the time of Mohammed's birth that caused him to seek a solution?

- What is Islam's position on the separation of church and state?

- What was the effect of the Ottoman Turks on Byzantium? On Christian Europe? On the present wars in the Balkans?

- What in your opinion will be the future course of Islam? Will it become more militant or will it join the one world of modern technology and consumerism?

- Use news items from contemporary events to illustrate friction between the U.S. and Islam concerning the role of women, religion and government, consumerism, and western science.

- What are the forces of Jihad and McWorld at work in Islam today?

Chapter 11 ▶ ▶
THE WEST AND THE REST

One way of looking at the world's cultures is to divide them into western culture and eastern culture. Rudyard Kipling wrote these familiar words:

> East is East and West is West,
> And never the twain shall meet.

But today "the twain have met"—in one sometimes clashing but nevertheless common communication network and world culture. "East" and "West" have almost become mere geographic directions again rather than meaningful terms of politics, civilization and culture.

Yet Kipling was right. The old West and another old East never did meet. Europe of the Colonial expansion, and the mysterious East of tribal village, of illiterate peasant, and of Confucian mandarin have not met. Both have disappeared.

At the time Kipling wrote, for 250 years, all great powers had been European. It has been taken for granted that political and economic control over entire countries with millions of inhabitants anywhere in the world could be arranged by European states without consulting anyone else. This imbalance of power could not last. Today's European union is an acknowledgement of the end of the old system of European nation state power and the beginning of a new arrangement in the world. One arrangement may be the grouping of the world into trading blocks; i.e., European Union, NAFTA and SEATO; a progression from the Polis or city state of the classical world to the nation state which started in Europe in the 1500s to a new trading block system.

While world markets, the multinational corporation and global communication systems are all today's reality, not so apparent are the cultural exchanges. One of the main events we are witnessing today is the formation of a world culture overlay on traditional cultures.

The world order that is following the European colonial period may well be anti-western; but it will quite definitely not be un-western in culture. Every single one of the new countries in the world today is trying to change into a western-style state, economy and society, and sees the way to do this goal in the theories, institutions, sciences, technologies and machines the west has developed. The great division between the GDP's of the world's poor nations and the world's rich nations can only by closed by the application of western science and management methods and all political leaders realize this. Everywhere countries are being led by people trained and educated in American and European schools, and western in their thinking, and training. In our description of the rejection of British rule in India, it was the Gandhis and Nehru's educated in England who led the way. And, of course, the Communism of China is western—a heresy, but one that could only have grown out of a western tradition.

As late as 1950, Western Europe and the United States had a virtual monopoly on industrial and military technology, knowledge and skills. To assume things would continue this way didn't seem unreasonable. Technology is not created in a vacuum, but the result of values, cultural traditions which were distinctly western. Yet—beginning with Japan—industrial and military technology has proven to be far easier to learn than was supposed. All over the world, non-western peoples are rapidly industrializing and rapidly building western-style armed forces. The technological monopoly of the United States and Europe has been broken for good. The fastest growing industrial country in the world for the last few years has been Communist China, while South Korea, Malaysia and Chile show remarkably rapid development.

There is another exchange. While western ideas are capturing the East, there is a very high interest in non-western cultures in the West. Today there is great interest in the cultures of native Americans, and in their ancient civilizations in Central America and in the Andes. And there is influence of Japan on American art, architecture and design. Perhaps most interesting is the strong new interest in eastern religious thought, meditation, and Zen-Buddhism.

More and more historians and school history courses stress that "world history" is not simply "European history." While we have lost some of the old certainty of superiority and self-centeredness, it is also true—and much more important—that every society in the world is borrowing from western traditions to build their future.

We can look on the interchange between the rest of the world and the West in two segments. During the first contacts, the West tried to get the rest to accept the western way of life in its entirety, including its religion as well as its technology, and this attempt did not succeed. Later, the English, Dutch, and French offered to the same peoples a worldly version in which religion had been left out and technology, instead of religion, had been made the central feature. This technological element, which had been made separate from the Christian core of western civilization during the Enlightenment, did succeed in pushing its way into traditional societies that had previously refused to swallow the complete version. Today Chinese business leaders could remain Confucian in their value sys-tem and even anti-western in their sentiment while getting all the technology and latest management techniques they can buy or steal from the United States.

The great world cultures prior to the mid-1700s remained virtually unchanged in their basic outlook and philosophy. What happened in Europe, on the contrary, was something new and explosive. While the few contacts before 1700 were more as equal to equal, after the 1700s, this was no longer true. While the rest of the world remained unchanged, Europe was attempting "to make all things new."

Today there is a great urgency that the cultures of the world come to an understanding. We have previously lived in a world where foreign cultures lived isolated in their separate worlds. Now, however, we are jostled together with people of very different cultures, traditions, and backgrounds, and we are looking for ways we can work together as we have no other choice. Cooperation is going to be impossible without some mutual understanding. Therefore, we have to look at the past in order to understand the origins of our values which are being brought to play all sides in this new global cultural contact. For the last four hundred years it is we of the West who have been doing the conquering and directing, sure of the superiority of our own ideas and way of life.

Today western ideas are by necessity being faced by both Islamic and Far eastern leaders. Often these ideas based on concepts of individualism are rejected on the assumption their cultural history makes them incompatalbe. For example, our Judeo-Christian tradition focused on one God which builds on individual responsibility is the foundation stone of our political and economic life. Anybody facing a single all-powerful God feels his special individuality. It was this assertion of man's individual responsibility that produced the Reformation which was key in the development of western democracy. However, in the world of Confucianism, Buddhism or Shinto gods are a collection of relatively vague beings on the misty edge of life. What really matters in the ordering of people's conduct is the concept of the family. It is the family that gives a sense of continuity, as you pay your respects to the ancestors who shaped your children's bodies. Out of the family comes the rules of what you may and may not do. And the family is not just father, mother, a couple of children and the ancestors. It extends to a wider sort of family, once the feudal lord and his dutiful followers, now the political or industry leaders. When you read the comments in the Appendix, this attitude may explain some of the critical views of today's fragmented American society and why concepts of family, loyalty and authority are so emphasized outside the West. But it should not lead us to believe that the West and the rest of the world will live in two separate cultural capsules or that only in Western culture will individualism and democracy thrive. India, the home of a very different culture, is still a democracy. South Africa, Turkey and Malaysia give hope for a deeply rooted democratic ideal that every human being is entitled to an equal say in how he is governed, and should not be denied it by others who claim that the business is best left to them. To believe the idea that the people should control the government, not the other way round, and that all sane adult human beings are equally entitled to share in the exercising of that control is surely of universal application.

It should be noted that plenty of Americans and Europeans feel the strong appeal of a more group valued society. Individualism can become anarchy and in an increasingly urbanized world violence and the tools to express it, make anarchy very frightening. But there is no substitute for individual energy and individual decision making to drive the new global information centered organizations.

The gap between Islam, Confucianism and the West may not be as wide as some believe. The individual and the community do not have to be irreconcilable concepts. The old battle between authority and liberty continues, but in most places liberty seems to be on the advance. Also, we must remember that although peoples may differ in culture they are above all human beings with much more in common than differences.

▶ Religious Thought

Let's look at a few aspects of the encounter. In the area of religious thought. Indians thought the material world was illusion and one escaped from it into the limitless ocean of Being. In China, the material world was the real substance of man's life and could be restored to harmony by obedience to the moral law. It would then revolve in orderly fashion, unchanged in the perfect pattern established thousands of years before. Both attitudes limited the range of thinking about the world and material reality—the Hindus by rejecting its importance, the Chinese by an inborn conservatism.

But in the Judeo-Christian and Greco-Roman tradition, Europe had a different attitude toward the universe. The Jews had the idea that man could find God's purpose in this world in time and in history. They did not regard material things as being largely meaningless, or as already fixed by a standard perfection achieved in the past. They believed in a progressive unfolding of God's purpose in time. (See Chapter 3, "Linear and Circular Time.") In it lay the seed of personal freedom, belief in progress, concern with material things—all of which are dominant ideas in the development of western culture.

The Greeks possessed an overwhelming curiosity about all things human, a belief, expressed most fully in the philosophy of Aristotle, that man could find in natural circumstances and in the structure of the world, matters of overwhelming interest in their own right and evidence, at the same time, of a divine order and harmony. Reason was the tool of this searching curiosity and its end the demonstration of an orderly universe. The world makes sense. Intellectual search and scientific achievement—two of the outstanding features of western culture come from the Greek approach, finding Divine order in the universe.

▶ Political Thought

In the area of politics the Western approach inherited from the Greek city states was different. In trading communities all along the Mediterranean, the Greek cities saw the emergence of the merchant class as an effective political force, and the first steps towards legal, constitutional, and representative government. In the 1500s in Europe, a dynamism unknown before in human history enters the world as the first Portuguese boats round the African cape on their way to India and points East. The old order would be challenged. The foundations of the world would be recast.

The rest of the world was confronted with something completely different, completely unexpected, completely inexplicable, and from their point of view, quite dangerously destructive. In the world's theocratic states, all men's activities were theoretically of a religious character and the purpose of human life was to conform to the great religious cycles of which night and day, the seasons, agriculture, birth and death were all manifestations. With this attitude toward existence, it seemed natural that the rulers took on religious sanction as autocratic representatives of God on earth.

In China, dynasties received the "Mandate of Heaven" and lost it again but the change of ruling family left the governmental forms untouched. The Emperor, with his religious attributes and functions, ran a very large empire by means of a large bureaucracy. Corruption and invasion weakened the system, and good government restored it. But its forms were unchanged. This was the pattern in all the world.

Least of all had there been any change in the basic world economic structure. Everywhere were large or small self-supporting communities, in which agriculture was the basic wealth, the land tax the basic form of revenue, and in which trade was confined to the luxuries and the unessential elements of life. Thus, through changes of rulers and catastrophes of war and invasion, droughts and famines, and religious movements, the basic world structure was not much changed through thousands of years.

How was what was happening in Europe different? In the first place, the development of Christianity led Europe away from one of the root characteristics of Oriental religion—the quality of otherworldliness. The trend of Christian thought was away from the belief that this world is unimportant, or an illusion, or bound by any absolute fatality to an unbreakable wheel of destiny. On the contrary, Christians tended to see the world as a testing ground, a creative area in which men could prove themselves and try to discover the purposes of God. From their Jewish heritage, Christians had received the idea of God's purpose in the world being made known in history.

History, therefore, was not simply a fatality or a succession of meaningless events. It was more like a drama, a drama in which a part was played out in time by both God and man. Time itself therefore became important. Time was something which you could not neglect. Time was not an illusion. Rather it was the theater, the stage, upon which God's purpose was being worked out.

And from this religious inheritance we owe a basic concept of our modern world, and that is the idea of progress. Progress, which is a concept alien to all other cultures, came from the Jews, with their insistence upon the purposefulness of history—and became a part of Christendom or Europe.

▶ Individuality

Another divergence from traditional thought came about in the Western approach to the individual human being. The Greek concept of a citizen with rights and the Jewish concept of the sinner with personal responsibility held in embryo the belief in personal individual freedom which appeared for the first time in history in Europe. In this notion of personal responsibility and of each soul having a role to play in God's plan, there is inherent some notion of equality.

This notion of spiritual equality was bound to have a great effect upon politics, and it has been one of the underlying elements in the development of constitutional government. The idea of the government itself being under law, and the idea of all sections of the community enjoying freedom and responsibility to take part in government are the essence of our constitutionalism.

In our day we have seen some of the horrible consequences produced by the concentration of power in Nazi Germany and Soviet Russia, and we are not likely to underestimate the supreme significance of the division of church and state power which was built into the foundations of western society. In its most typical form in the Middle Ages, in the fight for supremacy between the pope and the emperor, it gave all manner of free cities and corporations and guilds the chance of playing the one authority off against the other, and of establishing their own independence; in this way western society avoided the dominant political form of the traditional organization—the single theocratic order. This society of a pluralist character, which did not fit into a single theocratic model, proved to be of infinitely greater strength and growth than societies set firm in a single unchanging pattern.

One reason for European vigor was intellectual curiosity. However unworldly and ascetic were some aspects of the medieval church, the central teaching of Christianity had not deviated from its Jewish heritage. Time and the world were not illusions.

The world was the setting for man's struggle for perfection. What happened in time had significance, and the material universe was a reflection of God's glory. The Renaissance (Chapter 6) restored the old Greek curiosity in material things and generated a passion for exact knowledge which was the forerunner—in such observers as Leonardo da Vinci—of the scientific revolution.

Earlier societies—the Greeks above all—had made considerable discoveries about the universe. But they had not used them to manipulate material things by applying science, through machines, to raw materials. The European genius was applied science. Desire for wealth is not the whole reason for England's industrial revolution. Oriental merchants and bureaucrats piled up huge fortunes, but their capital went into jewels and concubines, not more factories and machines.

One decisive reason for the rise of industrialism in the West was the Protestant Puritan tradition which combined the idea of religious merit with hard work and allowed men to see virtue in accumulating vast fortunes and then in not spending them on worldly temptations. Capital ceased to be for enjoyment. It became the instrument of further work and the crucial capitalist cycle of saving and development was set in motion.

Thus in every field of human activity, the Europe which thrust itself out over the world after the 1500s was a new phenomenon. Its religion was becoming this-worldly. Its trading governments were either in the first stages of limited democracy—as in Britain and Holland—or, as in the case of France, were loaded with philosophical ideas preparing to blow despotic government to the skies.

Any idea of a single theocratic civilization had vanished with the coming of the Reformation, leaving a group of strongly competing nation states. And the economies of the main trading communities—once Portugal and Spain had been replaced—were tending toward an entirely new type of organization—the industrial system. European society, in spite of its material inferiority in the Middle Ages, suddenly took on a power of growth and change and dynamism, for good and for evil, that is today changing the world.

Before considering its impact on the world in detail, it is important to remember that the European impact, had, like all human activities, its good and its bad sides. On the one hand, it made for growth, excitement, and individual achievement on a unique scale. On the other hand, it unleashed forces of aggression and destruction, with which we are still living.

On the side of creation and progress, western culture gives us individual freedom and the concept of constitutional government. It has a spirit of free inquiry, of scientific curiosity, and of humanist idealism. In the economic field it has given us the application of science to raw materials in industry, and through industry, at long last, mankind has seen the first possibility of moving the great mass of people out of back-breaking work and poverty. All these things have been accomplished, and stand to the credit of the immense outburst of creative energy from Europe.

But for every high, creative, and promising achievement brought into the world, there was a darker side. It is essential for us in western culture to realize this double-edgedness of its performance. We tend to think only of the good. We show insufferable complacency. We lecture Third World nations on their international behavior. We fall into attitudes based upon the most pretentious and unsubtle habit of dividing every issue into black and white and claiming the white for ourselves. All this is death to our relations with the world, where we must show a decent humility and perspective or lose all influence and respect.

▶ Nationalism

One of the destructive forces Europe unleashed on the world was bigoted nationalism. Against the political vision of free, constitutional government, we must set the dark side of nationalism. Nationalism is intimately connected with democracy. Nationalism in the modern sense was unknown in the rest of the world. All affairs of state and public policy were settled by the ruling dynasty. The mass of people had no particular concern with either government or state affairs, even if in wars and invasions they often suffered the consequences. In such conditions, there are no motives for identifying yourself with the State in the same intimate way as you do, say, with family or clan or tribe.

Dynasties came, dynasties went, but the ordinary peasant and the ordinary townspeople simply carried on their traditional life as best they could.

Under such conditions, nationalism in the modern sense does not develop. In Europe, where the effort was made to bring more and more sections of the population into an active part in government and a responsible role in the community, the sense of belonging together as part of a nation state could develop. It could grow into creative patriotism. It could also become an aggressive and narrow nationalism.

In the West, unhappily, the development of nationalism ran out of control to become the curse of the world. This curse has plunged the world in this century into two world wars killing maybe 50 million, has spread the spirit throughout the world of national aggression, and made the nation state into a false god and heresy that has destroyed its followers physically and spiritually.

Let us take another instance of the two sides of the western achievement. Our spirit of scientific inquiry and our rationalism have not only liberated large sectors from superstition, but have done so without any necessary threat to a truly religious or spiritual concept of life. To believe that the whole of nature is orderly and gives expression to God's laws which may be uncovered by human reason—which is the underlying concept of science—is entirely compatible with the religious approach to life. But, in the Western world, so-called scientific thinking has often meant a complete wiping-out of the sense of religious purpose and of religious faith in men's lives. It has left either an unthinking materialism or a vacuum of faith that leaves a big void in sensitive lives.

▶ Western Impact on India, China and Japan

If you take three great cultures—India, China, and Japan—and study the impact Western life has had on them, you will see the extent to which it has taken them and shaken them with such violence that little is left intact of their traditional structure.

The fate of India under the impact of Western expansion was to come completely under the control of one Western power, Great Britain. They say that the British acquired their empire by absence of mind. Certainly as far as India is concerned, British control was not part of a long-drawn-out and determined scheme of imperial conquest.

One of the chief reasons why the British took over was the weakness of India itself. The structure of the Indian administration was near collapse after the fall of the Mogul Empire in the mid 1700s. Commercial rivalry between, Britain and France, led the British and the French to back rival kingdoms in India, in order to get trading concessions for themselves. Having begun to play politics, the British found that, in fact, when they had thrown out the French, large sections of India had almost by default come under their direct control.

British rule had in some ways a beneficial modernizing effect. It brought into an Asiatic country concepts of modern administration which, if a modern economy is to be built, are essential. At the same time, some of the bases for a modern economic system—communications, railways, irrigation—were laid and there was a beginning of industry. So much for the gain. But at the same time, bringing India into contact with the highly developed industrial system of Britain did mean the collapse of its old economic structure.

An earlier balance had existed—at a very poverty-stricken level—between the peasant producing the basic means of the community and the artisans providing consumer goods from their own handicraft for small local markets. The coming of industrial goods from the factories of Britain meant the destruction of the old labor intensive artisan structure of India. Of course, the same problem was present in England at the beginning of the Industrial Revolution.

Western concepts streamed in, carried by administrators and missionaries—Christian values, humanistic ideals, rationalism. At the same time there was a growth of nationalism of the Western form. This led tragically to a new spirit of rivalry and hatred between the Muslim and Hindu communities of India. That led to the division of India into three countries.

The impact of the West on India has had its good and bad side, but one thing is certain—there can be no return to the old static theocratic society of traditional India.

While no western power took over the government of China as they did in India, nevertheless the effect of the western impact changed the whole basis of traditional Chinese society. Christian missionaries weakened the old Confucian concentration of authority in family and throne. Western political ideas—of republican government and active citizenship—came in to discredit the dynasty and remove "the Mandate of Heaven." The old agriculture and handicrafts of the villages were destroyed by the coming of western goods as in India, which broke up the local industry and established a new modernized economy in the coastal ports dominated by Europeans.

In Japan, the reaction was totally different. First the Japanese excluded the West completely for two hundred years, and then, on the old principle, "If you can't beat 'em, join 'em," they were able with the Meiji restoration, in an incredibly short time, to transform their old despotic government into something similar to a modern political democracy.

By remarkable accomplishment, unequaled probably in the history of economics, they built an entire modern economy. They even followed the Europe example of aggressive imperialist trade and war. Yet, in spite of Japan's ability to keep its independence, the western impact resembled that of India or China, for it swept away forever the old economic system and political structure.

Wherever and whenever the western culture hit, it destroyed the old order. Whether it took over a country completely, as in India, the Americas, Australia, or Africa, whether it merely disintegrated the regime, as in China, or whether it stimulated the local people to put up a Western form of government—whatever it did, the old order passed almost without trace.

In our time, the direction of our shaken world will be decided. We are living in a time of turmoil in the Far East and Islam. We are far, far removed from the distant period when cultures could live alone. We have passed the period when a powerful and aggressive Western way of life came in to break up the old world structure. We now face the question of which direction world culture will take. In this discussion, I would advise the reader to review the three possible cultural patterns presented—a world of growing tribal strife, one world united by information and business or Jihad and McWorld.

Direct western control of the world is over. And it should be pointed out that Western imperialism always had plenty of opponents at home. In fact, the United States, emerged a nation whose whole significance consisted in throwing off the colonial pattern and declaring the freedom of man. Today, however much we might wish to be isolated from the world or however much we might wish to say that Islam, Africa and Asia are beyond our concern, modern science, technological change and the whole shrinking of the world have made such an attitude impossible.

Today western culture is under attack by many. The fact remains that Western culture has been an instrument whereby hopes of personal freedom have replaced the old despotisms, and the prospect of economic advance has appeared in place of the old hopeless poverty of the masses. Although the West has much to be ashamed of, in its aggressiveness and conceit, it would be a great error if we now went to the opposite extreme and thought western culture had no contribution to make. There is nothing that the world needs more than the great western traditions of freedom, law, and personal responsibility.

▶ The Western Revolutions

The material well-being of the human race has improved more in the past two hundred years than it did in the preceding five thousand. Until the mid-1750s, people in most areas of the world were living essentially with the same agricultural way of life as the early civilizations of Sumer and Egypt. They were still using the same wood and bricks to erect their buildings, the same oxen and horses to transport themselves and their belongings, the same sails and oars for their ships, the same homemade fabrics for clothes, and the same candles and torches for light.

But everywhere today metals and plastics are as common as stone and wood; the railroad, the automobile, and the airplane have replaced the oxen, the horse, and the donkey; steam, diesel, and atom power drive ships in place of wind and labor; many synthetic fabrics compete with the traditional cottons, woolens, and linens; and electricity has replaced the candle and become a source of power for many tasks at the flick of a switch.

The beginnings of this great material change are to be found in the scientific and industrial revolutions, those great changes in man's way of life that had their start in Europe and are still changing the world. The agricultural revolution of early times made cities and thus civilization possible, but then more or less stopped its change.

Scientific technology, on the other hand, is cumulative and change continues to lead to more change. When you think what has happened in the past couple of hundred years, or if you like the past 50, you get some feeling for the changes we may expect in the future. And scientific technology is now worldwide, changing old ways of life and creating new industries and replacing old.

▶ The Scientific Revolution

Europe's scientific revolution was rooted deep in the past. The beginnings go back to the ideas we discussed coming from the ancient Greek philosophers, who passed it on to the Romans. Even in the Middle Ages the scientific attitude wasn't dead. Medieval men studied the properties of natural materials and the geography of the earth to help agriculture and trade.

Besides, there were good religious reasons for studying science. We pointed out the Judeo-Christian position that to study nature was to study God's work. As early as the thirteenth century, Roger Bacon, a Franciscan friar, evolved a plan for the conduct of research which was essentially the scientific method: of investigation by experiment. Bacon justified his plan by asserting that since the creation of the world was God's handiwork, studying that world could be considered a form of piety.

But the flood of discoveries and new ideas called the scientific revolution came later. They started in the closing days of the Renaissance, chiefly in Italy. Humanist scholars, eager to restore the classical texts of ancient Greece and Rome, revived not only their literary masterpieces but also their scientific work. The Renaissance was the rediscovery of the Greeks and Romans, and that included Greek science. The Renaissance humanists opened the way to a more precise observation of the world and showed more interest in it. The medieval focus was on the spirit.

But science was to move beyond the Greeks and authorities like Aristotle. More and more, as the sixteenth century progressed, men began to think that things were true in science because their own experience told them so—through observation and experiment rather than authority. Copernicus substituted a stationary sun for a stationary earth in his system of the universe, and thus became the father of modern astronomy. Vesalius' superb descriptions of the human body, drawn directly from his own medical experience, surpassed those of all previous anatomists in accuracy of detail and daring of method.

To justify and explain the new discoveries, new philosophical explanations were constructed. This joining together of science and philosophy was of decisive importance to the scientific revolution: it led the best minds of the age from philosophy into scientific inquiry and gave science the sanction of reason. It made the great discoveries of Galileo, Robert Boyle and Newton part of a consistent pattern. It would be the application of these results of the scientific method that would lead to European global dominance.

In this regard we have a striking example of western technology being applied, the recent war in Iraq. American warships in the Persian Gulf could accurately and with impunity launch missiles over 200 miles with deadly accuracy. When a British soldier with an automatic rifle confronted a Zulu warrior with a spear, the results did not rest on bravery.

Why did this world-changing development in applied science take place in Europe? More than the rediscovery of the Greek and Roman sciences led to the explosion of the scientific revolution. One reason seems to be a tradition of respect for the practical arts of spinning, weaving, ceramics, glass making, and most of all, the increasingly important arts of mining and metallurgy. All these crafts in Renaissance Europe were in the hands of free workers rather than of slaves as in classical times.

Recall our discussion of St. Benedict and the dignity of labor, the Christian "To work is to pray." The higher status of the Renaissance craftsman allowed him to strengthen his ties with the scholar. Each had an important contribution to make. The craftsman had the old techniques evolved through trial and error. The scholars provided the facts, speculations, and procedures of rediscovered antiquity and of medieval science. The two got practice and theory together, and they produced an explosive combination.

A strong prejudice existed in ancient times against combining creative learning and manual work. This prejudice, which probably arose out of the ancient association of manual labor with slavery, held back the application of science.

The first major advances occurred in the field of astronomy which would be of great importance to Europeans related as it was to geography and navigation. Copernicus took up the idea of some ancient philosophers that the sun, rather than the earth, was the center of the universe, and then he demonstrated that this provided a simpler explanation of the movement of the heavenly bodies than did the traditional system of Ptolemy. Galileo supported Copernicus by using the recently discovered telescope to see what actually was in the heavens. Here we see the new attitude at work: *Don't rely on authority, but use actual observations.* We will discuss two outstanding examples of the new men.

▶ Newton and Darwin

A towering genius of early science was the Englishman, Isaac Newton. In addition to his pioneering work in optics, hydrodynamics, and mathematics, he discovered the law of gravitation: *"Every particle of matter in the universe attracts every other particle with a force varying inversely as the square of the distance between them and directly proportional to the product of their masses."* —A clear concise statement of a law of nature: nature makes sense.

Here was a sensational and revolutionary explanation that helped explain the universe. Newton had discovered a fundamental cosmic law that could be proved mathematically and applied to all matter, from the minutest object to the universe at large. Nature appeared to be a gigantic mechanical object operating according to certain natural laws that could be found by observation, experiment, and calculation. All branches of human knowledge could be broken down into a few, simple, uniform laws that rational persons could discover using the scientific method. People began to apply the analytical method of Newtonian physics to the entire field of thought and knowledge, to human society as well as to the physical universe.

As Newton's discoveries dominated thought of the nature of the physical universe, Charles Darwin dominated later social thought when he discovered the laws governing the evolution of humanity itself. His doctrine of evolution holds that animal and vegetable species in their present diverse forms are not the fixed and unchangeable results of separate special acts of creation. They are capable of change. And they are the natural outcomes of a common original source.

Darwin believed that the chief manner in which variation took place was by natural selection. There was bitter opposition in certain quarters, particularly among the clergy. This was understandable, because Darwin was denying the act of divine creation; man was receiving some blows to his pride. The Copernican system of astronomy had removed the earth from its central place in the universe, and now Darwinism seemed to deny human beings their central place in the history of the earth.

Despite opposition, Darwinism triumphed and deeply affected western thinking. Its emphasis on survival of the fittest and struggle for survival fitted in perfectly with the aggression of the times. Nationalistic empire builders in all countries believed that Darwinism offered them support and justification. They held that in politics, as in nature, the strongest are victorious and that warlike qualities decide who will win in the international "struggle for survival."

In economic life Darwin was used to justify free enterprise and rugged individualism. The "Haves," comfortable and contented, used Darwin to oppose greater social equality. They argued that their wealth was justified because they had proven themselves "fitter" than the shiftless poor.

And in business, the absorption of smaller concerns by big business was justified as part of the "struggle for survival." Darwinism was used to justify imperialism. The argument was that colonies were necessary for the prosperity and survival of a great power. Moreover, native peoples, judged in terms of worldly success, were weak, inferior, and in need of the protection and guidance of the superior and stronger Europeans. And you will recall its application by the Japanese.

The application of Darwin's theories to the social scene is known as Social Darwinism. Darwin himself had never dreamed that his findings would be exploited in this fashion. They were because they nicely supported the materialism spreading over Europe and America.

As Europe developed, science became an increasingly important part of western society. At the beginning, science was still a bit of a curiosity. But soon it was creating new industries and basically changing the whole European way of life. Beyond Europe, the scientific revolution was affecting the entire world. It made Europe's domination of the globe possible. Also it provided the basis for the West's intellectual predominance in the nineteenth century. European art or religion or philosophy did not affect non-Western peoples very much because they were advanced in these fields. But they had made no such advances in science and technology. Only the West had mastered the scientific method and used it for material advancement. No non-Westerner could deny this fact or look down on Europeans as uncouth barbarians who happened to have a certain superiority in sailing ships and firearms.

Reluctantly all cultures have had to recognize the importance of Europe's scientific revolution. Today the primary aim of so-called developing countries is to also reap the fruits of this unique revolution themselves. When we speak of western culture being carried to a foreign country, like Japan or India, we do not mean so much the planting of our Judeo-Christian and Greco-Roman traditions. We mean the application of science and the scientific method of problem solving, hypothesis, experiment, law.

In addition to the advance of science, no two events more profoundly altered the shape of present western culture than the political revolution of the United States and France and the Industrial Revolution, which got its start in England. "Modern" history begins with these major changes. Developments of the nineteenth and early twentieth centuries—the rise of the middle class, the decline of the old, ruling aristocracies; the growth of class consciousness among urban workers—all had their roots in these two revolutions. The political and Industrial Revolutions took place at about the same time and affected many of the same people—though in different ways. Together they resulted in the overthrow of absolutism, mercantilism, and the last vestiges of feudalism.

▶ The Industrial Revolution

What we refer to as the Industrial Revolution started in the midlands of England after 1750. It brought about a basic change from a rural, handicraft economy to one dominated by urban, machine-driven manufacturing. The fact that it was a Euro-

pean revolution was not accidental. Although Europe was, in the mid-Eighteenth century, a continent still predominantly agricultural, poor, and illiterate, it was not backward. European merchants were already established as the world's foremost manufacturers and traders. This wealthy class was depended upon to support the state, and these men had for the most part gained political clout and the ability to defend their property.

Written contracts were replacing custom and written laws were helping merchants, bankers, traders, and entrepreneurs gain the confidence that they lived in a world that was stable, rational, and predictable. On this belief, they moved out with self-confidence and in hopes of increasing their own, and their country's, prosperity. Only in Europe was found this class of independent and confident people that could make possible the industrial revolution.

The Industrial Revolution refers to a breakthrough in productivity. And that productivity again rested on the use of mechanical power to replace human and animal power. Power is the key, cheap and abundant power that can be used for an infinite variety of tasks. A mechanized factory system was created that produced goods in vast quantities and at rapidly diminishing cost, so it was no longer dependent on existing demand but could create its own demand. For example, the Model T Ford, produced in large quantities, created a mass market for them.

Throughout history men and women have accepted the evils of famine, shortage, disease and drought as facts of life that were fixed and unchangeable. Today, instead, as a result of the Industrial Revolution, the belief has arisen that something can be done about changing the nature of things. The unbelievable poverty of the Asian world can be corrected; all countries can learn how to expand and their economies grow. It is the change from fatalism to hope, from resignation to expectation, and this is perhaps the biggest revolution that a country can make.

These desires—to copy western prosperity and eliminate poverty—are driving poor countries' policies. The benefits of industrialization must be achieved because modern science and the multinational enterprise have wiped out the old economic system and have vastly increased the birth rate. The choice now is: modernize or perish. The village economy was destroyed by the coming of the machine and by the arrival from the West of cheap industrial goods. Only if the world economies become as dynamic as their birth rate is there any hope of avoiding catastrophic famines of the old type. Thus there is really no choice for the world; they must modernize and grow or fail.

The scientific revolution we described and the Industrial Revolution grew together. An example is the development of the steam engine. It provided badly needed power to operate machines and locomotives and, at the beginning, to pump water out of mines. James Watt combined technical ingenuity and scientific knowledge to improve the steam engines to a reasonable level of efficiency. If the relatively unlimited power of the steam engine had not been available, the Industrial Revolution might well have petered out. It might have amounted to a mere speed-up in textile manufacturing, as happened in China, where similar technical advances had been made centuries earlier. But the growth of the industrial revolution will be based on power: steam, motor, electric, and nuclear.

The science that made the most progress during the first half of the nineteenth century was chemistry—partly because of its close association with the textile industry, which experienced such rapid growth during those decades.

The Newton of chemistry was Antoine Lavoisier (1743–1794), whose law of the conservation of matter is comparable to the law of gravitation:

> "... although matter may alter its state in a series of chemical actions, it does not change in amount; the quantity of matter is the same at the end as at the beginning of every operation, and can be traced by its weight."

Lavoisier's successors in the nineteenth century made discovery after discovery that had important practical applications: Justus von Liebeg for chemical fertilizers; W. H. Perkin for synthetic dyes; and Louis Pasteur for his germ theory of disease, which led to the adoption of sanitary precautions and so brought under control old scourges like typhoid, diphtheria, cholera, and malaria.

Coal not only yielded coke but a valuable gas that was used for illumination. It also gave a liquid, or coal tar. Chemists discovered a veritable treasure trove in coal tar: hundreds of dyes, aspirin, saccharin, wintergreen, disinfectants, laxatives, perfumes, photographic chemicals, high explosives, and essence of orange blossom, all made from black coal tar through the magic of chemistry. These discoveries were to create many new businesses.

Whereas Germany led the world in the nineteenth century in applying science to industry, the United States was the pioneer in developing mass-production techniques. These were of two varieties.

One was the making of standard interchangeable parts and the assembling of these parts into the completed unit with a minimum of handicraft labor. The classic example is Henry Ford's endless conveyor belt. Car parts traveled along the belt and were assembled into the Model T by workers who were transformed into cogs of the machines.

The other production technique was the manipulation of large masses of material by means of advanced mechanical devices. The prime example of this method is the steel industry. These few examples illustrate the nature of the marriage of science and industry that has grown to become a world-wide transforming phenomenon by creating a world economy and multinational business enterprises.

Some Effects of the Industrial Revolution

An effect of the Industrial Revolution on Europe was a sharp increase in population. In spite of the emigration overseas of millions of Europeans during the nineteenth century, the population of the continent in 1914 was well over three times that of 1750. The reasons for this population explosion were both economic and medical.

Most deaths in earlier centuries had been due to infectious diseases, with the biggest toll always with the poor. With more productive farming, nutritional levels rose, natural resistance to disease rose correspondingly, and mortality rates dropped correspondingly. Famine in Europe became a memory of the past. Even if crops failed, the new railway networks insured adequate supplies from the outside.

At the same time the Industrial Revolution made possible improved sewage systems and safer water supplies, which further lowered mortality rates. On top of this, vaccination and other medical discoveries further reduced death rates.

Europe's population climbed steeply from 140 million in 1750 to 463 million in 1914. This rate of increase in Europe was so much higher than in the other regions of the world that it altered the global population balance. It also illustrates what will happen to the rest of the world as a result of modernization.

The Industrial Revolution led also to an unprecedented urbanization of world society. The size of cities had depended on the amount of food that the surrounding land could produce. With the Industrial Revolution and the factory system, a mass influx flooded the new centers of industry. The large new urban populations could be fed because food supplies now could be brought from all parts of the world. Technological and medical advances eliminated the plagues that previously struck crowded cities and even made city living relatively pleasant. The most important of these advances were the availability of pure water, the perfecting of centralized sewerage and waste-disposal systems, assurance of an adequate food supply, and prevention and control of contagious diseases.

The growth of cities continues and is a feature of present-day demographics. The huge size and problems of the mega cities, such as Mexico City, makes us wonder if limits have not been reached. The future of the city is a major world problem.

The Industrial Revolution, with its efficient use of human and natural resources on a worldwide scale, has brought about an increase in productivity that is without any precedent in all history. By the latter part of the 1800s the entire world felt the impact of the increasing productivity. The wool of New Zealand, the wheat of Canada, the rice of Burma, the rubber of Malaya, the jute of Bengal, all fed the busy factories of western Europe and the eastern United States. For the first time there was an intermeshed and constantly expanding global economy.

The Industrial Revolution also is responsible for changing values. In the discussion of time (Chapter 3), a difference between concepts and attitudes toward time was emphasized. Americans say that "time is money" and the German, Japanese as well as American value punctuality. A large part of the westernized world's attitudes are a result of the industrial revolution. Similar attitudes toward time exist among societies that are industrialized and those that are not.

About everyone is aware of the exploitation and suffering in the early days of industrialization.

The tenant farmers were kicked off their farms, and the weavers and other craft people were wiped out because they couldn't compete with the new machine-made goods. These people, and others like them, faced shock moving to the city, finding employment, adjusting to an unfamiliar environment and to strange ways of living and working. They were completely dependent on their employers, for they had no land, no cottage, no tools, and no capital. In short, they had become mere wage earners and had nothing to offer but their labor. Hours were long and the work was hard. This flocking to the cities continues unabated to this day. Vast slums surround Mexico City, Buenos Aires, Cairo and Calcutta, to name a few, and populations have soared by the millions. And still they come, for as bad as it is in the city, it is better than the country. The city represents progress and hope.

But the real hardship for a countryman comes in getting used to the discipline and monotony of tending machines in a factory. The workers came and went at the sound of the factory whistle. They had to keep pace with the movements of the machine, always under the strict supervision of an ever-present overseer. The work was monotonous—pulling a lever, brushing away dirt, mending broken threads.

The factory system introduced our modern concept of time. The factory day starts at 8:00 A.M.; the plane leaves for Houston at 3:23 P.M.; you have 30 minutes for lunch along with a 10-minute break at 10:00 A.M. and 3:00 P.M.; you are paid by the hour, i.e., time is broken into components. This attitude so ingrained in our thinking seems like a time obsession to the non-industrial societies of India, China, Africa and Latin America.

In the period before 1750, the Europeans had only a few footholds in Asia and Africa. Their major holdings were the Americas. Because the Americas and Australia were relatively empty millions of Europeans immigrated to fill their empty spaces. The Industrial Revolution was largely responsible for the mass migrations.

Increased productivity and advances in medical science led to the sharp increase in European population described that found an outlet in migration overseas. Persecution and disaster like the Irish potato famine and the availability of rail and ocean transport combined to produce a mass migration unequaled in human history to that date.

By and large, the British emigrants went to the dominions and the United States; the Italians, to the United States and Latin America; the Spaniards and Portuguese, to Latin America; and the Germans, to the United States and, in smaller numbers, to Argentina and Brazil. The result of this mass migration has been the almost complete Europeanization of Siberia, Australia, and the Americas, all of which have become part of European culture. The Indian population in Latin America managed to survive but as a minority.

The Industrial Revolution was largely responsible not only for the Europeanization of overseas territories but also for the creation of the huge European colonial structure of Asia and Africa. The great wave of empire building after 1870 was known as the new imperialism. It made a large part of the earth's surface subject to a few European powers.

This new imperialism and the Industrial Revolution were tied together by the growing desire to obtain colonies that might serve as markets for the rising volume of manufactured goods. The industrialized European countries were soon competing with each other for markets.

In the process they raised tariffs to keep out each other's products. Soon it was being argued that each industrialized country must have colonies to provide "sheltered markets" for its manufacturers.

The industrial European powers not only owned vast colonial territories outright, but we read how they also dominated those economically and militarily weak areas that were not actually annexed such as China, the Ottoman Empire, and Persia. Latin America also became dependent on the great powers, though in this region military action by Europe was discouraged by the American Monroe Doctrine. The great Russian Empire also came to be dominated economically to a very large extent by western Europe.

So we see that Europe's control extended not only over its actual empires but also over other extensive dependent regions. In fact, more European capital was invested in the dependent countries than in the colonies.

In this manner most of the earth's surface and most of the world's population had by 1914 come under the direct or indirect domination of a few European countries, including Russia, and the United States. This was a development without pre-cedence in human history. Today, in the late twentieth century, much of the global turmoil represents the inevitable reaction to this European domination.

Certainly world productivity rose greatly when European capital and skills were combined with the raw materials and labor of the underdeveloped regions. The combination produced, for the first time, an integrated global economy.

It is, however, understandable that colonial peoples were not very impressed by increased productivity or by the wages paid by foreign companies. They were more impressed by the level at which they subsisted, compared with Western levels. They also resented being cast always in a subordinate role. These dissatisfied people have supported movements to bring about radical change that we see around the world today. One of the ways they have chosen to get their way is to copy European nationalism.

▶ The Political Revolution

In addition to the use of applied science, and the Industrial Revolution, Europe underwent a political revolution that continues to affect the world's value system. The French Revolution of 1789 was introduced by a period called the Enlightenment. The term Enlightenment owes its name to the fact that the leaders of this movement believed that they lived in an enlightened age, as opposed to the Dark Age that preceded it. They viewed the past largely as a time of superstition and ignorance, and they thought that only in their day were human beings at last emerging from darkness into sunlight. It was the Europe of the Enlightenment that invented the terms and history concepts of Dark Ages and Middle Ages.

One basic characteristic of this Age of Enlightenment was the idea of progress, an idea that we have inherited. With the Enlightenment, it began to be optimistically assumed that the condition of humanity would steadily improve, so that each generation would be better off than that which came before.

How was this unceasing progress going to come about? The answer was simple and confident: by the use of humankind's reasoning powers. Faith in reason was a basic feature of the Enlightenment. It is often called the Age of Reason.

The two key concepts of progress and reason, were well defined by people who were known as the philosophes or philosophers. Their thinking had been much influenced by the law of gravitation that Newton had demonstrated. The philosophes believed in the existence of natural laws that regulated not only the physical universe, but these natural laws could also apply to human society. These laws were immutable like Newton's Laws of Physics and needed to be discovered.

Acting on this assumption, they proceeded to apply reason to all fields in order to discover the natural laws that operated in each. They subjected all the established institutions and traditions to the test of reason. Thus the philosophes subjected the old regime in France, that had developed over the centuries, to a barrage of devastating criticism. More important, they worked out new principles to use to build a new society based on reason.

Their key slogan in economics was *laissez faire*—let the people do what they will, let nature take its course. This opposition to government intervention was a reaction to the rigid regulation of economic life generally known as mercantilism. The ideal wealth for a country was created by exporting more than was imported. In the early period of building the nation state, mercantilism had been accepted as necessary for national security. But by the Eighteenth Century it seemed outdated and limiting.

The classic account of laissez faire was made by the Scotsman Adam Smith in his famous work *An Inquiry Into the Nature and Causes of the Wealth of Nations* (1776). He argued that individuals are motivated by self-interest as far as their economic activities are concerned, that the national welfare is simply the sum of the individual interests operating in a nation, and that each man knows his own interest better than does any government official.

In religion the key slogan was Voltaire's, *"Ecrasez l'infame!"*—"Crush the infamous thing," or stamp out religious fanaticism and intolerance, as represented by the Catholic Church. The philosophes rejected the traditional belief that God controls the universe and by His will determines the fate of humanity.

Instead, they wanted a natural religion that followed the discoveries of reason. There was an unprecedented growth of skepticism regarding "revealed" or "supernatural" religion. For the first time since Christianity created Europe as Christendom, a definite break had occurred with the Christian tradition.

For government, also, the philosophes had a key phrase—*"the social contract."* The contract theory of government was not new. The English political theorist John Locke, the principal thinker behind the American Constitution, had formulated it in his *Essay on Civil Government* (1690), in which he defined government as a political contract between rulers and ruled.

But the French philosopher Jean-Jacques Rousseau changed it into a social rather than a political contract. For him it involved an agreement among the people themselves. In his major political work, *The Social Contract* (1762), Rousseau justified revolution as a restoration to the sovereign people of its rightful power.

The slogans *"ecrasez l'infame," "laissez faire,"* and *"social contract"* meant the overthrow of traditional church, business, and government. The philosophes thought of themselves not as Frenchmen or Europeans but as members of the human race. They thought and acted in global rather than Western terms. They sought to discover social laws that had universal application, like Newton's laws of the physical world. Their challenge was meant to be for the world.

The American Revolution

In America the Revolution of 1776 was the first demonstration of these new doctrines in action. The American Revolution arose primarily out of claims for American colonial self-government. Not all of the American colonists favored violent revolution. The conservatives wanted to maintain loose relations between the mother country and the colony, while the radicals wanted to give the colonies complete control of their own affairs. They also wanted a political change inside the colonies in favor of the common people and ideas set forth by the philosophes. On this point the conservatives were violently opposed. They wished to retain upper-class leadership after English tradition. In the end the radicals had their way, thanks to the blunders of inept officials in Britain.

The American Revolution is significant to our world view not because it created another independent state, but because it created a new and different type of state. The Declaration of Independence proclaimed, *"We hold these truths to be self-evident: that all men are created equal."* Now the American people, both during and after the revolution, passed laws to make this declaration true in real life as well as on paper.

Ideas on the rights of man were now put into practice. Large estates were divided. Voting rights were given to all men (but not women). Many state governments passed laws forbidding the importation of slaves. Church and State were separated, and freedom of religion became the law of the land. All thirteen states adopted constitutions that included bills of rights, which guaranteed the natural rights of citizens.

These changes were not so far-reaching and fundamental as those that were brought about later by the French and Russian revolutions. These later revolutions, and particularly the Russian, involved far deeper social and economic reorganization. Nevertheless, the American Revolution had a profound impact.

The establishment of an independent republic in the New World was widely interpreted in Europe as meaning that the ideas of the Enlightenment were practicable—that it was possible for people to establish a state and a workable system of government based on the rights of the individual. America became a symbol of freedom and of opportunity throughout the world, looked up to as a country that had at last broken with the past.

The French Revolution

The French Revolution was more radical than the American Revolution. The French Revolution marked not only the triumph of the middle class but also the full awakening of the masses. Middle-class liberalism came to the fore, but so did nationalism with its appeal to the people in all sections of society. And indeed, "the people" became a main player in history for the first time, and this continues to be so.

This great change happened because France was a country of such gross inefficiency and inequality that the machinery of government slowly came to a standstill. The breakdown of government gave the ambitious and dissatisfied a chance to make its successful bid for power. The old regime in France was aristocratic in its organization. The clergy and nobility representing 2 percent of the total population, owned about 35 percent of the land and enjoyed most of the benefits of government patronage. In addition, they were exempted from almost all taxes.

The burden of taxation fell especially on the peasants. The peasants accounted for over 80 percent of the population but owned only 30 percent of the land. The middle class also were thoroughly dissatisfied with the old regime. They resented being snubbed by the nobility; treated as second-class subjects by the crown; and excluded from the higher posts in the bureaucracy, church, and army. In short, they wanted political power and social prestige to match their growing economic importance.

Strangely it was the nobles who started the revolution when they tried to seize opportunity to regain power from the king. The pinch for money became so acute that the king finally summoned the Estates-General to meet in the spring of 1789. The nobility assumed that they would be able to control this body and thereby regain a dominant position in the government. But their assumption proved completely wrong. The meeting of the Estates-General led, rather to the unleashing of a revolution that was to sweep away established institutions and ruling classes in France and most of Europe.

The revolution came under the control of the common people in Paris. The masses were successful in imposing their will and molding the direction of change. The masses that now ran the revolution in France were not the riffraff of the streets. They were the lesser bourgeoisie, made up of shopkeepers and heads of workshops. Mobs roamed the streets, demanding cheaper bread. On July 14 they stormed and destroyed the Bastille, an ancient royal castle in Paris and a symbol of oppression. That is why Bastille Day continues to be celebrated in France as Independence Day is in the United States. The fall of the Bastille marks the appearance of the masses on the historical stage.

Mass revolution occurred in the countryside as well as in Paris. The peasants took up arms, and in many parts of the countryside they tore down fences, seized lands, and burned manor houses. Laws were passed that ended all feudal dues, the privilege of tax exemption, the right of the church to collect tithes, and the exclusive right of the nobility to hold office. Church lands were confiscated, the judicial and administrative systems reorganized, and the Declaration of the Rights of Man and Citizen declared.

This declaration set forth certain fundamental principles concerning liberty, property, and security— "Men are born, and always continue, free and equal, in respect of their rights. . . . The Nation is essentially the source of all sovereignty . . . law is an expression of the will of the community . . . liberty consists in the power of doing whatever does not injure another. . . ." "The right to property being inviolable and sacred, no one ought to be deprived of it." This declaration contained the essential message of the revolution. The declaration carried the revolutionary slogan of "Liberty, Equality, Fraternity" throughout Europe, and eventually to all the world.

The French Revolution was a profound social revolution. It marked the beginning for the first time in history of mass participation in government. The principles of this revolution are still stirring the downtrodden and oppressed of the world.

Nationalism and the Nation State

One of the outcomes of the revolution was the spread throughout the world of nationalism and the glorification of the nation state. One could argue that the master institution produced in the West in the last six hundred years is the Nation State.

Perhaps this tribal feeling represented by the nation is the deepest of all our emotions. From the very beginning of organized life among mankind the sense of belonging to one group and not belonging to another has been enormously strong. Then, as civilizations developed, the old feeling of the tribe or clan developed into the idea of loyalty to the clan chief and loyalty to a king and his heirs.

In our modern world these old, long-established, deep-rooted groupings have taken a new and deadlier form. In the European nation state, formed along language lines, the idea grew up that people who spoke the same language were related and anyone who did not was an alien. One of the

first things Protestants did was translate the Bible from Latin to the national language.

This extreme concept of solidarity by language has been at the root of a great many troubles in Europe ever since the first modern nation states England, France, Spain, and Portugal. It has added a racial edge to war and world politics.

Nationalism grew also because of the new democratic idea that everyone has a stake or is a part of the country, rather than just the subject of some ruler. Each citizen's own private and personal fortunes are involved in what happens to the country. Democracy and nationalism grew together. Each citizen shares in the economic interests of the state. The modern nation state grew to a point of complete, unchecked sovereignty. And this was the political unit through which Western culture has, in the last four hundred years, been carried out into the world.

The spirit of nationalist aggression first came to the notice of the world in the shape of bitter national struggles between different trading groups; between Portuguese and Dutch, between French and British. They were amazed and indeed disgusted to see that there was virtually nothing that a merchant of one European nation would not do to a merchant of another nation provided he could get rid of his competition.

Later, the nations of Europe had developed their industrial strength, and national rivalry was now used as part of a pattern establishing colonial rule over foreign lands. One of the reasons why the Japanese excluded all foreigners for over two hundred years was that they realized that political control usually followed European traders. European business and exploitation, capitalism and imperialism, became synonymous in the minds of many of the world's peoples.

The habit of intense nationalism has now become worldwide because many have come to believe that this is the only way they can hold their own against super national powers. Asian, Islamic and African peoples are enshrining the Nation State. The Japanese led the way. In India, the spirit of exclusive nationalism led to the tragic split between Hindu and Muslim in which religion served as the basis for dividing the subcontinent into three states—Pakistan, India and Bangladesh.

Unfettered national sovereignty has come at a time when science, technology, and world business are making complete nonsense of any nation's claim, even the largest, to be totally sovereign and self-contained. Changes that have occurred in communications, in travel, in the whole organization of economic life point in one direction only: towards a world so small and so integrated that it must find some form of social and political order which transcends all these supposedly sovereign units. We have reached the peak of nationalism just when, from the point of view of industrial, economic, and social organization, exclusive nationalism has become completely impractical.

It might help if we realize nationalism is of recent origin. It did not exist in recognizable form in the Middle Ages. At that time the Catholic Church created an organization, to which all western Christians belonged; and one language, the Latin language, which all educated people used. Mass allegiance to a nation was, during those centuries, unknown. Instead, most people considered themselves to be first of all, Christians; second, residents of a certain region such as Burgundy or Cornwall; and only last, if at all, French or English.

The rise of national languages and the use of these languages for a national literature were the breakaway from the Catholic Church of several national churches. And the formation of several large, homogeneous, independent states —England, France, Spain, and Portugal—laid the basis for the rise of nationalism. Nationalism did not assume its modern form until the mid-1700s, when the European middle class came to share power. They did so in the name of the nation, comprised of citizens aware of their common interests.

The Rights of Man

Another important aspect in the political revolution was the freeing of the individual from class, church or governmental restraint. Liberal doctrines of individual rights were first clearly formulated and implemented during the English Revolution. At that time, these doctrines were primarily those of religious toleration and of security of person and of property against the arbitrariness of the crown.

Specifically, carrying out these doctrines involved parliamentary control of government, and existence of independent political parties, and the recognition of the need for, and the rights of, opposition parties.

On the other hand, the right to vote was limited by property qualifications, so that those without property, who made up most of the population, were left voteless. Thus, liberalism in seventeenth-century England advanced middle-class interests.

Rights were further defined and applied as the American Revolution brought about substantial advances in restricting slavery, extending religious toleration, broadening the franchise, and establishing constitutional government. The American Constitution adopted in 1791 was based on the principle of the separation of powers in order to prevent tyranny—by having the executive, legislative, and judicial powers check and balance each other.

Even more advanced in its liberal tenets than the American Revolution was the French. Its Declaration of the Rights of Man and Citizen is the classic statement of eighteenth-century liberalism, proclaiming in patriotic words the liberties of the individual.

The liberalism that emerged from the English, American, and French revolutions took the institutional form of constitutional parliamentary government. As the nineteenth century passed, liberalism, like other historical movements, changed appreciably in character. It would not continue to concern itself mainly with middle class property interests at a time when the masses were becoming more politically active as a result of increasing education and trade-union organization. Consequently, there was a shift from the early classical liberalism, which represented middle class interests, to a more democratic variety. Equality before the law was joined by equality before the ballot box.

Hitherto intervention by the government in economic and social matters had been regarded evil and futile meddling with the operation of natural laws (per Adam Smith). This theoretical proposition, however, did not jibe with the facts of life as far as the workers were concerned. Civil liberties and the right to vote did not relieve them from the poverty and insecurity produced by unemployment, sickness, disability, and old age. So there developed pressure for social reforms. Under this pressure a new consensus developed that recognized the responsibility of the state for the welfare of all its citizens.

The first country to set the modern pattern was Germany, which adopted social-reform programs, including old-age pensions; minimum-wage laws; sickness, accident, and unemployment insurance; and regulation of hours and conditions of work. These reforms were the prelude to the welfare state that has become the accepted government form of the modern nation state.

More recently the role of the state in providing aid to its citizens is being more carefully scrutinized. First, the welfare programs have grown enormously expensive; second, they can have a negative effect on the competitive position of the state in a globally competitive market; and last, and perhaps the most important, they seem to create a permanently dependent underclass with intractable problems for society.*

Note

*A real classic on the rise of Europe and its implication is *"The Rise of the West"* by William H. McNeill. His global point of view is used throughout this book. Also for a clear exposition of global history, L. S. Stavianos' world history books divided into the world before 1500 and the world after 1500 is hard to beat. I am particularly indebted to him for his delineation of the industrial and political revolutions and their worldwide implications.

Worksheet ▶

CHAPTER ELEVEN

Define or identify:

• The Industrial Revolution—country, date, principles

• The Political Revolution—country, date, principles

• The Noble Savage

• The rights of man

• The Age of Reason

• The substitution of animal power with mechanical power

• Industrial time

• Rich industrial—Poor agricultural

• Adam Smith—The Wealth of Nations

- Encrasez l'infame

- 1789, The French Revolution

- Reign of Terror

- "We hold these truths to be self-evident: that all men are created equal."

- Philosophe

Explain:

- Why is the separation of the power of church and state so important in European development?

- What was the difference between the Europe of 1500 when the first contact with the world was made and the Europe of 1750?

- How did Newton and Darwin change our idea of man and the universe?

- How has the industrial revolution changed our attitudes toward time, the family and the role of women?

- How did the Industrial Revolution affect population?

- What was the good news and the bad news of the Industrial Revolution?

- "Man is born free and is everywhere in chains."

- The American revolution, "We hold these truths to be self-evident; that all men are created equal." What causes prejudice and what are some solutions?

- The world can be divided into rich industrial North and poor agricultural South. Name some countries that would fall into each category.

- What are some common characteristics of the Triad; Europe; North America and Japan?

- Besides our western culture which has as a root value in the Judeo-Christian tradition, each of the other cultures has a root moral ethical system: India- Hinduism; China-Buddhism,Confucianism and Taoism; Islam-Islam.

- Why might we say that the industrial and political revolution of Europe are at the root of many conflicts we see between the West and the rest of the world?

Discuss:

- "East is East and West is West." How has this saying of Kipling been proven wrong?

- Why in the Judeo-Christian tradition are material things not regarded as meaningless? How does this turn into Western ideas on progress? On science?

- What has been the negative side of the rise of the nation state and nationalism?

- Outline the western impact on India, China, Japan or Islam and what has been their reaction to this challenge?

- How is the industrial revolution changing all the world's countries and cultures, Japan, China, Thailand?

- What are some ways the political and industrial revolutions of Europe have changed and are continuing to change the world.

- In what ways do you see the principles of the rights of man affecting our attitudes today. Women, race, the handicapped, sexual preference, equal access.

- I read in the newspaper India is being westernized. What do they mean?

- How does modern science play an integral part of industrialization?

- Is there a connection between the western revolutions and population growth?

· What does the author see as the negative side of the nation state and nationalism?

· If you were in power in a poor underdeveloped country, what are some steps you might take to improve your lot?

Chapter 12 ▶ ▶

WHAT IS YOUR CULTURE?

The bias of this presentation of world culture has been toward an intellectual, or spiritual emphasis as the keystone to understanding our world as opposed to a materialist, determinist one.

On one of the last pages of his last and most famous book John Maynard Keynes—by wide agreement the most influential economist of this century—observed that

"... the ideas of economists and political philosophers, both when they are right and when they are wrong, are more powerful than is commonly understood. Indeed the world is ruled by little else. Practical men, who believe themselves to be quite exempt from any intellectual influences, are usually the slaves of some defunct economist."

And again (how appropriate to the rantings of Hitler and Mussolini at the time).

"Madmen in authority, who hear voices in the air, are distilling their frenzy from some academic scribbler of a few years back."

Then came his affirmation:

"... the power of vested interests is vastly exaggerated compared with the gradual encroachment of ideas."

Writing four centuries before Christ the Greek Isocrates reflects on the Athenians:

"And so far has our city distanced the rest of mankind in thought and in speech that her pupils have become the teachers of the rest of the world; and she has brought it about that the term Hellenes signified no longer a race but an intelligence, and those are called Hellenes who share our education rather than those who share our common blood."

In other words, the Athenian leadership was a spiritual empire.

Geographically, Europe is no more than the small western promontory of the land mass of Asia. It is "Europe" solely because its frontiers mark the frontiers of Christendom. Racially, the United States is a melting pot of every nation under the sun. Only by force of an idea—the "proposition" that men are created equal and possess inalienable rights—has it risen to be the most powerful community in the history of man.

Both European society and its extension into the New World have been sustained by a unique faith in man—in his freedom, in his responsibility, in the laws which should safeguard him, in the rights that are his and in the duties by which he earns those rights.

If an exponent of the materialist explanation of history had been living and teaching by the shores of the eastern Mediterranean 1000 years before Christ and had been asked to forecast which people would be the next great influences of human affairs, he would no doubt have examined carefully the great societies around him—Egypt to the south, Babylonia to the east, the rising Assyrian power in the north, the Hittite community of Asia Minor, and the flourishing maritime empire of the Minoans.

He would have considered their relative economic strength, their differing military abilities, the pressure on them internally of rising population an externally of barbarian encroachment. Out of these calculations, he would have made his guess that in the next phase of history one or other power would exercise the greatest influence—Egypt perhaps because of its high degree of administrative organization, Minoan Crete for its maritime flexibility and commercial wealth, Babylonia for its elaborate economy, or perhaps Assyria for its addiction to naked aggression.

But our early materialist probably would have overlooked the Greeks and the Jews, yet these two people will be the people who form the future. For the ideas of the Greeks and the Jews will form our own western culture. For fifteen hundred years in western civilization, these two traditions have been at work and between them they have formed the intellectual and moral basis of our values.

For those who believe that all history can be determined by analyzing relative economic and military strengths, the Greeks and the Jews must be an extraordinarily difficult case. These two peoples possess such a unique individuality that they don't conform to any general scientific role, but rather stand for their own creative influences. Their great impact on western culture cannot be explained in economic or military terms.

The importance of the Greek achievement can best be judged by examining what the Athenians managed to do, to think, and to create between 600 BC and 300 BC, their Golden Age. Attica, as the area they controlled was known, was no bigger than the state of Massachusetts. The total number of citizens was never more than 100,000.

Athens itself was a small town. Yet this minute community was the home, within a few generations, of great legislators like Solon, Cleisthenes, and Pericles; of poets of the stature of Aeschylus, Sophocles, Euripides, and Aristophanes; of Thucydides, the greatest of all historians; of Phidias and Praxiteles, the first outstanding sculptors of the human body; of architects capable of designing the Acropolis; and of a brilliant line of philosophers including the great Socrates and Plato.

In the great areas of mental achievement, scientific inquiry, history, politics, and the arts the Greeks were doing things for the first time in the history of man. The intense influence they have exercised on all subsequent ages is a measure of their supreme genius.

Another insignificant power destined to lay the foundations of western culture was a small pastoral hill people of Judea whose immediate destiny was to be overrun by the Assyrian conquest of Babylon, to be scattered far from their capital Jerusalem, and to endure exile in the very heart of the enemy. Yet in the three thousand years that have followed the Babylonian captivity, history has been shaped by this small group while mighty Babylon has vanished into dust. The Jews, like the Greeks, are a unique fact in the development of man. No amount of explanation derived from environment or race or economic determinism can explain their special gifts.

There were other pastoral peoples in the Near East. If Marxist material explanations were all, they too should have produced similar insights into man's nature and destiny. But this particular race, living in this particular time of history, was to be the carrier of the new ideas. Like the great genius of a Leonardo or an Einstein, they remind us of the part of man that is free and creative, the element that cannot, by however elaborate a materialist explanation, be reduced to a mere projection of environment and heredity.

Perhaps the most remarkable of the insights contributed by the Jews was the break with the universal archaic idea of a history in endless cycles of repetition. (Remember our discussion of Indian time.) Because the idea of progress in history is still so strong in us in spite of disastrous wars of this century, it is difficult to realize what a startling break with accepted thought the Jews made when they saw in history not cyclical recurrence but progress along God's plan for the human race.

Yet with a never ending faith, they chose to change accepted history and to maintain against all experience and all apparent reason that God had chosen them, a small group of wanderers, to declare to the world the fact that history had a meaning and direction and that the meaning contained the message of the Jewish race.

Throughout history, those with a positive goal and a consistent aim have had their way. Like inspired artists, they have given vision and redesigned new patterns of human organization. At a time when the whole classical world of the Greeks and Romans was ending in calamity, the Greek and Jewish founders of western culture made their tremendous acts of faith in man and his destiny. The Greeks affirmed man's power to build a rational order, the Jews proclaimed him a partner with God in carrying out his divine plan.

If we believe people to be solely creatures of their environment, destined by the chance of birth and by uncontrollable forces on to the fatality of death—then they are ready to surrender their freedom, rights, and chance to achieve greatness. They are ready for dictatorship and the slave state. Everyone is lonely. No one is self-sufficient. Everyone is ready to rebel against meaninglessness in life. Everyone is haunted by death and is afraid. We all need to feel part of a wider whole and have great powers of dedication and devotion which must find expression in worship and service. Everyone looks for transcendence from a meaningless life to one that has significance.

If there is no greater outlet for these yearnings for purpose in life, people will worship the state, leaders or other false gods. For some, the need to worship is satisfied, in the worship of the self. Those who look for a god can nearly always be certain of finding a willing candidate. The French Revolution begins with the religion of human reason and ends with the dictator, Napoleon. Stalin took world Communism and shaped it to his personal will. In our own time Communism and the Nazism of Hitler have proved to be powerful religions and have brought back into advanced European states the identification of state and church. And their line could be added to with more recent monsters from Idi Amin, to Mao Zedong, and Sadam Hussein.

One of the products of ancient thought was the conviction that man's whole existence is bound to a fixed, revolving system, much as the workings of the stars, in which all is predetermined and all recurs. Buddhism saw man bound to a melancholy wheel driven by his own desires. In the midst of this conditioned cycle of recurrence, individual life is no more than a flash of consciousness playing on a vast and meaningless story of unending revolving change. We in the West through our Jewish-Christian tradition are convinced that time has meaning and that God works in history.

Many of the most characteristic features of this culture spring from our dynamic, history-conscious Christian tradition. The separation of church and state has helped to create a society in which all are free to enjoy their own appropriate rights. The notion of a moral law transcending kings and princes (the King was under God and the law) is another strong strand in our constitutional practice of government.

We created an American government under law. Freedom has its roots in the concept of each human soul enjoying infinite value in the sight of God. Along with this freedom is the necessity of personal choice and responsibility, and the realization that because all men are children of God they are brothers.

Our western culture, inheriting this vision of God, man, and history from its Jewish roots, has seen the whole of history as the unfolding of the drama of God's purpose for man—a drama in which man, with a free will, has an active part to play, changing himself and his environment into a closer reflection of God's plan. The fatalisms of antiquity are replaced by a new vision of personal and historical progress.*

I believe the driving forces of the future will be centered around our answers to values. What values? The United States will fill a role of leadership only if its material achievements are seen to express a value laden vision for a better life. And faith in our leadership will not be given because people believe it would be useful or "a good thing." Our faith in ourselves and our vision will return only when we discover our values and find they are true.

In some reading I ran across an account of a church synod taking place with barbarism on the loose in Europe. The report has words we must consider. "The towns are depopulated, the monasteries ruined and burned and good land converted into a desert. Just as primitive men lived without rule and without fear of God, subject only to their own passions, so today everyone does what he pleases in scorn of humans and divine laws and commandments of the church." Well, in Chapter One, I told you I was against the teaching of multiculturalism if it emphasizes the equality of all values. The Dark Ages of Europe as well as all barbarisms are the result of a lack of appeal to a higher authority.

Primitive men without rule and without fear, are subject only to their own passion. Anyone concerned about our future must be worried by the growing trend to violence, both in our entertainment as in our personal lives. As a teacher it seems to me I have noticed a growing trend toward crudity in language and a decline in everyday courtesies—the lubricant that allows us all to live together with less friction.

It is my hope that this book will have made you more tolerant and understanding, but also I hope you have at least made a start toward working out your own personal values. This should be a lifetime learning process that will give your life meaning and purpose. God had a plan for you. What is it?

Sixty years ago W. B. Yeats wrote a famous and prophetic poem.

> Things fall apart; the centre cannot hold;
> Mere anarchy is loosed upon the world,
> The blood-dimmed tide is loosed, and everywhere
> The ceremony of innocence is drowned;
> The best lack all conviction, while the worst
> Are full of passionate intensity.

The best lack all convictions. Where is our center? What are the values upon which we as a society can agree. Kenneth Clark closes his book *Civilization* stating:

> It is lack of confidence, more than anything else, that kills a civilization. We can destroy ourselves by cynicism and disillusion, just as effectively as by bombs.

Today we must ask ourselves in America whether the pride of material achievement has not brought our society to the verge of falling apart. Must we not search for values that will rebuild our faith, confidence and sense of purpose? And in our search for values which can be long and difficult we should take heart from the assurance given in the Bible, *"those who seek shall find, to those who ask shall be given and those who knock shall have the doors opened to them."*

Abraham H. Maslow lists some basic values confronting all men and women. How would you answer these questions?

> What is the good life?
> Who is the good man or woman?
> What is the good society and what is my relation to it?
> What are my obligations to society?
> What is best for my children?
> What is justice; truth; virtue?
> What is my relation to nature, to death, to aging, to pain, to illness?
> How can I live an enjoyable and meaningful life?
> What is my responsibility to my brothers?
> Who are my brothers?
> What shall I be loyal to?
> What must I be ready to die for?

Note

*Barbara Ward and Christopher Dawson have both maintained in brilliant fashion the proposition that Christian beliefs are the basis for western culture. "Faith and Freedom," by Barbara Ward is an excellent book upon which this chapter has drawn.

Worksheet ▶

CHAPTER TWELVE

Define or identify:

- Europe—Christendom

- The American "proposition"

Explain:

- Why would a determinist or a materialist have overlooked the Jews and Greeks, the founders of the western tradition?

- What is the danger if we believe we are simply products of our environment?

- When we say the United States is "a government under law" how does this tie to our Judeo-Christian and Greco-Roman values?

- The role of confidence in supporting civilization.

- How did the industrial revolution affect population?

Discuss:

- Do you agree or not that spiritual values prevail?

- "Things fall apart, the center cannot hold."

- What do you believe? Can you identify items in our Judeo-Christian tradition you feel are very important to preserve?

- "Greeks must live by law and those laws are framed by themselves." "Citizens enjoyed equality before the law."

- "In Christian metaphysics souls stand equal in the sight of God."

- What is the good life?

- What are some of your opinions on how American education should change in view of globalization and the knowledge of society?

Appendix ▶ ▶

WORLD CUSTOMS . . .
SOCIAL CONDUCT
AROUND THE WORLD_____

Oh wad some power the giftie gie us to
see oursels as others see us.
It wad frae monie a blunder
free us An' foolish notion
— Robert Burns

▶ Introduction

Each culture in the world operates according to an agreed upon value system: what are the rules? what and who should we admire? what is good and beautiful? Whoever we meet will be acting, often unconsciously, from a number of beliefs and accepted ways of acting learned from the group they identify. We have called these values, when shared by a group such as the Chinese, a culture. The culture acts as a guide to the actions and responses of those who identify with it.

In this section on world customs, we will lay down some general guidelines that will help us in the complex challenge of understanding other cultures actions and how we can best adjust to them. It is also hoped it will help achieve the first of the book's objectives, which was to simply create an increased awareness of cultural differences.

I would like to emphasize when dealing with a foreign culture, attitudes are more important than information. The essence of cross-cultural under-

standing is opening mutual communication rather than sending the right messages. Being well informed about another culture will not cover up the damage of arrogance, apathy or intolerance. The most important attitude is a sincere interest and caring along with an openness and desire to share information. Of course, the best is to both be well informed and have the right attitudes.

Chapter One, in outlining the aims of this book, stated the importance of mutual respect. *Important in our world view is the development of the idea of respect. . . . Respect is vital in all intercultural relations. Maintain your own cultural integrity. But treat others with respect.* This statement reflects the overriding theme of our discussion of world customs.

▶ American Values as Others See Them

A good place to start when dealing with intercultural relationships is a candid look at ourselves, to think of our values and try to see ourselves as others see us. Only when we can see that there is more than one approach to life and many different ways of behaving can we begin to experience the strong, pervasive influence of our own culture.

The United States is a continent-size country whose values have been influenced by people from around the world. We are a country of immigrants. In its early days, the country was strongly influenced by the English and other people from northern Europe; its laws are based on English common law and its language English. We emphasized the importance of language in forming culture (Chapter 3). Even though the United States has absorbed millions of people from countries around the globe, the core culture of the United States continues to have its roots in northern European or English culture. American culture is European and more specifically northern European at its base.

The U.S. has managed to absorb bits and pieces of many cultures to create a distinctively American culture. Americans, like other people, have their own distinctive way of acting. Generally, we are perceived to be open, friendly, informal, and optimistic. On the negative side, and this may be because of our size and economic strength, Americans tend to be self-centered and both ignorant and insensitive to foreign cultures.

For example, even though the U.S. shares borders with Canada and Mexico, most Americans know little of either country's history, and are completely (and unfortunately happily) in the dark when it comes to Islam, India or China. We all tend to think in stereotypes and while our picture of others is often superficial or false, it hurts when we find others also hold misleading stereotypes of us. We wish they would learn more or be more understanding. Lets look at some commonly held views of American values.

▶ American Culture and Society

The parts of our culture most foreigners question, misunderstand, or condemn include: our attitudes toward the family, our morals and ethics, the role of women, crime and violence, race relationships, and our emphasis on material possessions and success. We will discuss each of these in turn. Generally Americans have felt quite superior to the various world cultures, especially those not in Europe, probably because of our economic success. However, our own culture has not universally been held up as an ideal by the world.

A good place to start a healthy relationship is from a position of humility and awareness of how some of our unquestionably accepted values and institutions may appear in foreign eyes. While many American values are still admired and held up as examples to follow, many are being seriously questioned by those concerned with our social and moral decay. Many looking at America see a breakdown of the family, crime on the increase, an increasingly violent society ridden by drug abuse, and a society in decline. Others are offended by our narrowness and lack of cultural awareness when we are guests in their country.

A lot of foreign criticism comes from the fact that American values have changed rapidly in recent years. Our change from an agricultural to an industrial society along with all the gadgets, cars, and televisions, for example, has drastically changed patterns of living. We have not always been able to make successful social and cultural adaptations. The same problems and adjustments are now going on in Japan, Korea, China and other cultures as they modernize. America is a large and diverse country. It would be naive to assume we don't have our social and cultural problems. We should, however, remember we are a country open to new ideas and willing to seek solutions.

When we deal with people of other cultures, we should avoid the opposite errors of being overly critical or defensive. We should try to understand the foreigners' point of view and answer their questions with sincere and reasonable answers.

▶ The Family

Many of the changes in the American family are the result of the move to the city and increasing mobility. These changes are not peculiar to America, but take place whenever people change lifestyles. In a rural environment close family relationships develop as the family tends to work together, and relatives are close by. This is still the case in many poor agricultural areas such as India or Africa. As the move to the city takes place, the traditional extended family of grandparents and relatives is necessarily changed to what sociologists call the "nuclear family" of just the parents and children.

Again in a traditional family, the father as provider was the center of authority while the mother was fully occupied with the housework. Now in an industrial society such as the United States, this division of labor has changed. Women work outside the home and contribute to family support so that the old father-dominated home has been changed to one of partnership, and husband and wife work together as a team. To people from the more traditional societies, of course, this often appears that the family is breaking down and that women are not doing their job of running the home, and men have given up their role of running the family.

American children have been seen as having too much freedom and lacking discipline. To someone from an authoritarian tradition, American children seem to tell the parents what to do. There is some truth to this. In families separated by divorce, each parent, because of feelings of guilt, tend to be over-indulgent and afraid to apply discipline. There is no denying the father-mother-children relationships in the modern American family are very different from the past.

It is no longer expected for a man to control a woman. Not only is she a contributing partner, but she has her own choices. And it is much harder for parents to enforce their values in their children when they are being influenced so much by from television, schools, and friends outside the home. They are spending less time with the family than they would if they lived on the farm or in a small town.

The increasing educational level of women and opportunities for jobs and careers, the changing role of man as provider, and children educated outside the home have changed the nature of the American family. Father now washes dishes and generally shares in household chores, and Mother works outside the home. Many see mothers working outside the home as a major contribution to American family disintegration, feeling they have given up the key role of forming values and a sense of responsibility to others who really can't fill this role.

And, of course, the high American divorce rate is another major contributor to change in our family patterns. The problems of the changing family are not, however, uniquely American, but appear to be part of an industrialized lifestyle, whenever that occurs in the world.

It would be hard to exaggerate the effect of divorce on the traditional American family pattern. In traditional societies and here in America until recently, divorce was only very rarely possible. For one thing, there was no place for a single woman to go to find work. Also, the churches were against divorce and ready to condemn a divorced woman. This attitude is changing around the world, and is part of the industrial society's change which opens up freedom and opportunity.

As women get choices outside of the home for work and education, unfair and exploitive marriages are less and less possible. Women today do not have to put up with brutality, neglect, stupidity, and drunkenness, as they did when there were no other alternatives. Today, the move to the city is taking place even in the developing countries and divorce is increasing as people get real alternatives. The traditional family structure is under pressure today everywhere in the world.

With changing family patterns and the break-up of the extended family, old people have also seen their position change. In most of the world children take care of the old members of the family as, of course, they did until recently in the U.S. Now, more and more parents have decided that they do not want to be a burden on their children. Social welfare programs began with social security programs, pensions, government payments, and retirement schemes that reduced the older people's dependence on the young so that the choice of independent living is possible. Also people are living longer and remaining active. They do not want to be told what to do by their children. In America today, rarely do grandparents live with the families of their children; generally they prefer to maintain their independence and have the means to do so.

▶ The Role of Women

One of the dramatic changes in our culture in recent years has been the new role for women, thanks to the American women's liberation movement. Women in America have always had more freedom than in other cultures. For one thing, there was no servant class, and women always shared in the work, risk, and education in a way that was generally not the case in Europe, or even in the Asian or African cultures. American women always had a greater range of choices and freedom than elsewhere. Nevertheless, until recently the man was the dominant person or senior partner.

In recent times as more marriages have evolved into the partnership pattern, the woman's role as income earner is necessary to maintain the way of life the family wants. This has often put a strain on family life. Almost half of the American work force presently consists of women. One thing that is developing in America is more equality for women in terms of job opportunity and equal pay.

Women have also had their life changed by all the new labor saving equipment common in an American home. Automatic washers, gas stoves, microwave ovens have freed up time that was formerly spent on labor intensive chores. This new free time has allowed women to pursue outside interests, including education and a more varied life.

Most American women today certainly feel they want to be in control of their own lives. Women's liberation stands for women's desire to be seen as human beings deserving equal treatment with men and to have the same opportunities offered men.

On the average, women still earn less than men. But these discrepancies are slowly disappearing. More and more single women are expected to be as economically and socially independent as men.

Though not always socially or religiously acceptable, the new freedoms have made premarital and extramarital sex more common. The number of unmarried couples living together has tripled in the past ten years, and the divorce rate has doubled. In addition, many men and women choose to remain single. Still, the standard married couple remains the most preferred living arrangement, representing over 80 percent of all American households. The sexual freedom tolerated in the U.S. is seen as a sign of decadence by traditional or strongly religious-oriented cultures, such as Islam.

▶ Crime and Violence

Foreigners are repelled by what they see as the widespread use of drugs in the U.S. and are apt to interpret this as another instance of our breakdown of values, the family, and religious beliefs. Most agree that today's society is made less stressful by the comforting and support found in stable families and smaller, tightly-knit communities. Drugs have been used as a way of relieving this stress and loneliness. Again, there is no reason to see this as an American problem, but rather a problem of the modern fragmented and often rootless society.

It is interesting to note that many are forecasting a return to religion as more people feel alien-

ated in a competitive, individualistic world and look for somewhere to belong to receive support and guidance from a group.

Television and movies have helped spread the picture of America as a place of crime and violence. The entertainment industry is dominated worldwide by Americans and the image they have exported is violent. While a distorted view, it is also true we are living in a period of history filled with violence. Stable, close-knit communities have broken up, and the new widespread use of drugs has turned many law-abiding citizens to violent crime. The violence of television may also be contributing to violence by giving models of violence to the young.

▶ Race Relationships

Almost always a questioning of American culture will bring up the subject of race relationships. The place of blacks in America (as well as instances of other minority discrimination, particularly of Indians and Latinos) always has been given publicity by the world press. There is usually a lot of stereotyping involved. The U.S. is a mixture of many cultures with the English and north European cultural roots dominating. Many of our minority conflicts come from cultural clashes with this dominant one. Americans do have to admit there is bigotry in the U.S. based on fear and ignorance; on the other hand there is much progress in changing this.

Discrimination exists in all societies. The American Civil Rights movement is an example of American willingness to build an open and free society, and we can be proud of the initiative taken.

The treatment of native Americans or Indians is a particularly difficult part of history to rationalize to others. With the coming of the Europeans in 1492, the Indians were forced out of their native habitats and hunting and living areas, and the Indian population declined precipitously. The devastating effect was detailed in Chapter 7, "The Americas." Indians in the U.S. were forced to live on tribal reservations where they remained isolated. Unlike the blacks and Hispanics who remained in steady contact with the changing American scene, the Indian minority have been isolated in rural areas.

Things are changing. Indians can leave reservations any time, are full American citizens, and receive special treatment. However, still today many of the native Americans live on reservations, and the overall picture is one of a minority group behind in health and education, and basically underprivileged.

▶ Cultural Considerations

A broad area of criticism of American cultural values involves American self-centeredness as evidenced by our knowledge or interest in other peoples' cultures and our focus on money and success. Are Americans often uninformed about other countries and do they fail to show interest in their customs and history? Do many worship money and power and neglect family and community? While the answer is yes, it is also an oversimplification. American society is varied as are all others.

Newspapers and television programs are often superficial. They are designed to get readership from a mass audience. On the other hand, sources of in-depth special information have grown tremendously. Americans who wish to be informed have access to excellent sources of information, and the American free library system is unique in the world.

Americans have, it is true, not had a tradition of feeling part of a global community. Isolation has deep American roots. Even when sent on foreign assignments, Americans often tend to stay by themselves. They are notoriously bad at making the effort to learn a foreign language or to study a country's history.

While it is natural for any group to stay by themselves, our exclusiveness is often a valid criticism. The American school system is starting to pay more attention to world history, geography, and the multinational enterprise is emphasizing this need. Still the American student is apt to be taking driver training and athletics instead of learning world history and geography.

Foreigners see our public school system as undisciplined and its education superficial. In this they are not alone, as America comes to realize our public education is inferior by world standards. America has been a permissive society, and school has emphasized "being happy" and well adjusted rather than being prepared, disciplined, and trained to compete in a highly competitive world economy. The world's school system is elitist and focuses on educating the best and brightest for a leadership role. The American public school systems has been given the task of educating all citizens.

While American grade and high school education gets very low marks, the quality of American postgraduate education is generally considered the best in the world and continues to draw students from around the globe. The great American universities filled with foreign students show that segments of American education enjoy high prestige.

Are Americans shallow and without deep well-thought-through convictions? Many foreigners, especially intellectuals, think so. America does not have a tradition of intellectuals being highly respected. The people who settled this country were the educated middle class, not the aristocracy. People came to the U.S. seeking opportunity. They were often from the peasant class or religious minority groups. Many were down-and-outers looking for a new start. Some came as slaves.

These people put much more value on deeds than words. They worked very hard to make a living and get the material goods they dreamed about. This tradition of practical common sense and action is part of the American heritage. Americans generally are results-oriented and schedule their time to get things done. Schedules are made and followed and time commitments are taken very seriously. Promptness is a virtue, especially where business is involved. Being late for an appointment calls for an apology.

Americans also tend to want quick results. Wanting quick solutions, they are not used to waiting long periods of time for decisions and become anxious when decisions are not made promptly. This attitude puts them at a disadvantage when dealing with people such as the Germans, the Japanese, and Latin Americans, all of whom, for different reasons, take more time to reach decisions. American business people tend to think in short-term intervals. When Americans talk about the "long-term," they usually mean no more than two or three years instead of the 10, 20, or even 100 years of the Oriental.

Americans do prefer directness in communication, "Tell it like it is," "Don't beat around the bush," "Call a spade a spade" are very American phrases. Americans are uncomfortable with indirectness and sometimes miss subtle hints. This failure to perceive or understand nonverbal cues means that Americans often miss a build-up of tension and, as a consequence, fail to realize that something is wrong until a crisis develops.

Bragging and boastfulness are more common among Americans than other cultures where bragging is considered a sign of the uneducated. In manner, Americans often use humor to diffuse tensions on the job and in social situations. Good jokes are passed around and a good sense of humor is admired. Most Americans keep their social conversations light, and feel uncomfortable with serious philosophical discussions. Generally, Americans have little interest in discussing philosophy, which they consider too theoretical and personal.

American businesspeople like to deal with foreigners on a practical basis. They are often specialists dealing with classically educated foreigners who are often generalists. In their education, the foreign businessperson will have spent more time than the American studying history, philosophy, and culture. The more broadly educated foreigner may feel some contempt for the American who is a specialist and quite ignorant of history, language, and the arts.

Worth stating again is that too many foreigners have their impression of Americans formed from American movies and television. Often these paint a very distorted and not very complimentary picture of American lifestyle, family, crime, and cultural level. It should be remembered that we too often carry very distorted views of the foreigner put together from small bits of information about certain segments of their society.

▶ Some General Rules of Conduct

Greetings

First impressions are important, and we should observe some general rules to make sure we give notice that we respect local customs. Americans tend to be open and informal. Sometimes this informality and lack of respect for rank or social position can be considered disrespectful in other cultures. We are quick to use first names and disregard titles. As a general rule in greeting, as in many other areas of conduct such as dress, the prudent course is to be more formal. The rest of the world is more class conscious.

In the western or European tradition, which applies to all the countries in the western cultural realm, we shake hands when we meet. A professional person's title (e.g., Doctor, Professor, Director) is used in greetings before his or her last name. First names should not be used. In most of the world, only close friends or relatives use first names with each other. However, a young person is almost always greeted by his or her first name. Europeans will shake hands much more often than Americans. You should shake hands with everyone in the group in greeting. After the meeting when leaving a group, it is customary to shake hands with each member of the group and say a short goodbye to each person.

A variation on the simple handshake is found of the Latin, European, and American tradition is the abrazo or embrace. It is often used with a close friend one has not seen for awhile and among relatives and family. The abrazo consists of a warm handshake, a hug, a pat on each other's back, and often a light kiss on the cheek. Between women, the pat on the back is omitted.

Also, it is more common in other parts of the world to greet friends and acquaintances on the street or in offices with a friendly good morning, good afternoon, or good evening, *bon jour, buenos dias,* etc. Make an effort to learn these simple greetings in the foreign language. It says right from the start you are interested enough to make an effort to learn something about them.

In India the *namaste* is the traditional greeting. It is formed by pressing the palms together (fingers up) below the chin, and the term "namaste" (in the south, "namaskaram") is spoken. It is usual to show respect to add a slight bow. Indians do not usually shake hands with or touch women in formal or informal gatherings. This is a sign of respect for a woman's privacy. Indian men will, however, shake hands with Westerners, and educated women may do so as a courtesy as in all countries. It is polite to use titles such as professor and doctor, Mr., Shri, or the suffix "ji" with a last name to show respect. Indians usually ask permission before taking leave of others.

In Chinese tradition, and by extension in Korea and Japan, bowing is the form of greeting. The centuries-old teachings of Confucius on humility explain the Chinese practice of reserve and modesty in dealing with others. Aggressive, egotistical behavior is offensive. You should always understate the case when describing your accomplishments, rank, or possessions. Sincere compliments are given and appreciated, but the Chinese way is to deny praise and express unworthiness.

Polite conversation usually includes inquiries about one's health, business affairs, or school activities. Elderly people should be shown special respect in all actions and by a deep bow of respect. Bowing can be quite complex and it is not necessary to learn all the fine points, but generally the depth of the bow is an indication of respect. The western hand shake is becoming more common, especially in the main cities and business circles.

Among East Asians how one bows to another depends on whether the relationship is that of superior-subordinate or of equals. The person who is younger or of lesser rank bows more deeply than his counterpart, and permits a superior to straighten up first. This is true of women as well.

In Islamic countries there are several forms of greetings. The most common is a handshake and the phrase "peace be upon you." Often men will follow by extending the left hand to the other's right shoulder and a kiss to right and left cheeks. As in Chinese culture, the greeting used depends on the individuals' relationship with each other and their status in society.

Normally, you don't shake hands with women, and certainly you don't initiate the handshake. You may shake hands with an Arab several times in one day, each time you're apart for a while and remeet. Exchange greetings as you shake hands, and continue shaking until greetings are done, which may take several minutes. A simple "hello" is too abrupt for the Arab tradition; it lacks a proper show of sincerity and warmth.

Arabs are conscious of rank and expect rank to be acknowledged. Shake hands with the most important person first. You may see some Arabs use both hands to shake hands, with the four hands gently clasped into a ball. This gesture is usually used with old friends, not new acquaintances. But follow your host's lead. If he clasps your right hand with both of his, cover them with your left hand.

In greeting, as in other aspects of communication with other people, we have already noted respect as a vital element. In that regard we should emphasize how important it is to make an attempt to learn some of the others language. The minimum should be the proper greetings in the language of the country where you are a guest.

Learning some of the host country's language is one of the earliest and most visible signs of mutual respect. It shows you have taken the time and shown enough concern to have made the effort. When visiting a foreign country as a minimum learn the common greetings and thank you in the host country language.

▶ Time

Chapter 3 discussed various attitudes to time, and as was pointed out, different time values are one of the greatest sources of friction for businesspeople and tourists as they relate to other cultures. One aspect of this is that other societies differ in their sense of history. Most educations around the world strive for an historical perspective and an exploration of the roots of their values. In almost any subject from economics to law, textbooks go back in history 2,000 years to explore the roots of the subject. Americans are much more oriented to the future, which ties in with our ideas of progress and optimism. Americans put value on modern things.

For Americans, time is linear and segmented. We are very much aware of the hour, at work, lunch time, closing hour and with television, we have time broken into thirty-minute and one-hour segments with commercials of thirty seconds, precisely. We expect appointments to be kept exactly and are irritated if someone is twenty minutes late.

This approach to time is shared by many western Europeans and is part of the organization of time necessary for the Industrial Revolution. Industrial society emphasized that punctuality was a virtue and time was money. This typifies the attitudes of most North Americans, Swiss, Germans, and Scandinavians. In these western cultures, they tend to concentrate on one thing at a time. They divide time into small units and are concerned with promptness.

A part of the world accuses Americans, as well as other industrialized country citizens, of often putting schedules and profits before people. In many cultures, who makes a request or offer, and how it's made, may mean as much as, or more than, the proposition itself. Before business can be discussed, it is necessary for the participants to get to know each other.

We pointed out that this attitude of scheduled time is not peculiarly American, but is a part of the change of attitude brought about by the Industrial Revolution. To keep up with the ever-faster pace of change, Americans had to streamline time, and many of the time consuming, but human, elements were eliminated.

In many cultures which have not experienced the full impact of the Industrial Revolution, change and efficiency are not necessarily looked on as better. (The impact of the Industrial Revolution with its major cultural impact was discussed in Chapter 11.)

▶ Some Examples of Time Conflicts

Americans are apt to stereotype Latin Americans as always late while they view us as overly concerned about promptness. While not precisely true, we are time oriented. "time is money" we say; Time should be enjoyed, not spent. The Latin American can be puzzled by an invitation to a party which states in advance when the party will be over, proof that Americans are slaves to the clock. If everyone is having a good time, why would you want to stop just because the clock says it's time?

Even the industrialized Japanese see U.S. businesspeople as too time-bound and driven by schedules. This focus on schedules, they feel, can stand in the way of forming friendship bonds. The Arab concept of time is not the neatly segmented concept that we accept in the U.S. Arabs do not believe nature or human events should be or can be controllable by man through advanced planning, clock watching, and scheduling. The course of human events is determined by Allah alone, and His plan is unknowable and unpredictable.

▶ Formality—Hierarchy and Rank

Despite the changes resulting from the western political and industrial revolutions we described, class distinctions still exist in most of the world. Governing classes are proud of their history and accomplishments. Because of this feeling of class responsibility, educated people in positions of authority are expected to display good manners. Wherever we go in the world for travel or business, good manners will be a most important asset in helping gain acceptance. Americans tend to be very informal: we call each other by first names, allow younger people

to intrude on elders' conversation and generally disregard the traditions of others regarding status and position. This can make the foreigner feel acutely uncomfortable. They look for a degree of formality and politeness as a way of smoothing relations between people.

Most expect proper forms of address, and they are taken aback by the American custom of addressing a new acquaintance or a superior by a first name. We should make an effort to learn local customs so as not to needlessly spoil our acceptance or perhaps embarrass our foreign friends. If we don't spend the time needed to learn local customs, this could be interpreted as an example of our self-centeredness or feeling of superiority.

Here is a summary of some general rules of conduct in our contacts with foreigners:

—Use titles, not first names.

—Reduce the loudness of your voice and try not to attract attention. Americans tend to speak louder than others, and many find this offensive.

—Do not brag. It's best not to mention things about yourself unless specifically asked. Replies should be humble, not seem like you're praising yourself.

—Do not discuss money. It is out of place to mention income or what you might have paid for something. Discussion of personal wealth is considered very vulgar in all cultural traditions.

—Do not immediately ask personal questions. Inquiries about family, local politics, or religion should be left to the foreigner to initiate.

—Do not touch other people. This is especially true in the Far East. It is always better to keep a bit distant. This is especially true when dealing with women or older people.

—Never talk to someone with hands in pockets or with anything (e.g., chewing gum) in the mouth. It would also be impolite to slouch at a table or in a chair. Never put feet on chairs or tables with others present. Pointing with the finger, scratching, yawning, or using a toothpick in public are also considered bad taste.

—Do not talk about business at social situations. Business should be left for the office.

—Know enough about the other's culture so that you might at least be able to praise some of the country's great painters, poets, performing artists, historical periods, athletes, craftsmen, foods, and drinks. Do some homework.

—Be prepared to address some of the questions commonly asked of Americans. The beginning of this section outlines some background and information about key areas: family, morals and ethics, crime and violence, race relations, attitudes toward material possessions, and success.

—Avoid frankness or abruptness, especially in offering criticism of any kind. Loud, untactful, or rude behavior is usually regarded as very bad taste. Remember throughout the Far East the Confucian ethic of proper social and family relationships form the foundation of Chinese society. And this tradition emphasizes harmony and carefully avoids hurting the feelings of others.

—Greet everyone in any business or social occasion. In the European tradition, shake hands; in India and the Far East, bow. Leave no one out.

—When meeting with a group, especially in the Far East, greet the oldest person or the one of senior rank first, and so on down the line. Whoever has the most rank should start the greeting process.

—Latin Europeans may use two last names on business cards and in correspondence. For example, if a colleague's name is Juan Garcia Lopez, he is called Senor Lopez. Garcia is the father's name, Lopez the mother's. The mother's name is not used in conversation. In China the family name is placed first followed by a two syllable given name. General Chiang Kai-shek is General Chiang.

▶ Personal Appearance

In keeping with the generally more conservative attitudes around the world with the importance of status, an effort should be made to dress more conservatively and tastefully. You should try to dress well whenever you are in public. Even quite poor people spend money on good clothes so they can be well dressed in public. This is changing and American style casualness is now seen everywhere, but it is still a good bet to dress on the conservative side. Your first impression on people is very important and can be difficult to change.

Women especially should make an effort to be more conservative. In many parts of the world, shorts, low-cut dresses, and all types of revealing clothing are considered to be in poor taste and should not be worn in public. This applies to both the color and cut of your clothes, regardless of your sex.

Ties are always a must. Never enter a corporate or government office anywhere with an open-collar shirt. Lace-up shoes are better than loafers and black shoes more appropriate than brown. Men should not remove their jackets unless colleagues have already done so, and only then after asking permission. In cooler weather, dark suits—black, gray, or navy—white shirts and black shoes make a good impression everywhere. Evening socializing may be formal.

▶ The Role of Women

Women in America, especially in the last few years, have achieved a degree of freedom that is often in sharp contrast to other cultures. The treatment of women in the western world, has always been unequal and often oppressive, but even at its worst it was rather better than the rule of polygamy and concubinage that has otherwise been the almost universal lot of womankind on this planet.

The new position of women in American society is very much a part of the changing society brought about by what can be referred to as the first and second Industrial Revolutions. Briefly stated, the first industrial revolution enticed some women to leave the "inside" economy and enter the "outside" wage economy. Somewhat later, women benefitted from the establishment of public schools, where they were able to get an education along with male students. By the beginning of the twentieth century, women were winning the right to vote. In 1900, they had won the franchise in national elections in only one country; by 1950, they could vote in 69 countries; by 1975, in 129. Today women have the vote virtually everywhere.

Yet during the first half of the twentieth century, women did not achieve much from their access to voting booths. Women's rights appear to have been overshadowed by more immediate and traumatic concerns such as the Great Depression and World War II.

In the second half of the twentieth century, new horizons and new roles opened up for women, thanks largely to the effects of World War II and of the second industrial revolution. Contraceptives made available by medical technology have given women control over their own reproductive function. No longer are they inhibited by traditional assumptions about what "nature intended" concerning the social roles of males and females. Motherhood can be assumed or refused. And if assumed, planned parenthood leaves time for women, after raising their children, to renew old careers and even to begin new ones.

A key change in the status of women today is the opening of the doors to education. Global illiteracy is decreasing rapidly among women as well as men. In the developed countries, there are about equal numbers of males and females in school at all levels.

The most dramatic evidence of this worldwide trend has been in the U.S. where the contrast in education between male and female has long been the narrowest. With better education, women could also improve the contents in their paychecks. One of the dramatic effects has been the influx of women in the work force. In the United States, only 18.9 percent of adult women worked outside the home in 1890. Today, well over half do and most want to keep their jobs rather than return home as housewives.

This different role for women changes age-old patterns that are still firmly in place in most societies that have not become highly industrialized and some (as in Japan) that have. In the last few years, an impressive effort to raise the consciousness of men and women in the United States concerning sexist attitudes as revealed in speech, advertising, and hiring practices. Increasingly in clothing and fashion, in hobbies and careers, the line between what is suitable for a man and for a woman has become blurred.

For these many reasons Americans are often at odds concerning sex roles when dealing with other cultures.

▶ Latin America

Common in Latin America is the concept of machismo and the macho role for men. Machismo is an exaggerated expression of masculinity originally coined to describe Latin men. The classic portrayal of machismo is the bullfight: a test of human grace, quickness, courage, stamina, power, and respect. Machismo calls for a proud, aggressive, competitive stance in all important social matters. Characterized by personal dynamism, zest for action, and physical, sexual, psychic, and political potency; it's a Latin trait aligned with personalism. They differ in that personalism refers to the human being; Latin women have personalism, too. Machismo is specifically concerned with the man.

The father is head of the family: stern, aloof, and responsible. The North American in Latin America need not adopt any of the more blatant symbols of machismo, but should be aware of attitudes and the role of the male that machismo may demand. The male is expected to act strong and competent.

A woman who seems to be too independent or expresses opinions that contradict the male may call into question the machismo of the man. In this scheme of values, having many children is considered important proof of the man's virility and has the added result of requiring the mother to remain in her traditional domestic role.

A part of this attitude also assumes an almost inevitable sexual attraction between a man and a woman when they are together alone. Meanings can be read into relationships that in the U.S. would not arouse suspicion, such as being alone with another's wife, inviting a secretary to share lunch, dating a woman traveling alone. This attitude fostered the traditional custom of the chaperon.

The role of mother in Latin America or Latin Europe holds a very special and very important place. She depends upon her sons to take care of her in her old age, and it is part of the son's machismo to do so and to defend her honor at all times. Any implication of an insult to one's mother is a serious provocation. Americans are likely to feel that Latin men overdo their devotion to their mothers and fail to show sufficient respect for their wives; Latins are likely to regard Americans in the opposite way.

▶ Islam

Islamic cultures place a great emphasis on the private nature of women. Family honor is among the most important of Arab values. The greatest threat to it is the loss of chastity of a female member out of wedlock, or a married female relative caught in an extramarital affair.

As pillars of family honor, Arab women are what most Americans would consider overly protected. Not only are they vulnerable to the carnal thoughts of men but also to their own latent promiscuous desires. As such, they are a perpetual source of anxiety and trauma to their male relations, who see sexual temptation lurking in every shadow.

In the past, women were rarely permitted to leave the house. This was a matter of protection. Today women have become a common sight on streets in major cities. But most continue to appear veiled and fully cloaked in *abayas*—long, voluminous black robes hiding arms as well as legs—when in public. Moreover, even though Arab women, particularly those of Arab Gulf countries, are entering local work forces, and some who have been western-educated are wearing modest western dress to the office, they remain a sensitive subject best avoided in conversation.

▶ Far East

The traditional role of women in the Far East was one of complete subjection to the male. According to an old Chinese proverb, the most beautiful and talented daughter is not as desirable as a deformed son. Preference for boys was so open, in fact, that in upper-class families a cherished son was occasionally given a girl's name during his childhood in the belief that evil spirits, thinking the child a girl (and therefore less valuable) would pass him by. The birth of male heirs was considered a matter of utmost urgency and was sought by every possible magical, medical, and spiritual means. The birth of a daughter was greeted with considerably less enthusiasm, and peasant fathers, who were unwilling or unable to support yet another female, sometimes drowned newborn girls.

No matter what her circumstances, a woman could look forward to a life of subjugation—to her father and eldest brother in her childhood, to her husband and his mother after her marriage, and to her own sons upon her husband's death. (Her only opportunity for self-assertion came through her sons' marriages, when she too became a mother-in-law.)

Once married, she was known only by two surnames, her husband's and her father's, and regardless of her age or status, she was generally addressed as "aunt" or "grandmother." She could be divorced if barren, chronically ill, or neglectful of her father-in-law, and she was expected to live a life of perfect submissiveness as outlined in a T'ang Dynasty manual: *"A chaste woman must not go out often . . . and must work very hard. If asked to come, she must come at once; if asked to go, she must go quickly. If she fails . . . reproach and beat her. . . ."*

The classic Chinese beauty bound her feet from childhood, believing that her efforts to walk on deformed "lily feet" produced an alluring sway. Frequently promised in marriage at birth and generally married by the age of fourteen, a Chinese woman spent the major part of her life in total subservience to her husband and to the members of his family, particularly his mother. Chinese women were obligated to tolerate concubinage. Once widowed, they were expected to refrain from remarrying. Despite inequities, there is no evidence to suggest that the role of husband and wife in the typical marriage was not one of protective tenderness in both the husband and his wife.

Things are changing in Communist China and industrial Japan. Women are declaring that they have a right to their own careers and to share in occupations and diversions formerly monopolized by men. Coeducation is becoming the rule in higher education. The feminism of the West is making itself felt.

Still, old traditions don't die quickly. Only now and only rarely are women in Japan rising to executive positions in business. Traveling in the Orient on business, you do not dine with the wife of your foreign contact. If you did, politics and business would be an impolite subject in the presence of women. Women's place is still traditionally that of homemaker. This does not mean the woman may not have power. A wife of vigorous character is often dominant. Japanese women, for example, are responsible for family expenses to a degree many American husbands would feel oppressive.

By bearing a son a woman acquired greater importance, and when in the normal course of events she becomes a mother-in-law and a grandmother, she is regarded as being of more and more consequence and is treated with increasing respect. Throughout the Far East public displays of affection are discouraged. In dealings at all levels, business and social, a discreet distance should be maintained between men and women.

► India

The Indian people are deeply religious and family oriented. Physical purity is a great virtue. Marriage is sacred to most Indians and considered to endure beyond death. Chastity is a most treasured virtue. The divorce rate is the lowest in the world. The family is organized and male dominated. Family life emphasizes the authority of older over younger and man over woman.

Deference and propriety mark the relationship between spouses. The Hindu wife's lot in life demands that she give her husband and his family obedience and respect. The husband is her lord, both temporally and spiritually; emotional intimacy often develops only years after an arranged marriage. A woman may begin to gain respect and status in her husband's household with the birth of children, especially sons.

In the Indian village, which is where most Indians live, adult men and women are segregated at mealtime; men dine first, women and children later. As in other traditional cultures, the role of women in India is changing under the impact of western industrialization and political patterns. However, traditional patterns still exist. Even those the visitor might identify as modern city dwellers may compartmentalize their lives, returning from the office to traditional values where the rule of women is as it has been for centuries and the purity of caste marriage continues to be sacrosanct. The modern progressive laws passed by the Indian Congress in recent years conferring rights of divorce on men and women, fixing the minimum age of marriage, etc. have had limited effect.

As a general rule, then, in inter-cultural exchange, we must be aware that the role of women in most societies does not permit the degree of choice and liberty found in the United States. Maintain more distance and formality in male-female relationships. Women should dress more modestly. Men should emphasize politeness and deference.

► Interpersonal Relationships

Every person, in every culture, is both an individual, separate from others, and also a member of a cultural group. Cultural background influences whether the individualism is given emphasis, and if so, how much. Americans tend to be on the individualistic end of the scale. In this we differ greatly with older traditional societies such as Korea, India, most Muslim countries, and Africa where the group ranks in importance before the individual. In these cultures, the family, the tribe, the nation, or even organizations such as your profession or business form a "we" sort of value, where individual wishes are subordinated to the group.

For Americans the individual, not the group, is basic. So many of the values we think of as distinctly American—equality, democracy, freedom, privacy, and even progress—are bound up with the American view of individualism. Cooperation and teamwork are important, but we feel these should arise from the choice and desire of the individual. These different interpretations of the role of the individual in society can be a source of conflict. What we see as attractive individualism, may be interpreted as rude and anti-social. If we constantly stress our personal opinions, this can be seen as egotism. These differences can show up in many ways. We mentioned the Far Eastern bow and noted this was used to indicate relationships. In Japan, decisions are made by consensus, whereas we value the decision maker. Clothing is more apt to conform to one's group or status, and the family relationships take on greater significance.

► The Family

Many of the foreigner's biggest apprehensions about American culture center on the role of the family. Our value of individualism reflects an attitude toward the family. What is meant by "the family" and its relationship to the individual is very different from what one finds in most of the rest of the world. For Americans, "family" usually means parents and children, hopefully few. The family provides a kind of center for growing up, and young adults are expected to leave to go on their own. This pattern emphasizes independence for the parent as well as the child.

Family in the rest of the world, in sociology jargon the extended family as opposed to the nuclear family, typically includes many more relatives and particularly many more brothers and sisters who remain in close contact. While differences may be great, loyalty to each other and to the family is very strong. Young people are not encouraged to leave home, but to stay and help the family. It is typical of the value placed family in many cultures for them to feel that they cannot nearly know someone without knowing their family. In the same way, the Latin American, for example, may depend upon relatives or close friends to help "arrange things" if there is a problem, or to provide a loan or help in finding a job. The family is the primary network.

Since the sayings of Confucius have formed the base of Chinese culture now for over 2,000 years, and this culture covers all East Asia and forms a cultural unit, Confucius (in the five relationships those between ruler and subject, parent and child, older and younger brother, husband and wife, and friend and friend) laid down the pattern for harmony in society. A visitor to the Asian culture must observe and respect these relationships, as they help explain and guide conduct.

The virtues needed to make the relationships work are: filial piety, kindness, righteousness, propriety, intelligence, and faithfulness. Of these virtues, filial piety remains the most important. When Confucius lived, tyranny and warfare wracked China. The pervasive killing and human unhappiness inspired Confucius to create a set of moral guidelines for the civilized running of society. These guidelines gained acceptance both in China and beyond as an effective way to ensure peace and happiness in society.

Confucius saw the basic unit of society not as the individual, as we do in the U.S., but as the family. The concept of the family could be extended to any organization—a community, a corporation, a government, a nation—as the basic building unit to give the whole stability. For society as a whole to

remain stable, its basic building unit, the family, had to be stable. To ensure this stability, each family needed one set of commonly accepted rules on how each member should act. To keep the family going smoothly, Confucius advocated many rituals, customs, and codes of etiquette by which harmonious behavior could be expressed between individuals. (Refer to discussion of Confucius in section concerning Far Eastern culture in Chapter 9.)

No culture places higher value on the role of the family as a basic unit and harmonizer than Chinese-Far Eastern culture. Confucian relationships are reciprocal. For example, parents are just as obligated to provide for their children as children are obligated to obey and respect their parents, and, by extension, their substitute parents: teachers, employers, government leaders, and other authority figures.

Throughout the Far East, the Confucian ethic of proper social and family relationships form the foundation of society. An individual's actions reflect upon the whole family. In many areas three or four generations often live together as an extended family. Both young and old family members attend activities and spend much time together. Loyalty and cooperation among family members are highly valued. Parents exert great influence on the social and career choices of their children. Also the roles of father and mother are precisely defined. Father is the authoritarian provider and head of the family while mother runs the household. Family members are bound by a strong tradition of loyalty, obedience, and respect. Divorce is seen as a breakup of the family and thus society. Most moral teachers have placed a strong virtuous family as the basis for a healthy society. The value of a strong family was emphasized over the centuries in all cultures because of the human condition which includes war, famine or a plague. Without family to fall back on for strength a person perished. Everyone needs a home.

After the Second World War, the Japanese soldier returned without the benefits given to the American veteran. He was expected to go back to his family for support. The American poet Robert Frost said it very well in a poem in which he defined home. *"Home,"* he said, *"is where when you gotta go there they gotta let you in."*

▶ There Is a Difference

Cultures vary in how they direct people to look at a person's age, sex, and rank. American culture encourages us to play down such differences. For most cultures these differences are very important. To a greater extent factors such as age or rank or sex guide the foreigner's actions toward others. Where Americans may resent a person who is rank or class conscious or demands special attention, such behavior is not necessarily objectionable in other cultures.

Americans may equate attention to such matters with prejudice and discrimination. It does not agree with our faith in equality. We have learned that many old distinctions—race, sex, age, marital status easily become the basis of discriminatory behavior, and therefore references to these have been eliminated from job application forms. We've coined the word "Ms" to be co-equal with "Mr," and writers are now pressured to eliminate sexist or racist terms.

Other cultures are usually more hierarchical in society, in family patterns, religious orders, in politics, and in business. Americans tend to minimize differences between themselves and persons in subordinate roles, such as a maid or gardener. Such expressions of equality are not necessarily consistent with other things we do and say, and are definitely not consistent with what foreign cultures are used to. For example, a manager from the States may find it difficult to understand how employees might prefer to work for a dictatorial boss who patronizes his workers, rather than for an American who seems to delegate a good deal of responsibility in decision making. But the foreign worker feels more comfortable with the hierarchical structure.

In this regard, the American can also err at the other end of the social scale by failing to make sufficient fuss over persons whose age or rank or role demand attention. Doctors, lawyers, and engineers, of course, all have their own titles which they take most seriously, and expect others to as well. To make light of them is to make light of the person's dignity.

This hierarchial structure can reflect itself in many ways: In the use of language, in seating arrangements at social gatherings, in greetings to one another and hundreds of other ways. Some common status arrangements that should be remembered include:

(1) younger defers to older;

(2) female defers to male;

(3) student defers to teacher;

(4) the seller defers to the buyer;

(5) in any organization the lower rank defers to the higher.

All of this rank consciousness can be a source of irritation for Americans. For one thing, the very words used in attempting to describe the patterns we bristle at: "superior," "subordinate," or worse yet, "inferior." Americans usually infer that differences generally mean discrimination.

▶ Respect for Age and the Elderly

A rule of thumb in other cultures is to treat those older with more respect and deference than you would in American culture. The older person should not be interrupted when speaking, the older person should go through the door first, should sit at the place of honor, should be addressed by title. Who is an older person? Take it as a rough rule that someone 15 years older than you is an older person.

While this rule applies in all societies, it should be especially and carefully observed in the Orient. The Confucian tradition is especially respectful of elders as repositories of wisdom and deserve special consideration. (See Confucius and the 5 relationships.) Most traditional societies have honored the elderly for exactly the same reason: their experience. When a problem arose or decision to be made the family might ask "let's go ask Grandpa, he'll know." Of course in a modern American scene where the young person is debating the merits of an Apple Macintosh or IBM PC, going to ask Grandpa's advice would probably not be considered because Grandpa doesn't know. Our orientation puts more emphasis or growth and innovation, and the experience of the past is not pertinent.

An American in China might feel a lot less than complimented when his hosts find he is 40 years old and as an intended compliment say they thought he was at least 50. The Chinese are admiring wisdom and maturity more or less, as we might compliment a boy of 12 by saying you thought he was 14. The young boy would definitely feel complimented that you thought of him as so "grown up."

We put a great value on youth, not age, and millions of dollars are spent in America to appear more youthful. This Oriental respect for age not only affects family life where younger defers to older but also business, making it very difficult to place a younger worker in a position of authority over an older worker.

In the discussion of Confucius we talked of relationships "Older brother must be courteous, younger humble. Older friend must have wisdom, younger respect." The Japanese language has several words for brother, for example; one must choose between a world meaning "older brother" and one meaning "younger brother." The same is true for sister. Moreover, in the family the older brothers and sisters will be called by those terms, rather than by their given names. Being older in the Oriental tradition does not mean that one can do what one pleases. The senior age and respect carry special responsibilities toward the younger. Being older is not necessarily an enviable position. The younger is able to depend upon and lean on the older for support.

In Oriental firms there is usually a parallel between age and rank. A younger person may be more able than an older person, and everybody may recognize that, but the younger will still show deference to the older. This respect for age also extends to physical things; for example, an old tea pot is cherished because it is old. Firms that can advertise "founded in 1865" would hold much more confidence and respect than one founded in 1935. Age is interpreted as stability, wisdom, and proven reliability. Of course all these attitudes have parallels in all cultures. The teachings of Confucius make them deeply established in Asia.

▶ Face

Americans abroad are often unsympathetic and mystified by the foreigners' seeming horror at losing face. Asking a Latin American a piece of information such as how far it is to Guadalajara will usually get a definite and courteous reply indicating the exact mileage. However, it could be completely wrong. The Latin American wanted to please you and also did not want you to think he didn't know.

The difficulty Americans have in understanding "face" stems largely from the emphasis placed by American values on the individual. Other cultures, as we pointed out, will much more emphasize the group—the family, school, company, etc.—of which the individual is a part. From their perspective, therefore, how one treats others and is treated by them is of supreme importance. To slight another or to feel slighted, to cause embarrassment or be embarrassed, disturbs the delicate pecking order which is essential to feelings of worth and security. What others think of a person really does matter; it affects the position in the group.

▶ Last Words

In discussing differences between cultures, we should recall again the warning in the chapter, "What Is Culture?" While we should make every effort to develop our knowledge, and above all our respect for different cultures, we should remember to maintain our own cultural integrity. An American who "goes native" is an object of scorn. We should conduct ourselves basically according to our own American value system. We should avoid extremes in adjustment, not trying to make any change or trying too much.

You should certainly try to learn the proper way things are done in the foreign culture and adjust accordingly. Avoid being overly sensitive. Everyone has a tendency to be afraid and hesitant about trying something new because of fear of criticism. But remember that if you try to do what is appropriate in the foreign environment, even if what you do isn't exactly right, your thoughtfulness will still be at least appreciated and admired because you made the effort.

Observe the courtesies of custom and culture, but maintain your own cultural integrity.

Worksheet ►

APPENDIX

Define or identify:

- Linear time, circular time

- Macho and machismo

- Face

- Home is where when you got to go there they got to let you in

- Extended family, nuclear family

Explain:

- Some overall rules of thumb were presented were: Relationships tend to be more formal: Women play a more subordinate role than they play in the U.S.: Class lines are more rigidly drawn: Dress is more conservative.

- What are some concerns of other cultures about America's: family disintegration; crime and violence; race relationships; the role of women; consumerism?

- Why would it be a good idea to learn some of the language and history of a country you were going to visit?

- Greetings in western, Indian and Chinese culture.

- What is the traditional attitude toward meal time? Why would two hours spent on dinner not be considered a waste of time?

- In which countries would being on time be very important and in which countries would there be more leeway?

Discuss:

- As you meet people from other cultures, what are some of the salient points to remember?

- The role of respect in relationships.

- The attitude toward age in America, China and India.

- Knives and forks, chopsticks, hands.

- Use of titles, personal appearance.

- Should one discuss business at a dinner party?

- What is the reason the family has played such a key role in the traditional society?

- How has the industrial revolution changed attitudes toward time, women and family?

- As you now go out into the workplace and meet other value systems and cultures, what are some of the rules of conduct you have learned that you will remember and put into practice?

- Outline some specific things you would especially keep in mind in China, India and Islam.

- A central theme has been the rise of the West and the impact of western or European values on the ancient cultures of India, China and Islam. Discuss differences you would expect when traveling out of our culture to the three other cultures in terms of greetings, taboos, status of women, religion, time, eating habits and foods, eating oranges, attitudes toward nature, older people, humility, and work.

Selected Bibliography ▶▶

The Religions of Man, by Huston Smith
Harper & Row Publishing, Inc. 1958
10 East 53rd Street
New York, NY 10022

Faith & Freedom, by Barbara Ward
Image Books, 1958
Doubleday and Company, Inc.
New York, NY 10022

The Rise of the West, by William H. McNeill
The University of Chicago Press, 1963
Chicago, IL

L. S. Stavrianos
The World to 1500, 3/e, 1982
Prentice Hall
Englewood Cliffs, NJ

L. S. Stavrianos
The World Since 1500, 1966
Prentice Hall
Englewood Cliffs, NJ

F.S.C. Northrop
The Meeting of East and West
The MacMillan Co. 1947
New York, N.Y.